India of Aurangzib

India of Aurangzib

Topography, Statistics and Roads, Compared with the India of Akbar

WITH EXTRACTS FROM
THE **KHULASATU-T-TAWARIKH**
AND THE **CHAHAR GULSHAN**
TRANSLATED AND ANNOTATED

By

JADUNATH SARKAR, M.A.

GYAN

Published by

GYAN

Gyan Publishing House
5, Ansari Road
Daryaganj, New Delhi-110002
Phone: 011-47034999, 9811692060
E-mail: books@gyanbooks.com

Distribution Network
gyanbooks.com
India, USA, Canada, UK, Australia, France

ISBN : 978-81-212-6764-9 (HB)
First Published, 1901

2nd Impression 2022

Printed at: Gyan Press, Delhi.

INDIA OF AURANGZIB
Author: JADUNATH SARKAR

INDIA OF AURANGZIB

(TOPOGRAPHY, STATISTICS, AND ROA

COMPARED WITH THE INDIA OF AKBAR

WITH EXTRACTS FROM

THE KHULASATU-T-TAWARIKH

AND THE CHAHAR GULSHAN

TRANSLATED AND ANNOTATED

BY

JADUNATH SARKAR, M.A.,

PROFESSOR OF ENGLISH LITERATURE, PATNA COLLEGE.

1901.

ABBREVIATIONS.

A. } ...The *Ain-i-Akbari*, trans. by Blochmann and Jarret
Ain } (Bibliotheca Indica).

A...The *Indian Atlas* (see p. 167).

A. & C. Gaz. ...*The Agra and Calcutta Gazetteer*, 4 vols. (Calcutta 1842).

Al-Badaoni...The *Muntakhabu t-Tawarikh*, trans. by Ranking and Lowe (Bibliotheca Indica).

Bayley...*Gujarat*. (W. H. Allen, 1886).

C...The *Chahar Gulshan*

Cunningham...*History of the Sikhs*, 2nd ed., 1853.

Dorn...*History of the Afghans*, 2 pts. (O. T. F., 1829–36).

Duff...*History of the Mahrattas*, 3 vols. (1826).

Elliot...*History of India*, by Elliot and Dowson, 8 vols.

Ferishta...Briggs's translation, 4 vols. (1829).

I. G. or *Imp. Gaz.* ...The *Imperial Gazetteer of India*, 2nd edition.

K...The *Khulasatu-t Tawarikh.*

L. }
Letts } ...Letts's *Popular Atlas*.

Malcolm...*History of Persia*, 2 vols. (1829)

m...miles.

m...mahals.

n...footnote.

Rajasthan } ...Tod's *Rajasthan*, 2 vols (Indian Publication Society,
Tod } Calcutta, 1897–99)

Rev. Res. ...The *Revenue Resources of the Mughal Empire*, by E. Thomas.

Stein...*Memoir on Maps of Ancient Kashmir* (Asiatic Society of Bengal).

Stewart...*History of Bengal*, (Calcutta, 1847).

Tieff. ...Tieffenthaler's *Geographie de l' Indoustan* (being Vol. I of Bernoulli's *Description de l' Inde*, Berlin, 1786).

PREFACE.

THIS book is an attempt to present the topography and statistics of Mughal India, as far as we can learn them from the Persian works, *Khulasatu-t-Tawarikh* (1695 A D.), *Dastur-al Amal* (1700 A. D. ?), and *Chahar Gulshan* (1720 A. D. ?),—all three of which are in manuscript. These sources of information have been Abul plemented by Abul Fazl's *Ain-i-Akbari* (Blochmann and Jesuit translation) and the Jesuit missionary Tieffenthaler's revenues *of de l' Indoustan* (Bernoulli's French version), which, though detailed ed in 1786, was based on Persian works fully half a century several in date. A very detailed comparison has, also, been checked an between the India of Akbar and, broadly speaking, the India for Aurangzib. The revenues of the several provinces of the revenues Empire have been given separately for ten different periodsn, and the time of Akbar to that of Tieffenthaler ; and thus revenues of given in Thomas's *Revenue Resources of the Mugha* supplemented been supplemented and partly checked. The various *Inaoustan* the main roads of Mughal India have been traced on comparison Tavernier's *Travels*, the *Chahar Gulshan*, Tieffenthaler's statistical *de l' Inaoustan*, and an old Indian *Gazetteer* of 1842. Finallyf old topographical and statistical portions of the *Khulasatu-t-Tawir*, the and the *Chahar Gulshan*, (178 pages), have been here *Travels* of for the first time and copiously annotated.

The title of the book, therefore, does not fully exp title an contents. Its size, too, gives an inadequate idea of the making has involved, especially in making out proper names and difficult viated Arabic word-figures (*raqam*) from badly-transcribed into sian manuscripts If the net result of the researches nature of in this work be imperfect and wanting in finality, manuscripts difficult nature of the subject and our want of the materials materials will be taken into consideration before involved our pronounced upon it.

The Hunterian spelling has in most cases been adopted here, especially when a name occurs for the first time ; but the current spelling of the names of famous places has been retained. The two '*kaf*'s have been represented by *q* and *k* respectively. All corrections and suggestions, especially from those who have access to better MSS of the two Persian works translated here, will be thankfully received.*

My thanks are due to Khan Bahadur KHUDA BUKHSH KHAN of Bankipur, to whose enlightened courtesy I am indebted for the use of a MS of the *Chahar Gulshan*, and to Maulvi ABDUL IAI of Patna College, with whom I read the *Khulasat* and revised portion of the *Chahar Gulshan*.

JADUNATH SARKAR.

such communications should be sent to me addressed Ghoramara, P. O. District, Bengal.

CHAPTER I.

SCOPE AND MATERIALS.

Author's apology.

Nobody can be more sensible of the imperfections of this book than the author. But he hopes that nobody who knows what it is to translate a Persian work bristling with obscure geographical names from a single and incorrectly transcribed manuscript, will be hard upon him for these imperfections. In antiquities continual supersession is the rule. The path of the Indian antiquarian is, moreover, beset with peculiar difficulties. It is seldom that the requisite materials are all accessible to him. He has to settle the texts of his authorities, few of which have been printed and fewer still edited. He is expected to correct and identify wrongly-spelt proper names, though he has often no second manuscript to collate with the one lying before him. Then, again, he can expect very little help from brother-antiquarians, because the field is large and the labourers few Pandits and Maulavis are of little assistance except in throwing light on the grammar or explaining the probable meaning of the text. They are ignorant of historical criticism ; the usual materials on which the antiquarian works being obscure books and not classics, they are never studied as text-books or even read for pleasure by our Pandits and Maulavis. The historical student in India is thrown almost entirely on his own resources. He may, therefore, claim a partial, if not a plenary, pardon for his sins. To expect perfection in such a branch of study is hardly more reasonable than to ask a goldsmith to give a proof of his professional skill by prospecting for gold, digging the mine, extracting and refining the ore, and then making the ornament.

Our task is, therefore, often a thankless one. The very nature of the subject precludes any high degree of excellence,—at least what would be regarded as excellence by those familiar with the brilliant results achieved by the students of European history ; and the Indian antiquarian for all his pains is rewarded with censure. In spite of the great risk of failure, I have been tempted to step into the field, by the importance of the subject treated here. A contribution to our knowledge of it, thougb imperfect, may still have its value.

Importance of the Subject.

The *Ain-i-Akbari* gives "the Administration Report and Statistical Return of Akbar's government as it was" in 1594 A D., with a minuteness of detail and accuracy of information which leave little to be desired. But, for the remaining century and a half during which the Mughal Empire lasted, we have no statistical record in English. With the consolidation of the British Power in India we again emerge into light. We have the works of Rennell, Buchanan-Hamilton and other explorers of the early British period. The East India Company was renowned for its liberal patronage of literature dealing with India, and we are in no want of materials for a statistical study of India even before the publication of Hamilton's *East India Gazetteer* (c. 1830.) There is, thus, a gap in our knowledge of Indian topography and statistics for the period extending from 1595 to 1760 A. D.

Our Materials: (a) Persian works,

This gap ought to be filled up, for there is no want of materials for a study of this period from the point of view indicated above First, there are the professed attempts at the description of India made in contemporary Persian works, like the *Khulasátu-t-Tawárikh* and the *Chahár Gulshan*, extracts from which have been here translated. Unfortunately, these are the only contemporary works of the class we need. Elliot names another, the *Hadiqatu-l-Aqalim*, but it is much later in date. Secondly,

(b) Side-lights,

there are incidental mentions of facts that are important for our study, in the Persian histories of India. But they are so scattered and the books in which they occur have been so seldom correctly edited, that I have not been able, within the time at my command, to work these materials up with anything like fulness. Indeed, an exhaustive study of these side-lights on Indian topography would, in the present state of our materials, take up decades. Lastly, we have the works of European travellers mostly accessible to our readers,—Bernier and Tavernier, Mannucci, and Tieffenthaler. The *Geography of Hindustan* of the last is very valuable, being based on several Persian topographical works and the author's own observation during his long residence in India ; but its extreme scarcity and French garb* have made it less known in India than Bernier's *Travels*. From these works we get, among other things, details of the Mughal revenue which have been embodied by Thomas in his *Revenue Resources of the Mughal Empire*. Rennell's Atlas (Folio, 1781), invaluable as it otherwise is, does not strictly fall into this class. It treats of British India.

(c) Travels.

The Khulasatu-t-tawarikh.

Author.

Elliot calls the author "Subhán Rái Khattri, an inhabitant of Pattiala." (viii. 5) In the Bengal Asiatic Society's *Catalogue of Persian Works*, he is named Sujan Rai But on the last page of the Society's MS. D. 156 (which I call the A-text), the author's name is spelt carelessly and looks like "Saján Rái Nahdari."† Among the pious founders of Batala, our author mentions a "Sujan Singh Qanongo" (p 85 of my translation), but we cannot know for certain whether that person was the same as our author. His birthplace was mistaken by Elliot for Pattiala, whereas it was really Batala, a town in the Gurdaspur district of the Panjab. (p 83 of translation).

Date.

From internal evidence the date of composition seems to have been some year between 1695 and 1699 A. D. (i) On page 12 we read cannot know for

* *La Geographie de'l Indoustan*, ecrite en mentions a "Sujan Singh Le Pere Joseph Tieffenthaler, being the 1st vol. of same as our author. the et geographique DE L'INDE," by M. Jean but we cannot know for

† He is here described as "an inhabit: Gurdaspur district of the Panjab. Persian, and Sanskrit learning, and was the person was the same as: Elliot epoch in pleasantness of style and literary skill."

intervened between the death of the Saint Mahiu-d-din Abdul Qadir Gilani (in 561 A H.) and the writing of this book. This gives 1111 A. H (1699 A. D.) as the date of the work. (ii) On p. 81 we are told that the book was written more than 40 years "after the commencement." If we take the expression to mean the commencement of Aurangzib's reign, the date would be later than 1107 A H. (1695 A. D.) But if it means the commencement of the work of embanking the Ravi at Lahor (in the 4th year of the reign), the date would be 3 years later, *i e*, 1698 A. D. (iii) On p. 90 we are told that the book was written in the 23rd year of the pontificate of Guru Govind. *i. e.*, in the 40th year of Aurangzib's reign (1107 A H., 1695 A D.) Col. Lees writes, "The author brings his narrative down to the end of the year 1107 A. H. It was continued for some years later by another hand" (Elliot viii. 8.) I find that MS. D 156 ends with the death of Aurangzib, evidently an addition by a copyist. Elliot tells us, "It was written in 1107 A. H. (1695-6 A. D) and occupied two years in its composition" (viii 5) and also that the author wrote in the 40th year of the reign of Aurangzib.

Style. Its style is the corrupt one characteristic of an age of decadence. It is rhetorical without ceasing to be prosaic; the embellishments have a tinsel glitter. The author has borrowed certain set phrases which he uses every now and then. Assonance, which is the vice of most Persian writers, degenerates into mere jingle in his hands. Hence the repetitions which in the translation may strike the reader as meaningless

Scope. "It is a well-known general history. The *opening chapters* which are *the best portion of the work*, give a good account of the products of Hindustan, and its geography, as known in the time of Aurangzib." The author's account of the early kings of Delhi is brief, and that of the first four Mughal Emperors copious. He has said very little of Shah Jahan, and "he closes with the period when Aurangzib has succeeded in getting rid of his rivals and has no longer a competitor for the throne." (Elliot, viii, 6.) It is, however, with these opening chapters that we are here concerned. In the MS. used by Elliot (Quarto, 19 lines to the page), they occupy pp.12-99. In the A-text (Folio, 19 lines to the page), they cover 104 pages,—from leaf 6 page 2 line 1 (which I briefly put as 6 *b*. 1) to leaf 58 page 2 line 12 (which I express by 58. *b*. 12). This portion is subdivided in the following manner ;—

(1) Description of Hindustan. commencing from 6. *b*. 1. (2) The Province of Shah Jahanabad or Delhi, 17 *b*. 9 (3) Akbarabad or Agra, 24. *b* 14. (4) Allahabad, 26. *a*. 3. (5) Oudh, 27 *a*. 8. (6) Bihar, 28 *a* 17. (7) Bengal, 29 *b*. 18. (8) Orissa, 31 *b*. 13. (9) Aurangabad, 32 *a* 13 (10) Berar, 32 *b*. 16. (11) Khandesh, 33 *a* 17. (12) Malwa, 33 *b* 12. (13 Ajmir, 34 *a* 18 (14) Gujrat or Ahmadabad. 35 *b*. 6. (15) Thatha. 37 *b*. 10. (16) Multan, 38 *b* 17. (17) Lahor, 41 *b* 1. (18) Kashmir, 52 *b* 5. (19) Kabul, 55 *b*. 3, ending at 58 *b*. 11, where the "History of the Kings of Hindustan" commences. Of the above, the first chapter of 22 pages (6 *b* 1—17 *b* 9) gives a general description of Hindustan, its flowers, fruits, sages, and hermits, in a florid and bombastic style. But the account is so vague, so barren of facts, and written in terms of such extravagant praise, that I did not consider it worth printing in my translation The curious will get a sample of it in the "Description of Hindustan" extracted by Elliot (viii. 3) from the *Mukhtasiru t Tawarikh*, which is identical in language with the account given by the *Khulasat* The description of the *Subah* of Kabul, occupying 6 pages of the A-text, has also been omitted from my translation, as Kabul is outside the geographical limits of India. My translation, therefore, covers nearly 76 pages of the text, or exactly 1438 lines

Heads of information.

In the account of each of the 17 *Subahs* here translated, our author first describes, more or less fully, the chief towns, holy places, and other interesting localities of the province, with the lives of its saints. Then comes an account of the chief manufactures, crops, and rivers ; and last of all the boundaries of the province, the names of its chief districts (*Sarkars*), the number of its subdivisions (*mahals*) and its revenue in *dam* ($\frac{1}{40}$ of a rupee.) The descriptions of the towns are in many cases borrowed from the *Ain-i-Akbari* either *verbatim* or in a modified form. But in several instances, notably in the province of the Panjab, our author supplements the *Ain-i-Akbari* with original information. As he was a native of the Panjab, he naturally gives an original account of it; but the farther we proceed from the Panjab the more does he draw on the *Ain*, till at length his accounts of provinces like Bengal, Orissa, and Kashmir, become mere transcripts of the *Ain*. In the century that intervened between the *Ain* and the *Khulasat*, changes occurred in the Mughal Empire, and many of them have been embodied by our author; but, unfortunately, the expansion of the Mughal Empire under Aurangzib finds no statistical record in the *Khulasat*. Possibly the statistics of the newly annexed *Subahs* had not yet been compiled, or probably they were not accessible to our author, though the author of the *Chahar Gulshan*, writing half a century later, used them. Where the *Khulasat* supplies any additional information, I shall notice it in my detailed account of the several *Subahs*. The names of the *Sarkars*, the numbers of the *mahals*, and the amount of the revenue, as given by our author, enable us to institute an interesting comparison with the *Ain*, that is, to make a comparative study, however rude and incomplete,—of the India of Akbar (1594 A. D) and the India of Aurangzib (1695 A. D.).

Originality.

The Asiatic Society of Bengal has two manuscripts of this work, numbered respectively D. 156 and D. 157 in the *Catalogue of Persian Books*. The former (which I call the A-text) was copied "on the 10th of the month of Zi-qada in the 9th year of the reign of Muhammad Shah [1728 A.D.] at the time of the feast of *Nau-roz* in the evening of Saturday" (Colophon) It is a thick folio volume, 19 lines to the page, transcribed in a legible hand and fairly correct, though omissions and errors (especially in the spelling of proper names)

MSS.

occur on almost every page. The more important of these have been noticed in the foot-notes of my translation. The second manuscript, D. 157, (which I designate the B-text), is a modern copy, incomplete, full of mistakes, and so badly written as to be hardly legible ; most of the proper names in it are incomprehensible, as the dots have been omitted. It has, however, been of use in supplying the more important of the omissions in the A-text. The Bankipur Oriental Library of Khan Bahadur Khuda Bukhsh Khan has a MS.* of this work, but it is incorrect, without rubrics, and written in a hurried and careless hand. This fact, coupled with my want of leisure, prevented me from using it in collating the text.

The Chahar Gulshan.

"This work, which is also known as *Akhbáru-l-Nawádir* (Accounts of Rare Things), was composed by Rai Chatar Mán Káyath in the year 1173 A.H. (1759 A.D.), the last sheets being finished only a week before his death. As it was left in an unconnected shape, it was arranged and edited, after his death, by his grandson, Rai Bhán Rai Raizada in 1204 A. H. (1789 A.D.) The editor has added nothing to his grandfather's labours." (Elliot, viii. 255). In the Preface of the Khuda Bukhsh MS the editor is, however, named "Chandar Bhán Munshi Káyath Saksina (?), entitled Ráizáda." In the (lithographed) Persian Catalogue of Khuda Bukhsh, the author is described as "Rái Chatar Man Rái, of the tribe of Káyath Sakina, who was in the service of Ghaziu-d-din Khan, Wazir of the Empire," and the date of composition is given as 1173 A.H. On the last page of this MS. we read that the book records Indian history down to the reign of the Emperor Mahiu-d-din Shah Jahan the

Author.

Date.

* It is thus described in his Persian Catalogue of Oriental Works, "Written in the Nasta'liq hand, neatly but with many mistakes,—the first page gilt, with borders of vermillion,—on Kashmiri paper,—copied in the year 1234 A H." (1818 A.D.)

Second, who "increased the splendour of the throne in the year 1173 A.H., with the help of the Wazir of the Empire, Ghaziu-d-din Khan *alias* Shahábu-d-din Khan, at the time of the second invasion of Ahmad Shah Abdali"

Style.

The style is terse and precise. The sentences are short and simple, some of them being without verbs. The whole work looks like a set of notes reduced to the smallest compass, rather than a finished treatise. It is refreshing to meet with a writer free from that "indirection of speech" which was considered a merit in Persian compositions and that vague rhetorical display and pretence which disgusts us in so many minor writers.

Scope.

The *Chahar Gulshan* or "Four Gardens" is a condensed history of India, with descriptions and statistics of the several provinces and the lives of holy men. The following is an analysis of the work.*

Book I.

I. The kings of Hindustan (N India) from Judhishthira to Shah Jahan the Second (1759 A.D.), with a statistical account of the several *Subahs*, their chief towns, forts, rivers, rulers, and saints: (1) DELHI 3. *a* 14—its kings 3 *b*. 4—Saints 21 *a* 10—Hindu Shrines 36 *b*. 5—Melas 37 *b* 4—Chhattars 39 *a*. 5—Rivers and canals 39 *b*. 11—Mines 40 *b*. 6—Statistics of the province 41 *a*. 4—Detailed statistics of the Sarkars 41 *b* 1. (2) AGRA 42 *a*—its rulers and saints *a* 5—Forts, buildings, &c 44 *a*. 1—Hindu shrines *a*. 12—Rivers 44 *b*. 12—Mines 45 *a*. 9—Provincial statistics *a*. 13—Delailed statistics of the Sarkars 45 *b*. 4 (3). PANJAB 46 *a*. 7—its kings *a*. 15—Saints 46 *b*. 1—Hindu Shrines 47 *a*. 9—Forts and buildings 47 *b*. 14—

* The leaves are numbered as in the Khuda Bukhsh MS. Each page has 15 short lines as a rule, but the statistical figures are written in a finer hand and then more lines are put in the page, some of them being written crosswise. In such cases I have not given the exact number of the line (which is sometimes impossible to determine), but the number which the line would have had from its position if the page contained the usual 15 lines only. The reader will thus be able to see at a glance in what portion of a page a certain line is situated.

Mosques and gardens 48 *a*. 9—Doabs and rivers 48 *b*. 7—Mines 49 *a*. 7—Provincial Statistics *a*. 12—Detailed Stat. 49 *b*. 3 (4) MULTAN, 50 *a*. 1—its rulers *a*. 8—Saints 50 *b*. 3—Forts 51 *b*. 2 —Prov. Stat. *b*. 6—Detailed Stat. 51 *a*. 13. (5) THATHA, 52 *a*. 9 —its kings and Jáms 52 *b*. 9—Prov. Stat. 53 *a*. 8—Detailed Stat. *a*. 13. (6) KASHMIR, 53 *b*. 4.—its kings *b* 11—Lakes, hills, shrines and springs 56 *a*. 12—Mines and rivers 57 *b*. 10—Prov. Stat. 58 *a*. 4—Detailed Stat. *a*. 13. (7) ORISSA, 58 *b*. 2.—Saints *b*. 7—Temples *b*. 8—Prov. Stat. 60 *a*. 1.—Detailed Stat. *a*. 8. (8) BENGAL, 60 *a*. 12—its rulers 60 *b*. 8—its divisions and neighbouring countries 62 *a*. 2—Prov. Stat. 63 *a*. 4—Detailed Stat. *a*. 11—Rivers 63 *b*. 6. (9) BIHAR 63 *b*. 11—Kings and Saints *b*. 14—Rivers 64 *a*. 15—Hindu Shrines 64 *b* 13—Provincial Stat. *b*. 15—Detailed Stat. 65 *a*. 5. (10) ALLAHABAD, 65 *b*. 2—Kings *b*. 6—Saints *b*. 10—Hindu holy places 67 *a*. 2—Forts 67 *b*. 2—Mines *b*. 7—Prov. Stat. *b*. 13—Detailed Stat. 68 *a*. 6. (11) OUDH, 68 *b*. 7—Holy tombs 69 *a*. 2—Kings and Saints *a*. 7—Hindu holy places *a*. 11—other towns 69 *b*. 3—Prov. Stat. *b*. 7—Detailed Stat. 70 *a* 1. (12) AJMIṚ, 70 *a*. 10—Kings and Saints *a* 13—Forts and mines 71 *a* 2—Prov. Stat. 72 *a*. 7—Detailed Stat. *a* 13. (13) GUJRAT, 72 *b*. 12—Kings and Saints 73 *a*. 6—Hindu holy places 74 *b*. 11—Cities 75 *b*. 2—Prov. Stat. 76 *a*. 8—Detailed Stat. 76 *b*. 2 (14) MALWA, 77 *a*. 1—Kings *a*. 5—Cities 79 *b*. 1—Prov. Stat. 80 *a*. 11—Detailed Stat. 80 *b*. 4. (15) Kabul, 81 *a*.—Swad 84 *a* 1 to *a* 12.

Book II. II An account of the Five *Subahs* of the Deccan, with their rulers, saints, chief towns, forts, and Hindu holy places. The Deccan, 84 *a*. 13—(16) BERAR, 84 *b*. 11—Provincial Statistics 85 *b*.—Detailed Stat. 86 *a*. 3. (17) KHANDESH 86 *a*. 14—Prov. Stat. 87 *b*. 6—Detailed Stat. *b*. 9. (18) AURANGABAD, 87 *b*. 13—Prov. Stat. 88 *a*. 13—Detailed Stat. 88 *b*. 1.—Crops 88 *b*. (19) BIJAPUR, 89 *a*. 3—Prov. Stat. 90 *b*. 14—Detailed Stat. 91 *a*. 1—Nagarkot fort *a*. 8.—Revenue in money *a*. 14. (20) HAIDARABAD, 91 *b*. 2—Conquest of Golconda 92 *a*. 8—Prov. Stat. 94 *a*. 5—Detailed Stat. *a*. 10

(21) BIDAR, 94 *b.* 11—Prov. Stat 95 *a.* 7—Detailed Stat. *a.* 10—Industries and fruits *a.* 15—The SULTANS of the Deccan 96 *a.* 1.—The FORTS of Aurangabad 116 *b.* 2—of Khandesh and Berar 117 *a.* 7—of Bidar *a* 10—of Bijapur *a.* 12—of Haidarabad 117 *b.* 14—The SAINTS of the six Subahs of the Deccan 118 *a.* 6—Hindu shrines, Springs, and Rivers 119 *a.* 10 to 120 *a.* 11.

Book III.

III. The Distances and Stages, or a ROAD-BOOK showing the stages on the roads leading from Delhi to the different chief towns of India. 120 *a.* 12 to 125 *a.* 15.

Book IV.

IV. An account of the Hindu FAQIRS including the Sikh Gurus, the last in the list being the successor of Ajit Singh, 125 *b.* 1 to the end of the book.

Value of its information.

The book contains "so much information in a small compass that it resembles the ocean placed in a cup. The historical part is a mere abstract, and of no value; but the work has other points of interest, especially in the matter of the Biographies of the Muhammadan saints, which are written in a true spirit of belief, though the writer is a Hindu. The accounts of the Hindu fakirs, the Itineraries, and the Statistical Tables of the 22 Subas are also useful, though it is to be regretted that the latter are not given in sufficient detail to enable us to institute safe comparisons between its results and those given in the *Ain-i-Akbari.*" (Elliot viii, 255.)

The portions translated.

The topographical notices in Bk. I. are mostly a repetition of the corresponding portions of the *Ain-i-Akbari*, though necessarily in an abbreviated form. I have, therefore, merely given the names of the places in my translation, without quoting the descriptions in full. But in some places additional information is supplied, and every such item I have translated. The details of fairs, amusements, and other things, which are mostly vague and rhetorical, have been omitted by me. Nor have I translated the dry and short chronicles of the kings, or disturbed the holy repose of the saints[*] in the pages of my authority. My translation of Bk.I. is thus an abridged one, though the statistical and topographical points—the only materials of value—have been given with sufficient fulness. Bk. II. has been translated almost fully, though some of the topographical notices in the chapters on Aurangabad and Berar are merely copied from the *Ain* and the *Khulasat*. The accounts of the kings and saints have again been omitted, as also the history of the siege of Golconda,—because the siege of Bijapur, here translated in full, forms a good specimen of this kind of composition. In both these Books, the detailed statistical tables of the *Subahs* have presented an insurmountable difficulty,[†]

Mistakes in the Text.

They are evidently written by a person other than the transcriber of the rest of the book, and in a very small and illegible hand. Moreover, though the headings 'Sarkar,' 'Area,' 'Revenue' &c are put down in every column, yet in several cases the names of the *Sarkars* and the figures for the area and revenue are not given, the spaces being left blank. Then, again, the numbers are not expressed by numerals, but by Arabic letters which represent figures according to the system called *raqam*[‡] In the Khuda Bukhsh MS. one particular word-figure has puzzled me. It does not correspond to any of the figures given in the *Muktab-nama*, but looks like 3 and 7 joined into one. This letter seems to have been written over and altered by some other hand after it was first put down. In his statistics, our author first gives the total area, revenue, &c. of each *Subah* (province) written *fully in words*, and then in the detailed account (*tafsil-i-sarkárán*) the separate area, revenue &c of each of the *Sarkars* (divisions) composing the *Subah*. But these latter when added together do not always agree with the provincial total given above in the same chapter. I have

---

* Except in the case of Shaikh Mina, the patron saint of Lucknow, of whom the *Ain* (Vol. III.) gives no account.

† Thomas has noticed a similar discrepancy between the Provincial total and the *taqsim-jama* in the *Dastur al-Amal* (*Rev. Res.* pp 40 and 41).

‡ Thomas, *Rev. Res.* p. 45 *n*.

in every case pointed this out in my notes within square brackets at the end of each chapter in my translation of the *Chahar Gulshan.* The lists of the forts of the Deccan have been given in full, but only a few of these 260 places have been identified, because I had not the "Indian Atlas" sheets for the Deccan with me, and also because when a name was found on the Map similar to one in my text, I could not know whether it ever was a fort. Then, again, several places were found bearing the same or similar names, and in the corrupt state of my text I could not decide which of them was the place intended. Tieffenthaler gives lists of the forts of the Deccan They agree in many points with the lists of my authority, but differ from the latter in number and sometimes in names. Hence I conclude that both Chatar Mán and Tieffenthaler borrowed their lists from the same (unnamed) Persian work, the one with more and the other with less fulness. I have put the two lists side by side in my account of the Deccan.

Forts of the Deccan.

In the Road-book (Book III) we have 10 pages containing tables of the stages in the roads leading from Delhi to various other cities of the Empire, such as Bijapur, Atak, Kabul, Patna, Agra, Srinagar &c. I have reproduced the tables without any change, because, though each column is easy enough to follow, it is not very clear what is meant by the entries on the two sides or by the numerals used in some places. The latter evidently mean distance in *kos* from the last stage, but all the distances are not given. The Fourth Book has not been translated at all.

Road-book.

It will be thus seen that the 2nd and 3rd Books are of the greatest value to us. They supply such information as we cannot have from any other source. The same may be said of the Statistical Tables in Book I. also. Unfortunately these tables are in some cases evidently incorrect and in some others incomplete. I had no materials for supplying the omissions or rectifying the errors. Hence a comparison with the *Ain* would not be absolutely correct,

Originality.

Still, the ***Chahar Gulshan*** is of far greater value to us than the *Khulasat.* Though written in 1759 its statistics are evidently of an earlier date,—having been probably borrowed from some ***Dastur-al-Amal*** (Revenue Manual) of about 1720 A. D The author states that he cannot give the statistics of Bijapur and Haidarabad, "as Nizamu-l-mulk Asaf Jah during his viceroyalty carried away with himself the papers of every one of the six divisions of the Deccan." (p. 156) Asaf Jah first set up the standard of independence in the Deccan in 1720 A. D. Hence 1720 is the upward limit of the date of these statistics. In 1759, when the *Chahar Gulshan* was completed, the Empire of Delhi was a name only; the true Emperor was a fugitive; the Marathas had been enjoying much of the Deccan since 1716, and in 1725 they first crossed the Narbada under Baji Rao; the Panjab had been ceded to Ahmad Shah Durani eight years before. The statistics of this work obviously belong to a period when the whole Mughal Empire was still intact, the Emperor of Delhi still reigned in fact, and the provincial revenues were still paid into the Imperial Exchequer. The *Chahar Gulshan*, therefore, shows us the Mughal Empire as it was about 1720 A D.

Date of the Statistical Tables.

I had unfortunately to translate this work without any critical apparatus of the text. Though Elliot says that the *Chahar Gulshan* is common in India, I could not procure a second copy. The Asiatic Society of Bengal does not possess it. The only copy that I could get was the one in Khan Bahadur Khuda Bukhsh Khan's Oriental Library (Patna.) It has been neatly transcribed on Kashmiri paper, with a gilt front-page, by a man who was more remarkable for the beauty of his penmanship than the soundness of his Persian scholarship. Mistakes are numerous. In several places, esp. in the case of proper names (such as the towns which form the boundaries of *Subahs*), he has left blank spaces, as if he failed to make out the original which he transcribed. The copy is an octavo volume of 160 leaves, with 15 lines to the page, (except

MS.

in the case of the statistical tables, when more lines are compressed into a page.) Elliot mentions a MS. of 560 quarto pages with 13 lines to the page.

Before I could translate these two works, I had to edit them.

Emendation and Translation.

I first copied out the MSS. and settled and punctuated the texts, reading them with a Maulavi. Then I turned them into English, corrected the spelling of proper names, and elucidated obscure passages. In the latter work, Jarrett's translation of the *Ain-i-Akbari* (vol ii, and Dr. Stein's *Memoir on Maps of Ancient Kashmir* have been of the greatest service to me. The former, though inaccurate in some minute points (as I have pointed out in my notes), has been my guide all through the description of Hindustan, not only on account of the *Ain* having been the basis of the topographical notes of these two Persian works, but also on account of the scholarly notes of Col. Jarrett. Of Dr. Stein's *Memoir* it is impossible to speak too highly. But for it, the Persian accounts of Kashmir would have remained hopelessly obscure and confused. The *Imperial Gazetteer of India* (2nd Edition) was at my elbow while writing the notes.

Annotation.

I have added a marginal analysis to the *Khulasat* but not to the *Chahar Gulshan*,* as the latter is very much shorter and more condensed. In the foot notes I have tried with the help of modern sources of information and maps to throw light on the topography of Mughal India and to identify the places mentioned. In the latter work I have been only partly successful, as the corrupt condition of my texts made it impossible to Romanize correctly many of the proper names. I had to leave out, for want of space, much interesting matter, such as a contrast between then and now as regards the condition of particular places, old legends, &c ; but I have given references to other works which will guide the curious.

---

* The differentiation of the types (the antique being employed in the headings of my translation) will, I hope, supply this omission in the case of the *Chahar Gulshan.*

Maps. In the work of identifying old places, which has been done with different degrees of success in different parts, the following Atlases were before me: (1) Sheets marked "*Letts's Popular Atlas*," bound in one volume with the title of "Chatterjee's School Atlas" (George Gill & Sons, London, 1891) They are drawn on a scale of 35 miles to the inch, being neither too large nor too small for my purpose. Except for the representation of elevations forests &c. by colours and later additions (esp. railway lines), these sheets are identical with (2) "the *Atlas of India*, revised by J. Walker, selected from the Maps published under the superintendence of the Society for the Diffusion of Useful Knowledge" (Edward Stanford, London, 1853). This latter work has also been used by me, inasmuch as it is the oldest large-scale map of India and makes, of all the good maps we have, the nearest approach to the India of the Mughals. (3) That most useful publication, the *Indian Atlas* issued by the Surveyor-General of India on a scale of 4 miles to the inch, is so costly that one cannot complete Hindustan even after spending a hundred rupees. When it failed me, Letts's *Atlas* was consulted, sometimes with good results. (4) A very finely executed *Atlas of Southern India* (printed by John Walker, London, and issued by Pharoah and Co., Madras, *c.* 1854), on a scale of 16 m. to the inch, might have supplied my want of the *Indian Atlas* sheets for S. India. But the hopelessly illegible spelling of names in the Second Book of the *Chahar Gulshan* made it useless to me. (5) The *Agra and Calcutta Gazetteer* (4 vols, pub. by Rushton & Co., Calcutta, 1842), contains District maps of as much of Northern India as was then in British possession. But these plates have little to add to Letts's *Atlas*, which is a fuller, though later work. (6) Rennell's *Bengal Atlas* (Folio, 1781), though consulted, has been of only limited use, because it deals with Bengal and Bihar, of which provinces our authors Sujan Rai and Chatar Man, living up-country, had a very meagre and evidently second-hand knowledge.

Road-book.

The Itinerary or Road-book is the most valuable part of the *Chahar Gulshan*. Of the main routes of Mughal India we know something from Bernier, Tavernier, and Tieffenthaler, and the materials thus derived have been utilised in one of my own chapters. Elliot's translations from the Persian histories of India and Lowe's translation of Al-Badaoni, vol. II., throw side-lights on the stages and main lines of the old roads. But great as the value of Elliot's work is as a guide to the Muhammadan historians of India, it is not always reliable in its details, especially in the case of obscure proper names. Nearly all the histories which Elliot and Dowson dealt with were in unedited MSS., and the encyclopædic character of their work prevented minute attention to all its parts. For the purposes of a road-book, howover, minute accuracy in the spelling and identification of the names of places is of the utmost importance. Elliot has not tried to trace out all the places mentioned in his history, nor has he given their names in Persian characters as Briggs has done in the Appendix to his translation of Ferishta (vol. iv.). Such a course might in many cases have helped us to discover the correct name by tentatively varying the dots. Hence I have not been able to derive as much information from Elliot and Lowe as can be wished for. Rennell's *Bengal Atlas* is prefaced by a road-book* which, unfortunately, affords no help in elucidating the *Chahar Gulshan*, as the routes are different in the two works. The *Agra and Calcutta Gazetteer*, Vol. II. Pt. I., has one invaluable "Indian Road-book" covering 229 pp. and another (entitled "the Bengal and Agra Road-book") covering 37 pp., with an additional 19 pp.,—a total of 285 pages, containing detailed information about the distances between the stages, and the *nullahs*, *bazars*, toll-gates, ferries, wells, tanks, &c. on the route. From this source we get a good account of the main roads, before the old order

* The copy of Rennell's *Atlas* in the Library of the Asiatic Society of Bengal is wanting in this road-book.

had altogether disappeared from India, before railways were introduced, before the British dominions had extended beyond the Sutlej and the vast changes wrought by the annexation of the Panjab Sind and Burma and the Sepoy Mutiny, had taken place.

CHAPTER II.

THE MUGHAL EMPIRE : ITS EXTENT.

Subahs.

When in 1580, the 25th year of Akbar's reign, "the ten years' settlement of the revenue was made, His Majesty apportioned the Empire into *twelve* divisions, to each of which he gave the name of *Subah* and distinguished them by the appellation of the tract of country or its capital city. These were Allahabad, Agra, Oudh, Ajmir, Ahmadabad [*i.e.*, Gujrat], Behar, Bengal, Delhi, Kabul, Lahor, Multan, Malwah : and when Berar, Khandesh, and Ahmadnagar, were conquered, their number was fixed at *fifteen*." (*Ain.* ii. 115) The above list omits Kashmir, which was conquered in 1586. In the detailed account of the 15 *Subahs* given in the *Ain*, vol. II, no mention is made of Ahmadnagar, but Kashmir is added to complete the tale of 15 *Subahs*. In the *Chahar Gulshan* Ahmadnagar is included in the *Subah* of Aurangabad (see p. 151.) We may, therefore, conclude that Ahmadnagar did not form a *Subah* by itself. It should also be noted here that in Abul Fazl's time Orissa and Thatha were included in Bengal and Multan respectively, though they were afterwards constituted into separate provinces. Indeed, even Abul Fazl himself in the detailed account of the *Subahs* speaks of Thatha as a *Subah* and not *Sarkar* (*Ain*. ii. 339.) Akbar's 15 . himself in the detailed be valent to 17 *Subahs* of later times.

By 1695 this number had increased Kashmir is added to com the additional *Subah* (*Khulasat*). Abul *Chahar Gulshan* Ahmadnagar the date of the records in Aurangabad (see p. 151.) We may, number reached the maxim Ahmadnagar did not form a *Subah* by Bijapur, Haidarabad, and Bidar.

Sarkars and Mahals.

The following table will exhibit the numbers of the *Sarkars* (divisions of a province) and *Mahals* (sub-divisions) in the three periods* named above. I have omitted Kabul for the reasons already stated.

Subahs.	Number of Sarkars in A.D.			Number of Mahals in A.D.		
	1594	1695	1720	1594	1695	1720
1. Delhi ...	8	8	12	237	229	248
2. Agra ...	13	14	12	262	268	254
3. Allahabad ...	10	16	17	177	247	269
4. Oudh ...	5	5	5	133	197	149
5. Bihar ...	7	8	8	200	240	252
6. Bengal ...	19	27	28	688	1109	1243
7. Orissa ...	5	15?	12	99	233	258
8. Malwa ...	12	12	11	301	309	259
9. Ajmir ...	7	7	8	197	123	238
10. Gujrat ...	9	9	10	138	188	256
11. Multan ...	3	3	4	88	96	113
12. Thatha ...	5	4	4	53	58	60
13. Panjab ...	5	5	5	232	316	329
14. Berar ...	13†	10	10	242	200	200
15. Khandesh ...	1	5?	1	32	112	133
16. Kashmir ...	1	1	7	38	46	75
17. Aurangabad...	—	8	11	—	80	116
18. Bijapur ...	—	—	15‡	—	—	114‡
19. Haidarabad ...	—	—	12	—	—	96
20. Bidar ...	—	—	4	—	—	54
Total ...	123	157	196	3,117	4,051	4,716

* The figures for the third period are the Provincial Totals marked 'P' in the notes to my translation.

? indicates that the figures are of doubtful accuracy.

† The *Ain*, in the preliminary statement, gives the number of *Sarkars* as 16 and that of *mahals* as 242; but in the detailed account only 13 *Sarkars* are named and the *mahals* of these 13 make up the total of 242.

‡ These two figures are supplied from the *Dastur-al-amal* (D. 163) as the *C. Gulshan* is silent on this point.

Growth of the Empire.

We thus see that side by side with the outward expansion of the Empire caused by the annexation of new territory,—an expansion which is represented by the increase in the number of *Subahs*,—there was going on an internal growth in the old provinces. They were brought more under control, administration became more systematized, and sub-division of territory became more minutely developed. Thus, taking the same number of *Subahs* (viz. 16) as the basis of our comparison, we find that Akbar's 123 *Sarkars* had increased in a century to 149, and 25 years later to 154 *Sarkars*, while his 3117 *mahals* increased to 3971 in 1695 A.D. and to 4336 in 1720 A.D Including the newly acquired territory, the total number of *Sarkars* rose from 123 to 157 and 196, and that of *mahals* from 3,117 to 4,051 and 4.716 in 1695 and 1720 A.D. respectively.

Constant changes.

We shall see later on that changes were continually going on in the extent of the *Subahs*. A *Subah* of 1695 was not identical in extent with the *Subah* of 1594 bearing the same name, though the two had much in common. *Sarkars* were taken away from one province and attached to another, to suit new administrative needs, just as in British India, we see now and then a sub division taken away from one district and merged into another, or even a district transferred from one province to another. In this respect, as in many others, our present has its roots deep down in our past. It will be thus seen that the Mughal administration was not of a stereotyped character, it had not much of 'Chinese immobility.' It showed the same elasticity that characterises, and must characterise, every system that lasts centuries.

Area of measured land.

This administrative development is still more strikingly illustrated by the increase in the area (*raqba*) of measured land (*zamin-i paimuda.*) Unfortunately, the *Khulasat* is silent on this point, and so our comparison must be between the India of 1594 and the India of 1720, and even in this it must be limited to those *Subahs* of which the statistics are available. In the following table the area of measured land is given in *bighas* and *bisuas* (a *bisua* being one-twentieth of a *bigha.*) The *Chahar Gulshan* gives the "measured land" for Orissa as 9,01,26,259 *bighas*, a figure so obviously incorrect that I have suggested an emendation in my table.

Subahs.		Area in *bighas* in 1594 A D.	Area in *bighas* in 1720 A. D.
1.	Delhi ...	2,05,46,816—16	6,93,56,572—18
2.	Agra ...	2,78,62,189—18	5,58.79,207—2
3.	Allahabad ...	39,68,018—3	1,97,03,983—15
4.	Oudh ...	1,01,71,180	1,90,22,908
5.	Bihar ...	24,44,120	1,31,52,844—16
6.	Bengal ...	...	3,34.775
7.	Orissa ...	...	[91,26,259 ?]
8.	Malwa ...	42 66,221—6	1,29,64,538
9.	Ajmir ...	2,14.35,941—7	1,74,09,684
10.	Gujrat ...	1,69,36,377—3	1,27,49,374—6
11.	Multan ...	32,73,932—4	44,54,206—15
12.	Thatha ...	...	...
13.	Panjab ...	1,61,55,643—3	2,43,19,960
14.	Berar ...	...	2,00,28,100—13
15.	Khandesh ...	...	88,00,000—16
16.	Kashmir ...	...	...
Total for 16 *Subahs*		12,70,60,440	27,81,76,156—1*
17.	Aurangabad ...	...	2,55,70,950—9
18.	Bijapur ...	...	...
19.	Haidarabad ...	...	...
20.	Bidar ...	...	78,72,194—10
	Grand total ...	...	31,16,19,301 *

Progress of Land Survey.

We thus see that in the 16 Indian provinces of Akbar the area of measured land rose from 12,70,60,440 *bighas* to 27,81,76,156$\frac{1}{20}$ *bighas*, an increase of nearly 119 p. c. Not only were provinces left unsurveyed by Akbar—such as the newly conquered Bengal, Orissa, Berar,

* Excluding the area of Orissa given within square brackets.

and Khandesh,—surveyed for the first time during the intervening 125 years, but progress was also made in the survey of the older provinces,—the result being an increase of the measured area in every province except Ajmir and Gujrat. If we include the four provinces annexed to the Empire last of all, we have for 1720 A. D., a total surveyed territory of 31,16,19,301 *bighas* as against 12,70,60,440 *bighas* in 1594 A. D.

CHAPTER III.

THE MUGHAL EMPIRE : ITS REVENUE.

Thomas's Estimates.

Mr. E. Thomas gives us seven different estimates of the revenue of the Mughal Empire between 1594 and 1707. His first authority is the *Ain-i-Akbari* (1594), his second the *Badshah-nama* (1648), his third and fifth the *Dastur-al-amals* (revenue manuals) of 1654 and a later and unknown date, his fourth Bernier (1665), his sixth Mannucci (1697), and his seventh Ramusio in Harris's *Voyages* (1707). From these I have chosen the first and the fifth for comparison with the revenue returns furnished by the *Khulasat* (1695) and the *Chahar Gulshan* (1720), because they are based on official records, as my two authorities are, though Thomas makes little of the former and prefers "to rely upon external testimony rather than upon the formal papers of the servants of the State : these latter usually refer to a given assessment or settlement of the land revenue for a term of years, without marking in any distinct way the incidental fluctuations of absolute collections, the loss of territory, or the spread of conquest .. whereas a competent witness at head quarters [like any of the European travellers] would be in a position to obtain exact information of the actual income for the current year, as it was reported, on immediate realization from the various divisions of the empire."* But the authors of the *Khulasat* and the *Chahar Gulshan* wrote far away from the capital ; hence, their source of information must

Dastur-al-amal

* *The Revenue Resources of the Mughal Empire*, pp. 40 and 41.

have been official records like the *Dastur-al-amal*. Their returns partake of the character of these official records in being "definite and distinct in their totals." A comparison of their figures with those of foreign observers 'at head-quarters" would not be fair. I am, also, inclined to assign a later date than Thomas,—say 1700 A. D.,—to the *Dastur-al-amal* MS. C. (Thomas, p. 41), because the figures supplied by it make a close approximation to those of the *Chahar Gulshan* and evidently belong to a period when the newly conquered *Subahs* of the Deccan had been fully settled.

Corrections of the Ain-i-Akbari.

Thomas, writing in 1871, had Gladwin's translation of the *Ain-i-Akbari* before him, as is evident also from his footnotes. In compiling my column of revenue for 1594 I have followed Jarrett's translation, converting the *dams* into rupees,* with the following modifications and corrections :—

(1) For Berar, the *Ain* (ii. 231) gives a total revenue of 64,26,03,272 *dams*. But by adding together the revenues of the 13 *Sarkars* of the province we get a total of 64,60,07,264 *dams*. The former sum has been accepted as the difference between the two is slight (Rs. 85,099-12-10 only.)

(2) In the revenue of the Panjab, Jarrett has dropped the final zero in the rupee equivalent of the *dams* (ii. 315).

(3) In the revenue of Multan the rupee equivalent of the *dams* is 37,85,090 and not 3,78,590 as given by Jarrett (ii. 328.) But by adding together the *taqsim jama* of the *Sarkars* we get a total provincial revenue of 20,16,75,418 *dams* (Rs. 50,41,885), which I have adopted. Thomas, however, raises the amount to 38,40,30,589 *dams*. (*Rev. Res.* p. 13).

(4) The total revenue of Thatha is given as 66,15,393 *dams*. This is evidently incorrect, because the *taqsim jama* of the *Sarkars* amount to 6,62,51,393 *dams* (ii. 339.) I have accepted the latter sum.

(5) The revenue of Kashmir is explicitly given as 6,21,13,040

* In converting *dams* into rupees in the following tables I have taken every fraction above 12 annas as an entire rupee.

dams (ii. 368) ; but on the preceding page we are told that Kazi Ali's revenue was 7,46,70,411 *dams* and Asaf Khan's assessment less than that amount by 8,60,034 *dams.* This ought to yield a revenue of 7,38,10,377 *dams* (Rs. 18,45,259-6-10.) I had, however, to accept the first-mentioned sum.

Hence, my figures for Akbar's revenue will be found to differ somewhat from those given by Thomas. His total of Akbar's revenue excluding Kabul is Rs. 13.38,38,552 against my Rs. 13,21,36,831 for the same number of provinces.

In the column for the *Dastur-al amal*, MS. C., I have followed pp. 42 and 43 of Thomas and not pp. 52 and 53, as some of the figures of the latter pages unaccountably differ from those given in the former. In all subsequent quotations from this source, pp, 42 aud 43 will be followed in preference to pp 52 and 53 of Thomas.

Dastur, MS. C.

In the column for the *Chahar Gulshan*, the revenue of every *Subah* is the rupee equivalent of the provincial total in *dams* and not of the *taqsim jama* of the *Sarkars* added together. In the case of Bijapur, however, I have given the "collection in cash" (p. 156)

Kabul, Qandhar, Badakhshan, and Balkh have been left out of my calculations, as they are outside the frontiers of India.

REVENUE IN RUPEES IN A. D.

	Subahs		1594 (*Ain-i-Akbari*)	1695 (*Khulasat*)	1700 ? (*Dastur-al-amal* MS. C.)	1720 ? (*Chahar Gulshan*)
1.	Delhi	...	1,50,40,389	1,86,58,375	3,05,73,753	2,64,65,892
2.	Agra	...	1,36,56,257	2,45,45,000	2,40,29,175	2,24,16,110
3.	Allahabad	...	53,10,695	94,01,525	1,05,33,673	72,55,806
4.	Oudh	...	50,43,954	66,13,500	69,89,490	83,10,015
5.	Bihar	...	55,47,985	95,18,250	73,58,613	94,60,434
6.	Bengal	...	1,18,18,167	1,15,72,500	1,31,15,903	1,40,72,725
7.	Orissa	...	31,43,316	1,01,02,625	43,21,025	—
8.	Malwa	...	60,17,376	92,25,425	1,02,08,667	90,04,593
9.	Ajmir	...	72,10,039	1,38,84,000	1,50,74,500	1,75,29,829
10.	Gujrat	...	1,09,20,557	1,45,94,750	1,34,13,125	1,32,57,233
11.	Multan	...	50,41,885	61,15,375	49,95,057	45,90,786
12.	Thatha	...	16,56,285	23,74,250	17,20,025	17,32,938
13.	Panjab	...	1,39,86,460	2,23,34,500	2,23,25,985	1,45,29,765
14.	Berar	...	1,60,65,082	1,51,81,750	2,31,63,625	2,25,60,000
15.	Khandesh	...	1,13,82,356	1,10,90,475	1,05,00,000	1,15,00,750
16.	Kashmir	...	15,52,826	31,57,125	69,47,784	53,20,502
17.	Aurangabad	...	—	1,29,07,000	2,95,93,375	2,95,00,002
18.	Bijapur	...	—	—	5,63,68,178	3,36,84,771
19.	Haidarabad	...	—	—	2,50,70,875	2,73,20,875
20.	Bidar	...	—	—	2,05,13,750	1,55,13,750
	Total		13,21,36,831	20,12,76,425	33,68,16,584	29,40,76,776

Total Revenue.

We may make a further study by comparing the total revenue of India proper at *all* the dates mentioned by Thomas with the totals suppiied by the *Khulasat* and the *Chahar Gulshan*. The authorities are cited within brackets after the years :—

1594 (*Ain-i-Akbari*) ...	Rs. 13,21,36,831	(for 16 *Subahs*.)	
1648 (*Badshah-nama*)...	„ 21,15,00,000	(„ 19 „	)
1654 (*Dastur-al amal*)	„ 26,35,12,752	(„ 18 „	)
1665 ? (Bernier) ...	„ 22,06,70,500	(„ 18 „	omitting Bengal.)
1695 (*Khulasat*) ...	„ 20,12,76,425	(„ 17 „	)
1697 (Mannucci) ...	„ 38,30,39,552	(„ 21 „	omitting Bengal.)
1700 ? (*Dastur*, MS. C.)...	„ 33,68,16,584	(„ 20 „	)
1707 (Ramusio) ...	„ 29,77,70,876	(„ 20 „	)
1720 ? (*Chahar Gulshan*)	„ 29,40,76,776	(„ 19 „	omitting Orissa.)

CHAPTER IV.

THE PROVINCES :

1. DELHI.

Extent

Under Akbar this province extended 165 *kos* in length from Palwal to Ludhiana, and 140 *kos* in breadth from the frontier of Rewari to Kumaon, or 130 *kos* from Hissar to Khizrabad. (*Ain*. ii. 278) The *Khulasat* and the *Chahar Gulshan* merely repeat the above description of its limits.

Divisions.

The *Sarkars* (divisions) and *mahals* (sub-divisions) of which this province was made up at different periods may be learned from the annexed table :

1594	A. D.	(Authority : *Ain* ii)	8 *Sarkars*,	237	***mahals***
1665 ?	„	(„ Bernier)	16 „	230	***parganas***
1695	„	(„ *Khulasat*)	8 „	229	***mahals***
1700 ?	„	(„ *Dastur-al-amal* *)	12 „	261	„
1720 ?	„	(„ *Chahar Gulshan*)	12 „	248	„

* The *Dastur-al-amal* I have used is MS. D. 163 of the Library of the Asiatic Society of Bengal. It is referred to by Thomas on p. 40 line 3 of the footnote (*Rev. Res.*) Owing to the carelessness or ignorance of the copyist of this MS. I have shared Thomas's difficulty in discriminating the badly formed *raqams* or abbreviated word-figures. I suppose the date of this work to be about 1700 A. D.

I now give the names of the *Sarkars** with the number of the *mahals* belonging to each :

(1594)		(1695)	(1720)	
Delhi	48*m*.	Delhi	Delhi	51
Badaon	13	Badaon	Badaon	20
Kumaon	21	——	Kumaon	7
Sambhal	47	Sambhal	Sambhal	49
Shahranpur	36	Shahranpur	Shahranpur	28
Rewari	12	Rewari	Rewari	11
Hissar	27	Hissar	Hissar	28
Sirhind	33	Sirhind.	Sirhind	38
		Narnol	Narnol †	15
			Tijara	18
			Srinagar	7
			Faizabad	12

Thus we see that the extent of the province was changed in each of the two latter periods, first by substituting one *Sarkar* for another of Akbar's list, and secondly by the incorporation of new *Sarkars* with it. Yet, the authors of the *Khulasat* and the *Chahar Gulshan* slavishly followed Abul Fazl in defining the boundaries of the province, though the latter's demarcation could not truly apply to the new state of things. The 2nd of the above tables will also show the comparative numbers of *mahals* for the *Sarkars* taken separately, in 1594 and 1720

Area and Revenue.

The total area of measured land for the entire province increased from 2,05,46,817 *bighas* in 1594 to 6,93,56,573 bighas in 1720. Below is given comparative view of the areas and revenues of the *Sarkars* common to the *Ain* and the *Chahar Gulshan*, though some of them are included in different provinces in the two works.

* Tieffenthaler, in his account of Hindustan, merely repeats the "divisions" of the *Ain*. His account of the Deccan comes from another source. The date of his statistics must have been much earlier than that of the publication of his work (1786.) Where he merely repeats the *Ain* I do not quote him.

† The *Ain* includes Narnol and Tijara in the Province of Agra. Faizabad is now included in Oudh.

Sarkars	Area in *bighas* in A. D.		Rev. in Rs. in A. D.	
	1594	1720	1594	1720
Delhi ...	71,26,108	1,21,456	30.75,315	61,63,043
Badaon ...	80,93,850	1,65,928	8,70,426	29,22,244
Kumaon ...	——	——	10,10,942	4,20,000
Sambhal ...	40,47,193	47,53,321	16,73,536	35,41,843
Shaharanpur	35,30,370	36,29,315	21,95,991	27,27,682
Rewari ...	11,55,011	13,95,535	8,80,566*	10,26,983
Hissar ...	31,14,497	71,48,184	13,13,872	22,09,483
Sirhind ...	77,29,466	1,57,86,388	40,19,763	60,81,227
Tijara ...	7,40,001	2,00 376	4,42,511	8,07,322
Narnol ...	20,80,046	68,04,356	12,51,167	19,20,819

Here we notice an increase of the measured area in every *Sarkar* expect Delhi, Badaon, and Tijara, while the revenue shows a marked increase everywhere except in Kumaon. The total Provincial Revenue was

in 1594	(*Ain*. ii. 285) ...	Rs.	1,50,40,389
1648	(*Badshahnama*) ...	„	2,50,00,000 †
1654	(*Dastur-al-amal*) ...	„	3,89,70,978 †
1665	(Bernier) ...	„	1,95,25,000 †
1695	(*Khulasat*) ...	„	1,86,58,375
1697	(Mannucci) ...	„	1,25,50,000 †
1700	(*Dastur-al-amal*, MS. C.)	„	3,03,23,753 †
1707	(Ramusio) ...	„	3,05,48.753 †
1720	(*Chahar Gulshan*) ...	„	2,64,65,892
	(Tieffenthaler, p. 135)...	„	3,05,73,753

Places of Note.

I give below an account of the places of note in this province, indicating within brackets in which of the three works,—the *Ain*, the *Khulasat*, and the

* This is not given separately in the *Ain* (ii. 293); but I have worked it out by subtracting the revenues of the other 7 *Sarkars* from the total provincial revenue.

† All these figures are taken from Thomas, pp. 52 and 53, except the figures for 1700 which are taken from pp. 42 and 43 of his work, for a reason already stated.

Chahar Gulshan (marked A, K, and C respectively), they are mentioned.

(i) TOMBS of Muhammadan Saints : *Panipat*, the burial-place of Abu Ali Qalandar *alias* Sharfuddin ; *Sirhind* that of Fariduddin Sani and Muhammad Masum Kabuli ; *Sadhaura* that of Shah Qames ; *Sunam* that of Shaikh Taiwi (K) ; *Hansi* that of Jamal-ud-din, the successor of Fariduddin Ganj-i-shakkar (A & K.) and *Badaon*.

(ii) Hindu HOLY PLACES : (1) *Thaneswar* (A, K, & C), near which flows the Saraswati, one of the sacred rivers. In the neighbourhood is the lake of Kuru-kshetra in which vast crowds of pilgrims bathe. (2) *Har-mandil* or *Hari mandir* (A, K, & C) in the city of Sambhal ; here Kalki, the last Incarnation of Vishnu, will be born as the son of a Brahman. (3) *Nának-math* or *Nának-matá*, (K & C) near Sambhal, was a holy place of the Sikhs. Tieffenthaler thus describes it (i. 140). "Nanakmatha, a place celebrated for the hand (or writing) of Nanak carved on a tree,—30 m from Barili, 18 short miles from Philibhit, and 3 m. from the nearer bank of the Garra" (4) *Prabhás kund* (A & C), a hot-water spring in the hill of Islamabad. (5) A hot-water spring near the town of *Sahna*, 14 *kos* from Delhi (A & C), "the peculiarity of which is undoubtedly due to a sulphur mine." (A.) (6) Near *Narnol* is a sacred well which overflows of itself when the conjunction of the moon occurs on a Friday. (A & C.) (7) *Hardwar*, *Hrishikesh*, *Badrinath*, and *Kedarnath*, in the Himalayas, near the source of the Ganges. The first three are mentioned by K. and all of them by C. ; but, curiously enough, the *Ain* has nothing to say about any of them,- not even Hardwar,—though the *Kumbh mela* there must have been as famous in Akbar's time as in Aurangzib's. (8) *Jog-máyá* (C) near the garden of Mihr-parwar Begam. (9) *Surajkund*,* a sacred reservoir near the Serai of Khawajah Bakhtawar Khan, south of Delhi (C) (10) *Nagam-budh* where the Fish Incarnation of Vishnu appeared (C.) (11) *Parsun*,

* There is another *Surajkund* in Oudh (*Ain* ii. 173).

the hermitage of Rishi Paráshar, 2 *kos* west of Faridabad, south of Delhi. (C) (12) *Pinjaur*, 30·48 N. 78·59 E, contained the shrine of Bhimá Devi (K) (13) *Bhupa ?* an old shrine on the bank of the Saraswati, 10 *kos* from Thaneswar (C).

(iii) Famous GARDENS: (1) The garden of Hafiz Rakhnah at Sirhind (A) (2) The garden of Fidai Khan Koka at Pinjaur (K), "laid out on the natural slope of the ground in six separate and successive terraces, one below another."

Delhi City.

Delhi was the capital of Hindustan and the intellectual and political centre of all India, during the empire of the Mughals. Under Akbar's grandson it was renamed after the reigning monarch, and it is by this name of *Shah-Jahanabad* that it is spoken of in K. & C., and indeed in all later Persian histories. An idea of the splendour, wealth, and population of the metropolis may be gathered from the *Khulasat*, which breaks into poetry in the description of it. The city was commanded by a red sand-stone fortress, and enclosed by a stone wall and a broad ditch, while the river Jumna washed its feet in the eastern side. Firuz Shah's canal flowed through the city and spread freshness and verdure along its margins. The population of Delhi was cosmopolitan. Trade, education, diplomacy, administration, pleasure, and curiosity alike drew to it vast crowds from remote regions. The bazar, especially the *Chandni Chauk*, contained the produce of every country in the world, for here thronged the rich and the gay, here the "wealth of Ind" changed hands. The *Khulasat* mentions the *Jama Masjid* and the Imperial Bath only among the grand public buildings, but omits the Pearl Mosque and the Audience Halls built by Shah Jahan.

Its Environs.

Glorious as Shah-Jahanabad was, it was situated in the grave-yard of Indian capitals. In its neighbourhood had sprung up capitals and royal palaces in every age of Indian history. The *Khulasat* enumerates sixteen such, and the record of former dynasties and their royal seats stretches through the epochs of Mughals and Pathans, Rajputs and Pandavas, till it is lost in the twilight of fable. On the fall of a dynasty or the desolation by fire or plague of one city, or at the changing caprice of the reigning despot, the site was changed and the capital was shifted to a place a mile or two off, where a new capital soon sprang up, only to share the fate of its predecessors when its short day of glory was over. Thus the environs of Delhi, for miles and miles round, are littered over with historic ruins, among which the lamp of the antiquarian may help us to discover the vestiges of the past The suburbs were not only rich in such ruins, but during the later Empire boasted of the villas of the rich and the mansions of the nobles, each reposing in the midst of its extensive gardens and clusters of trees.

Tombs.

Other gardens there were in the suburbs which enclosed the tombs of nobles and ministers, scholars and saints. "Within and around this large town are the tombs of many of the former kings ; but the most famous is the sepulchre of the Emperor Humayun. The tombs of nobles, ministers, scholars, and accomplished persons, situated within orchards and gardens, are too many to be enumerated. There is *a separate city formed by the tombs* of the departed" (p. 10 of translation.) Here, far off from the din and dust of the city, were their "places of sleep" as the *Khulasat* touchingly calls their tombs. If the wrangle of the school, the controversy of the church-porch, the rivalry of the council-chamber, the intrigue of the Court, and the strife of the stricken field were fitly represented by the big roaring city where they had passed so much of their lives, surely, these graves,—each standing apart within its grassy compound, each shaded by green trees, far away from the noise and bustle of the metropolis,—were also emblematic of the silence and peace of that sleep in which they await the judgment of their Maker.

Fairs

The *Chahar Gulshan* gives a long acconnt of the *melas* and *chhattars*,—15 are separately named,—held near Delhi, in which devotion and trade were combined. Primarily religious gatherings, they were soon converted into fairs, in which the pleasure-seeker and the trader outnumbered the devotee and the pilgrim. Such fairs were held near Hindu shrines and Moslem saints' tombs alike (pp. 123 and 124). But the Ganges Fair at Garh Mukhteswar seems to have surpassed all others in grandeur and merriment, while in point of sanctity and true devotion the *Kumbh mela* at Hardwar was, as it still is, at the head of all Indian fairs. As we read the account of these numberless fairs and gatherings round Delhi, we almost forget that the *Chahar Gulshan* was written in 1759. The gay and fickle butterflies of the capital seem to have turned the year into one long holiday and spent their lives in a round of merry-making and sight-seeing, as if Nadir Shah's invasion were not a thing of living memory to them and the spear of the Maratha and the long knife of the Durani Afghan did not yearly glitter before their eyes.

Mines. In the hills of Kumaon were mines of gold, silver, lead, iron, copper, orpiment and borax (*Ain.* ii. 280 and *Khulasat* p. 16 of trans.)

Crops. "Cultivation depends upon rain and irrigation, and in some places on wells. In certain tracts tillage yields 3 crops in the year. The fruits of Iran, Turan and Hindustan grow in plenty" (*Khulasat*, p. 22, and *Ain*, p. 278).

Manufacture. No manufacture is mentioned in any of these 3 works, except that of rose-water at Pinjaur in K.

2. AGRA.

Extent The length of this province was 175 *kos* from Ghatampur to Palwal, and its breadth [100 *kos*] from Kanauj to Chanderi in Malwa. (*Ain.* ii. 179) K. & C. merely repeat the above boundaries, though evidently inapplicable to the altered *Subah* of Agra of their times

Divisions. The province was divided into *Sarkars* and *mahals* in the the following manner :

1594	...	13 *Sarkars*,	262 *mahals*	
1665	...	14	„	216 *parganas*
1695	...	14	„	268 *mahals*
1700	...	22*	„	244 „
1720	...	12	„	254 „

I next give the names of the *Sarkars* with the number of the *mahals* belonging to each :

(1594)		(1695)	(1720)	
Agra	33*m*	Agra	Agra	48
Kalpi	16	Kalpi	Kalpi	14
Kanauj	30	Kanauj	Kanauj	30
Kol	21	Kol	Kol	13
Gwalior	16	Gwalior	Gwalior	23
Irij	16	Irij	Irij	20
Bayanwan	27	Satuan	Bayanwan	30
Narwar	5	Narwar	Narwar	23
Mandlaer	14	Mandlapur	Mandlaer	15
Alwar	43	Alwar	Alwar	43
Sahar	7	Bari ?	Sahar	7
Tijara	18	Tijara	—	
Narnol	16	[Two not named]	Sanor	6

Here it should be noted that the *Ain* includes *Narnol* in Agra, but K. & C. include it in Delhi. *Tijara* is placed in Agra by A. & K. and in Delhi by C., the latest of the 3 works. A. & C. mention the *Sarkar* of *Bayanwan*, for which a note in the *Ain* adds the variant Sanwan, evidently the same as the *Satuan* of K. K. mentions by name only 12 out of its 14 *Sarkars*. Alone among the 3 works, K. mentions a *Sarkar* named *Bari*, and C. another named *Sanor*.

Area and Revenue. The total area of measured land increased from 2,78 62,190 *bighas* in 1594 to 5,58,79,207 *bighas* in 1720.

* This may be a copyist's error for 12.

I give below a comparative study of the areas and revenues of the *Sarkars* common to 1594 and 1720.

Sarkars.	Area in *bighas* in		Rev. in Rs. in	
	1594	1720	1594	1720
Agra ...	9,10,07,324	2,00,97,473	47,95,481	1,50,601 ?
Kalpi ...	3,00,023	47,92,565	12,33,918	10,00,028
Kanauj ...	27,76,674	54,62,569	13,14,615	25,01,386
Kol ...	24,61,730	26,69,310	13,74,823	11,14,239
Gwalior ...	11,46,465	41,46,148	7,42,091	24,90,453
Irij ...	22,02,125	33,43,777	9,44,510	22,24,046
Bayanwan ...	7,62,014	12,49,197	2,11,482	8,84,183
Narwar ...	3,94,353	41,46,147	1,05,833	4,09,002
Mandlaer ...	65,642	47,92,462	93,452	5,00,534
Alwar ...	16,62,012	24,57,410	9,95,805	23,98,356
Sahar ...	7,63,474	14,27,148	1,47,939	6,13,689

Here an increase of the measured area is noticed everywhere except in the *Sarkar* of Agra, the increase being more than tenfold in Kalpi and Narwar. The area of Kol in 1594 is wrongly given in Jarrett's translation, the final zero having been dropped by oversight. The revenue of the *Sarkar* of Agra in 1720 cannot be correctly stated, as the leaf containing it is partly wormeaten. The rise in the revenue is most marked in Gwalior, Bayanwan, Narwar, Mandlaer, and Sahar,—there being slight decreases in Kalpi and Kol only.

The total provincial revenue was

in 1594	Rs. 1,36,56,257	1697	Rs. 2,22,03,550
1648	,, 2,25,00,000	1700	,, 2,40,29,175
1654	,, 3,41,15,052	1707	,, 2,86,69,003
1665	,, 2,52,25,000	1720	,, 2,24,16,110
1695	,, 2,45,45,000	(Tieff. i. 169).	,, 2,80,44,004

(i). Muhammadan TOMBS: (1) At *Sikandra*, 5m. from Agra, is the tomb of Akbar (K). (2) In the *Taj*

Places of Note.*

* Henceforth in these topographical notes I shall leave out the *Chahar Gulshan* where it merely repeats the *Ain* or the *Khulasat*, which preceded it in date.

Mahal Shah Jahan lies buried by the side of the wife he loved. (3) *Kalpi* (A & K) contains the tombs of many saints. (4) *Gwalior* (K) holds the tomb of Shaikh Muhammad Ghaus. (5) At *Makhanpur* (K),—now in the Cawnpur District,—is the tomb of Shaikh Bahau-d-din, a place of annual pilgrimage. (6) *Char-bagh*,—now called Rambagh,—(A) opposite Agra on the other side of the Jumna, where Faizi lies buried.

(ii). HOLY PLACES of the HINDUS : (1) *Rangtah* (A) on the bank of the Jumna, near Agra. (2) *Mathura* (A & K) one of the most famous of the places of Hindu worship. The *Khulasat* adds that the celebrated temple of Keshava Rai was demolished by order of the Emperor Alamgir (in 1669 A.D.) and a mosque erected on the site. The *faujdar* Abdu-n-Nabi Khan built another mosque (the "cathedral" mosque) and a beautiful *ghat* called *Bisrant*. (3) *Kanori* (A) had hot springs.

(iii). TOWNS : *Fatihpur-Sikri*, (A. & K) a village 12 *kos* from Agra, was raised into an important and beautiful city by Akbar, who built here a fort, palace, mosque, college, religious house, &c. Near it is a lake, 4 miles square, on the bank of which the Emperor constructed a court-yard, a *minar*, and polo-grounds. It was to Akbar what Versailles was to Louis XIV. or St. Cloud to Napoleon I. On the death of Akbar the importance of the place declined. (2) *Kanauj*, (A & K), a very old city and a capital of Hindustan in ancient times. (3) *Gwalior* (A & K)—its impregnable fort was used as a state prison. This district was the home of good musicians (including the famous Tánsen) and beautiful women. (4) *Biana* (A & K.), a very old city, the importance of which entirely declined on the rise of Agra. It had a strong fort in which captive rebels used to be confined (according to the *Khulasat*), but which even in Akbar's time had fallen into disuse and was looked upon as a lumber-room of old curiosities (A).

Agra City.

Agra was formerly a village belonging to the sub-division of Biana. Sikandar Lodi (1488-1516) chose it for his capital and founded a city on the *left* bank of the Jumna. The citadel got the name of *Badal-garh.* Akbar made it his capital, partly to escape from the over-crowded and insanitary old site of Delhi and its intolerable heat, but chiefly because Agra occupied a more central position in the Empire. From Agra issued three main roads, one leading to Allahabad Patna and Bengal, another to the Deccan, and a third to Rajputana. Agra was, therefore, a far more convenient base of supplies in his Indian wars than Delhi. A campaign into Rajputana, Gujrat, or Ahmadnagar could be more readily undertaken from Agra. Taking advantage of the unoccupied site on the *right* bank of the river, he laid out a fine city, with "a royal palace, the residences of many of the nobility,...numerous mansions and gardens." "The Jumna flows through the city for four *kos*, and on both sides lofty buildings and charming villas have been built". Akbar's red sand-stone fort was built in 1566 A D. He beautified his new capital, fortified it, and finally gave it his own name,—for it is known as *Akbar-abad* in Muhammadan histories. But like all other royal favourites, Agra enjoyed glory and importance during one reign only. Jahangir did not share his father's love of this city ; he was more attracted by Lahor and Kashmir. Shah Jahan deserted it for Delhi and lavished his wealth in beautifying a new city there, which was named after him Shah-Jahanabad. But he made ample amends for it : he immortalised Agra by his priceless gift of the Taj Mahal. Aurangzib had, of needs, to shift the capital to his camp during the long and arduous wars in the Deccan, where cities soon grew out of Mughal encampments. At last he laid down his old bones in the scene of his toil, without being able to return to the capital of his fathers. Opposite Agra, on the other bank of the Jumna, was the pleasant garden of "Char-bagh, a memorial of Babar." In this suburb Abul Fazl was born, and here his brother Faizi, the poet-laureate of Akbar, lies buried.

Mines.

The *Ain* mentions copper mines at *Perath*, (in Narnol), *Singhana*, *Udaipur*, and *Kotputli*, silver mines at *Perath*, old and unremunerative copper and turquoise mines at *Toaah Bhim*,—[K. wrongly transfers the last description to *Kalpi,*]—an iron mine in *Gwalior*, and a red-stone quarry near Fatihpur.

Biana was famous for its *mango* (A), *wood-apple*, and *melon* (K)

Crops &c. "*Indigo* of the finest quality and excellent *hinna*" were also to be had here (A)

"Sugar of extreme whiteness" was manufactured at Biana and

Industries. a famous kind of sugar-candy at Kalpi. (A & K) Excellent carpets were woven at Fatihpur (A) and Alwar, the latter place producing articles of glass also. Agra was famous for its "gold and silver embroidery on turbans and on other kinds of cloth ..very nicely done." (K)

3. ALLAHABAD.

Its length from Sinjhauli (in the Jaunpur District) to the sou-

Extent. thern hills (the Kaimur range) was 160 *kos* ; its breadth from Chausa (on the Ganges) to Ghatampur was 122 *kos* (A. & K.)

The following were the *Sarkars* and *mahals* of which the pro

Divisions. vince was composed in different periods :

1594	...	10 *Sarkars*,	177 *mahals*
1665	...	17 „	216 *parganas*
1695	...	16 „	247 *mahals*
1700	...	17 „	269 „
1720	...	17 „	269 „
(Tieffenthaler)		9*	

Sarkars (1594)		(1695)	(1720)	
Allahabad	11*m*	Allahabad	Allahabad	11
Benares	8	Benares	Benares	9
Jaunpur	41	Jaunpur	Jaunpur	42
Manikpur	14	Manikpur	Manikpur	14
Chunar	13	Chunar	Chunar	15
Kalinjar	11	Kalinjar	Kalinjar	10

* All the *Sarkars* mentioned in the *Ain*, except Bhath-khora.

Corah	9	Corah	Corah	8
Ghazipur	19	[The other 9	Ghazipur	17
Bhathkhora	39	not named]	Bhathkhora	
Karrah	12		Karrah	12
			Barhar	18
			[The other 6 not named]	

The total area of measured land for the whole province rose from 39,68,018 *bighas* in 1594 to 1,97,03,984 *bighas* in 1720.

Area and Revenue.

Sarkars	Area in *bighas* in		Rev. in Rs. in	
	1594	1720	1594	1720
Allahabad ...	573.311	15,53,607	5,20,834	9,69,147
Benares ...	36,869	4.53,354	2,21,733	1,35,750
Jaunpur ...	8,70,265	54,51,119	14,09,852	25,97 088
Manikpur ...	6,66,222	21,01,324	8,47 913	15,06,270
Chunar ...	1,06,270	7,40,687	1,45,266	87.500
Kalinjar ...	5,08,273	43,38,324	5,95,987	11,75,001
Corah ...	3,41,170	13,57.817	4,34,939	14,39,183
Ghazipur ...	2,88,770	17,33,349	3,35,782	3,63,836
Karrah ...	4,47,557	14,17,127	5,67,051	9,29,140

Everywhere the area of measured land increased remarkably, the increase being most striking in the *Sarkars* of Benares, Jaunpur, Chunar, Kalinjar, and Ghazipur. As regards revenue, there was an unaccountable falling off in Benares and Chunar, but in the other seven *Sarkars* there is an increase, sometimes a great increase.

The total provincial revenue was

in 1594	Rs.	53,10,695	in 1697	Rs.	77,38,000
1648	„	1,00,00,000	1700	„	1,05,33,673
1654	„	1,31,97,029	1707	„	1,14,13,581
1665	„	94,70,000	1720	„	72,55,806*
1695	„	94,01,525	Tieff.	„	1,14,13,581

* This amount is of doubtful accuracy, as the *taqsim jama* of all the *Sarkars* taken together, exceeds it by more than 20 lacs of Rupees.

Places of Note.

(1) ALLAHABAD (A. K. & C.) is called *Praydg* in the Hindu Scriptures. The confluence of the two grand rivers, Ganges and Jumna, was very early recognised as a one of the holiest of places, and bathing here was regarded as a means of washing away all sins.* The third member of the Hindu riparian trinity, the Saraswati, which seems to have mysteriously disappeared after the early age of faith and which devotees of every place have sought to locate in their own neighbourhood,—was supposed to have here joined the other two rivers and thus given to Allahabad its name of *Tribeni* or 'the three braids of hair.' Akbar renamed the town *Illahabas* (A); but Shah Jahan changed the name into *Illahabad* (K.) Akbar's sand-stone fortress still exists and excites admiration by its strength and massiveness. Within the fort there is a very old tree called the *Akshaya-bata* or 'the imperishable banian tree.' The *Ain* does not mention it, though it must have existed from long before Akbar's time. Jahangir cut it down and fixed on the stump a caldron of iron (K.) But the tree grew again and shook off the obstruction. Both K. & C. mention that "in former times" there was a saw here, under which devotees used to place their necks and make a sacrifical offering of their heads "in the hope of final redemption and the obtaining of their desires in the next world. This practice was forbidden by Shah Jahan." As the *Ain* does not mention this act of self-immolation, it must have originated after Akbar's time. In *Magh* vast crowds of pilgrims assembled at Allahabad and daily bathed in the Ganges for one month (K. & C. but not A) A poll-tax was levied on the pilgrims by the Imperial Government. (K.) But, as all pilgrim-taxes were remitted by Akbar, this tax must have been re-imposed by one of his successors.

(2) BENARES, a very ancient and holy city, and a seat of

* As Kalidas says, "Internally purified by bathing at this meeting-place of the waters of the two Consorts of the Sea, one is exempted from re-birth after death, even though he may not have been spiritually enlightened." (*Raghu*, xiii.)

Hindu learning. K. & C. do not mention Aurangzib's iconoclastic acts. C. gives to the town an alternative name, Muhammadabad. (3) *Chunar* a strong stone fort. (4) *Kalinjar*, a lofty stone fortress containing the temple of Kal Bhairav. (5) *Jaunpur*, a large city. (A. & K.)

Mines.

An iron mine is mentioned near Kalinjar, and small bits of diamond were also found there by the peasants, evidently near the surface of the ground. (A. & K.)

Crops &c.

Melons and grapes were abundant *Jawári* and *bajra* did not grow, and *moth* was scarce. (A. & K.) In the forest near Kalinjar, ebony trees were found and many kinds of fruits grew spontaneously. (A. & K.) Wild elephants were caught in the village of Kantal (A) and in the forests near Chunar and Kalinjar (A. & K.)

Industries

Cloths, especially *jhona* and *mihrkul* were beautifully woven at Benares, Jalalabad and Mau (A. & K.) Woollen carpets were manufactured at Jaunpur and Zafarwal (A.)

4. OUDH.

Extent.

Under Akbar this province extended from the district of Gorakhpur to Kanauj, 135 *kos*, and from the northern mountains to Siddhaur, 115 *kos*. (A. K. & C.)

Divisions.

The following table will show the number of its *Sarkars* and *mahals* in different periods :

1594	...	5	*Sarkars*,	133
1665	...	5	„	149
1695	...	5	„	197
1700	...	5	„	105
1720	...	5	„	149

Sarkars (1594)		(1695)	(1720)	
Oudh	21*m.*	[The same names.]	Oudh	22*m.*
Gorakhpur	24		Gorakhpur	57
Bahraich	11		Bahraich	12
Khairabad	22		Khairabad	24
Lucknow	55		Lucknow	34

The province seems to have suffered no change of territory, because is was distinctly marked off from the neighbouring provinces by broad rivers.

Area and Revenue The total area of measured land rose from 1,01,71,180 *bighas* in 1594 to 1,90,22,908 *bighas* in 1720.

Sarkars	Area in *bighas* in		Revenue in Rs. in	
	1594	1720	1594	1720
Oudh ...	27,96,207	43,83,869	10,23,908	14,32,340
Gorakhpur	2,44,283	53,04,601	2,98,170	27,97,842
Bahraich ...	18,23,435	27,52,378	6,03,013	6,29,929
Khairabad	19,87,700	65,46,458	10,91,109	20,44,896
Lucknow...	33,07,426	——	20,17,904	13,80,000

Hence we see that in every *Sarkar* except Lucknow the area and revenue increased, Gorakhpur and Khairabad being very prominent in respect of this increase.

The total provincial revenue was

in 1594	Rs.	50,43,954	1697		——
1648	,,	75,00,000	1700	Rs.	69,89,490
1654	,,	90,99,571	1707	,,	80,58,195
1665	,,	68,30,000	1720	,,	83,10,015
1695	,,	66,13,500	Tieff.	,,	80,32,928

The *Khulasat* merely repeats the account of the *Ain* without adding a single item of its own.

Places of Note (1) *Ajodhya*, the birth-place of Ram, the hero of the Ramayan. It is a very old and sacred city, and had formerly a very large population. Near the city are two large tombs, vulgarly believed to hold Seth and Job. Muhammadans made annual pilgrimages to them. (2) *Rattanpur* was the place of burial of Kabir, who wanted to combine the Hindus and the Muhammadans into one sect. The place is now called *Maghar.* (3) *Bahraich*, an old town with many gardens in its environs Here are the tombs of two holy warriors of Islam,—Salar Masaud (sister's son of Mahmud of Ghazni) and Salar Rajab (father of Firuz Shah Tughlaq) Grand processions were formed by pilgrims to them. (4) *Nimkhar*, a large fort and a holy place of the Hindus. Near it is a reservoir, the *Brahmawart-kund*, in which the water boiled and eddied. In the same neighbourhood there was another sacred tank, in which the figure of Mahadeva was manifested on the sand. (5) *Charmiti*, where flames spontaneously issued from the ground at the *Holi* festival. (6) *Suraj-kund*, a place of pilgrimage. Elliot (ii. 549) identifies it with Asokpur, between Ajodhya and Gonda. (7) *Lucknow*, where Shaikh Mina lies buried. (His life is given in the *Chahar Gulshan*, see p. 135). (8) *Bilgram*, a small but healthy town, remarkable for the keen wit and musical skill of its inhabitants, and containing a well the water of which "increased intelligence and comeliness." (9) *Dokon*, a village near Bahraich, formerly containing a copper mint

Crops.

Excellent rice was produced here, especially the three varieties, *sukhdas*, *madkhar* [*'badrahkir'* acc. to K.], and *jhanuah*, which were matchless "for whiteness, delicacy, fragrance and wholesomeness." Rice was here sown three months earlier than in other parts of India. Game was plentiful.

Trade and Industries.

In the environs of Ajodhya gold was obtained by sifting dust. Fish was speared by men in boats on the Sai river. A brisk trade was carried on with the people of the Himalayan region, who brought, on the backs of men goats and hill ponies, gold, silver, copper, musk, the tail of the yak cow (*qutas*), and other things, and carried back in exchange cloth, amber, salt, ornaments, glass and earthen ware, &c. (see p. 32).

---

5. BIHAR.

Extent. The length of the province from Telia-Garhi to Rohtas was 120 *kos*, and its breadth fron Tirhut to the northern (? southern) mountains, 110 *kos*. (A.)

Divisions. The province was composed of the following *Sarkars* and *mahals* :—

1594	... 7	*Sarkars*,	200 *mahals*
1665	... 8	„	245 *parganas*.
1695	... 8	„	240 *mahals*.
1700	... 8	„	250 „
1720	... 8	„	252 „

Sarkars (1594)		(1695)	(1720)	
Bihar* (Patna)	46 *m.*	[The last 6 *Sarkars* of the *Ain* are repeated, but the other 2 *Sarkars* are not named.]	Bihar	58
Monghyr „	31		Monghyr	40
Champaran	3		Champaran	3
Hajipur	11		Hajipur	11
Saran	17		Saran	27
Tirhut	74		Tirhut	102
Rohtas	18		Rohtas	7
			Shahabad	12

Hence we learn that Shahabad was constituted as a *Sarkar* after the time of Akbar.

Area and Revenue. The provincial total of measured land increased from 24 44,120 *bighas* in 1594 to 1,31,52,845 *bighas* in 1720.

Sarkars.	Area in *bighas* in		Rev. in Rs. in	
	1594	1720	1594	1720
Bihar ...	9,52,598	67,09,647	20,04.910	43.535
Monghyr ..	——	12,78,698	27,40,649	10,05,575
Champaran	85,711	——	1,37,835	2,40,603
Hajipur ...	4,36 953	——	6,83,276	11,33,185
Saran ...	2,29,053	22,37,856	15,04,[illegible]00	8,83 220
Tirhut ...	2,66.464	——	4.79,494	7,37,080
Rohtas ...	47,335	10,45,275	10,20,487	7,07,050

* The *Sarkar* of Bihar must not be identified with the modern Sub-division of Bihar.

The revenue column for 1720 is very incorrect, because the detailed revenue (*taqsim jama*) of the *Sarkars* total up to 21,84,21,981 *dams* only, whereas the revenue of the province taken as a whole is given as 37,84,17,380 *dams* (see p. 135.) Hence a comparison between 1594 and 1720 would not be safe in this particular.

The total provincial revenue was

in 1594	Rs.	55,47,985	in 1697	Rs.	1,21,50,000
1648	„	1,00,00,000	1700	„	73,58,613
1654	„	1,36,32,523	1707	„	1,01,79,025
1665	„	95,80,000	1720	„	94,60,434
1695	„	95,18,250	Tieff.	„	1,01,79,525

Places of Note

(1) *Patna*, the capital of the province; most of its houses were roofed with tile (A. & K.) It was named *Azimabad* by Prince Azimu-sh-shan when he was Governor of Bihar, 1703 A. D. (2) *Gaya*, a famous Hindu shrine where the Hindus offer *pindas* of grain and water to the souls of their ancestors. (A.&K.) (3) *Baidyanath* (K) in the hilly region, has a famous temple of Mahadeva, at which miracles were wrought (see p. 36.) The *Khulasat* tells a remarkable story of the way in which the priests of the temple imposed on the credulous, among whom the author of the work was one. The *Ain* does not mention the place. (4) *Tirhut* was for a long time "a seat of learning and a centre of Hindu culture." (A. & K.) (5) *Rajgir* had a quarry of stone. (A) (6) *Rohtas*, a strong and lofty fort (A & K.) (7) *Monghyr*, the border district between Bengal and Bihar (A. & K.)

Crops &c.

Long pepper grew in the jungles of Champaran; in that district the seed of the vetch *mash* was cast on unploughed soil, where it grew "without labour or tilling." (A & K.) Tirhut had an excellent breed of buffaloes, which often proved more than a match for tigers. (A & K.) This district was also famous for its curd; the milkmen were prevented by a superstitious dread from adulterating milk. (A & K.) Orange-groves stretched for miles and miles here (A.) The jack-fruit grew to a large size in Hajipur. (A & K.) All over the province excellent rice was grown. Poor people ate a kind of pulse named *khesari* (A. & K.) Sugar-cane grew well and in plenty. Betel-leaf, esp. the *maghi* variety of it, was one of the famous articles of the place. (A. & K) No mention is made of indigo cultivation—now so widely spread over N. Bihar—by any of our three authorities. Rent was paid in cash and not by division of crops between landlord and tenant. (*Ain.* ii. 151.)

Animals.

Elephants were numerous, horses and camels less procurable. (A. & K.) This fact would surprise those who have seen the vast assemblage of horses at the Sonepur fair now-a-days. A fine species of Barbary goat was bred here. Fighting-cocks and game were abundant. (A & K.)

Industries.

Stone ornaments were carved at Rajgir near Gaya. (A) Good paper was made in this district. (A. & K.) Gilt glass (A. & K.) and various kinds of cloth (K) were manufactured in this province. But the paper and cloth industries have now died out. The *saligram* stone, worshipped by the Hindus as a form of the Deity, was found in plenty in the Gandak (K) and Son (A) rivers.

6. BENGAL.

In Akbar's time, what little of Orissa was possessed by the Mughals was regarded as a part of the province of Bengal though in a succeeding reign it was formed into a separate *Subah.* For the purpose of comparison Orissa will be always considered in this book apart from Bengal.

Extent.

Bengal was 400 *kos* in length from Chittagong to Telia-Garhi, and 200 *kos* in breadth from the northern hills to the southern frontier of the *Sarkar* of Madaran.

Divisions.

The account of Bengal in the *Chahar Gulshan* is very unsatisfactory. The provincial totals of *Sarkars* and *mahals* are given as 28 and 1243, but the totals formed by adding up the detailed statistics are 31 and 959 respectively. Moreover, the *Sarkars* are not treated separately, but the statistics given are for the *Sarkars* joined together in groups of two and two. To add to our difficulties, several names are so carelessly written in the MS as to be almost illegible. A comparative study of the revenues and areas of the *Sarkars* in 1594 and 1720 is impossible, as the *Chahar Gulshan* is silent on these points.

1594	...	19	*Sarkars*,	688 *mahals*
1695	...	27	"	1109 "
1700	...	34	"	485 (?) "
1720	...	28	"	1243 "

Sarkars (1594)	(1695)	(1720)
Udner (Tanda) 52 *m.*	[The 1st 15 *Sarkars* of the *Ain* are repeated, but the other 12 *Sarkars* required to complete K's total of 27 *Sarkars* are not named.]	Udner
Fatihabad 31		Fatihabad-Madaran 14
Jannatabad (Gaur) 66		Jannatabad in Bengal 73
Tajpur 29		Tajpur-Pinjara 26
Pinjara 21		Pinjara Barbakabad 47
Barbakabad 38		Barbakabad-Bazoha 5
Bazoha 32		Bazoha 2
Sonargaon 52		Sonargaon-Balgaon 72 *
Sylhet 8		Sylhet-Ghoraghat 16
Sharifabad 26		Sharifabad-Khalifatabad 15
Sulaimanabad 31		Sulaimanabad 31
Ghoraghat 84		Ghoraghat-Mahmudabad 98
Madaran 16		Madaran-Sonargaon 52
Bagla 4		
Chatgaon 7		
Mahmudabad 88		Mahmudabad and Fatihabad 38
Khalifatabad 35		Khalifatabad and Bankar 24
Purnia 9		Purnia 11
Satgaon 53 †		Satgaon-Farmandihi 7
		Udaipur
		Tajpur in Bengal 30
		Jannatabad in Kamrup 55
		Mahkar in Kamrup 15
		Dakhankol-Sharifabad 29
		Bihar-Dakhansikol
		Salimabad near Bihar 2
		Balgaon-Salimabad 37
		Jannat-Sylhet 124
		Maljih*-Jannat 1
		Tappa Kori-Maljih 25
		Farmandihi Tappa Kori 4
		Khuldabad-Satgaon 53
		Sulaimanabad-Khuldabad 53

* The *Ain* mentions *Bangaon* and *Maljipur* as two of the *mahals* of the *Sarkar* of Barbakabad. (ii 137)

† Blochmann, in the *Journal of the Asiatic Society of Bengal*, (1873, Pt. I. p. 209), thus identifies the Sarkars of Bengal under Akbar: Sarkars North and

Area & Revenue

The *Ain* does not give the area of measured land in Bengal, probably because it was a province the conquest of which had been completed only a few years before the book was written. The *Chahar Gulshan* gives the total measured area as 3, 34, 775 *bighas*, a figure very much smaller than that for other *Subahs*. The total provincial revenue was

in 1594 Rs. 1,18,18,167			in 1700 Rs. 1,31,15,903	
1648 ,, 1,25,00,000			1707 ,, 1,31,15,906	
1654 ,, 1,14,46,450			1720 ,, 1,40,72,725	
1695 ,, 1,15,72 500			Tieff. ,, 86,21,200*	
1697 ,, 4 00,00,000			(for Bengal and Orisa.)	

Places of Note

The *Khulasat* merely repeats the main portion of the information supplied by the *Ain*. The only point in which it is original is the statement that Dacca or Jahangir-nagar was the seat of government at that time, and that it was a beautiful, populous, and spacious city with a thriving trade in "the products of the seven climes." In Akbar's time the provincial capital was Tanda. FORTS : (1) *Bagla*, situated in the Sundarban. The rivers here are tidal ; in 1584 a terrible inundation took place in this *Sarkar* in which many houses and

East of the Ganges: (1) Lakhnauti or *Jannatabad* [=Malda.] (2) *Purnia*. (3) *Tajpur*=East Purnia and West Dinajpur. (4) *Panjarah*=Dinajpur (5) *Ghoraghat*=Dinajpur, Rungpur, and Bogra. (6) *Barbakabad*=Maldah, Rajshahi, and Bogra. (7) *Bazuha*=Rajshahi, Bogra, Pabna, and Dacca. (8) *Sylhet* (9) *Sonargaon*=W. Tipara and Noakhali. (10) *Chittagong*. Sarkars in the Gangetic Delta : (11) *Satgaon*=24 Parganas, W. Nadia, and S. W. Murshidabad. (12) *Mahmudabad*=N. Nadia, N. Jessore, and W. Faridpur. (13) *Khalifatabad*=S. Jessore and W. Bakarganj. (14) *Fathabad*=Faridpur, S. Bakarganj, and the islands at the mouth of the Meghna. (15) *Bakla*=Bakarganj and Dacca. Sarkars South of the Ganges and West of the Bhagirathi : (16) *Tandah* or Audambar=Murshidabad. (17) Sharifabad=Burdwan. (18) *Sulaimanabad*=N. Hughli and portions of Nadia and Burdwan. (19) *Madaran*=W. Birbhum, Burdwan, and W. Hughli.

* "According to the latest Register of the Empire", as Tieffenthaler adds. (i. 437).

boats were destroyed, and two lacs of living beings perished. (2) Lakhnauti or *Gaur*, the ancient Hindu and early Muhammadan capital of Bengal, was abandoned for its unhealthy climate. Humayun named it Jannatabad. Akbar's general and governor, Munim Khan, was attracted to this town * by its fine buildings; but he died here (1576). From that time forward it was shunned as death. † It had a brick fort and several monuments of great antiquity. In the neighbourhood were a lake, from which the city was protected by an embankment and a poisonous tank, the water of which condemned criminals were forced to drink. (3) *Mahmudabad*, a fort in the midst of a swamp. (4) *Tanda*, the seat of government from 1564 to 1592 A D. (5) *Dacca*, the seat of government from 1609 to 1704, when Murshidabad took its place. *Rajmahal* (named Akbar-nagar) was the provincial capital from 1592 to 1608 A. D. and again from 1639 to 1660.‡

PORTS : (1) *Chittagong* was named Islamabad by the Subahdar Islam Khan Mashedi in 1638 A D. § Christian and other merchants flocked here. There was a belt of forests at the back of the town. (2 & 3) *Hughli* and *Satgaon*, two ports, a mile apart from each other. Both of them were occupied by Europeans as early as Akbar's time.

Crops, Tenure, &c.

"The staple food of the people is rice and fish ; wheat, barley and other grains are not esteemed wholesome" (A) To this K. adds, "Nay more, they have not even the custom of eating bread Having cooked *brinjals* herbs and lemon together, they keep it in cold water and eat it the next day. It is very delicious when mixed with salt. They carry it to distant places and sell it at a high price." (p. 41). So many varieties of rice were cultivated that if only one grain of

* *Al Badaoni*, ii. 220.

† Cf. the pun of Nizamu-d-din, "*az Gaur ba-gor raft*, from Gour they went to the *gor* (grave)." Elliot, v. 395 *n.*

‡ All these dates are from Stewart's *History of Bengal.*

§ Stewart's *Bengal.* But Khafi Khan gives the date as 1665 A. D. (Elliot, vii. 275).

each kind were taken the specimens would fill a pitcher. Some tracts yielded three harvests in the year.

The tenants were very submissive, and paid their rent in cash in eight monthly instalments. It was not customary, as in Upper India, to divide the crops between government and tenant, nor to subject rent-free lands to assessment.

Fruits &c.

The *mango* grew in the Sundarban and elsewhere, nearly all over Bengal. There was a creeper bearing the mango in Kampur The *orange* grew in Barbakabad and Sylhet. The latter district also produced the *sangtarah* (a fruit like the orange), the China root, and aloes-wood. *Betel-nut* of the finest quality grew in Bengal. (Noakhali is still famous for it.) Mahmudabad produced long *pepper* and Hugli *pomegranate*.

Animals.

Wild *elephants* roamed over the forests of Khalifatabad and Araccan. Sharifabad was famous for "a beautiful species of *cattle*, white in colour, of a fine build," and carrying loads up to 15 maunds, and for Barbary *goats* and fighting cocks. Hill-*ponies* were numerous in Ghoraghat. Pegu was famous for its white elephants. Araccan had the *gayal*, an animal sharing the characteristics of the cow and the buffalo; but no cow or buffalo was found there; horses were scarce and camels dear.

Mines.

At Harpah in the *Sarkar* of Madaran, there was a mine yielding small diamonds An iron mine existed in Bazoha. In Pegu were mines of ruby, diamond, gold, silver, copper naphtha, and sulphur.

Industries &c.

Silk and sack-cloth (jute) were manufactured in Ghoraghat, *ganga-jal* cloth in Barbakabad, and fine muslin in Sonargaon. Bengal was famous for its mattresses, some of which were so nicely made as to "resemble woven silk." One variety of it is named by K. *sital-pati*, a name which it still retains. Boat-building was highly developed in this land of rivers and creeks. Boats "are of different kinds for purposes of war, carriage, or swift sailing. For a siege they are so adapted that when run ashore, they* overtop the fort and facilitate its capture. The *sukhasan*, a crescent-shaped litter with a moveable top of cloth, carried by men on poles, was a favourite conveyance of the rich. Horsemanship was rarely practised in this province.

The houses were made of bamboos ; but some of them were so elegantly built as to cost Rs. 5,000 ; these, however, lasted long. Salt was in great demand and was brought from great distances. Diamonds and precious stones were among the imports. Eunuchs were numerous in Ghoraghat and Sylhet. Kamrup was celebrated for the beauty and sorcery of its women, of which wonderful tales were told. (p. 43.)

7. ORISSA.

In the *Ain-i-Akbari* Orissa is included in the province of Bengal, but K. and C. regard it as a separate province. Its boundaries are not laid down in the *Ain*, and hence the two later works are silent on this point. The *Ain* only tells us that when Orissa was added to Bengal the length of the latter was increased by 43 *kos* and the breadth by 23 *kos* (ii. 116) K. & C., however, assign to this province a length of 120 *kos* and a breadth of 100 *kos*.

Extent.

Divisions.

The province was composed of the following divisions :

1594	..	5 *Sarkars*,	99	*mahals.*
1665	..	11 ,,	12	*parganas*
1695	..	15 ,,	233	*mahals*
1700	...	13 ,,	214	,,
1720	..	12 ,,	258	,,

The *Ain* mentions the following *Sarkars* : Jalesar (28 *mahals*), Bhadrak (7 *m*), Katak (21 *m*). Kalang Dandpat (27 *m*), and Rajmahendri (16 *m*) K. & C. merely repeat these without mention-

* Evidently the *goloi* or stern to which the rudder was tied and which had a sort of poop on it.

ing the names of the other *Sarkars* required to complete their lists. The two later writers evidently had no original information of Orissa, but merely copied the *Ain.*

The *Chahar Gulshan* assigns to the province an area of measured land amounting to 5,95,079 *Birsinghi bighas*, which it converts into 9,01.26,259 *Akbarshahi bighas.* The latter figure is evidently incorrect. Our usual comparison of the areas and revenues of the several *Sarkars* in 1594 and 1720 is impossible here, as C. does not supply the necessary information. The total provincial revenue was

Area and Revenue.

in 1594 Rs. 31,43,316		in 1697 Rs	57,07,500
1648 „ 50,00 000		1700 „	43,21,025
1654 „ 56,39,500		1707 „	35,70,500
1665 „ 72 70,000		1720 „	[not given]
1695 „ 1,01,02,625*		Tieff. „	35,70.525

The *Ain* says that there were 129† brick forts in the province. K. & C. merely repeat the account of the *Ain.*

Places of Note.

(1) *Katak*, a stone fort and the seat of government. It contained a nine storied palace of Rajah Mukund Deo‡ (2) *Puri*, temple of Jagannath. (3) *Kanarak*, temple of the Sun, with 28 other temples in the neighbourhood.

Customs &c.

The staple food consisted of rice, fish, brinjals, and herbs. Rice was cooked, steeped in water, and laid aside to be eaten the next day. Betel-leaf grew in plenty. The people lived in reed huts, anointed their bodies with sandal rubbings, and wore golden ornaments like women. The women adopted a tropical simplicity of dress and had a poor name for chastity. Books were written on palm leaves with a dry steel pen, quill and ink being rarely used. Cloth was manufactured and eunuchs were procurable in this province.

* An incredibly large sum. † 29 according to K. & C. ‡ *Ain.* ii. 127.

8. MALWA.

Extent. Its length from Garha (Mandla) to Banswara was 245 *kos* and its breadth from Chanderi to Nandurbar 230 *kos* (A. and K.).

Divisions. The province was made up of the following divisions :—

1594	...	12 *Sarkars,*	301 *parganas.*
1665	...	9 „	190 „
1695	...	12 „	309 *mahals.*
1700	...	11 „	117 „
1720	...	11 „	259 „

Sarkars (1594)		(1695)	(1720)	
Ujjain,	10 *m*	[The first 9 *Sarkars* of the *Ain* are repeated, but the other three are not named.]	Ujjain	13
Raisin	35		Raisin	38
Chanderi	61		Chanderi	49
Sarangpur	24		Sarangpur	24
Mandu	16		Mandu	23
Hindia	23		Hindia	13
Gagron	12		Gagron	12
Kotri Paraya	10		Kotri Paraya	9
Bijagarh	29		——	
Kanauj	57		Garh*	55
Mandesor	17		Mandesor	16
Nandurbar	7		Shahabad †	7

Area and Revenue. The total area of measured land increased from 42,66,221 *bighas* in 1594 to 1,29,64,538 *bighas* in 1720.

* Garh is the same *Sarkar* as the Kanauj of the *Ain*, (see p. 142 *n.*)

† May be a copyist's mistake for *Nandurbar*.

Sarkars.	Area in *bighas* in		Revenue in Rs. in	
	1594	1720	1594	1720
Ujjain ...	9,25,622	42,02,057	10,95,699	13,11,816
Raisin ...	1,59 617	89 850	3,45,260	20.35,408
Kanauj ...	——	——	2,51,927	5,53,250
Chanderi ...	5,54.278	——	7,75,944	23,12,090
Sarangpur ...	7,06,202	39,93,213	8.24 872	2,56,791
Mandu ..	2,29,970	17,05,818	3,44.725	7.36,189
Hindia ..	89,574*	4,91,627	2,90,274	28,625
Mandesor ...	——	43 400	1,71 535	6,53,515
Gagron ...	63,529	6,63,374	1,13,39[illegible]	4.36,067
Kotri P. ..	1,90.039	6,12,508	2,00,798	4,55,592
Nandurbar or Shahabad	20,59,604	10,59.586	12,54,056	2,25,000

The total provincial revenue was

in 1594 Rs.	60,17,376	in 1697 Rs.	99,06,250
1648 „	1,00,00.000	1700 „	1,02,08,667
1654 „	1,39,32,933	1707 „	1,00,97,541
1665 „	91,62,500	1720 „	90,04,593
1695 „	92,25,425	Tieff. „	1,14,13,581

The *Khulasat* merely repeats the *Ain* without adding a single item of original information.

Places of Note.

(1) *Ujjain* the capital was a very large city and a holy place of the Hindus Here the famous Vikramaditya reigned in the days of yore. In its environs were 360 temples and many summer-houses built in former times. (2) *Chanderi*, a large town with a stone fort. It is said to have contained 14,000 stone houses, 384 bazars, 360 *serais*, and 12,000 mosques ! (3) *Mandu* had a large fort and many old buildings. It was the capital of the local Muhammadan dynasty from 1387 to 1526, and contains the tombs of the Khilji

* This is evidently incorrect, as by adding together the areas of the several *mahals* of this *Sarkar* we get a total of more than thrice this figure. (*Ain*. ii. 207).

kings. (4) *Dhar*, an old town and the capital of the celebrated Rajah Bhoj. (5) *Garha* (Mandla), the ancient capital of the Gond dynasty, was situated in a wooded region. (6) *Tumun*, a village on the Betwa, where mermen were seen ! It had a large temple from which no sound could issue. [The *Khulasat* names it *Numan* and says that a perennial spring of water (and not merman) was found here]

Crops &c.

Wheat, poppy, sugar-cane, mango, melon, grape, (the last two grew specially well in Nandurbar), fine tamarind (in Bijagarh), and betel-leaf were the chief products of this province At Hasilpur (in the *Sarkar* of Mandu) and Dhar, the vine bore twice a year. Wild elephants abounded in Bijagarh, Hindia, and Garha

Industries &c.

Cloth of the best texture was woven here. The philosopher's stone was believed to have been found in this province ! No person of any class whatever, was without arms. High and low alike gave to their children, up to the age of 3, opium to eat.

9. AJMIR.

Extent.

Its length from Ambar to Bikanir and Jesalmir was 168 *kos*, and its breadth from the frontier of the *Sarkar* of Ajmir to Banswara (in Sirohi) 150 *kos*. (A. & K.)

Divisions.

The province was subdivided in the following manner :

1594	... 7	*Sarkars*,	197 *parganas*
1695	... 7	,,	123 *mahals*
1700	... 8	,,	217 ,,
1720	... 8	,,	238 ,,

Sarkars (1594)		(1695)	(1720)	
Ajmir,	28 *m.*	[The same as the *Sarkars* of the *Ain.*]	Ajmir	30
Chitor	26		Chitor	35
Rantambhar	73		Rantambhar	83
Jodhpur	22		Jodhpur	27
Nagor	31		Nagor	31
Bikanir*	11		Bikanir	...
Sirohi	6		Kumbhalmir †	...
			Jesalmir	8

Here we see that Bikanir and Jesalmir were regarded as two distinct *Sarkars* and the headquarters of another *Sarkar* was removed from Sirohi to Kamalmir, after Akbar's time.

Area and Revenue. The total area of measured land decreased from 2,14,35,941 *bighas* in 1594 to 1,74,09,684 *bighas* in 1720

Sarkars.	Area in *bighas*		Rev. in Rs.	
	in 1594	in 1720	in 1594	in 1720
Ajmir ...	56,05,487	64,25,670	15,54,585	2,66,194
Chitor ...	16,78,801	9,35,507	7,51,191	24,63,044
Rantam ...	60,24,196	82 64,551	22,45 614	30,85,359
Jodhpur ...	......	......	·,63,219	66,30,000
Nagor ...	80,37.450	17,83,354	10,09,746	19,89,017
Bikanir & Jesalmir	......	......	1,18,750	2,50,000 2,18,250
Sirohi or Kamalmir	......	......	10,51,936	1,27,000

The area of measured land shrank very considerably in Nagor and in a less degree in Chitor, but it increased in Ajmir and Rantambhar. The revenue of Ajmir showed a great decline in 1720, but that of every other *Sarkar* increased, the increase being most striking in Chitor, Jodhpur, and Sirohi. The total provincial revenue was

* Under Akbar, Bikanir and Jesalmir together formed one *Sarkar* (*Ain.* ii. 277.)

† *Kamalmir* is 50 m. N. E. of Sirohi.

in 1594	Rs.	72,10,039	in 1697	Rs.	2,19,00,002
1648	„	1,50,00,000	1700	„	1,50,74,506
1654	„	1,62,19,042	1707	„	1,63,08,634
1665	„	2,19,70,000	1720	„	1,75 29 829
1695	„	1,38,84,000	Tieff	„	1,63,08,642.

Here the *Khulasat* adds a good deal to the information supplied by the *Ain.* The *Subah* was made up of the three Rajput States, Mewar, Marwar, and Haraoti (Bundi-Kota), acc. to the *Ain.* FORTS: Ajmir, Jodhpur, Bikanir, Jesalmir, Amarkot, Abu-garh, Jhalor. Chitor, Kamalmir, Mandal, and others (A.) The residence of the governor was at Chitor. (A.) Near Ajmir was the fort of *Garh-i-Bithli*, the memorial of the mythical Rajah Bithal. In the environs of the city were a large lake named *Anasagar* and a natural spring named *Jhalra*, on the bank of which last was the tomb of Khawajah Muainu-d-din Chishti, to whose shine Akbar so often went on pilgrimage. *Pushkar*, a large lake 3 *kos* from Ajmir, was considered one of the holiest sheets of water in India (K.) *Sambhar* contained a lake from which excellent salt was extracted (K.) The *Khulasat* describes the process in detail, though the *Ain* is silent on this particular.

Places of Note

Jawari, *moth* and *lahdarah* (A, but *bajra* acc to K) were grown in this province (A & K.) The revenue was always paid in kind. and amounted to $\frac{1}{7}$ or $\frac{1}{8}$ of the produce (A. & K.) The people lived in conical bamboo huts (A).

Crops &c.

At *Chainpur* and some other places (A & K) there were copper mines, which the *Ain* describes as "extremely profitable." At *Jawar*, 24 m. S. of Udaipur, was a zinc (or lead?) mine (A.) In the *Indian Atlas* we find "copper and lead mines" 6 m. S. of *Chenpuria* (25 12N 74·29E.) The *I. G.* speaks of the zinc mines of *Jawar* as now unworked. K mentions an iron mine at *Gaugarh*, a dependency of Chitor; the name cannot be traced in the *Indian Atlas*, which, however, gives a *Gangrar* a few miles N. of Chitor.

Mines

10. GUJRAT.

Extent. Its length from Burhanpur to Dwarka was 302 *kos*; and its breadth from Jhalor to Daman 260 *kos*, or from Edar to Cambay 70 *kos*. (A)

Divisions. The following were its divisions:

1594	...	9 *Sarkars*,	138	*mahals*
1665	...	9 „	190	*parganas*
1695	...	9 „	188	*mahals*
1700	...	10 „	216	„
1720	...	10 „	256	„

Sarkars (1594)		(1695)	(1720)	
Ahmadabad,	28 *m*	[The first 8 *Sarkars* of the *Ain* are repeated, but Sirohi* is given instead of Sorath.]	Ahmadabad	34
Pattan	16		Pattan	16
Nandod	12		Nandod	12
Baroda	4		Baroda	4
Broach	14		Broach	14
Champanir	9		Champanir	10
Surat	31		Surat	37
Godhra	12		Godhra	11
Sorath (Kathiawar)	12		Sorath	63
			Islamnagar	15

Area and Revenue. The total area of measured land decreased from 1,69,36,377 *bighas* in 1594 to 1.27,49,374 *bighas* in 1720.

Sarkars.	Area in *bighas*		Rev in Rs.	
	in 1594	in 1720	in 1594	in 1720
Ahmadabad .	80 24,153	63,76,319	52 07,675	67,78.179
Pattan ...	38,50,001†	24,23,308	15,08,127	10,16.184
Nandod ...	5 41,818	...	2,19,940	...
Baroda ...	9 22,212	9,85,415	10 28,647	7,30,296
Broach ...	3,49 771	28,69,141	5.46,141	14.12,540
Champanir ...	80,337	3,72,184	3,75,247	8,18,567
Surat ...	13,12,816	7.23,000	4,75,879	19,65,571
Godhra ...	5,35,255	...	85.465	40,502
Sorath ...	13.20,014	...	15,85.934	11 71,259

* Evidently a mistake for *Sorath*, as *Sirohi* has been already included in the Subah of Ajmir. † Wrongly given as 3,85,00,015 in *Ain.* ii. 254; I have corrected it to 38,50,000 *bighas* 15 *bisuas* by adding together the areas of the *mahals*.

Here we notice a marked falling off of area in the *Sarkars* of Ahmadabad, Pattan and Surat, and an increase in Baroda, Broach, and Champanir. The revenue shows a great decrease in Pattan, Baroda, Godhra, and Sorath, and enhancement in Ahmadabad, Broach, Champanir, and Surat. The total provincial revenue was

in 1594	Rs.	1,09,20,557	1697	Rs.	2,33,05,000
1648	„	1,32,50,000	1700	„	1,34,13,125
1654	„	2,17,32,201	1707	„	1,51,96,228
1665	„	1,33,95,000	1720	„	1,32,57,233
1695	„	1,45,94,750	Tieff.	„	1,13,68,728

K. merely repeats A., adding only five new facts of very minor importance. (1) *Pattan* (Anhilwarra) was the Hindu capital from 746 to 1194 A. D. It had 2 forts. (2) *Champanir* was the next capital,—that of the Muhammadans,—from 1494 to 1560. It had a fine fort. (3) *Ahmadabad*, founded in 1412 by Sultan Ahmad, was the seat of the governor under the Mughals. It had 360 *porahs* (see p. 61*n*) and 1000 stone mosques. Abul Fazl records that in his time only 84 of the former were in a flourishing condition. In its environs were *Rasulabad* (the burial-place of Shah Alam Bokhari), *Batwa* (that of Qutb-i Alam) and *Sarkhej* (that of Ahmad Khattu, and Sultan Ahmad and other princes.) (4) *Mahmudabad* had beautiful buildings, villas, and game preserves; it was founded by Sultan Mahmud Begarra. (5 & 6) *Salir* and *Mulir*, 2 famous forts in the Nosari District. (7) *Junagarh* had a stone fort. (8) *Osam*, a hill-fort. (9) *Girnar*, another hill-fort

Places of Note.

HOLY PLACES OF THE HINDUS; (1) *Sidhpur* on the Sarsati, a place of pilgrimage. (2) *Barnagar* had 3000 pagodas, each with a tank. The residents of the city were mostly Brahmans. (3) *Somnath* (also called Pattan) held the famous emblem of Shiva. It had a stone fort and a capacious harbour. Near it were *Phal-katirath* (the Shrine of the Arrow), where Krishna was mortally wounded in the foot by a hunter with an arrow. The *pipal* tree on the bank of the Sarsati under which he died, gave the name of *Pipal-sir* to the place, which was highly venerated. (4) *Mul*,* where a miracle annually took place in the temple of Mahadeva, (see p. 65). (5 & 6) *Paranchi* and *Korinar*. (7) *Palitana*, where there were many Jaina temples and a fort. (8) *Dwarka* (also called Jagat) had a famous shrine of Krishna, who was believed to have reigned here after leaving Mathura. (9) *Girnar* had many Jaina temples in its environs.

PORTS: (1) *Cambay*, where many merchants congregated. (2) *Surat*, a famous emporium and the place of embarkation of pilgrims to Mecca. (3) *Broach*, another famous port, known in Sanskrit at *Bharukaccha* and in Greek as *Barugaza*. The *Ain* names 21 others.

Crops &c. The revenue was assessed by valuation of crops, survey being seldom resorted to (A.) *Jawari* and *bajrah* were the staple crops and formed the principal food of the people. Wheat was imported from Malwa, and rice from the Deccan. (A & K.) On the whole, the province was rather backward in agriculture; but "fruit trees were so numerous that the country might well have been called an orchard" (p. 66) There were numerous mango-groves. Figs, musk-melons, grapes, and pineapples grew in plenty, the first three especially in Kathiawar and the last in Surat. Baglana was famous for its peaches, apples, grapes, pineapples, pomegranates, and oranges (A., or "lemons and mangoes" acc. to K) Excellent indigo was produced and exported to European Turkey Hedges of prickly pear were set up around the fields, and hence the country was difficult to traverse. (A & K.)

Animals. Fine oxen were bred in Kari and Pattan; a pair often sold for Rs. 300 (K 'Rs. 500'), and those of the latter place travelled 50 *kos* in 12 hours! In Cutch (A. 'Navanagar') camels, goats, and horses of a peculiar breed were found. K. throws light on the origin of the last: "It is said that

* So named by K. A., however, calls it *Mul Mahadeo* and Bayley *Madhopur*.

once upon a time a merchant was conveying Arab horses by way of the river [or ocean ?] when the ship was suddenly wrecked and a few of the horses reached the bank on planks, and thus arrived in this country. The breed of those horses is still here." (P. 66) In the Bhadar river the fish were so delicate that they melted when exposed to the Sun (A & K) Leopards abounded (A), and were often trapped and trained to hunt (K)

Industries.

This maritime province has been famous from ancient times for its trade and industries. The vast number of its natural harbours (each an emporium), its contact with diverse foreign nations, and (probably) its backwardness in agriculture, all caused the energies of the people to be directed into the channel of industries. A large number of artisans carried on painting, seal-engraving, and inlaying mother-of-pearl on boxes and inkstands. Stuffs of gold embroidery, such as *chirah* (coloured-turban), *fotah* (loin-band), *jamahwar* (flowered woollen stuff), *khara* (undulated silk cloth), velvets, and brocades were skilfully woven (A. & K) Good cloth was manufactured at Pattan (A) and *alchah* at Broach (K.) Various stuffs of Turkey Persia and Europe were finely imitated here (A.& K.) Swords, daggers, (esp. the *jamdhar* and *khapwah*), bows and arrows were well made, Somnath being noted for its good swords Rare perfumes (A & K.) of many kinds were manufactured, Nosari being famous for "a manufactory of perfumed oil, found nowhere else." (A) A brisk trade was carried on in jewelry and in silver [K. 'gold'] imported from Turkey and Iraq. Salt was extracted from the Rann (A. & K.), the salt duty being levied in Jhalwarah (A).

Houses &c.

"The roofs of houses are usually of tiles and the walls of burnt brick and lime... The walls [in some houses] have hollow spaces between" (A & K), "and there are secret paths for going in, so that in time of need men can seek their safety by escaping by means of these paths" (K.) "Some wealthy men, having built vaults, cover the buildings with lime and mortar in such a way that the pure and clear rain water enters into the cave which has been made like a tank." (K.) The *Imp. Gazetteer* (i. 97) speaks of the practice as still current, but the *Ain* does not mention it.

11. MULTAN.

Length from Firuzpur to Sewistan 403 *kos*, breadth from

Extent. Khatpur to Jesalmir 108 *kos*. [K. '125 *kos*']

Divisions. The province was sub-divided in the following manner:

1594	... 3	*Sarkars*,	88 *mahals*
1665	... 4	"	96 *parganas*
1695	... 3	"	96 *mahals*
1700	... 4	"	103 "
1720	... 4	"	113 "

Sarkars (1594)		(1695)	(1720)	
Multan,	47 *m*	[The 3 *Sarkars*	Multan	53
Dipalpur,	29	of the *Ain* are	Dipalpur	24
Bhakkar,	12	repeated.]	Bhakkar	15
			Sewistan	21

Here we see that the *Sarkar* of Sewistan, which in 1594 was included in the *Subah* of Thatha, had by 1720 come to be incorporated with the *Subah* of Multan.

The total area of measured land rose from 32,73,932 *bighas*

Area and Revenue in 1594 to 44,54,207 *bighas* in 1720.

Sarkars	Area in *bighas* in		Revenue in Rs. in	
	1594	1720	1594	1720
Multan ...	5,58,649	——	13,47,908	31,80,684
Dipalpur ...	14,33,767	44,54,207	32,33,354	6,59,931
Bhakkar ...	2,82,013	——	4,60,623	6,09,681

The area of the *Sarkar* of Dipalpur as given by the *Chahar Gulshan* is the same as that given for the entire *Subah* in the same work. Hence this figure must be incorrect, though a trebling of Akbar's measured area in a century and a quarter would not in itself have been impossible. The total provincial revenue was

in 1594	Rs.	50,41,885	1697	Rs.	50,25,000
1648	„	70,00,000	1700	„	49.95.057
1654	„	84,60,529	1707	„	53,61,073
1665	„	1,18,40,500	1720	„	45,90,786
1695	„	61,15,375	Tieff.	„	51,59,999.

Here K. adds a great deal to the information derived from the

Places of Note

Ain. (1) *Multan,* one of the oldest cities of India. In Sanskrit *Mulasthanpur.* The *Malli* of this place offered a stout resistance to Alexander. In Mughal times the city had a brick fort and a lofty minaret. Here were the venerated tombs of Shaikh Bahau-d-din Zakaria and others (A. & K.) Among the 'others', K. mentions Shaikhs Sadru-d-din, Ruknu-d-din, Yusuf Kurdezi, Musi Gilani, and Shamsu-d din Tabrizi. (2) The tomb of Sayid Zainu l-Abidin, the father of Sultan Sarwar, 4 *kos* S. of Multan, and a place of pilgrimage in summer. (K.) (3) *Sakhi Sarwar,* the burial-place of Sultan Sarwar (a holy warrior of Islam), and his wife and son, 40 *kos* W. of Multan (K.) The *Khulasat* gives a long account of the miracles wrought at their tombs (p 74.) (4 *Uch,* the burial-place of Shaikh Jalal, grandson of Sayid Jalal Bokhari (K.) (5) *Ajodhan* (modern Pak Pattan), west of Multan, contains the tomb of Shaikh Faridu-d-din Ganj-i-shakkar (K.) (6) *Bhakkar* (Bukkur), an impregnable fortress on an island in the middle of the Indus, identified by some with Mansurah (A & K.) (7) The *Lakhi Jungle.*—In the rainy season the *Sarkar* of Dipalpur becomes flooded. And "when the water subsides, so many jungles spring up all over this land, owing to the great moisture, that a pedestrian has great difficulty in travelling" and a rider greater still. (K.) The *Imp. Gazetteer* tells us that this interior upland is "interrupted at places by an impenetrable jungle impassable alike for man and horse."

The wise *Diwan,* Rajah Todar Mal, anticipated the modern

policy of Buffer States by absolutely surrendering to the Baluchis the territory between Kot Korur and Dhankot, to which the Imperial government had a nominal right, "fixing them as a strong barrier between Hindustan and Khorasan, and thus setting up a firm rampart on the confines of the two countries." (K)

As the Indus every year ate away its banks or shifted its channel, the houses on the two banks were built of wood and straw and not brick or stone.

Industries &c

Zabti or assessment of crops at special rates was the custom here. Flowered carpets, *satranjis*, and *chhints* with figures, were woven in Multan, and Arab horses were brought for sale from Iraq by the Qandhar route. (K).

12. THATHA.

For a long time it was an independent country. Akbar annexed it and made it a part of the *Subah* of Multan. But it was recognised as a separate *Subah* in the following reign, and possibly even in Akbar's time.*

Extent.

Length from Bhakkar to Kach and Mekran 257 *kos*, breadth from Badin to Lahori Bandar (port) 100 *kos* or from Chando (in Bhakkar) to Bikanir 60 *kos*. (A.)

Divisions.

The province was subdivided in the following manner :

1594	...	5 *Sarkars*,	53	*mahals*
1665	...	4 „	54	*parganas*
1695	...	4 „	58	*mahals*
1700	...	4 „	59	„
1720	...	4 „	60	„

* The *Ain* (ii. 339) speaks of Thatha as "the fourth *Sarkar* of the *Subah* of Multan", but a little below it is spoken of as a *Subah* : "This *Subah* contains 5 *Sarkars*." Tieff. gives all the *Sarkars* of the *Ain* except Hajkan.

Sarkars (1594)		(1695)	(1720)	
Thatha,	18*m*	Thatha	Thatha,	24
Nasirpur	7	Nasirpur	Nasirpur	10
Hajkan	11	—	Hajkan	14
Sewistan	9	Sewistan	—	
Chakar-Hala	8	—	Chakar-Hala	10
		Amarkot	—	

The *Chahar Gulshan* includes Sewistan in Multan. In the *Ain*, Amarkot is only a *mahal* of the *Sarkar* of Nasirpur. The area of measured land is not given either by A. or C.

Revenue

Sarkars	1594	1720
Thatha	Rs. 6,50,000	7,99,391
Nasirpur	„ 1,95,865	3,01,421
Hajkan	„ 2,94,614	2,04,237
Chakar Hala	„ 1,27,135	4,30,388
Sewistan	„ 3,88,670	3,15 740

The total provincial revenue was

in 1594	Rs. 16,56,285		in 1697	Rs. 60,02,000
1648	„ 20,00,000		1700	„ 17,20,025
1654	„ 22,3c,750		1707	„ 22,95,420
1665	„ 23,20,000		1720	„ 17,32,938
1695	„ 23,74,250		Tieff.	„ 17,20 420

Places of Note

The *Khulasat* supplements the *Ain* in four points only, all of them of minor importance. Otherwise, it merely repeats the main portion of the information supplied by the *Ain* (1) *Brahmanabad*, now in ruins, was the ancient capital of the province. It had a grand citadel with 1400 towers. Then *Alor* became the capital. and last of all (2) *Thatha*, also called Debal (A. & K.) The *Khulasat* adds that Thatha was a great emporium of trade, pearls and other articles being much imported. (3) *Niklaj*, 70 *kos* from Thatha on the sea-coast, contained a shrine of Durga, the sanctity of which was enhanced by its difficulty of access. "*Sanyasis* naked from head to foot, having chosen a life of hunger and thirst, reach this place and perform worship. The journey in going and coming back occupies more than 15 days and involves many hardships." (K.)

The staple food of the people was rice and fish ['and curd,' K.]

Crops &c. Excellent *shali* rice grew here. The revenue was realised by division of crops, the share of the State being one-third (A. & K) In the Manchur lake, fishermen lived on floating rafts or artificial islands. Mangoes grew in the province, and the wild melon was found in desert tracts.

Animals. Fine camels were abundant and a good breed of horses was also procurable (A.) Game, especially wild-asses, hares, hog-deers, and wild boars, were hunted. In the Indus river was found a very sweet-flavoured fish called the *pala* (A. & K.) Other kinds of fish were dried and exported in boats Fish-oil was extracted and used in boat-building.

Mines. There were some iron mines and salt pits, which (the *Khulasat* adds) yielded a large revenue. Near Thatha was a quarry of yellow stone which was used in building.

The *Ain* gives and the *Khulasat* repeats, a long and interesting account of the Sorcerers (called 'Liver-eaters') of this province. (Pp 68, 69). It is curious to observe how closely the English superstition about witches resembled the Indian.

13. PANJAB.

Extent. Length from the Sutlej to the Indus 180 *kos*; breadth from Bhimbar to Chaukhandi, 86 *kos*. (A.)

Divisions. The province was divided into *doabs* insteads of *Sarkars*.

1594	...	5 *doabs*,	232* *mahals*
1665	...	14 *Sarkars*	314 *parganas*
1695	...	5 *doabs*,	316 *mahals*
1700	...	——	458 "
1720	...	5 "	329 "

* The *Ain* (ii. 315) gives 234 *parganas* in the preliminary statement, but by adding together the *mahals* of the *Sarkars* we get 232 *mahals*.

Sarkars (1594)		(1695)	(1720)	
Jalandhar Doab,	60 *m*	[The 5 *doabs*	Jalandhar Doab,	69 *m*
Bari „	52	of the *Ain*.]	Bari „	57
Rechnau „	57		Rechnau „	49
Chinhat „	21		Chinhat „	22
Sind Sagar „	42		Sind Sagar „	48
			Kangra „	63

The total area of measured land rose from 1,61,55,643 *bighas* in 1594 to 2,43,19,960 *bighas* in 1720.

Area and Revenue

Sarkars	Area in *bighas* in		Rev. in Rs. in	
	1594	1720	1594	1720
Jalandhar ...	32,70,303	39 39,518	31 09.130	35.93 751
Bari ..	45,80,003	52 39,857	35.70,204	49,33,751
Rechnau ...	42,53,148	98.52,010	43,01,192	10,66.088
Chinhat ...	26,33,210	40,41,809	16.12,560	23,17,218
Sind Sagar ...	14,09,929	12,56,771	12,97.805	35.14.984
Kangra ...	—	...	—	14,51,346

The total provincial revenue was

in 1594	Rs.	1,39,86,460	1707	Rs.	2,06,53,302
1648	„	2,25,00,000	1720		1,45,29,765 excluding Kangra.
1654	„	2,72,43,994			1,59,81,111 including Kangra.
1665	„	2,46,95,000			
1695	„	2,23.34.500			
1697	„	2,33,95,000	Tieff	„	2,24,53,304.
1700	„	2,23,25,985			

Places of Note

The chapter on the Panjab is by far the longest and most important in the *Khulasat*, whereas the account of the same province in the *Ain-i-Akbari* is very meagre and incomplete In treating of the Panjab, Abul Fazl is silent on the industries, fairs, important cities, holy men, and other points on which he has usually a wealth of information in the case of other *Subahs*. On the other hand, the author of the *Khulasat* was a native of the Panjab, and he has lovingly recorded every piece of information he could collect about his own province. His account is, therefore, accurate, full, and up to-date. and nowise inferior to the best descriptive chapter of the *Ain*. A brief summary only is possible here ; for the full account the reader is referred to my translation (pp. 80—111.) The few points supplied by the *Ain* are marked 'A', all the rest, though unmarked, being supplied by K I have no space in this chapter for the succession-list of Sikh Gurus (pp. 88-90) and the detailed description of the courses of the six rivers of the Panjab (pp. 102-110), which K. furnishes.

Lahor

CITIES : (1) *Lahor*, supposed to have been founded by Lava, the son of Ramchandra, the hero of the Ramayan ; hence its other name Lahawar (A. & K.) In the later Hindu period, Sialkot became the provincial capital and Lahor fell into decay But Malik Ayaz, the favourite of Mahmud of Ghazni restored the town and defended it by a fort, and it again became a capital and remained so under the last two Ghaznivide kings. Under Tatar Khan, a noble of Bahlol Lodi, it again became the seat of government. Subsequently it was repaired and enlarged by Akbar. (A. & K) Jahangir loved it particularly, and he increased its beauty and importance in various ways. He lies buried at *Shahadra*, on the other bank of the Ravi, and near him sleeps his brother-in-law and minister, Asaf Khan. Near Lahor Shah Jahan laid out the famous garden of *Shalimar*—which was one of the wonders of India. Aurangzib constructed a bund, 2 *kos* in length, to prevent the encroachment of the Ravi upon the town. He also built a lofty stone mosque at a cost of 5 lacs of Rupees. But the cathedral (*jama*) mosque of Wazir Khan is more celebrated. The saint Pir Ali Hajuri lies buried in this town.

Other Cities.

(2) *Jalandhar* contains the tombs of the saints Nasiru d-din and Abdulla Sultanpuri. (3) *Guru Govind Chak* had a large garden and tank to which pilgrimages were made annually. (4) *Ramtirath*, a holy place. (5) *Batala* (in the modern Gurdaspur District) was the birth-place of the

author of the *Khulasat.* A long and minute account of its foundation, history, buildings, and holy men, has been given in pp. 83-87 of my translation. In its environs were the tombs of many holy men. (6) At *Dhianpur,* near Batala, lived the Hindu saint Babalal, who was much respected by Dara Shekoh. (7) *Achal,* 2 *kos* from Batala, contained the shrine of Kartik, the son of Mahadeva. At the vernal equinox a *mela* took place here, of which a graphic description has been given in pp. 91-93. (8) At the foot of the hill-fort of Kangra is *Nagarkot,* containing the shrine of Bhavani. Pilgrims visited it in September and February. Some of them, in order to gain their wishes, used to cut out their tongues (A., but K. adds that others severed their heads) before the idol, but the lost limbs were restored miraculously, and the men lived. (A. & K.) (9) *Jawalamukhi,* 10 *kos* from Nagarkot ; here tongues of flame issued from the ground and were worshipped as a manifestation of the Devi (A. & K.) (10) *Sialkot,* supposed to have been founded by Shalya (a hero of the Mahabharat,) and restored by Shalivahan (the founder of the Shaka era), an old fort being traditionally ascribed to the latter. In later times it was repaired by Shahabu-d-din Ghori, Man Singh, and Masdar Khan Faujdar in succession. Among the 'pious founders' of the town were many members of the Jaina tribe of Bhabra. In the rainy season, when its canal over-flowed, the townsmen merrily disported themselves in the water on inflated skins. It was a seat of Muhammadan learning, the school kept by Maulana Kamal and his descendants being especially famous (11) *Dhonkal,* 4 m. S. of Wazirabad, a place of pilgrimage (12) *Purmandal,* 14 m. S. E. E of Jummu city, had a temple of Shiva, to which pilgrims, mostly hill-men, flocked in the month of Baisakh. (13) *Sodhra,* 4 m. N. E. of Wazirabad. Near it Ali Mardan Khan, the famous engineer of Shah Jahan founded a city named *Ibrahimabad* after his son, and laid out a fine garden, watered by a canal issuing from the Tavi river. (14) *Gujrat,* a town founded in the reign of Akbar, as the headquarters of a separate *pargana* created by detaching villages from the *pargana* of Sialkot. Shah Daula,a holy man of this town, whose illumination of mind was believed to have led him to discover hidden treasure,—spent large sums in adding buildings and bridges to the town and otherwise increasing its splendour. One of these bridges is given in the *Indian Atlas* (p. 98 of translation.) (15) *Balnath Jogi* (or Tilla), a hermitage and resort of Jogis, where pilgrims assembled on the Shiva-ratri. (A. & K.) (16) *Atak Banaras,* a famous fort built by Akbar, was the ethnic frontier of India. "It is a city ... midway between Hindustan and Kabulistan, so that on this bank the manners, customs, and language are Indian, while on the other bank are the houses of the Afghans and Afghan customs and speech" Just below it the Indus swept violently through a narrow channel. The danger of the passage was increased by two jutting precipices of black slate, which formed a whirlpool between them. Many boats were wrecked here. The name of the rock (*Jalali*) originated in a *bon mot* of Akbar (p. 109) (17) There was a sacred lake (named *Kota Chhina* ?) in the *mahal* of Makhiala. It rivalled in sanctity the Pushkar lake of Ajmir.

Crops &c.

The Panjab was a very fertile province (A.) Cultivation depended upon irrigation from wells (A. & K.) Very good water-wheels were constructed by mechanics here. The autumn crops depended upon rain (K.) Musk-melons could be had all the year round. (A) Excellent vine, mango, rice, and sugar-cane grew here. Snow was brought down from the northern mountains (A) by the rich to cool their drinks. Horses of good breed were procurable, esp. at *Awán* (A., or 'Astpur-mati' according to K.)

Industries.

On this point the *Ain* is absolutely silent, and all our knowledge comes from the *Khulasat*. *Bajwara* ($1\frac{1}{2}$ m. from Hoshiarpur) was famous for its cloth manufacture, esp. *sirisaf*, *adhars* (?), *doriah*, *panch-tolia*, *jhona*, white *chirah*, and gold-embroidered *fotah*. At *Sultanpur* in the Jalandhar doab, *chhint*, *dolai*, and embroidered cloths were finely made. *Sialkot* was celebrated for the manufacture of paper (esp. silk-paper and a variety called the *Man-singhi*), embroidered cloth (esp. *bafta, chirah, fotah. sozani. adsaka* (?), table-cloth, tray-covers, and small tents), and weapons (the *jamdhar, katari*, and lance.) At *Gujrat* were manufactured swords, *jamdhars*, and embroidered cloth. A species of horse resembling the Arab, was bred here, some of them selling for a thousand Rupees each. Near the salt mines of Shamsabad, trays dishes lamps and other fancy-articles of rock-salt were made (A). Similar art-ware was also manufactured from sweet lime in that region.

Mines

The *Ain* mentions copper and iron mines at Saket and Mandi in the Jalandhar doab, salt mines at Dhankot on the Indus and at Makhiala and Shamsabad. The *Khulasat* mentions the last two places only, and gives a long account (pp. 100, 101) of the extraction of rock-salt near Shamsabad and the names of the best mines (Keora and Khura.) From the *Ain* we learn that the merchants purchased rock-salt from the mines at $2\frac{3}{5}$ to $9\frac{3}{5}$ pies a maund, the landlord charged a royalty of 4 annas on each porter of salt (i.e., on say $1\frac{1}{2}$ maunds), and the State levied a duty of $11\frac{1}{3}$ pies on every maund. Thus, a maund of salt at the pit's mouth cost in all from 5 annas $1\frac{3}{5}$ pies to 5 annas $8\frac{14}{15}$ pies ; a little *less than* $5\frac{1}{2}$ *annas on an average was the cost price of rock-salt in Akbar's reign.* There was also a quarry of sweet lime in this region (K). In Jummu there was a mine of tin (*qal'i*) "Taking gravels from the river Tavi and setting them on fire, tin of unparalleled whiteness, hardness, and durability" was made (p. 98.) "In some places in the northern mountains, there are mines of gold, copper, brass, and iron, which yield revenue to the Imperial government" (K.) In certain rivers, esp. the Bias and the Jhilum, gold.—(the *Ain* adds 'silver, copper, *rui*, zinc, brass, and lead')—was obtained by washing sand. (K.)

14. BERAR.

Extent.

Length from Pitalwari to Wairagarh 200 *kos*, breadth from Bidar to Hindia 180 *kos* (A. & K.)

Divisions. The province was divided in the following manner :—

1594 ...	13* *Sarkars*,	242 *parganas*	
1665 ...	20 ,,	191 ,,	
1695 ...	10 ,,	200 *mahals*	(No *Sarkar* named.)
1700 ...	12 ,,	251 ,,	
1720 ...	10 ,,	200 ,,	
Tieff. ...	13		

Sarkars (1594)		(1720)	
Gawil,	46 *parganas*	Gawil,	46 *mahals*
Panar	5	Panar	4
Kherla	35	Kherla	24
Narnala	34	Narnala	37
Kallam	31	Kallam	28
Basim	8	Basim	8
Mahur	20	Mahur	21
Pathri	18	Pathri	11
Mahkar	4	Mahkar	22
Pitalwari	9	Pitalwari	9
Manik-durg	8	——	
Telingana	19	——	
Ramgarh	5	——	

We do not know the area of measured land under Akbar, but in 1720 the province had 2,00,28,100 *bighas*.

Area and Revenue The *Chahar Gulshan* does not give the *taqsim jama* or revenue of the different *Sarkars*, hence a detailed comparison with the *Ain* is impossible. The total provincial revenue was

in 1594	Rs.	1,60,65,082	in 1697	,,	1,58,07,500
1648	,,	1,37,50,000	1700	,,	2,31,63,625
1654	,,	1,47,65,000	1707	,,	1,53,50,625
1665	,,	1,58,75,000	1720	,,	2,25,60,000
1695	,,	1,51,81,750	Tieff.	,,	2,03,50,625

* See *ante* xxvi. *n* †.

Places of Note

K. and C. merely reproduce the account of the *Ain*, the first in a very abridged form and the second more fully; the only item of information that they add is that monkeys abounded in the country! TOWNS: (1) *Ellichpur*, the provincial capital, produced a beautiful flower named the *bhum-champa*. (2) *Shahpur*, a city which grew out of the encampment of Prince Murad, son of Akbar. (3) *Kherla*, a fort on a plain, containing a hillock which was worshipped. HILL FORTS: (1) *Gawil*, (2) *Panar*, (3) *Narnala*, (4) *Mahur*, containing a temple of Jagad-dhatri), (5) *Ramgarh*, (6) *Manikdurg*, (7) *Pitalwari*, which had 24 temples cut in the sides of its neighbouring hills.

There were a petrifying well near Kherla and a petrifying spring near Melgarh. Lake *Lonar* (Sanskrit *Lavaneshvar*) was considered sacred by the Hindus and named Vishnu-Gayá, one of the three Gayás of the world. Near it a spring flowed in a miraculous manner out of a rock shaped like a cow's mouth (p. 145).

Animals.

A great part of the province was covered by forests; the chief inhabitants were savage races like the Gonds, except in the western side where there were Rajput settlers. Wild elephants abounded near Kherla, Wairagarh, and Ramgarh; buffaloes were numerous near Kallam, Mahur (where they yielded half a maund or more of milk each), Indor, and Narnala.

Mines, &c.

Mines of steel and other metals existed near Indor and Narnala. Near Wairagarh were diamond mines, (the *Imp. Gazetteer* adds 'ruby mines'); but they are no longer worked. Figured cloth was woven at Wairagarh; excellent stone utensils were carved at Indor and Narnala; the materials for the manufacture of soap and glass were extracted and salt-petre produced from the Lonar lake Lustre was given to weapons of steel by dipping them in the water of a spring in Gawil.

The following forts belonged to this province :

Forts.

(*Chahar Gulshan.*)	(Tieffenthaler, i. 365)
Gáwil	Gawil
Kámla	Khelna
Nárnala	Parnala
Náuagarh	Golconda
Báila ?	Manda
Bábhalgarh ?	Hámgarh

15. KHANDESH.

Extent. Length from Boregaon (adjoining the *Sarkar* of Hindia) to Laling (near Dhulia) 75 *kos*; breadth from Jamod (in the modern Akola District) to Pal (adjoining Malwa) 50 *kos*, and in some parts 25 *kos* only.

Divisions.

1594	...	1	*Sarkar*	32 *mahals*
1695	...	5	„	112 „
1700	...	3	„	134 „
1720	...	1	„	133 „

Area and Revenue The area of measured land in 1594 is not given by the *Ain*, that in 1720 was 88,00,001 *bighas*. The total provincial revenue was

in 1594	Rs.	1,13,82,356	in 1697	Rs.	1,11,05,000
1648	„	1,00,00,000	1700	„	1,05,00,000
1654	„	1,24,23,250	1707	„	1,12,15,750
1665	„	1,85,50,000	1720	„	1,15,00,750
1695	„	1,10,90,475	Tieff.	„	78,15,755

Places of Note K. and C. merely repeat the account of A., the first adding two unimportant points (viz., the growth of aloes near Burhanpur and the weaving of *alfia* cloth in this province), the second adding what is more important,—a description of Ahmadnagar and a legend about its capture. This province was named *Khán-desh* or 'the country of the Khán' from Nasir Khán (named Ghizni Khán by A. and Gharib Khán by K.), who ascended the throne in 1399, first assumed the ensigns of royalty, and received the title of Khán from his suzerain, the king of Gujrat. (Ferishta). In Akbar's time, Prince Daniál was appointed Viceroy and the province was re-named* after him *Dan-desh*, a name which it soon lost. (1) *Talnir*, a strong fort was the first capital (1382—1480) ; (2) *Burhanpur* next succeeded. In Akbar's time (3) *Asir*, a strong hill-fort conquered by Abul Fazl, was the seat of the Governor. There were many gardens near Burhanpur ; sandal-wood ('and aloes,' K.) grew here. It had a large population including thriving artisans of various classes. (4 & 5) *Pipaldol* (in Jamod) and *Malkámad*, 2 hill-forts. HOLY PLACES of the Hindus : (1) Near *Adilabad* was a holy lake in which King Dasaratha expiated his sin (the accidental shooting of a hermit's son.) Tieffenthaler describes Adilabad as 'a city surrounded partly by stone walls, with a small and very old fort, situated on the bank of the Parna,' (p. 368). (2) *Damarni* ('Amarni,' C.) contained a tank in which a hot spring constantly bubbled up. (3) Near the town of *Chopra* the Tapti and the Girni united, and there was the holy shrine of *Rameswar* at their confluence. (4) Near the village of *Changdeo*, the Tapti and the Purna mingled together. It was called *Chakra-tirtha* † and contained an idol of Shiva, about which a legend was told. Near it was a spring of miraculous origin (A & C.)

Crops.

The peasants were docile and industrious ; scarcely any land was out of cultivation ; the villages were very populous and flourishing (A.) *Jawari* was the chief cultivation,—in some places three crops of it were raised in the year. Rice of good quality and betel-leaf in abundance grew here (A., K., and C.)

Industries.

Good cloth stuffs were woven in the province, especially *sirisaf* and *bhiraun* (K. 'and *alfia*') at Dharamgaon.

* Cf. the title of *Azimabad* given to Patna by its Governor, Prince *Azimu-sh-shan*, in 1703 A. D.

† Tieffenthaler mentions in his chapter on Oudh (p. 276) *Chakratirtha*, 'a reservoir on the bank of which is a temple sacred to *Bheroun*' (Bhairava or Shiva)

Forts

	(*Chahar Gulshan*)		(Tieffenthaler, p. 365)
1.	Burhanpur	...	same
2.	Asirgarh	...	same
3.	Rudi Manik *	...	Aurang-garh
4.	Hargarh	...	Marg-garh
5.	Maura-garh	...	Móra
6.	Parnala	...	Paniala
7.	Fatihabad	...	Narabad
8.	Bhatnir	..	Balissar
9.	Mul	..	Maol
10	Mujha	...	Múlar
11.	Sultangarh	...	Auréngarh
12.	Sanula	...	Pania-gola
13.	Songarh	...	Sonda *or* Púnda

16. KASHMIR.

Extent Length from Qambar Ver (Phamber ?) to the Kishan-Ganga, 120 *kos*, breadth from 10 to 25 *kos* (A) or 80 *kos* (K.)

In Akbar's time the whole country was regarded as one *Sarkar*, but Abul Fazl found it convenient to retain the old division into two tracts—the Mar-ráj in the east (with 22 *mahals*) and the Kamráj in the west with 16 *mahals*),—with further subdivisions, as given below. These last were evidently mistaken by C. (p. 132) for a division into 7 *Sarkars*.

Divisions

1594	...	1	*Sarkar*,	38 *mahals*
1665	...	5	„	45 *parganas*
1695	...	1	„	46 *mahals*
1700	...	—	„	53 „
1720	...	7	„	75 „
Tieff.	...	—	„	44 *parganas*

* Tieff. (p. 484) mentions a fort named *Rudar Mál* in the *Subah* of Aurangabad.

(1594)	(1720)
Mar-ráj Tract (22 *mahals*)	Environs of Kashmir, 36 *m*
Srinagar city, 1 *m*	Kamraj, 22 *m*.
East of Srinagar, 3 *m*	Srinagar, 3
N. E. 7	N. 7
S. E. 11	S E. 11
Kam-ráj Tract (16 *mahals*)	[The other *mahals* are not accounted for.]
N. W. 2 *parganas*	
S. W. 12 „	
[The other two *mahals* are not accounted for.]	

Revenue. The total provincial revenue was

in 1594	Rs.	15,52,826	in 1697	Rs.	35,05,000
1648	„	37.50,000	1700	„	69,47.784
1654	„	28.59,750	1707	„	57,47,734
1665	„	3.50,000 ?	1720	„	53.20,502
1695	„	31,57,125	Tieff	„	25,00,000

Places of Note. The *Khulasat* has merely copied much of the account of the *Ain*, adding only one item of original information: "The soil is of two kinds: (1) soft and moist, and (2) hard and black"! Still more evident is the ignorance of the author of the *Chahar Gulshan* concerning Kashmir. As the whole chapter deals with marvels and miracles, and the account of the *Ain* itself is far from correct, a summary of it has not been given here. But I should like to draw the reader's attention to the extracts from Dr. Stein's *Memoir* quoted in the foot-notes of my translation.

17. AURANGABAD.

Authorities for the Deccan. At this point we are deserted by the *Ain* and the *Khulasat*. A comparison between the Deccan of Akbar and the Deccan of Aurangzib is impossible, because only a very small portion of the Deccan owned the sway of Akbar. Still, a description of the Deccan after its annexation to the Mughal Empire is not without interest or importance. The author of the *Khulasat* tries to give an account of the *Subah* of Aurangabad; but the *Ain*, which he has so long faithfully copied, now fails him, and he shows his own ignorance. His account of Aurangabad is not worth the paper it is written on. It is exactly like an article such as a clever sub-editor would write in the 'silly season,' when hard pressed for 'copy' in the midst of an absolute dearth of news. The whole of p. 49 of my translation contains nothing but vague rhetoric. The only useful things that the author gives are the history of Daulatabad and the extent and revenue of the province.

Happily, Tieffenthaler comes to our aid here His account of the Deccan is taken from some Persian works which he does not name, but which seem to have included a *Dastur-al-amal* (called by him 'a register of the empire') and the sources of the *Chahar Gulshan.* Henceforth I shall place the two (T. and C.) side by side in my description.

Extent

The province of Aurangabad had a length of 150 *kos* and a breadth of 100 *kos* (K.) East of it lay Berar, west Salhir and Mulhir (in the Nosari District), south Bijapur, north Burhanpur and the river Pambra (C)

Divisions.

1665	...	8 *Sarkars,*	79 *parganas*
1695	...	8 ,,	80 *mahals*
1700	...	14 ,,	140 ,,
1720	...	11 ,,	116 ,,
Tieff.	...	14 ,,	140 ,,

The following are the 11 *Sarkars* mentioned by the *Chahar Gulshan*: (1) Daulatabad (or Aurangabad), 19 *mahals*, (2) Ahmadnagar, 20 *m*, (4) Jalna, 10 *m*, (4) Islamabad Kokan 7 *m*, (5) Sholapur, 3 *m*, (6) Jooner ? 13 *m*, (7) Pattan ? 3*m*. (8) Sir ? 1 *m*, (9) Purainda ? 19 *m*. (10) Sakha ? 11 *m*, (11) Fatihabad, 11 *m*. Tieffenthaler incidentally mentions the following "principalities and governments" as belonging to this province: (1) Sopán in the Kokan, (2) Baglána, (3) Javár, a district between Baglana and

Kokan*. He speaks of Ahmadnagar (or Balghat) as a province distinct from Aurangabad and yielding a revenue of Rs. 1,64,12,500 (i. 490).

The total area of measured land in 1720 was 2,55,70,950 *bighas*.

Area and Revenue. (C) The total provincial revenue was

in 1648	Rs. 1,37,50,000		in 1707	Rs. 2,58,73,622	
1654	„ 1,26,79,000		1720	„ 2,95,00,002	
1665	„ 1,72,27,500		Tieff.	„ 2,57,51,225	
1695	„ 1,29,07,500		Tieff.	„ 2,51,24,125	
1700	„ 2,95,93,375	(Thomas, p. 42)			
1700	„ 2,60,71,119	(*Dastur*, MS. D 163)			

Places of Note (1) *Daulatabad,* anciently called Dhárá-nagari, and then Deogir When Muhammad Tughlaq made it his capital, he re-named it Daulatabad (1338 A. D.) The Mughal forces captured it in 1632 A. D. (2) At the village of Khirki, 10 m. from it, Aurangzib founded a new city which he named after himself *Aurangabad.* This was the provincial capital under the Mughals. Here are Aurangzib's palace and the mausoleum of his wife. (3) *Ahmadnagar.* C. describes

Ahmadnagar. this *city* in the account of Khandesh, but includes the *Sarkar* of Ahmadnagar in the *Subah* of Aurangabad Near the city were two famous gardens, the *Fara-bagh* and the *Bihisht-bagh* Tieffenthaler thus describes them: "Ahmadnagar is a large and populous town, 2½ m. in circuit, 5 stages distant from Aurangabad and Satara alike It is adorned with magnificent buildings and is watered by a canal which conducts water to the houses. There are many gardens in and around it, of which the principal, named Farabagh, is 2000

* He further (i. 505) speaks of the following cities of the *Kokan* as having formerly belonged to Nizamu-l-mulk (*sic*), but been afterwards annexed by Aurangzib to the province of Aurangabad : (1) *Kaliani* ; with 499 villages, (2) *Bimbri*, with 463 v. (3) *Janol* with 170 v. (4) *Aminabad*, with 180 v. (5) *Karnala* with 123 v. (6) *Kunbhal* with 22 'places' (7) *Nagina* with 249 v. (8) *Goshala*, with 63 'places,' (9) *Kunch*, (10) *Vergorna*, with 116 v. (11) *Nasrapur* with 50 v. (12) *Vabra*, with 31 v. and (13) *Sablak* with 151 villages.

yards in circuit. In the centre of it is a tank 528 yards in circuit and fed with water brought from the hills by subterranean canals. In this tank is a large and lofty building with a high cupola and 320 rooms. Another garden, named Paradise [*i.e.*, Bihisht-bagh] is 612 yards long (?) and has an octagonal tank, from the middle of which rises a magnificent edifice." (Condensed trans. of p. 490.)

Crops &c.

The province was famous for its sugar-cane (esp., the soft and black variety) and mango. Cocoa-nut grew in abundance, and so also did betel-leaf, rice, and the flower *keora.*

Forts.

The *Chahar Gulshan* (p. 162) mentions 144 forts as belonging to this province, while Tieffenthaler (i. 479) gives 141 only. I have put the latter within brackets by the side of those names of the former of which they seem to be variants The numbers are those which the forts bear in my translation

1. Kaliáni (Kalián)
2. Bakhári (Muktari Sewai)
3. Puri (Gohòra)
4. Qila Manik (Mánik)
5. „ Masi (Bassi)
6. „ Balgarh (Malgarh)
7. „ Manranjan (same)
8. Mankar-garh (Malak-garh)
9. Sarmar-rái (Marmardarái)
10. Bhamri (Kasmari)
11. Dhánkhora (Dhán Bavára)
13. Barálaf (Rássef)
14. Bahrángarh (Bheroun-garh)
15. Barili (Parli)
16. Durg-garh (same)
17. Sardári (Sorwári)
18. Rámpuri (Rajoui)
19. Ratan-garh (same)
20. Sárdá-durg (Sarádurg)
21. Sakatrú (Bhenkara)
22. Son-garh (Loungarh)
23. Surpál-durg (Sorandurg)
24. Koliána (Gopála)
25. Kúr-garh (Górgarh)
26. Kalána } (Calaya)
    Khora } (Catóra)
27. Kanak-durg (Cantdurg)
28. Ghosála (Gossála)
29. Mát-garh (Mángarh)
30. Mánik-garh (same)
31. Madh-garh („)
33. Mandal-garh (Mandan-garb)
34. Mulk-garh (Merg-garh)
36. Haidar-garh (same)
37. Manpál-garh (Betal-garh)
38. Mór-garh (Súrgarh)
39. Isá-garh (Alfagarh)
40. Go-ganj (Cocandeh)
42. Deodand (Deodita, commonly called Deotana)

43. Uniri (Aondbari)
46. Chándbari (Chandiri)
47. Dhák (same)
48. Koplás (Keláss)
49. Konkána (Gangána)
50. Udurg (Aod durg)
51. Bisrám-garh (Rámgarh)
52. Bhúri (Bavani)
53. Saudágir (Songarh)
54. Padam-durg (Padam-garh)
55. Partab-garh (same)
56. Púrna (Torna)
57. Chandan-garh (same)
58. Raj-garh („)
59. Rajdurg („)
60. Karúr (Karód)
61. Khanderi (same)
62. Kotwal-garh (Khewal-garh)
63. Kalman-gaih (Kalje-garh)
64. Kánu (Kámóri)
66. Makarand-garh (same)
67. Dabdal-garh (Didan-garh)
68. Wánúba (Darssona)
69. Bansli (Beli)
70. Sakota (Masnóna)
71. Ahangarh (Rengarh)
72. Bandá-garh (Massandgarh)
73. Kijr garh (Kanjar-garh)
74. Suádas (Massudak)
75. Harsal (Marsél)
77. Begampur (same)
78. Daulatabad („)
79. Ajláu (Achala)
80. Ahmadnagar (same)
81. Islamabad or Jalná (or Chakla)
82. Azim-garh (Azimgarh or Mór)
84. Amúr (Anbór)
85. Aud-gir (Aud-garh)
86. Usa (Ossér)
87. Undh (Aonda)
88. Islamabad or Ráiri(Islam-garh or Rápari)
89. Anjráni (Anjerai)
90. Alang (same)
91. Anki-banki (Atki-patki)
93. Bahadur-garh or Bikapur („ or Nandagaon)
94. Bula (Turia)
95. Buhár (Lossiára)
96. Sardári (Sarfarázi)
97. Báni-garh (Maga-garh)
98. Malih (Paniala)
99. Sálih (Pend)
100. Puraínda (Barbada)
101. Nand-gaon (see 93)
102. Bhim-garh (Pemgarh)
103. Bamar-bank (Bandeka)
104. Warangal-dári? (Portugál Bári or the garden of the Portuguese)
105. Júdhan (Jódhi)
106. Jaula (Jurna)
107. Chándpur (Jawand-dór)
108. Parand (Márand)
109. Chanún (Chówal)
110. Dharat (Dérp)
111. Dabhra (Déra)
112. Rajmand (Rajend)
113. Ráikot (same)
144. Rásanj (Rámsej)
115. Rúla (Dola)
116. Sadhu-durg (Madhór-durg)
118. Sagar-garh (same)
119. Son-garh („)
120. Sholápur (Sewapur)
121. Qandhár (same)
122. Fatihabad or Dhári („ or Dhárgarh)
123. Gulbarga (same)
124. Khadása (Gundána)
125. Kahan-garh (Khatan-garh)

126. Kálubi (Khanoti)
127. Khajar-bajar (Kanjar-manjar)
129. Kurang (Kórand)
130. Gúldhar (Calóssora)
131. Kánra (Kandana)
132. Kurang (Koárand)
133. Kalul-garh (same)
134. Kar-garh (Mer-garh)
135. Lauh-garh (same)
136. Muftahu-l-fatuh (same)
138. Márkand (Markandeo)
139. Máhuli (same)
140. Manik-ganj („)
141. Máhúr („)
142 Nal-durg („)
143. Sarbas (Harbans)
144. Harchand-garh (same)

The following forts are mentioned by the *Chahar-Gulshan* only :—

12. Dargáhi-khora
32. Balá
35. Basant-garh
41. Bháskar
44. Unak-danda
45. Mulk-garhi
65. Bari
76. Aurangabad
83. Buna
92. Ahuhat
116. Sinkhar
128. Nakhra
137. Badh.

The following forts are mentioned by Tieffenthaler alone :

Dilkána
Kúnch (Kúnja ?)
Arsgir
Asse-ewar
Mukund-garh
Mal-gir
Ao-garh
Amóra
Górek-chand
Madma-kund.

18. BIJAPUR.

Extent. North of it lay Aurangabad, in the south Adoni and the Krishna river, in the east Gulburga, and in the west Tull-ghat (in Kokan) (C.) According to Tieffenthaler (i. 498) its length extended from the Tamira river to Setubandh Rameswar, and its breadth from Chaul* and Dhabul† to the frontier of Orissa.

Divisions. Neither the *Chahar Gulshan* nor Tieffenthaler gives all its *Sarkars* and *mahals* ; but the *Dastur-al-amal* assigns to the province 15 *Sarkars* and 114

* A port about 8m. S. of Kolaba. † A port due west of Satara.

mahals. Tieffenthaler incidentally mentions the following divisions :

1. Bijapur ('domain')		7. Lakmir ('principality')	
2. Deughi	(„)	8. Gadak	('district')
3. Ossa ('district')		9. Balsar	(„)
4. Sholapur ('canton')		10. Badam	(„)
5. Dhar	(„)	11. Kokan.	
6. Sikhar	(„)		

The *Chahar Gulshan* incidentally names two *Sarkars* only,—(12) *Nurkal* and the *Kokan*.

The Kokan was sub-divided into the following *parganas*.

The Kokan. Here Tieffenthaler (i. 506) helps us to correct the *Chahar-Gulshan* (pp. 155 & 156 of translation).

	(*Chahar Gulshan*)				(*Tieffenthaler*)			
1.	Kubir or Bhagundá, 748 *mauzas*,	Rev.	Rs.	4,91,819	Kóta or Pounda, 749 villages,	Rev.	Rs.	4,91,812
2.	[Not named] 92*m*,	„	„	63,763	Khelna, 92 vill ,	„	„	81,226
3.	Muzaffarabad, —	„	„	1,66,875	Túrghod	„	„	18,125
4.	[Not named] —	„	„	45,000	Solwála, 50 vill ,	„	„	72,500
5.	Kodana, 56*m*,	„	„	71,332	Pachaiben, 50 vill.,	„	„	71,352
6.	Sarangah —	„	„	33,750	Ragná, 100 vill.,	„	„	33,750
7.	Khaló, 235*m*,	„	„	1,66,875	Barzapur, 235 vill ,	„	„	1,86,875
8	Sáhli, 52*m*,	„	„	45,000	Sári, 72 vill.,	„	„	45,000

The total provincial revenue was

in 1697	Rs.	5,00,00,000
1700		5,63,68,178 (acc to Thomas, p 43)
		5,63,70,688 (acc. to *Dastur*, MS. D. 163.)
1707	„	2,69,57,625
1720	„	3,36,84,771 ('cash realisation.')
Tieff.	„	5,88,87,500 ('acc. to a Register of the Empire')
		2,48,75,000 ('the [actual] annual revenue')

Places of Note. (1) *Bijapur*. C gives a long account of its siege and capture. Here the most noticeable thing is Aurangzib's suspicious habit and mean-mindedness, which we may contrast with Akbar's frank spirit and large hearted kindness in dealing with conquered enemies.* (2) *Torna*, a hill-fort situated on the top of a hill, (18·14 N. 73·17 E.) The walls were of stone, and about 5 yards in thickness. Of its two gates only the northern one was kept open. It was 1395 yards in circuit, with 24 towers and 389 parapets. A ditch 9 yds. broad surrounded the fort, but it ran dry in summer (3) *Nagarkot*, a fort on a plain, buit by Ram Raja, ruler of the Karnatik. (C). Tieffenthaler (pp. 503 and 504) thus describes it : "It is situated on a slight elevation, on the frontier of the Karnatik, close to the further bank of the Kahati river. It has two gates,—one in the S. E, the other in the North towards the river. The ditch runs east up to the bank of a tank. It contains two wells into which one descends by steps. The wall has been constructed with irregular stones. The fort is 24 or 30 miles from Bijapur, according to the road followed. The circumference of the walls is 1475 yds. with 1422 embrasures. There are in all 18 towers ; the ditch is a dry one. The gate is about 14 yds. broad and 7 yds. deep. The interior parapet of the wall is 3 to 1½ yards (thick)

Crops, Industries, &c. Not given separately for this province.

Forts

The *Chahar Gulshan* (see p. 164) mentions 120 forts, while Tieffenthaler gives 131 in his list (i. 497). I have put the latter within brackets. The numbers are those which the forts bear in my translation.

1. Bijapur (same)
2. Islam-garh (")
3. Alang (Aland)
4. Achalpur (Amelpur)
5. Amalánk (Ankalang)
6. Rewni (Anóli)
7. Aniraj-durg (Bijraj-durg)
8. Andarud (Endór)
9. Ast-garhi (Amel-giri)
11. Táru (Márvi)

---

* "In this year (1588), Sadik Khan [Akbar's] governor of Bhakar, under orders, proceeded to attack the country of Tatta...Jani Beg, ruler of Tatta,... sent envoys with suitable gifts to the Imperial Court. The Emperor took compassion on him, and sent a *farman* to Sadik Khan, saying, "I bestow the country upon Jani Beg. Withdraw from its occupation." (Elliot, v. 456) Jani Beg was created a noble of the court, commanding 5,000 horse.

Similarly, the king of Kashmir, on making his submission to Akbar, was enrolled among the nobles of the Empire and granted a large *jagir* in Bihar.

12. Panch-durg (Bije-durg)
14. Mahim-garh (Bhim-garh)*
15. Sudar-garh (Búndár-garh)
16. Badnur (Badlór)
17. Sák-durg (Sáldurg)
19. Bái-buzáni (Rúi-boráni)
22. Banli (Bhaou)
23. Sálliki (Sankali)
24. Sadh-garh (Sidh-garh)
25. Nupar-garh (Lópar-garh)
26. Sapandan-durg (Mandan-garh)
27. Susar (Sawái)
28. Siáh-durg (Sita-durg)
29. Kalki (Kalanki)
30. Kisan-garh (Kapál-garh)
31. Lakhmir (same)
32. Lúmsi-garh (Lússigarh)
33. Nádar-garh (same)
34. Bhál-garh (Nahál-garh)
35. Mahammat-garh (Bhemat-garh)
36. Mandhi-garh (Mohib-garh)
37. Nándu-garh (Nandi-garh)
38. Bálápur (Malápur)
39. Harang (Marand)
40. Dangpur (Délpur)
41. Bhúkhan-garh (Púhar-garh)
42. Múdgal (Múkel)
45. Mandpál (Nandpál)
47. Bundi-kotha (Londi kot)
51. Bundi } (Sundí-kot)
52. Kotpur }
54. Rasúl-garh (Rehú-garh)
55. Kandal-garh (Kúndan-garh)
56. Kulár-garh (Kólár)
57. Júb-garh (Jeri-koh)
58. Bhúm-garh (Bhúm-Shankar)
59. Rahim-garh (same)
60. Ruin-garh („)
61. Shah mandar (Sáda-bandar)
62. Wazir-garh (same)
63. Viláit-garh („)
64. Huma (Holia)
65. Banká balá (Makábalad)
66. Harbans-garh (same)
67. Chandan-garh (Chanda-garh)
68. Mahál-garh (Samán-garh)
69. Gulaband-garh (Calanedh-garh)
70. Gandharb-garh (same)
71. Mor-garh (Múrka)
72. Naulpur (Lolpur)
73. Mardán-garh (same)
78. Asgharnagar or Akluj (Assad-nagar or Aklúj)
80 Imtiáz-garh (Ambar-garh Rúdoli*)
81. Kabúrah (Kalóra)
82. Máráni (Márdhani)
83. Banal-garh (Bangarh)
84. Básuámin (Lessúhan)
85. Baldá garh (same)
89. Bánsi (same)
90. Máthúra (Mahóra)
91. Núrgal (same)
92. Mangalkot („)
95. Rajbans-garh (Rajsissgarh)
97. Anmál-garh (Birpál-garh)
98. Sánkúla (Sangóla)
99. Sadhúr (Sidhpur)
100. Sadánand-garh (Sodanand laka)
101. Sribast-garh (Sirimast-garh)
102. Harkona-garh (Hargovand)
103. Kanúl-garh (Nakpur-garh)
104. Martazá-bád (Martazabad, commonly called *Merch*)
105. Mangal-band (Mangal-garh)

* A mistake for *Adoni*.

107. Baldatpai (Baland-garh)
108. Máham (Manjan)
110. Sabanján-garh (Sobans-garh)
111. Mandal garh (Mándar-garh)
112. Mahmángarh (Masnad garh)
113. Nasirabad (same, also called Darbár)
114. Nandpál (same)
115. Dárá-garh (Dárú-garh)
116. Bijúli (same)
117. Huli-garh (Múli-garh)
118. Hali-hál (Beli-jál)
119. Huli-honúr (Holipúr)
120. Húnmali (Bhúbali)

The following forts are mentioned by the *Chahar Gulshan* only :

10. Rang-durg
13. Him-durg
18. Naumadár-garh
20. Mákhárái
21. Mákhárali
43. Súṣal
44. Barad
46. Saubat-durg
48. Gokalpur
49. Chhilam
50. Luná
53. Khua
74. Súram-sakh
75. Kumbar-álál
76. Khadi
77. Ladhásadha
79. Azimnagar or Malkápur
86. Bikánur
87. Bhus-garh
88. Padishạh-pur
93. Khabrá
94. Dhubri
96. Athsli-garh
106. Múdgal
109. Haidar-garh.

The following forts are mentioned by Tieffenthaler alone :

Sahodar-garh
Barjit-garh
Malcau
Jelda
Jankari
Raouli
Rámkha
Ráheli
Langha
Mandak
Múki-garh
Músseljera
Búdand-durg
Kúdiloya
Hakim-kóta
Lálgarh
Lál-kúndi
Pendála
Islam-garh
Shergarh
Sakágarh
Mandanbórd
Dadharsa
Díwar-durg
Rehli
Sera
Shah durg
Sarnála
Rajhúr or Firuznagar
Kamarnagar or Karnún
Kandurg
Kachandar-garh
Gadak
Máúkl
Máheli
Machandar garh
Nasratabad-Bangar

19. HAIDARABAD.

Its boundaries are not given either by C. or by Tieff.

Divisions. 1700 ... 18 *Sarkars*, 129 *mahals*
1720 ... 12 " 96 "

The *Sarkars* of 1720 with the number of their *mahals*:

1. Devar-konda,	18 *m*	8. Kulpur	8
2 Warangal	10	9. Rajmahendri	12
3. Rajgopal	8	10. On the further side of the Krishna	19
4. Kam-bhim-mandi	5	11 On this side of the Krishna	6
5. Ibrahimpattan	—		
6. Nizampattan	5		
7. Muhammadanagar	5		

Revenue. The provincial revenue* was

in 1697 Rs 5,00,00,000
1700 " { 2,50.70,875 (acc. to Thomas, p 43)
2,73.37,500 (acc. to *Dastur*, MS D 163.)
1707 " 2,78.34,000
1720 " 2,73,20,875
Tieff. " 2,77,82.500 (i. 494)

Industries &c. The only places of note that are mentioned by C. are Haidarabad and Golkonda. No account is given of the crops, industries, &c. of this province separately. But we incidentally learn from C. that Haidarabad was famous for the handicrafts, which were established there by King Abul Hassan, and that the State derived large revenues from [the tax on] the juice of the date-palm (toddy) and from the diamond mines.

Forts. The *Chahar Gulshan* assigns to the province 54 forts and Tieffenthaler (i. 494) 57 'forts and castles.' The latter are placed within brackets. The numbers are those borne by the forts in my translation.

* The revenues given by Thomas (p. 53) for 1648, 1654, and 1663-66 for the *Subah* of Haidarabad were really derived from Telingana, before the kingdom of Haidarabad (Golconda) was annexed. Hence, they would be misleading in our comparative study.

2. Danúr-garh (Devar-garh)
3. Muhammadabad (same, also called Golkonda)
5. Khúlás (Kóláss)
6. Martaza-nagar (same, also called Kotta)
7. Kalúh-bádar (Katiladam)
8. Makha (Messi-maka)
9. Kúmal-garh (Gopal-garh)
10 Mustafa-nagar (same)
11. Haidar-nagar (Haidar garh)
13. Kúbháúli (Ghámeli)
14. Tubal-kandan (Dan-kundar)
15. Mandakrápur (Mandak)
16. Hasab-nasab (Jétpat)
17. Kanji-kúp (Kichikossand)
18. Jangal-pet (Jangal-bar)
19. Másrúr (Mauvar)
22. Sadah-danam (Sidham)
23. Habur (Ranór)
25. Wálmák (Danbág)
28. Karúdh (Karóda)
29. Bansi dhar (same)
30. Harmali (Barnála)
31. Urksla (Ardhakamla)
32. Uárun (Darán)
34. Khulirah (Khelna)
35. Karáb-kali (Ghirbán-kali)
37. Kumin (Gópi)
38. Ubúr (Devar)
39. Panchla (Bejila)
40. Lundhái (Lúliáni)
41. Korúr (Karór)
42. Kalápur (Kalanór)
43. Kúli (same)
45. Abdulla-garh (same, also called Ourdgarh)
46. Bidli-garh (Tili-garh)
47. Sundam-bár (Londam-bár)
49. Kharam-war-dar (Dorod-dar)
50. Khajla (Jejela)
53. Dharam-rám (Diraj Ram)

The following forts are mentioned by the *Chahar Gulshan* only :—

1. Haidarabad
4. Rasápur
12. Basant-núnam
20. Naumalgarh
21. Golkonda
24. Arganúr
26. Makah-kúr
27. Bhu-garh
33. Mánkal
36. 'Absi
44. Bámin
48. Manjá-durg
51. Nimi
52. Khim
54. Kúni

The following forts are mentioned by Tieffenthaler only :—

Shewnagar
Ghóra
Kalankór
Darnokl
Barzapur
Kádernák
Kalól
Lodam
Kalwa
Hétbálam
Lágaum
Sewar
Jamteli
Dandoros
Alighir-patan
Loki-bálam
Kardad
Karan-garh

20. BIDAR.

Extent. East of it lay Haidarabad, west Aurangabad, S. W. Gulburga, and north Burhanpur. (C.)

Divisions. The *Chahar Gulshan* and the *Dastur-al-amal* agree in giving to this province 4 *Sarkars* and 54 *mahals*, the former naming them.

Sarkars (1720) Bidar, 8 *mahals*
Kallian 2
Rumgarh 1
Mandir 43

Area and Revenue. The total area of measured land in 1720 was 78,72,194 *bighas*. The provincial revenue was

in 1700	Rs.	1,32,68,558 (acc. to Thomas)
	„	1,32,68,568 (acc. to the *Dastur*, MS. D. 163)
1707	„	93,24,359
1720	„	1,55,13,750
Tieff.	„	93,24,374

Forts. C. and Tieff. assign to this province the same 5 forts: *Bidar* (also called Muhammadabad), *Ramgir*, *Firuzgarh*, *Kalian*, and *Muzaffarnagar* or Balkhi ('Balighir' acc. to Tieff.)

Fruits of Deccan. *Nutmeg* and *Cardamom* grew in abundance in the Deccan. European *almond* grew in Haidarabad. *Plantain* grew in plenty, and there were many varieties of it (see p. 162) *Betel-nut*, though plentiful, had a very good flavour and high prices were paid for it. The *corinda* grew well in certain places. It was much relished by the Emperor Aurangzib. (C) This was quite in keeping with the sour temper of the man who "inhibited" music.*

Industries of Deccan. Bidar gave its name to a beautiful kind of gold and silver inlaying on pots In several places of the Deccan, cloth was well woven, esp. the gold *badla*, *dopatta*, bordered *korta*, *chirah*, *sarpech*, *kamar-band*, and *chhint* (C.)

* "The minstrels and singers of reputation in the service of the court were

CHAPTER V.

THE ROADS.

The *Chahar Gulshan* gives the stages of the following 24 roads, of which the first 13 have been traced either fully or in great part. Of the remaining 11 roads, a few of the stages have been identified, but they not not enable us to trace accurately the alignment of these highways. In the case of some of the latter class, we encounter the further difficulty of not knowing for certain where the road begins and where it ends and the relative positions of the different stages.

Roads mainly traced.

1. Agra—Delhi.
2. Delhi—Lahor.
3. Lahor—Gujrat—Atak.
4. Atak—Kabul.
5. Kabul—Ghazni—Qandahar.
6. Gujrat—Srinagar.
7. Lahor—Multan.
8. Delhi—Ajmir
9. Delhi—Barili—Benares—Patna.
10. Delhi—Kol.
11. Agra—Allahabad.
12. Bijapur—Ujjain.
13. Sironj—Narwar.

Roads partly traced.

14. Aurangabad—Ujjain ?
15. Golkonda—Asir—Hindia.
16. Hindia ?—Sironj.
17. Narwar ?—Gwalior—Dholpur ?
18. Dholpur—Agra ?
19. Multan—Bhakkar.
20. Srinagar—Atak.
21. Ajmir—Ahmadabad ?

Roads not traced at all.

22. Surkhab—Kabul.
23. Qandahar ?—Multan.
24. Qandahar ?—Atak.

---

made ashamed of their occupation, and were advanced to the dignities of *mansabs*. Public proclamations were made prohibiting singing and dancing. It is said that one day a number of singers and minstrels gathered together with great cries, and having fitted up a bier with a good deal of display, round which were grouped the public wailers, they passed under the Emperor's *jharokha-i-darsan* or interview-window. When he inquired what was intended by the bier and the show, the minstrels said that Music was dead, and they were carrying his corpse for burial. Aurangzib then directed them to *place it deep in the ground*."—From Khafi Khan. (Elliot. vii. 283.)

[The stages are given on the left, one below another; those that have been identified are printed in *Italics*, while unidentified and doubtfully transliterated names are printed in Roman type, the last having a note of interrogation after them. When not otherwise stated, the italicized places have been found in the Maps (see *ante* xxiii.). The distance in mile given after a stage is its *distance from the stage immediately preceding* it.]

1. AGRA to DELHI, 80 *kos*.

Sikandra, 5 m. N.W. of Agra Here is the tomb of Akbar.
Farah-Serai, 13½ m N.W. W. of the last stage.
Jhandipur, 3 m N.
Ganú-ghát ? a *pucca* Serai on the Jumna.
Koila-Serai, 5 m N of Jhandipur; it is on the Jumna
Naurangabad, not given in the *Atlas*, but the *A. & C. Gazetteer* places it 9½ m. from Farah, *i e*, 1½ m. N. of Koila.
MATHURA, 6 m. N. of Koila.
Akbarpur, 12 m N.W.
Chátá, a *pucca* Serai, 6 m. N
Deotána, 3 m. N. W.
Kosi-Serai, 3½ m. N. W.
Hodal, 8 m. N. W
Banchári, 3½ m. N.
Khataila, 4 m. N.
Mitnaul, 2½ m. N.
Khera Serai, 2½ m. N. (also named Baminee Khera)
Palwal, 6 m. N. This was the frontier town between the provinces of Delhi and Agra.
Baghaula, 4 m. N
Pirthala, 2½ m. N.
Sikri, 3 m. N.
Ballab-garh, 5 m N
Faridabad, 5½ m. N.
Serai of Khawajah Bakhtawar Khan. This man, a favourite eunuch of Shah Jahan, built 2 villages named after himself. (Elliot, vii. 150)
Badarpur. Tavernier mentions *Badalpura*, 8 *kos* S. of Delhi.

Neither name is found in the *Ind. Atlas.* But there is a *Madanpur*, 8 m. N. of Faridabad.

Tank of Raja Kishan Das, 11 m from the Turkoman gate of Delhi (*A. & C. Gaz*).

Serai of Mahábat Khán.

Barapula

DELHI, 16 m. N. of Faridabad as the crow flies.

The following stages are given by *Tavernier* (Ball's trans. i. 104):—Agra—Goodki Serai, 6 *kos.*—Shaiki Serai (near Mathura), 5 *kos*—Koti Serai, 16 *kos*—Palwal, 15 *kos*—Badalpura, 18 *kos*—Delhi, 8 *kos*.

Tieffenthaler mentions the following stages :—Agra—Sikandra —Gaugath, on the further bank of the Jumna, (=the Ganú-ghát of the *Chahar Gulshan* ?)—Renka, opposite Gaugath,—Runkuta, 8 miles from Agra,—Chandipur (=Jhandipur), 12 m. from Agra—Aurangabad, on the Jumna, 3 m. on,—Mathura—Chaomao, a Serai 6 m. from Mathura—Cháta, a fortified Serai,—Horel (=Hodul), 12 m. from Chaomao—Palwal, 12 m. on—Faridabad—Delhi (Pp. 206 & 207).

The *Agra and Calcutta Gazetteer* (1842) mentions the following stages :—Agra (Cantonment)—Nurcutta, 12 m.—Furrah, 10 m—Muttra (Cantonment), 13 m.—Jeyt, 10 m.—Chattah, 12 m.—Horul, 15 m.—Baminee Khera, 15 m.—Peertal, 13 m.—Faridabad, 13 m.—Kissen Dass ka Talao, 10 m.—Delhi (Cantonment), 11 m.

2. DELHI to LAHOR.

Badli, 7 m. N. W. of Delhi.

Narela, 8½ m. N. N. W.

Sonepat, 11½ m. N. W.

Ganaur, 9 m. N.

Samalkha. 8 m. N.

Panipat, 10½ m. N.

Gharaunda, 10 m. N.

Serai-Pul, evidently a Serai near the bridge (*pul*) over the Western Jumna Canal, in the 6th mile from Gharaunda (*A. & C. Gaz.*).

Karnal, 10 m. N. of Gharaunda.

Taraori, 9 m. N. N. W.

Azimabad, is given in Letts's *Atlas* in the very locality in which Taraori is given in the *Indian Atlas*. After it the Nai river is crossed.

Thanisar, 13 m. N. N. W. of Taraori. Here the Saraswati river is crossed.

Shahabad, 13 m. N.

Umballa, 16 m. N. N. W. After it the Ghaggar river is crossed.

Serai-Nún.

Serai Hajjam.

Todar Mal ?

Aluwa, 18 m. N. W. of Umballa.

Sirhind, 11 m. N. W.

Khanna, 10½ m. N. W. W.

Serai-Lashkar Khan, 20 m. from Sirhind (*A. & C. Gaz.*)

Douraha, 25 m. from Sirhind. (*A. & C. Gaz.*)

Ludhiana, 14 N. W. After this the Sutlej is crossed.

Phulour, 11 m. N N. W.

Nur-mahal, 12 m. W.

Nakodar, 7 m. W.

Dakhni, 5 m. N. W, (also named Jahangirpur). Here is the old bed of a river (the Bias ?).

Sultanpur, 13 m. W. Here the Kalna river is crossed immediately west of the town, and the Bias river 6 m. further N. W. at the ferry of Baoo-pur.

Fatihabad, 13 m. N. N. W., as the crow flies.

Naurangabad, 7½ m. N. W. of Fatihabad and 4½ m. S. E. E. of Tarn Taran.

Nuru-d-din-Serai, 8 m. N. W.

Serai-Amanat Khan, 11 m. N. W. W.

Darkah Pul ? Is it a mistake for *Kunchnee-ka Pul*, 8½ m. N. W. of Hosheear Nugur (A. 30), on the high road from Amritsar to Lahor ?

Hushiar-Nagar, 5 m. N. of Serai Amanat Khan and 21 m. E. of Lahor in a straight line.

Shah ganj.

LAHOR.

Tieffenthaler gives the following stages:—Delhi—Narela, 12 miles—Sonepat, 6 m.—Ganor, 6 m—Panipat, 12 m.—Karnal, 14 m.—Azimabad, 7 m.—Thaniswar, 9 m.—Shahabad, 12 m.—Umballa, 12 m.—Serai built by Nilkanth, 10 m.—Sirhind, 10 m.—Machiwara, on the further bank of the Sutlej, 14 m., [the frontier of the province of the Panjab]—Rahon, 8 m.—Rajaga, 10 m.—Serai Nuruddin, 10 m.—Adinanagar, 15 m.—Patiala, 12 m.—Kalanór, 12 m.—Serai Amanat Khan, on the road to Atak,—Shahdara, 15 m. from Kalanor—Lahor, 2 m. (Pp. 146 & 113) Or, from Ludhiana to Phulour, 12 m.—Nakodar, 12 m.—Sultanpur, 12 m.—The Bias, 7 m.—Govindwál, 5 m.—Serai Amanat Khan, 13 m.—Lahor, 12 m.

The *Agra and Calcutta Gazetteer* (1842) gives the following route:—Delhi—near Alipur, 10 m.—Barotah, 10 m.—Burki Choki, 13 m.—Somalkha, 11 m.—Panipat, 12 m.—Garaunda, 10 m. Karnal, 12 m.—Lilakheri, 10 m.—Thanisar, 13 m.—Shahabad, 14 m.—Kotkuchua, 8 m.—Umballa, 9 m.—Rajpura, 13 m.—Pattarsi, 8 m.—Sirhind, 9 m.—Kunha ka Serai, 11 m.—Douraha ka Serai, 14 m.—Ludhiana, 14 m.—Phulour, 7 m—Noor Mahal, 14 m.—Kalke, 15 m.—Kapurthala, 10½ m.—Birawal, 14½ m.—Joondiala, 13½ m.—Amritsar, 12 m.—Bania-ka-Dera, 15 m.—Shalimar, 15 m.—Lahor City, 5½ m.

---

3. LAHOR to ATTOCK.

Shahdara, 3 m. N. of Lahor fort, on the other side of the Ravi.

Fazilabad, not found in the Maps, but Tieff. places it 12 m. N. of Lahor, where the *Indian Atlas* gives a "Pucka Surai in ruins."

Juáhir-pul? Probably "Pool Shah Dowla" on the Degh river, 22 m. N. of Lahor (A. 30).

Eminabad, 10½ m. N. N. W of "Pool Shah Dowla," and 9 m. S. of Gujranwala.

Hakimabadpur.

Ghukkar Cheemah, 10½ m. N. of Gujranwala.

Wazirabad, 10 m N. After this the Chenab is crossed.

Gujrat, 9 m. N.

Khwaspur, 11 m. N. N. W. of Gujrat and 6 m S W. W. of Daulatnagar. After this the Bhimber river is crossed.

Kinári. Probably *Kharian*, a pass 12 m. N. W of the last stage.

Khariala, 3½ m. N. W. of Kharian

Serai Alamgir, 3 m N. W. The Jhilum river is 1½ m. N. W of it.

S'aid Khán.

Naurangabad, given in the *Indian Atlas* (Sheet 29) as adjoining Serai Alamgir.

Chokuha There is a Chakoa, 9 m N. W. of Rohtas fort (A. 29).

Khurda Jalál. Tieff. mentions a *Serai-i-Jalal Khan*, 20 m. N. W. of Rohtas.

Mahsa?

Paka? Tieff. mentions a *Paka*, 10 m. N. W. of Serai i-Jalal Khan.

Rowat, 11½ m. S. E. of Rawal Pindi.

Laskari?

Rawal Pindi.

Hazira? Tieff. mentions a *Khurja*, 5 m. N. W. of Rawal Pindi.

Kalapani. Kala-ka-Serai, 17 m. N. W. of Rawal Pindi, as the crow flies.

Hassan Abdal, 9 m. N. W.

Madrota, 19 m. N. W. W.

ATAK, 7½ m. W., on the eastern bank of the Indus.

Tavernier (i. 91) gives the following stages:—Wazirabad—Kariala or Sarai-i-Alamgir, 16 *kos*—Tulpuri, 19 *kos*—Rawat, 16 *kos*—Kalapani, 16 *kos*—Atak, 16 *kos*.

Tieffenthaler gives the following routes :—

Lahor.	Lahor.	Lahor.
		Elchi Serai, 4 m.
Shahdara, 2 m.	Firuzabad, 6 m.	Fazilabad, 8 m.
Shah Daulatpur (?= Shah Daula Pul) 12 m.	Pool-i-Shah Daula, 6 m.	Pool-i-Shah Daula, 6 m.
Eminabad, 12 m.	Eminabad, 6 m.	Eminabad, 6 m.
	Cutcha Serai, 6 m.	
	Ghakkar Chima, 6 m.	Ghakkar Chima, 12 m.
Wazirabad, 12 m.	Wazirabad, 6 m.	Wazirabad, 12 m.
(P. 113)	(P. 114)	(P. 86)

Then, Wazirabad - Gujrat 5 m.—Khawaspur, 8 m —The Jhilum, 8 m.—Rohtas, 5 m —Chokuha, 10 m.—Serai-i-Jalál Khán, 10 m.—Paka, 10 m —Rawat, 10 m —Rawal Pindi, 7 m.—Kurja, 5 m.—Kalapani, 5 m.—Hassan Abdal, 5 m,—Dingaron Serai, 6 m.—Mandróta, 5 m.—Atak, 5 m.

The *Agra and Calcutta Gazetteer* (1842) gives the route detailed below ;—Nowrangabad Serai—Jhilum city, 2 m.—Rohtas, 11½ m.—Udurana, 8½ m.—Bukrala, 8½ m.—Tumako, near Dhumak, 9½ m.—*Pucca* Serai on the right bank of the Kassi Nadi, 14 m. —Manikyala, 12½ m.—Hoormak. 9½ m.—(after crossing the Sohan river) Rawal Pindi, 2 m.—(after crossing the Kali Nadi) Jani-ka-Sang, 13½ m —Vab, 14 m.—Burhan, 8 m.—Shamsabad, 13 m.—Atak, 10 m

4. ATTOCK to KABUL.

Khairabad, on the western bank of the Indus, opposite Attock.

Qasári ? Evidently a mistake for *Niri*, 4½ m. N. of Khairabad.

Akora, 10 m. N. W. of Khairabad, as the crow flies.

Sindh ? Probably a mistake for Nowshera, 9 m. W. of Akora.

Khan-khanan.

Peshawar, 22 m. W. of Nowshera.

Jumrood, 11½ m. W. This fort is only 3½ m. east of the mouth of the Khyber Pass.

Dah-ghulámán ?

Ali Masjid, 10 m. W. of Jumrood.

Landikhana, 12½ m. N. W.

Dhaka, 7½ m N. N W. ; on the southern bank of the Kabul river, at the western mouth of the Khyber Pass.

Surkh diwar. The *A. & C Gaz.* mentions the ruins of this place, between Bareekab (9½ m. S. E. of Ali Boghan) and Ali Baghan.

Ali-Boghan, 31 m. N. W. W. of Dhaka.

Jalalabad, 7½ m. N. W. W., on the southern bank of the Kabul river, or 'the stream (*nahar*) of Surkh-áb' according to the *Chahar Gulshan*. The Surkh river falls into the Kabul, a few miles west of Jalalabad.

Jái ?

Chárbágh-khurd ; there is a Balabagh, 12½ m. S. W. W. of Jalalabad.

Chárbágh-kalán

Serai Chilla ?

Gandamak, 29 m. S. W. of Jalalabad.

Malik Ali

Jagdalak, 17 m N. W. of Gandamak.

Bárang-badehát ?

Sar-dahana. Not given in the Maps. Tieff. places it (Sher-Dahan) 5 m. from Jagdalak.

Tazin, 5 m. E. of Qahar Jabbar

Qahar Jabbar, 16 m. S. W. of Jagdalak.

Khurd Kabul, 6 m W

But-khak, 10 m. N.

Bagrami, 5½ m. W.

KABUL Fort, 6 m W.

Tavernier (i 91) gives the following stages :—Atak—Nowshera, 19 *kos*—Peshawar, 14 *kos*—Khairbari ?, 14 *kos*—Dakka, 6 *kos*—Ali Baghan, 17 *kos*—Nimla-bagh, 19 *kos*—Barikab, 17 *kos* Kabul, 19 *kos*

Tieffenthaler (p 72) lays down the following route :—Atak—Khairabad—Néri, 3 m.—Akóra, 4 m.—Girdab, 4 m.—Naushera,

4 m.—Shahabad, 8 m.—Júigúsar, 4 m —Peshawar. 3 m.—Jamrud, 7 m.—Ali Masjid, 8 m —Landikhana, 8 m.—Haft Chah, 8 m.—Dagá, 5 m.—Barikáb, 6 m.—Jalalabad, 10 m.—Fatihabad, 6 m.—Nimboul, 6 m —Gandamak 6 m.—The Surkh-ab, 6 m.—Jagdalak, 6 m.—Sher-dahan, 5 m.—Tazi, 8 m. Khurd Kabul, 5 m —Budakak, 5 m —Kotalieklang 4 m.—Kabul, 3 m

The *Agra and Calcutta Gazetteer* mentions the following stages :—Attock—Khyrabad, 2 m —Akora, 10 m.—Nowshera, 10 m.—Pubbee, 9 m.—Peshawar, 12 m.—Howulsur, 8½ m.—Near Kadam, 6½ m.—Ali Masjid, 11 m.—Landikhana, 13 m—Dhaka, 8½ m.—Hazarinow, 8½ m.—Char Debr, 11½ m.—Ali Boghan, 14 m.—Jalalabad, 6½ m.—Sultanpur, 8½ m.—Fatihabad, 7½ m.—Siffaud Sung near Gandamak, 11½ m.—Surkhab, 9½ m.—Jagdalak, 13 m.—Kutta Sung, 7 m.—Baba Esaw,—Near Tazeen, 8½ m.—Khurd Kabul, 12½ m.—Boothak, 9 m.—Kabul, 8½ m.

5. KABUL to QANDAHAR.

Sufid-sang

Char-asia, 9 m. S. of Kabul.

Laghmán ?

Deh-nau.

Danbara ?

Bakhsáwand ?

Haft-asia.

Shash-gaon, 3 m. S.

Sher-i-dana, 3 m. S. ; a mountain pass.

Mausoleum of Sultan Mahmud, marked *Roza* in the Map, a little north of Ghazni.

Ghazni Fort, 11 m. S. of Sher-i-dana.

Dera *Nani*, 12 m. S.

Karábágh or Farábágh ?

Bárik-diwár ? Here was the frontier of Qandahar.

Shastal.

Ab-i tazi, 5 m. S.

Sar-i-asp, 16 m. S. W.

Kalat Ghilzai, 10 m. S. W. Qandahar is 75 m. S. W. of it.

The stages of the last 75 miles of this road are not given.

Tavernier (i. 91) gives the following stages :—Kabul—Shiganu (?=Shashgaon), 40 *kos*—Karabagh, 17 *kos*—Masur, 17 *kos*—Ab-i-Tázi, 6 *kos*—Kalat-i-Ghilzai, 8 *kos*—Shahar-i-Safa, 12 *kos*—Qandahar, 10 *kos*.

Tieffenthaler and the *A. & C. Gazetteer* do not describe this road.

6. LAHOR to KASHMIR.

From Lahor to Gujrat, as in 3. From *Gujrat* :—

Daulatnagar, 12 m. N. of Gujrat

Bhimbar, 16 m. N., on the western bank of the Bhimbar river.

Chauki Hati, not given in the Atlas, but Tieff. places it 4 royal miles (*i e.*, 7 ordinary miles) N. of Bhimbar and speaks of its having a cave with 2 elephants carved on the rock.

Nowshera, 16 m. N. of Bhimbar, on the western bank of the Tawi river.

Changiz-Hati, Tieff places it 4½ m. N. of Nowshera, but the *Indian Atlas* gives *Chingas Serai* 5½ m. N. N. E. of Nowshera.

Ináyetpur, probably *Moradpur*, 7 m N.E of Chingas Serai (A. 29)

Rajaor, 16 m. N. N. E. of Nowshera.

Thana. Thanna Bazar, 12 m. N. (A. 29).

Baramgula, 5 m N. N. E. There is a waterfall here.

Poshána. 2 m. from Baramgula, acc. to Tieff.

Serai-Ali Mardán Khan, or Serai-Muhammad Kuli, 3½ m. onward, acc. to Tieff.

S'aid Hala ? or Serai Sokhta, acc. to Tieff.

Hirpur, 10 m. N. of Poshana (Tieff.)

Shádimarg, or Shajamarg, 6 m. from Hirpur, acc. to Tieff.

Khanpur, 18 m. N. N. E. of Hirpur (Tieff) and 11 m. S. of Srinagar (Stein's Map).

Srinagar, 11 m. N.

Another road goes from Rajaor to Kashmir :—

Rajaor

Saifabad.

Poonch, 42 m. N. N. W. of Rajaor, as the crow flies.

Aliabad. Walker's *Atlas* has *Shookrabad*, between Poonch and Oori.

Oori, a well-known gorge, 17 m. N. of Poonch.

Bhamiar, 8½ m. N. E. E.

Báramula, 10 m. E Srinagar is 30 m. E. of it, as the crow flies.

Tieffenthaler, (P. 87) gives the following route :—Wazirabad—Gujrat, 5 m.—Daulatnagar, 8 m—Kathra (a fort built by Issatiar Khan) 5 m.—Bhimbar, 5 m—Sahatabad, 12 m—Nowshera, 10 m. —Serai-i-Zangiz, 10 m.—Rajawar, 10 m.—Thana, 10 m.—Baramgula, 7 m.—Poshana, 6 m.—Serai Aliabad—Serai Sokhta—Hirapur, 10 m. from Poshana—Shajamarg Serai, 6 m.—Khanpur 6 m.—Kashmir (*i e*, Srinagar) 6 m.

He quotes the following route from *The History of Shah-Jahan* (probably the work of Abdul Hamid Lahori or that of Muhammad Salih Kambu) :—Bhimbar—Chauki Hati, 4 royal miles (=7 ordinary miles)—Nowshera, 3½ m.—Changiz Hati, 4½ m.—Rajawar, 5½ m.—Thana, 4½ m.—Baramgula, 3½ m.—Poshana, 2 m.—Serai i-Muhammad Kuli, 3½ m.—Serai Sokhta (a *pucca* Serai), 3½ m.—Hirapur, 3¾ m.—Shajamarg 4 m.—Khanpur, 3 m.—Srinagar, 5 m. (P. 88).

Tieffenthaler (P. 89) speaks of the following route as generally followed by merchants :—From Nazibgarh, (a fort built by the Afghan Nazib)—Alamnagar—Dharampur—Shahranpur—Tajpur—Gular—Nahn (at this place the road enters into the mountains) Bilaspur—Jala—Zoali—Haripur—Makrota—Bissuli—Badroa—Kishtawar—Srinagar.

7. LAHOR to MULTAN.

Abul Hassan.

Aurangabad.

Nowshahra, 42 m. S. W. of Lahor.

Mopalkee, 13½ m. S. W.

Satghara, 14 m. S.

Kamal, Khan Kumalwala, 19½ m. S. W. W; or it may be *Kot Kumalyuh*, 30·43·30 N. 72·43 E. (A. 17).

Chauki Fatu, probably *Jhook*, 11½ m. N. E. of Harappa.

Harappa, 30·38 N. 72 56 E.

Chichawatni, 11½ m. S. W. W.

Ali *Sahwa*, probably *Sahwa Gureeb*, 6 m. W.

Talumba, 21 m. W.

Sard, 19 m. W. in Walker's *Atlas*; not given in the *Indian Atlas*, in which it ought to be N. of *Serraie Siddhoo*.

Khalid, not found. Walker gives a *Kulalpur*, 8 m. N. W. of *Sird*.

Mardánpur, probably *Mundalpoor*, 14 m. S. S. W. of Kulalpur, and 36 m N. E. of Multan (Walker, Sheet xii.).

The stages of the remaining 36 miles are not given in the *Chahar Gulshan*.

Tieffenthaler (P. 119) gives the following stages:—Lahor—Katpur—Guzar Serai—Noshahra—Satghara—Harpan (Harappa)—Maktúnpúr—Kanpur—Multan; the total distance is 120 or 160 miles.

8. DELHI to AJMIR.

Serai Alawardi, 16 m. S. W. of Delhi, and 1 m. N. of the Gurgaon Railway Station.

Pataudi, 19½ m. S. W.

Rewari, 13 m. S W.

Kot, 44 m. S. S. W.

Putli, 1 m. S. W.

Barduráyán ?

Chuksar, probably *Jubner*, 13½ m. N.N.E. of Sambhar (A. 33 S E)

Sámbhar, a city on the S. E. bank of the Sambhar lake.

Múranda, probably *Momana*, 10½ m S. W of Sambhar city.

Sarsará, probably *Horamara*, 11½ m. S. W. of Momana, and 24 m N. E. of Ajmir.

21. AJMIR to AHMADABAD.

(120 *kos*, acc. to the *Chahar Gulshan.*)

Jhalor, 147 m. S. W. of Ajmir, as the crow flies. Jhalor was the frontier town between the provinces of Ajmir and Gujrat. The other stages are not given in the *Chahar Gulshan.*

In Akbar's time the under-mentioned routes were followed (Elliot, v.) :—

Nagor.	Ajmir	Ajmir.
Mirath.		Mirtha.
		Jitaram.
		Sojhat.
		Páli
		Bhagwanpur.
Sirohi.	Jhalor.	Jhalor.
Pattan Nahrwala.	Haibatpur.	Pattanwál.
Disa fort.		
Ahmadabad.	Ahmadabad.	Ahmadabad.

We also learn from the *Tabqat-i-Akbari* that from Bhagwanpur the road by Sirohi was shorter than the road by Jhalor. (Elliot, v. 362).

Tieffenthaler (P. 332) lays down the following route :—Gujrat (*i.e*, Ahmadabad)—Pethapur, 12 m.—Mesána, 12 m.—Sitapur, 20 m.—Palhanpur, 6 m.—Bilmál, 20 m.—Jhalor, 20 m

9. DELHI to MORADABAD and BENARES to PATNA.

Delhi. Cross the Jumna.

Shahdara, 3 m. E.

Serai Basant ?

Ghaziu-d-din-nagar (acc to Letts's *Atlas*) or *Ghaziabad* (acc. to the *Indian Atlas*), 8 m. E. of Shahdara. In coming to this town the Hindun river has to be crossed.

Dasna, 6 m. E.

Kálan deh-ni ?

Hapúr, 16 m. N. E. E. of Dasna. After this place, the Kali river is crossed.

Bagsar, also called Gangadharpur. 13½ m. N. E. E. of Hapur.

Rath-Sahi ? "bridge of Bábá Dargahi, a follower of Guru Nanak" (*Ch Gulshan*).

Garh-Muktesar, 6½ m. E. of Bagsar, on the western bank of the Ganges.

Bagri, 13 m. N. E E.

Amroha, 10½ m. N. E. E.

Moradabad, 18½ m. E. on the western bank of the Ramganga, and 46 m N. W. of Barili.

From this point we lose all trace of the road, as given in the *Chahar Gulshan*, and have to pick it up at *Rai Barili* which is 234 m. S. S. E. in a straight line.

Rai Barili, on the eastern bank of the Sai river, 49 m. S. E. E. of Cawnpur and 79 m. N. N. E. of Allahabad.

Selon, 21 m. S.

Kharah ? probably *Kurrah*, on the western bank of the Ganges, 26 m. S. of Selon.

Dia Mái ?

Kurrah is only 3 m. N. of the Agra-Allahabad road, and Diamái was probably the point in this road at which it was joined by the road from Rai Barili. From Diamái we lose all trace of the latter road, but at Benares we pick it up again.

Benares.

Serai Said Rázi

Ghazipur, 39 m. N. E. of Benares; on the left bank of the Ganges.

Buxar, 24 m E., on the right bank of the Ganges, which river is crossed at Chausa, 7 m S. of Buxar

Ranisagar 25 m. N. E E. of Buxar, and 20 m. W. of Arrah.

Bisambhar. There is a *Bisumhurpur*, 10½ m. N. N. E. of Arrah and a little west of the place where the Son falls into the Ganges.

Patna.

Tavernier (i. 118) went from Benares to Patna by the following route :—Benares—Bahadurpur, 2 *kos*—Sadráza-ki-Serai, 8 *kos*—Mohaniá-ki-Serai, 6 *kos*—Khurmábad, on the Koodra river, 8 *kos*—Sasseram, 4 *kos*—Daudnagar, 9 *kos*—Arwal, on the Son, 10 *kos*—Aga Serai, 9 *kos*—Patna, 10 *kos*.

The *Agra and Calcutta Gazetteer* gives the following stages:—Benares—Chobepur, 12 m.—Syedpur, 11 m.—Nandganj, 12½ m.—Ghazipur, 10 m.—Muhammadabad, 14 m.—Near Kuruntadee, 13 m.—Near Buxar, 2½ m.—Chota Bhojpur, 10 m.—Rani Sagar, 13 m.—Gajrajganj, 12½ m.—Arrah, 8½ m—Kuttesur, 11 m.—Dinapur, 14½ m.—Patna, 11 m

10. DELHI to KOIL.

Delhi ; here cross the Jumna.

Patparganj, 3½ m. S. E. of Delhi, on the eastern bank of the Jumna.

Chalera, 5 m. S. E E.

Pucca Serai of *Bhagel*. 3½ m. E. of Chalera. After this cross the Hindun river.

Begampur, 5½ m. S. E. of Bhagel.

Serai Khási. There is a *Kasna*, 6 m S. E of Begampur.

Sikandrabad, 15 m S E. E of Begampur.

Khurja, 16 m. S.

Well of Sitaram.

Chandaus, 11½ m. S. of Khurja.

Koil, 18 m. S. E. of Chandaus, and 2 m. S. of Aligarh.

Harduaganj, 6 m. E.

The *Agra and Calcutta Gazetteer* gives the following stages :—Delhi (Cantonment)—Patparganj, 8 m—Surajpur, 14½ m.—Sekandra, 14 m.—Choolah, 10 m.—Khurja, 7 m - Somnathganj, 14 m.—Aligarh 15½ m.—Koil, 2 m.

---

11. AGRA—ALLAHABAD—BENARES.

Tomb of Wazir Khán.

Firuzabad, 24 m. E. of Agra, as the crow flies.

Shikohabad, 11 m. S. E E.

Etawah, 34½ m. S. E.

Rájpur, 52 m. S. E.. and 13 m. N. N. W. of Kalpi.

Koorarah, 29 m. S. E. of Rajpur and 18 m. S. E. E. of Kalpi.

Hutgaon, 90 m. S. E. of Kalpi, and 52 m. N. W of Allahabad.

Shahzadpur, 32 m. N. W. of Allahabad, on the southern bank of the Ganges.

Fatihabad, probably *Fatihpur*, 9 m. N. W. of Allahabad.

Allahabad.

The following stages are evidently on the road from Allahabad to Benares, though the *Chahar Gulshan* does not explicitly say so :—

Báns Barili.

Hanuman nagari. There is a *Hanumanganj* 10 m. E. of Allahabad.

Malikpur.

Shah-Jahanpur.

Sandha, 27 m. W. of Benares.

Mullá Lúsad-wáli ? Probably *Mirza Murad*, 14 m. W. of Benares.

Here the *Chahar Gulshan* abruptly stops, without giving the remaining stages to Benares.

Tavernier (i. 113) travelled by the following route :—

AGRA—Firuzabad, 9 *kos*—Serai Murlidas, 9 *kos*—Etawah, 14 *kos*—Ajit Mal, 12 *kos*—Sikandara, 13 *kos*—Sankal, near Musanagar, 14 *kos*—Sherúrábad, 12 *kos*—Serai Shahzada, 10 *kos*—Hutgáon, 13 *kos*—Aurangabad, 9 *kos*—Alumchand, 9 *kos*—Allahabad, 8 *kos*—Sadul Serai (Sydabad ?), 16 *kos*—Jagadis Serai, 10 *kos*—Baboo Serai, 10 *kos*—BENARES, 10 *kos*.

Tieffenthaler (P. 240). lays down the following route :—Allahabad—Handia, 12 m.—Gopiganj, 9 m.—Mirza Morad, 10 m——Benares, 8 m.

The *Agra and Calcutta Gazetteer* gives the following stages :—AGRA (cross the Jumna)—Etimadpur, 14 m—Firuzabad, 13½ m.—Shekohabad, 12½ m.—Murlidhar-ka-Serai, 8½ m.—Jaswant-nagar, 14½ m.—Etawah, 9½ m.—Bukiwar. 14 m.—Ajitmal, 11 m.—

Ooria, 14 m.—Sikandra, 10½ m.—Shah Jahanpur, 10 m.—Boghni, 7 m.—Musanagar, 10½ m.—Ghatampur, 12 m.—Jahanabad, 10½ m. —Kajwa, 13 m.—Khuapur, 10½ m.—Fatihpur, 10 m.—Munda-ke-Serai, 13 m.—Chauki-ke-Serai, 13½ m.—Daranagar, near Karrah, 14½ m.—Kusia, 10½ m.—Mufti-ka-Púrwa, 15½ m.—ALLAHABAD, 13½ m.—Jhoosee, 4½ m.—Sydabad, 13½ m.—Ooj-ke-Chauki, 13½ m. —Gúsiá, 13½ m.—Tamashabad, 10½ m.—Mohun ke-Serai, 11½ m. —BENARES, 7 m.

12. BIJAPUR to UJJAIN.

Bijapur Fort.

Bijapur City.

Kanwalápur. Not found in Letts; it may be a mistake for *Sholapur*, which is 60 m. N. of Bijapur.

Nandgáon. There is a *Nimbgaon* 18·5 N. 74·58 30 E., about 100 m. N. N. W. of Bijapur.

Chambhargoonda, 38 m. N. N. W. of Nimbgaon, and 33 m. S. of Ahmadnagar.

Izdabad, probably *Kalarabad* or Mandavgáon, 17 m. N. N. W. of Chambhargoonda.

Ahmadnagar fort, 19 m. N. of Mandavgaon.

Bihisht-bagh, a garden north of Ahmadnagar. After this the Pain-Ganga river is crossed. From this stage we lose sight of the road and have to take it up again, 140 m. north, at Bhikhangaon.

Durjanpur.

Three villages in succession (not named).

Cutcha Serai.

Bhikhangaon. 21 49 N. 76 1 E.; 39 m. N. N. W. of Burhanpur.

Gogdon, 14 m. W.

Multhan, 7 m. N.

Serai Málchand, probably *Balkhar*.

Akbarpur, an important ferry over the Narbada, 25 m. N. W. of Gogaon, and 12½ m. W. of Mandlesar.

Jahangir-nagar.

Núnhara. There is a *Lunhera*, 2½ m. west of Akbarpur, on the opposite bank of the Narbada. Elliot refers to it (vii. 18) as Lonihara

Dikthan, 30 m. N. of Akbarpur.

Dipalpur, 19 m. N.

Fatihabad or *Jharolia*, 14½ m. N. N. E, across the Gamhir river.

Garden of Aurangzib.

Darband or the Gate of Ujjain ?

Ujjain, 12½ m. N. E of Fatihabad.

14. AURANGABAD to UJJAIN ?

Aurangabad.

Pulmari, 14 m N.

Pathri.

Alund, 13 m. N. E. of Pulmari.

Serai Kámún.

Sailur, 8 m. N. E. of Alund.

Golagáon.

Fardápur. Elliot speaks of it as a pass midway between Aurangabad and Burhanpur (vii. 498), or about 32 *kos* from Aurangabad (vii. 307), which would be near Ajunta.

Pass of Fardápur.

Serai-i-Hatam Beg.

Bikhári ?

Idulabad, 37 m. N. N. E. of Ajunta, and 5 m. E. of the junction of the Purna and the Tapti.

From this point to Ujjain, 150 m N., we lose sight of the road.

Antri.

Bahári ?

Ujjain City.

Firozpur village.

Serai-i-Sultan Mahmud.

15. GOLKONDA—ASIR—HINDIA.

Golkonda.

Bidar, 67 m. N. W.

Qandahar, 68 m. N.

Ellich pur, 166 m. N. N. E.

Takht-bahzád ?

Asir, 77 m. W. of Ellichpur ; the Tapti is crossed 10 m. E. of it.

River Mándhár ?

Serai Mándhár ?

Mánduh. This cannot be the Mandu of Malwa.

Dáudnagar

Serai-Bir ?

New Serai

Serai

Serai-Bhrangana ?

Serai *Chinpur*, 36 m. N. E. of Asir.

Serai-Nim

Charwa, 18 m. N. N. E of Chinpur.

Serai-Beli ?

Serai-Bijhula. Tavernier calls it *Bichola* and places it 4 *kos* S. of Hindia.

Hindia, 27 m. N. of Charwa, on the right bank of the Narbada.

Tavernier followed the route given below :—Burhanpur—Piombi Serai, 5 *kos*—Pander (Mandwa), 3 *kos*—Balki Serai (Balwara), 6 *kos* —Nawel-ki-Serai, 5 *kos*—Kusemba, 5 *kos*—Chainpur, 3 *kos*—Charwa, 8 *kos*—Bichola, 8 *kos*—Hindia, 4 *kos*.

The *Agra and Calcutta Gazetteer* gives the following stages between Asir and Charwa :—Asir—Borgaon, 13½ m—Khirgaon, 9 m—Bamgarh, 8 m.—Gangapat (river), 11 m.—Gorapachhar (river), 11½ m—Charwa, 12 m.

16. HINDIA ? to SIRONJ.

Serai-Núrbari. Probably *Newardi*, 22½ m. N. of Hindia. (A. 53 S. W.)

Ichhawar, 37 m. N. of Hindia.
Sihor, 13 m. N.
Serai-Nimak.
Duraha, 15 m. N. of Sihor.
Bhath khira Serai, 30 m. N. E. It is an obscure village away from the modern roads as given in the *Indian Atlas*. Tavernier names it Hatiakhera
Cutcha Serai.
Nála Bhua nála. The river *Baha* has to be crossed midway between Bhatkera and Barda
Serai of Baróda village. There is a *Barda*, 15 m. N. of Bhatkera (A. 52. S. E) A village named *Baroda* is 8½ m. W. of Barda.
Serai Basant-baria ?
Serai Kánkar ? Probably *Gangakheri*, 14 m. N. of Barda, and 5 m. S. S. W. of Sironj.
Serai Niuária ?
Sironj, 19 m. N. of Barda, on the E. bank of the Kethan river.

Tavernier gives the following stages :—Hindia—Onquenas ? 4 *kos*—Tiqueri ? 5 *kos*—Toolmeden ? 4 *kos*—Nova Serai, 4 *kos*—Ichâwar, 4 *kos*—Sihor, 5 *kos*—Shaikhpura, 3 *kos*—Duraha, 3 *kos*—Hatiakhera 3 *kos*—Dilod, 4 *kos*—San Khaira ? 3 *kos*—Sironj, 12 *kos*.

13. SIRONJ to NARWAR.

Stone Serai.
Mogul Serai, 14 m. N. of Sironj.
Afghan-Serai.
Kachner Serai, 9 m. N. of Mogul Serai.
Shahdaura, 13 m. N.
Serai of Madh-kathi village ?
Kalabagh village, 16 m. N. of Shahdaura.
Serai Abul Hassan.
Túmádú-nagar ? Tieffenthaler calls it Búradú-nagar, and places it 6 m. S. of Kailaras and 8 m. N. of Nai Serai. At that place

the *Indian Atlas* gives *Budadanga*, 13½ m. N. of Kalabagh.

Rajhula village.

Serai S'aid. Probably a mistake for 'Serai-i-Sind,' some Serai near a ferry of the Sind river.

Serai Badridás. Evidently a mistake for *Kailaras,* (10½ m. N. of Budadanga), which was a stage in the routes of Tavernier and Tieffenthaler alike. The latter mentions a place with a similar name, *Badarwas,* "a village, being the frontier of the district [*Sarkar*] of Narwar, on the road from Narwar to Sironj." (P. 179) Badarwas is situated 8 m. N. N. W. of Kalabag. (A. 52. N. E.).

Sawari village. Evidently a mistake for *Sipri,* 15 m. N of Kailaras. Tieffenthaler calls it Sheopur, but Tavernier names it correctly.

Dongri, 8 m N. E. of Sipri. Midway between it and the next stage the Sind river is crossed.

Narwar City, 14 m. N. E. It is situated S. E. of a bend of the Sind river.

Tavernier travelled by the following route:—Sironj—Mughal Serai, 6 *kos*—Paulki Serai? 2 *kos*—Kachner, 3 *kos*—Shahdaura, 6 *kos*—Kalabagh, 6 *kos*—Akmati? 2 *kos*—Kailaras, 9 *kos*—Sipri, 6 *kos*—Dongri, 4 *kos*—Ghat [*i.e.*, ferry over the Sindh river], 3 *kos*—Narwar, 4 *kos*.

Tieffenthaler (P. 349) gives the following stages:—Sironj—Mughal Serai, 6 m—Shahdaura, 11 m.—Nai Serai, 7 m.—Buradunagar, 8 m—Kailaras, 6 m—Sheopur, 6 m.—Narwar, 12 m.

17. NARWAR—GWALIOR—DHOLPUR?

Maláncha Serai?

Nun River

Nun Village?

Nun Serai, 12 m. S. S. W. of Antri, on the N. bank of the Noon river.

Serai-i-Sardár Khan. Probably *Barki Serai,* 5½ m. S. of Antri.

Cutcha Serai.

Antri, 10 m. S. of Gwalior.

Serai Sarmast ?

Serai-i-Gajpati in the city [of Gwalior] ?

Gwalior is 40½ m. N. N. E. of Narwar in a straight line.

Serai-i-Khán daurán.

Serai-i-Awad Sing.

Serai-i-Mihr Ali.

Serai Sang ?

Garden of Khan Jahan

River Sankh. This river is crossed by the modern road 14½ m. N. N. W. of Gwalior fort.

Serai Kanwari. Evidently the place where the Kumari river was crossed, 10½ m. N. of the ferry over the Sankh river, which forms the preceding stage.

Dholpur, 36½ m. N. N. W. of Gwalior in a straight line ; 11 m. N. N. W. of the ferry over the Kumari river. The Chambal has to be crossed 2 m. before reaching the modern town of Dholpur ; the old fort of Dholpur, however, stood on the bank of the Chambal close to the ferry, which was formerly guarded as an approach to Agra.

Tavernier travelled by the following route :—Narwar—Barki Serai, 9 *kos*—Antri, 3 *kos*—Gwalior, 6 *kos*—The Sank river, 5 *kos* —Kuari Serai (on the Kuari river), 8 *kos*—Dholpur, 6 *kos*.

The *Agra and Calcutta Gazetteer* lays down the following route :—Antri—Jinsee, 12 m.—Gwalior Residency, 6½ m —Dunaila, 11m.—Hingona, 12 m —Dholpur, 13½ m

18. DHOLPUR—AGRA ?

Dholpur, after crossing the Chambal from the south This town is 50 m. S. of Agra.

Serai Sadiq. There is a *Sadiqpur*, 7 m. N N. E. of Dholpur.

Fatihabad

Serai Begam
Serai Shaikh
Serai Than ?
Serai Abu Said Hassan
Jamal-nagar
Serai-Sambhá ?
Serai-*Sikandra*, evidently Sikandarpur, 11 m. S. of Agra.
Serai Sara
Kakuba, 7½ m. S of Agra, and 4 m N. of Sikandarpur.
Serai Mulúkchand ?

Tavernier gives the following stages :—Dholpur—Mania Serai, 6 *kos*—Jajou-ka-Pul, 8 *kos*—Agra, 4 *kos*

The *Agra and Calcutta Gazetteer* lays down the following route :—Dholpur—Munia, 9 m —(after crossing the Banganga or Utangan). Jhajhur, 8½ m —Tehara, 5 m —Agra, 12 m

---

Tavernier travelled from **Surat** to **Burhanpur** by the following route :—Surat—Bardoli (Panoli), 14 *kos*—Ballor, 10 *kos*—Kerkoa (Begam Serai), 5 *kos*—Nawapur, 15 *kos*—Nandurbar, 9 *kos*—Dolmedan, 14 *kos*—Sind-khair, 7 *kos*—Talnir, 10 *kos*—Chopra, 15 *kos*—Sankh, 13 *kos*—Nabir ? 10 *kos*—Balleda, 9 *kos*—Burhanpur, 5 *kos*.

Tieffenthaler's route from **Qandahar** to **Multan** is reproduced below, as the road given by the *Chahar Gulshan* is hopelessly illegible and confused :—Qandahar—Koshaz, 41 m —Mastani, 46 m.—Ouchen, 28 m.—The Sindh river, 31 m.—Multan, 14 m "The road is 160 royal miles or 300 ordinary miles in length." (P. 75)

KHULASATU-T-TAWARIKH.

[The figures within square brackets indicate the leaves of the Bengal Asiatic Society's Persian manuscript D 153, while *a* or *b* stands for the front or back page of each leaf.]

I. DELHI.

The Metropolitan Province of Shah-Jahanabad.

[17. *b*.] We learn from many Indian and Persian histories that in ancient times the capital of the rulers of Hindustan was the city of Hastinapur, on the bank of the river Ganges. The spaciousness and extent of this town is spoken of as having been very great in that age. Though it is still inhabited, yet it has not so large a population at present. When, in the days of the Pandu and Kuru kings, a quarrel broke out between the two parties, the Pandus migrated from the city of Hastinapur to that of Indrapath,* on the bank of the river Jumna, and made it their capital.

Old capi and pala near Del

(1) Hasti pur

(2)

After a long period, in the year 440 of Vikramajit (383 A.D.), Raja Anangpal Tomar † founded the city of DELHI near Indrapath. After that, Rai Pithora,‡ in the year 1200 and odd of Vikramajit, built a fort and town after his own name. Sultan Qutbu-d-din Aibak and Sultan Shamsu-d-din Altamsh lived in the fort of Rai Pithora. Sultan Ghiasu-d-din Balban, having built

(3) Rai P thora

---

* Sanskrit *Indraprastha*.

† A text reads *Tonwar*. The *Ain* (ii. 300) gives the date as 429 Samvat (372 A.D.) and the name as *Tonwar*. Tod spells the name *Tuar*, and assigns 848 Samvat (729 A.D.) as the date. (*Rajasthan*, I. 92). For Anangpal, see Elliot, iii. 565 and *Ain*, ii. 212.

‡ Prithvi-raja, the Chohan king, who died in 588 A.H. (1192 A.D.) which is the year 1249 of the Vikram era.

another fort in 666 A. H. (1267-68 A.D.), named it *Sar-*
4) *ran.** Sultan Muizzu-d-din Kaikubad, having in the year
686 A. H. (1287 A. D.) founded on the bank of the river
Jumna another city with charming buildings, named it
(5) *Kilugarhi* ; † Amir Khusrau has celebrated ‡ it in his
book, the *Qiranu-s-Saadain.* Sultan Jalalu-d-din
Khilji having founded the city of *Kushk-lal,* § [**18a**]
(6) and Sultan Alau-d-din the city of *Kushk-Sairi,*|| made
(7) them capitals.

Sultan Ghiasu-d-din Tughlaq Shah founded the
(8) Tughlaqabad city of *Tughlaqabad* in 725 A. H. (1325 A. D.) Sultan
(9) Muhammad Fakhru-d-din Jauna, his son, having founded
another city, built a lofty palace with one thousand
pillars ; and other charming houses of red stone were
also constructed. Sultan Firuz Shah having in 755 A.H.
(10) Firuzabad (1354 A. D.) built a large town, *Firuzabad,* cut [a canal
and made] the river Jumna come near. Three *kos* from
Firuzabad is another palace containing a world-gazing
tower, which still stands on a hillock; the people call
it the *Lath* (Pillar) of Firuz Shah. Sultan Mubarak
(11 Shah founded Mubarakabad.

The Emperor Nasiru-d-din Muhammad Humayun
having in 938 A. H. ¶ (1531 A. D.) [re-] built and
decorated Indrapath, made it his capital under the
(12) Dinpanah name of *Dinpanah.* Sher Shah Afghan, having demo-

* So reads the A-text. Elliot has Shahr-Zaghan (the City Kite).

† In the A-text the word may also be read as *Kitlu-garhi.* I have followed Elliot (iii 126.) The *Ain* (ii. 279) has *Kelu-Khari.*

‡ See Elliot iii. 525.

§ 'The Ruby Palace', or 'the Red Palace'.

|| 'The Palace of Satiety'.

¶ A-text gives 938 A. H. Elliot reads 943 A. H. (viii. 11), but gives the correct date 939 A. H. in the description of the building of *Dinpanah* in V 124-126. *Dinpanah* means 'the Shelter of the Faith'.

ished the city of Ala [-u-d-din Khilji] known as *Kushk-Sain*, founded another. His son, Salim Shah in 953 A. H. (1546 A.D.) built the fort of *Salimgarh*, which is still extant, in the midst of the river Jumna, opposite the citadel of Shah-Jahanabad. (13) Sa garh

Although each of these kings founded a separate city and made it his capital, yet Delhi alone became famous in all parts of the country as the capital of the kings of Hindustan. In the year 1048 A. H. (1638 A. D.), corresponding to the 12th year from the glorious accession of the Emperor Shah Jahan, he founded a city near Delhi and named it Shah-Jahanabad. On this town being founded, all the cities of the former kings, which have been described above, lost their names and became famous under the general name of Shah-Jahanabad,—just as other rivers on uniting with the river Ganges get the name of Ganges. Its citadel is built very strongly with red stone and contains charming buildings, many palaces (which are the store-houses of pleasure), all sorts of houses (which are the lurking-places of cheerfulness), many kinds of seats (which are the abodes of repose), several pleasant porticoes, flowing canals, large tanks, spacious reservoirs of water, lofty fountains, gardens of eternal spring, trees loaded with fruits,—which everywhere [18 *b*] remind one of the land of Paradise ; and every part of the town rivals Paradise. Every one of its palaces looks more beautiful than the palace of a Kaiser (emperor); every one of its mansions ravishes the soul like the mansion of Kisra* (14) Sh Jahanab 1638 A. Its beau

[Verses :] Every spot of its soil is like Paradise ;
In every place there is a garden.
Its flower-beds are so pleasant, that one may say

* One of the titles of Naushirwan the Just.

That its lanes are the streets of Paradise.
Its air is heart-attracting and heart-captivating ;
Freshness is like a slave-child of this place.

Around it is a broad ditch full of pure water, so very clear that a grain of sand in it is visible in a dark night, and so very deep that its fishes rival the Fish supporting the universe.

[Verses :] At the bottom of its water,—so great is its purity,—
A blind man can count the fine sands at midnight.
Its depth is so great
That the earth seems to have disappeared from its bottom.

The river Jumna, flowing eastwards, acquires dignity and glory by kissing the feet of this fort, and goes onwards with a hundred kinds of splendour. A royal canal,* which has been cut from the hill of Sirmur, adds to the splendour of the streets and markets of the city and confers bounty on the citizens. Entering grand houses, it keeps tanks and reservoirs full to the brim and gardens fresh ; or issuing from fountains it forms a wonderful spectacle.

The Jumna canal.

[Verse :] On every side of that garden there is a canal,
Rising and falling like a party of drunkards.

A wall of stone aud mortar encloses the city. Its circumference is more than the imagination can comprehend ; and the number of the population within and around it is beyond the range of description. The men of Roum (Turkey), Zanzibar, and Syria, the English, the Dutch, the men of Yemen, Arabia, Iraq, Khorasan, Khwarizm, Turkistan, Kabul, Zabulistan,

Cosmopolitan population of Delhi

* Excavated by Firuz Shah in 1356 A. D. (Elliot, iv. 8.)

Cathay, Khotan, China, Machin,* Kashghar, Qalmaqistan, Tibet, and Kashmir and other provinces of Hindustan, have chosen their abode in this large city, and, having learnt the manners and speech of this place,—which is the place of origin of the Hindustani language,—they engage themselves in their own business and trades. The classes of its population agree together like prose sentences, and the manners of its people are harmonious like the verses of poetry. Its heart-ravishing houses have perfect beauty and charm; its soul-refreshing pleasure-houses possess grace and happiness; [19 a] its streets look like the flower-beds of a garden in ornament and beauty; the squares of every ward of this town are beautiful and heart-ravishing like the squares of a garden; every one of its houses and mansions looks like flower-beds of eternal spring; in every lane and street are canals filled to the brim with water of a sweet taste; the roads of its bazar are bright and heart-attractive like the veins of jewels; its shops are full of happiness and beauty like the two eye-brows of beloved ones. In this bazar,—where all precious and rare things of every country port and city and all wonderful articles can be had,—are bought and sold at one place the rubies of Badakhshan and sparkling pearls and sapphires, lustrous pearls of Oman, bright pearls, corals, and other lustrous jewels of sea and mine; at another place various kinds of cloth, merchandise, weapons, food-stuffs and drink, perfumes, and other articles which men require. At another place, many kinds of dry and fresh fruits of every country excite a sweet sensation and pleasure in the membranes of the stomachs of fastidious lovers of good cheer. Elsewhere elephants

The Bazar in Delhi.

* *Mahachin* or Greater China, a named applied to China. (*Ain* ii. 118 and Elliot. i. 45).

of renown, wind-paced horses, and swift sumpter camels and other animals in thousands and thousands, yield profit to the buyers and sellers. Every day the bustle of the buying and selling of all commodities is great, and the crowd of buyers and sellers is beyond limit or calculation; somuch so, that you may here collect in one day all the royal articles suitable for the requirements of a kingdom; and the necessary outfit of a thousand soldiers can be got together in one hour, without the delay of preparation.

[Verses :] The men of Iraq and Khorasan have placed before them their commodities without limit;

Europeans, having come from Europe, have arranged rare imports in order before them.

On every side sits a jeweller, having caused the oceans to lament [the robbery of their gems.]

On every side have been set a hundred lustrous rubies; in every shop is a mine of Badakhshan.

From a single shop can be offered for our inspection the articles of the seven climes.*

Although in every lane, bazar, square, and street they have erected mosques, temples, monasteries, and colleges, (from which men derive the benefits of this world and the next, and gain material and spiritual advantages),—yet in the centre is the Emperor's Jumma mosque, strongly built with red stone in the year 1060 A. H. (1651 A. D.), corresponding to the 24th year of Shah Jahan's reign. It is so high that the voice of its *muazzin*† reaches the ears of the deni-

Jumma Musjid.

* The Arab geographers regarded the whole world as divided into seven climates. (*Ain* ii. 115 *n.*)

† The crier who summons the people to prayer in a mosque.

zens of the sky. [19*b*] It is so spacious that a world may be put within it. Its pulpit is high like the dignity of the summit of the noble law of Muhammad. Its arches are the places of adoration of men of religion. Its cupolas lift their heads up to the dome of heaven. Its *minars* reach the ramparts of the sky. Its doors are open to all, like the doors of the liberal. Its interior is ready to impart bounty like the interior [*i. e.*, heart] of holy men. Its porticoes and cells are places for the peformance of austere devotions. Its turrets and pulpits are the lecture-rooms of good men. Its quadrangles are free from impurities, like the hearts of the pure-hearted. Its reservoirs of water are full of bounty like the ambition of high-minded men.

[Verses :] From its quadrangle another bounty can be derived ;
In its reservoir one can get the water of *Kausar*.*
On account of its height the sky appears to be one of its steps ;
The Moon and the Sun are under its shadow.
Its portico is the altar of the Children of the Faith ;
It is a counterpart of the mosque of *Aqsa*.†

Among the good buildings is the Imperial Bath. What an excellent bath, well situated and inscribed with pleasure! Its air, like the air of New Year's Day, refreshes the spirit, and like the days of April scatters bounty. Its hot-rooms create warmth like the excitement of pleasure. Its cool rooms give repose to fatigued constitutions. In temperateness it rivals the air of Paradise. Its dome vies with the upper sky. Its warmth, like natural warmth,‡ stimulates health. One grows robust from its coolnes, which is like the

Imperia Bath

* The river of nectar in Paradise.

† The Temple of Jerusalem.

‡ That is, the warmth of the body of a living being.

coolness of the body. The Sun wanders from sign to sign in the sky in longing for its tower. The Moon heartily desires it in order to get rid of her chill. Whosoever enters it, feels the different temperatures of the different seasons. He puts off the vestments of [worldly] ties ; he paces the path of retirement like lonely hermits, he chooses the path of purity and cleanliness like those who are pure in their nature. Many diseases are cured by the bath, such as disorder of the brain, heaviness of the limbs, yawning caused by crop-sickness, and dulness of the system. Many kinds of happiness are gained in it, such as cheerfulness of spirit, freshness of the brain, liveliness of the heart, and purity of the body. The tempering of water and heat is [always] a difficult matter. But in this wonderful place water and fire issue harmoniously blended together. No other place is free from wind and dust ; but this is a rare place, as wind and dust cannot enter here.

[Verses :] In it water and fire work together ;
Air and dust are away from its door.
In it there is a sky named *Hammam* (bath)
[20. *a.*] The Moon and the Sun are called the *gul* and *jam** (rose and cup.)
In this world, from the temperateness of its constitution,
The elements have been [harmoniously] blended together.

Praise of Delhi in prose,

In short, it is a city of perfect spaciousness and extent ; a capital city and the centre of the kingdom. Travellers of the seven climates and tourists of the habitable world cannot point out any other town on the surface of the earth so spacious or so largely populated.

* Our author probably means that the bath may be likened to the concave roof of heaven, and that the rose and the cup play the parts of Sun and Moon in this heaven.

The city of Stamboul (Constantinople,) the capital of the Sultan of Roum, which is famous for its largeness and extent, is not a tenth part of a tenth part of this city. The cities of Kazwin * and Isfahan, the capitals of the Sháh of Persia, which are famous for excellence and beauty, do not come up to even a single quarter of this city. Eloquent and accomplished poets and eloquent masters of condition and speech † have described the beauty of this unparalleled city in heart-ravishing verses, prose pieces, and odes. Among them are the following :— and in verse.

[Verses :] It is a great city, exactly like heaven,
The centre of India, and the capital of kings.
Like the circuit of heaven it enhances pleasure.
Like a garden in spring it exhilarates the spirit.
Its inhabitants are all like favourite sons,
Accomplished, ingenious, and learned.
All of them are victorious in battle and conquerors of the world ;
All of them are of a nature acceptable to the Lord of the world.
All of them have the dignity and rank of *Khans* ;
All possess the elegance and pomp of a king ;
All are sagacious like Abu Ali ; ‡
All of them repeat the name of God like the angelic host.
All are layers of healing ointment on wounded hearts ;
All are free from the troubles of the times.

* Situated a little to the west of Teheran.

† That is, wise men.

‡ Abu Ali Husain bin Abdullah bin Sina, better known as Avicenna, b. 980, d. 1036 A. D.

All are sweet-voiced like David ;
All distinguished in their respective arts and professions.
All with the face of Yusuf and the love of Zuleikha ;*
All with the disposition of Farhad † and the taste of Shirin.
All closely united to the persons of their desires,
All intoxicated with the wine of happiness.

Within and around this large town are the tombs of many of the former kings; but the most famous is the sepulchre of the Emperor Humayun, which is situated in the Kilugarhi of Kiqobad, on the bank of the river Ganges. The tombs of the Nobles, Ministers, Scholars, and accomplished persons—each of whom was in his own days reputed perfect,—situated within orchards and gardens, are too many to be enumerated. There is a separate town formed by the tombs of the departed. There are so many saints' tombs,—the manifestations of blessing,—that their number cannot be expressed in writing.

Tomb of Humayun.

Among them, situated two or three *kos* from the town is the tomb of Khawajah Qutbu-d-din Bakhtiar Káki, ‡ [20. *b*.] the son of Khawajah Kamalu-d-din Ahmad Musi. It is said that his birth-place was Ferghanah. When a child, he felt attracted to God. His Holiness Khizr § happened to pass by him and the mirror of his understanding became polished. In the 18th year of his life in this world of dreams, he got the rank of successor from Khawajah Muinu-d-din

Tomb of Qutbuddin Bakhtiar Kaki

* The wife of Potiphar.

† A celebrated Persian statuary, famous for his love of Shirin (Malcolm's *History of Persia*, I. 129.)

‡ Also known as *Ushi* from his birthplace. Born 585. A. H. For his life see Dorn ii. 2-5 and *Ain*. iii. 363.

§ A prophet. (*Ain*. iii. 375).

Chishti * and set out on his travels. Having reached Baghdad, he gathered grace from many saints in that country. Coming to Multan he met Shaikh Bahau-d-din Zakaria. † In the reign of Shamsu-d-din Altamsh, he came to Delhi, in order to meet Khawajah Muinu-d-din Chishti, his preceptor. That true preceptor, by divine inspiration came from Ajmir to Delhi for the purpose of meeting him. The interview pleased both of these members of the court of God. They lived together for some time. After a few days, Khawajah Muinu-d-din went back to Ajmir, but Qutbu-d-din elected to live at Delhi and thereby conferred much grace upon the men of this world. Afterwards on the morning of the 14th Rabiu-l-Awal, 633 A. H. (1235 A. D.), ‡ he left this fleeting world.

Tomb of Nizamu-din Auliya.

In this quarter is also the tomb of that manifestation of light, Shaikh Nizamu-d-din Auliya, § *alias* Muhammad bin Ahmad Danial. Born in the country of Ghaznin in 632 A. H. (1234 A. D), he, on reaching years of discretion, came by chance to Budaun and there acquired the usual learning. Gaining victories in disputations, he became famous under the name of Nizam the Disperser of Assemblies. In his 20th year, he went to the town of Ajodhan || and became the disciple of Shaikh Faridu-d-din Ganj-i-Shakkar. ¶ Having got in his hand the key to the treasury of Reality, he departed for Delhi, in order to guide the people. Having conferred grace on many seekers [after spiritual knowledge], he gained great eminence. His disciples were famous men, namely, Shaikh Nasiru-d-din

* Born 537 A. H. d. 633 A. H. (*Ain.* iii. 361).

† See *Ain* (iii 362) for his life.

‡ According to Niamutu-llah, 603 A. H. (Dorn, pt. II. 5.)

§ See *Ain.* (iii. 365) for his life.

|| Or Pak Pattan in the Panjab.

¶ See *Ain* (iii 363) for his life.

Mahmud surnamed the Lamp of Delhi and Amir Khusrau in Delhi; Shaikhs Alau-l-Haq and Akhi Siraj in Bengal; Shaikh Ojihu-d-din Yusuf at Chanderi; Shaikhs Yakub and Kamal in Malwa; Maulana Ghias at Dhar; Maulana Maghis in Ujjain; Shaikh Hisamu-d-din in Gujrat; Shaikhs Burhanu-d-din and Muntakhab and Khawajah Hasan in the Deccan; and in [21. *a.*] many other places. And even now all his descendants and vicars are successfully acting as spiritual guides to the people of this country. In short, His Holiness marched away from this perishable world to the eternal world at 9 A. M. on Wednesday, the 18th of Rabiu-s-Sani, in 710 A. H. (1310 A. D.) He gained greater fame for saintship than all other saints of Hindustan. The genealogy of this member of the Court of God goes back to the saint of saints, His Holiness Miran Mahiu-d-din Abdu-l-Kadr Gilani, * who is said to have been one of the Sayids descended from Husain, and in the fifth generation form Shaikh Shibli. † Near Baghdad is a village named Jil which was the residence of His Holiness; hence he is known as *Jilani*, and also as *Gilani.* Born in 471 A. H. (1078 A. D.), he was unrivalled in his age in customary and spiritual learning. He inherited the mantle of saintship of Shaikh Abu Said Mubarak. His greatness of character, amiability of speech, wonderful acts, and impressive miracles arrested the attention of the world. Crowds of people came to him from all sides of the earth with material and spiritual desires, and, by placing the yoke of faith on the shoulders of their souls, gained their desires. In 561 A. H. (1165 A. D.) in his ninetieth year, His Holiness hastened from the perishable to the eternal world. Five hundred and

Mahiuddin Abdul Kadr Gilani.

* See *Ain*, iii. 357.

† The *Ain* has "spiritually connected with Shibli through four intermediaries."

fifty years have passed away from his departure up to the writing of this book, and his auspicious name is still living, and in every part of the world numbers of men still repose their faith in him.

Paniapt tomb of Abu Ali Qalandar

In short, thirty *kos* from Shah-Jahanabad is PANIPAT, an old town. In this town is the revered tomb of Abu Ali Qalandar.* This Shaikh in his fortieth year came to Delhi and gained the happiness of meeting with Khawajah Qutbu-d-din Bakhtiar, and for twenty years acquired secular knowledge, when he attained to a passion for God, and the mirror of his soul became illuminated. Having thrown into the water of the Jumna all books of worldly learning, [21. *b*] he set out on travel. Going to Turkey, he conversed with Shamsu-d-din Tabrizi, Maulana Jalalu-d-din Rumi (who has written spiritual *Masnavis*), and other holy men of that country, and was greatly benefited. After his travels, returning to his own country, he led the life of a recluse at Panipat, and from that place passed on to the eternal world. His many miracles are his memorial. The tomb of this Manifestation of Light is an object of pilgrimage to the people of the world.

Sirhind

SIRHIND is an ancient town, and a dependency of *Samanah*.† Sultán Firuz Sháh, in his own reign, in 760 A. H. (1359 A. D.) separated it from Samánah and made it an independent *parganah* ; and its population and splendour daily increased. Although many favourites of the court of God have their tombs here, yet, among the saints of the present time Shaikh

* Better known as Sharafu-d-din of Panipat. For his life, see *Ain*, iii. 368.

† Samanah is mentioned in the *Ain* (ii. 296) as one of the mahals of the *Sarkar* of Sirhind in the *Subah* of Delhi. It is now in Patiala.

Faridu-d-din Sani and Shaikh Muhammad Masum Kabuli repose in this town. Both of these great saints had the gratification of guiding men in the time of the Emperor Shah Jahan; numbers of people are spiritually benefited by reposing their faith in him.* Even now his descendants are seated in the seat of adoration.

Sadhaura,

At Sadhaura † is the place of sleep of Shah Qames, who enjoyed the honour of saintship in his life-time.

Sunam.

At Sunam ‡ is the tomb of Shaikh Taiwi, an object of pilgrimage to people.

Hansi.

At Hansi, which is an old town, is the tomb of Shaikh Jamalu-d-din, the successor of Shaikh Faridu-d-din Ganj-i-Shakkar. In short, there are so many tombs of eminent saints in this province that they defy calculation. I have selected only these few.

As I have done writing about the holy places connected with the Muhammadan saints, a few of the Hindu shrines situated in this province ought to be described. Twenty *kos* from Sirhind, on the skirt of the hills, is a shrine, Ekhat Bhuayah (Kot Bhima?), associated with Bhima Devi, and from ancient times a place of worship of the Hindus.

Shrine of Bhima Devi

In the fourth year of Alamgir, (1661 A.D.) Fidai Khan Koka, one of the great nobles, made it his residence and named it Bejaur.§ By command of the Emperor, he expelled the Raja of this place from his ancestral home, [22. *a.*] laid out a pleasant garden with five terraces one above another, and built attractive

* The text has the singular number.

† Sadhaurah was a mahal of Sirhind and had a brick fort. (*Ain.* ii. 296.)

‡ *Ain.* ii. 296.

§ Different from Bajwara (42. *b.*), a village in Hoshiarpur District, Panjab, 1½ miles east of Hoshiarpur town. A very ancient place, and, originally the head-quarters of the Naru Rajputs. The fort was built by the Kangra chief Sausar. (*Imperial Gaz.*, i. 439.)

edifices and pleasant mansions. By bringing to this garden the canal which issues from the hill, he caused fountains to flow. They form a wonderful spectacle and a rare sight. The abundance and sweet scent of the 'red flower'—which is an expression signifying the rose—of this place are famous. The writer of this book went in the spring season to walk in this garden of eternal spring. On that single day, forty *maunds* of the rose-flower, according to the Alamgiri measure of weight, were taken to the rose-water factory. And it daily increased.

Rose-wa

Thanesw

Thirty *kos* south of Sirhind is the ancient town of *Thanisar*, and near it is a very large tank named KURU-KHET* (Kuru-kshetra). In Hindu books it is called *the Navel of the Earth*, and it is held that the creation of earthly beings began here. Looking upon it as an honoured place, they consider it an act of great merit to bathe in its tank. Although it is meritorious at all times to bathe in it, yet, on the day of the Solar eclipse large numbers of people, high and low, great and small, male and female, assemble here from all parts of the world and all sides of the country and from remote distances. They give away in charity many kinds of things, both in cash and kind, openly and secretly. Even if a man happens to be a stingy miser or an empty-handed person or a pauper, he on that day and at that place practises liberality beyond his means and capacity. Besides the aforesaid lake, there are many tanks reservoirs and wells in the out-skirts of the city and in many other places. The river *Sarsati* passes by this town. The ancient books mention the names of all places which are associated with the old devotees. [A space] about forty *kos* [in area] is considered holy because the Pandus and Kurus—who reigned over the

Bathing the tank Kuruksh

* See *Ain.* ii. 281 *n.*

people of Hindustan—fought in this place and drank the draught of martyrdom.*

Sambhal

Forty *kos* east† of the capital is the old town of SAMBHAL; within it is *Har Mandir*,‡ an ancient place of worship. It is believed that the last man, the manifestation of divine light, will be born here. [22. *b*.]

Nanak Math

Near it is a place called Nanak Math, where the followers of Baba Nanak assemble and chant his praise.

Kamaun: mines

Northwards lies the mountain of KUMAUN, containing mines of gold, silver, copper, lead, iron, arsenic, and borax. The musk-deer, *qutas*§ cow, hawk, falcon, pony, and wild honey are plentiful here. The landholders of this place, by reason of the inaccessibility of the mountain and the impregnability of their strongholds, do not obey the rulers of Hindustan.

The Jumna: its source

There are two large rivers in this province. The first is the JUMNA. Its source is unknown. After issuing from China and traversing difficult mountainous countries, it reaches the country of Leh, as travellers report.

Leh:

It is said that gold abounds in this country. Many bits of stone have the property of the Philosopher's stone, i.e., on touching them copper, iron, and other metals are turned into gold.

Philosopher's stone

As this stone cannot be distinguished, the people of this country put iron shoes on their goats, sheep, and kine, and send them to graze on the hills. Very often the shoes of these grazing animals become golden by contact with that stone. The vases, kettledrums, and other articles and utensils of the king of this country are of gold.

* The word originally meant death in a religious war, then, death in any sort of battle.

† A-text reads *north*, but has a marginal correction *east*.

‡ The *Ain* reads *Hari Mandal* (ii. 281.) Elliot (viii. 304) mentions 'Nanak-math in the skirt of the hills.' A-text reads 'Nanak-mata.'

§ Jarrett explains it as the *Yak* cow. (*Ain*. ii. 172.)

In short, this river after leaving this place, reaches the territory of SIRMUR. The king of this country proves his obedience and holds himself and his kingdom in safety by sending by the river highway boat-loads of ice as a present to the Emperors of Hindustan and their nobles and ministers. Therefore, all people, high and low alike, call him the Ice-King (*Barfi-Rajah.*) Near the city of Sirmur the river leaves the hill and descends to the plain. The Emperor Shah Jahan ordered a palace to be built at this place on the bank of the swelling torrent. The high grandees and other Imperial officers having each built a house worthy of his condition and rank, a heart-ravishing city has been formed, which is famous under the name of Mukhlispur.* The Emperor often travelled to this pleasant place, [**23**. *a.*] and enjoyed great happiness.

Sirmur,

Shah Jahan's pleasure-house at Mukhlispur

From this place branches off a royal canal, which may be styled one-half of the river Jumna. It runs up to the metropolis Shah-Jahanabad ; it does good to the crops of many *parganahs*, confers freshness on the gardens in the suburbs of the capital, lends happiness to the streets and bazar, and enhances the splendour of the Imperial palaces. The above river, after emerging from the hill and adding splendour to many tracts, reaches the foot of the city of Shah-Jahanabad. On its bank is situated a fortress containing charming houses and the mansions of the nobles. Fifteen leagues from this place, it reaches the feet of the towns of Mathura, Gokul, and Sri Vrindavan. Then it arrives at the capital Akbarabad (Agra.) In this town also there are Imperial and baronial palaces on the bank of the river. Issuing thence, it flows by the fortified town of Etawah, and then the city of Kalpi.

Jumna canal.

* Literally, the 'Beloved or Pure city.'

Next it comes to the city of Akbarpur,* the birth-place of Rajah Birbal of Akbar's time. On its bank stand the lofty spacious and strong houses of that Rajah. The river CHAMBAL unites with the Jumna near Akbarpur, and the rivers Betwah, Dhasan,† and others— which come from the direction of Gondwanah —fall into the Jumna apart from each other. Thence going to the *mahal* of Malkusah‡ it unites with the waters of the Ganges at the foot of the fort of Allahabad.

Union with the Chambal

and the Ganges.

The Ganges: its course.

The second is the GANGES. Nobody knows its source; but the Hindus believe that it descended from heaven, as old and authentic works say. After issuing from heaven and descending on the hill of Kailas, it leaves the latter and reaches the country of China. It is stated in the *Shahnamah* of Firdausi that the residence of Prince Siaus§ the son of Kikaus Shah and son-in-law of Afrasiab, was on the bank of the river Ganges. After leaving China it arrives at *Badri*‖ in the mountains. The region [is called] *Himanchal*,¶ that is 'The Circle of Ice.' Hindus look upon the dissolution of the elementary body at this place as a cause of redemption in the next world, so much so that

Badri,

* A petty village, 79°23 E. 26°31. N. (Atlas, sheet 68,) near which the Jumna and the Chambal unite. There is another Akbarpur, the head-quarters of a *tahsil* in Cawnpur district, midway between Cawnpur and Kalpi, but it is far away from the river. (*I. G.* i. 138.)

† The *Dhassan*, a tributary of the *Betwa* (Atlas, sheet 69 S. W.)

‡ In the *Sarkar* of Kanauj (*Ain.* ii. 185.) Elliot spells it *Malkonsah* (iv. 416.)

§ Saius went over to Afrasiab (King of Turan), married his daughter Feringees, and received as her dowry the countries of Chin and and Khoten, of which he fixed Kung as capital. (Malcolm's *History of Persia*, I. 30.)

‖ Better known as Badrinath, a peak in the Garhwal district, containing a shrine of Vishnu. (*I. G.* i. 410.)

¶ Literally, 'the skirt of snow.' The usual name is Himachal, the mountain of snow.

the Pandus, who were the rulers of the people of this country, [23. *b.*] abandoned their bodily frames at this place. It is situated in this very mountain. In this hilly region the banks of the river are so high that the water can be hardly seen. The crossing is not done in boats. At appointed places they firmly tie thick ropes to trees on the two banks and use this as a sort of bridge. People come and go over it. In the language of that country, it is called *chhakna.** The crowds of men who come to Badri on pilgrimage from all sides of the world, if they once gaze at this spectacle, become alarmed and frightened in crossing the river. Rope bridg

In short, this river having come out of the hill of Badri, reaches the foot of the city of Srinagar,† the residence of the king of that country. Thence it passes by HRISHIKESH, and issues from the hill at Hardwar. Although according to the holy books the river Ganges should be worshipped from its origin to its end, yet HARDWAR is described as the greatest of all holy places [on its banks.] Every year, on the day when the Sun enters the sign of Aries,—which is called *Baisakhi*,‡— people from every side assemble here. Especially in the year when Jupiter enters the sign of Aquarius (otherwise named *Kumbh*)—which happens once every 12 years,—vast numbers of people assemble here from remote distances.§ They consider bathing, giving alms, and shaving the hair and beard at this place, as acts of merit, and the throwing of the bones of the dead into the Ganges [as the means of] salvation of the deceased. Its water is carried to distant places as a valuable

Hrishikes

Hardwar

Kumbh mela

* Hunter calls it *chika* (*I. G.* viii. 65.)

† The chief town of Garhwal District.

‡ Baisakh, a Hindu month, from the middle of April to that of May.

§ *Imperial Gazetteer*, v. 333.

Praise of Ganges water

present. It is a most wonderful fact that if the water is kept in a pot even for a year, it does not acquire a bad smell or change its colour. Undoubtedly its water, which is pleasant to the taste, free from impurity like the hearts of the pious, and full of grace like the souls of God's chosen ones, equals in purity and sweetness the water Kausar * and rivals in delicacy and agreeableness the water of Salsabil.† Its perfect purity makes it suitable to men of all constitutions. Many benefits [24. *a.*] are derived from it; that is to say, it confers health and recovery on the sickly, and the benefits of medicine in the case of long-standing diseases. It causes stoutness and cheerfulness in the healthy. It gives purity to the unclean stomach and brightness to the internal heat; it increases the appetite and stimulates the sexual energy. It makes the amber-coloured face look like the ruby, and the saffron-complexioned face purple. This is the reason why the kings of Hindustan and the great nobles, wherever they may be, drink the water of the Ganges.

Towns on the Ganges

In short, this river after leaving Hardwar and flowing by the BARHA ‡ of the Sayyids, arrives at the foot of the fort of Hastinapur, which in olden times was the capital and had a population covering a space of some leagues in length and breadth. Thence, passing by the forts of Muktesar, Anup-shahar, Karanbas, Soron, and Badaon, § (which are famous places), it reaches Kanauj,

* The river of nectar in Paradise.

† A fountain of pure water in Paradise.

‡ A cluster of twelve villages in Muzaffarnagar District, held by a famous family of Sayyids or descendants of the Prophet. (*Ain*. i. 390).

§ Garh-Muktesar, a *mahal* of the *Sarkar* of Delhi (*Ain* ii. 287). Anupshahar, a town in a *tahsil* of the same name in the N. W. P. (*I. G.* I. 294.) Karanbas, is described in *Imperial Gazetteer* vii. 465. Soron, 78'49 E. 27'53 N., is given in Atlas, (sheet 68).

an ancient town, and increases the splendour of that country. Leaving this place and passing by Sirajpur, Khajwah, Manikpur, Shahzadpur* and other *mahals*, it arrives at the foot of the fort of Allahabad. There the Jumna, coming with some other rivers, becomes united with it.

Thirty *kos* from this [junction], it reaches the city of Benares. Then passing by Chunargarh and some other *mahals*, up to the point where it reaches the foot of the city of Patna, 72 navigable rivers, having come down from the northern and southern mountains, unite with it at different places, at distances from each other; and they from one deep river whose bank cannot be seen. All these rivers get the name of Ganges. Thence passing by Jahangirabad, † Akbarnagar (*alias* Rajmahal,) Maqsudabad (Murshidabad) Mirdadpur, and Khizrahati, it reaches the foot of the town of Jahangir-nagar Dacca. After some leagues, it parts into two branches;—one, flowing east, gets the name of Padmavati ‡ and falls into the ocean near the port of Chatgaon; the other, turning south, branches off into three channels, of which the first is called Sarsati, the second Jumna, and the third Ganga. [24. *b*.] This third, with its thousand branches, joins the ocean near the port of Satgaon.§ The Sarsati and Jumna also fall into the ocean at the same place.

Patna

* All given in Lett's *Popular Atlas*, India, sheet 10.

† Rennell's *Bengal Atlas* gives *Janguira*, 18 miles w. of Bhagalpur (Sheet 2), and *Hazeryhutti*, 31 miles E. of Murshidabad (Sheet 6.) The Khizrahati of the text must be a mistake for Hazrahati (*Ain.* ii. 132.) Jarrett wrongly spells it *Khizrakhani* in the next page of the *Ain*. Mirdadpur not identified.

‡ The main stream of the Ganges in Lower Bengal is called the *Padma*.

§ Sanskrit *Sapta-gram* (seven villages), the ancient name of Hugli (*Ain* ii. 125).

Wickedness of dwellers on the Ganges

Travellers say that from its beginning (the emergence of the river from the hill) to its end (its reaching the ocean,) the inhabitants of its banks are all men of wicked professions, quarrelsome, thieves, highway robbers, shedders of blood, and oppressors of men. As on bathing in this river, sins become detached from the bodies of men, so these sins are certainly by transmigration born again on its banks in the form of men, and become the cause of such wicked deeds.

Agriculture

In short, in this province the climate is almost temperate. Cultivation depends upon rain and irrigation, and in some places on wells. In certain tracts, tillage yields three crops [in the year.] The various fruits of Iran, Turan, and Hindustan and fragrant flowers grow in plenty. The houses are lofty and built of brick or stone.

Extent

Eastwards lies the province of Akbarabad, westwards* that of Lahore, southwards Ajmir, and northwards the hilly region of Kumaun. From Palwal† in the direction of Akbarabad to Ludiana on the bank of the river Sutlej, the length is 160 *kos*‡ ; and from the *Sarkar* of Rewari to the hill of Kumaun, the breadth is 140 *kos*. The *Sarkars* are Shah-Jahanabad, Sirhind, Hisar-Firuza, Shahranpur, Sambhal, Badaon, Rewari and Narnal§—8 Sarkars, comprising 229 *mahals*. The

Revenue.

revenue of the province is 74 kror, 63 lac, and 35 thousand *dam* (Rs. 18,658,375.)

* A text omits the passage from "westwards" to "direction of Akbarabad." B-text supplies the omission.

† *I. Gazetteer*. xi. 21, and *Ain*. ii. 278.

‡ 165 *kos*, according to *Ain*. ii 278.

§ The *Ain* gives *Kumaun* instead of *Narnol*, the latter being a *Sarkar* of the province of Agra (ii. 193.) Now, deducting the revenue of Kumaun and adding that of Narnol, we get 61, 19, 99, 661 *dam* (Rs. 15,299, 991-8) as the revenue of the province of Delhi in Akbar's time. (*Ain*. ii. 285).

II. AGRA.

The Province of Akbarabad, the Seat of the Empire.

AGRA was originally a village, a dependency of the *parganah* of Biana. King Sikandar Lodi (1488-1516) considering it to be a pleasant place, made it the capital during his reign and founded a worthy city.* After that the town became known as BADAL GARH.† Subsequently, the Emperor Akbar, regarding it as the centre of the protected empire, laid the foundations of a stone fort of perfect strength; and a town of unparalleled spaciousness and extent became inhabited under the name of Akbarabad. Travellers [25. *a.*] have seen few such strong forts or large towns. The water of the Jumna flows through the middle of the town for 4 *kos*; and on both sides lofty buildings and charming villas have been built. Men of every race and country live in it; and articles of the seven divisions of the globe are bought and sold here. Various kinds of fruits, especially the melons of Persia and Turkistan, many kinds of flowers, and excellent betel-leaf are also found here. The air is delicious. Although its excellent artisans of every art and workmen of every profession are skilful in their respective trades, yet gold and silver embroidery on turbans and other kinds of cloth is very nicely done. Merchants, coming from [the other parts of] the kingdom and distant places, make purchases and gain profit. In short, this town has every ornament. There are in it the tombs of many great saints and eminent scholars; and the illuminated sepulchres of their Majesties the

Agra

Akbar's capital

Tombs of Akbar and Shah Jahan

* The Agra of the Lodis lay on the left bank of the river, while Akbar's city was on the right bank. (*Ain.* ii. 180 *n.*)

† According to Elliot this name was applied to the citadel of Agra (v. 491) and also to an out-work of Gwalior fort (v. 13).

Emperors Jalalu-d-din Akbar* and Shahabu-d-din Muhammad Shah Jahan† are situated near this town.

Biana

BIANA‡ was formerly a great city and had a strong fort, and captive rebels used to be confined in its fort. Its wood-apples and melons are excellent, and mangoes sometimes grow to one *seer* [in weight.]

Sikri

Akbar's buildings.

SIKRI was a village, a dependency of Biana, and 12 *kos* from Akbarabad. The Emperor Akbar, having at the instance of the greatest of eminent saints—Shaikh Salim,§—built a stone fort, strong houses, mosques, schools, and villas, and named it Fatihpur, made it a capital. Near it is a large tank, two *kos* in length and breadth alike, which confers bounty on the people. There are on its banks a royal platform, high turrets, arenas for elephant-fights, and ground for playing *chaugan*.|| Near it is a quarry of red stone; pillars, slabs, and other building requisites of every size that is desired, are taken out of it.

red stone quarry

Gwalior,

a state prison

GUALIAR is a populous place, with a pleasant climate. Its strength and impregnability are well-known, and prisoners sentenced to punishment are confined within it. The excellence of speech of its inhabitants, the singing of its musicians, the enchanting power of its singers, and the charm of its fair ones are famous. There are iron mines in some places in this district. In this town is the tomb of Shaikh Muhammad Ghaus,¶ who in his time had the rank of a saint.

iron mines

* At Sikandra, 5 miles N. W. of Agra city.

† In the Taj Mahal.

‡ Now a town in the Bhartpur State, Rajputana, 50 m. S. W. of Agra (*I. G.* ii. 418).

§ Shaikh Salim-i-Chishti, who died in 979 A. H.

|| Hockey, according to Blochmann's interpretation. (*Ain.* i. 297.)

¶ Died 970 A. H. (1562 A. D.) He had great influence over Akbar when the Emperor was young (*Al-Badaoni.* ii. 28 and 62.) For his tomb, see Fergusson, 576.

KALPI [25. *b.*] is a town on the bank of the river Jumna, and the burial-place of many saints. The sugar-candy of this place is famous. There is a cave containing mines of copper and turquoise, but the expense [of working them] is greater than the return. Kalpi Mines

MATHURA is an ancient town on the bank of the Jumna. It is the birth-place of Sri Krishna. Hindu books describe its great honour. It has been known as a place of worship from the beginning of its existence. In modern times, the temple of Keshav Rai* was famous, but it was demolished by command of the Emperor Alamgir and a mosque was built [in its place.] Abdu-n-Nabi Khan, the commandant of the forces, by building a flight of beautiful steps on the bank of the river Jumna, has increased the beauty of the city and conferred bounty on the townsfolk ; this place is called Bisrant (Repose.) He has made his name celebrated also by building a high mosque† in the middle of the city. Muttra Hindu temple demolished Ghat

KANAUJ is an ancient town on the bank of the river Ganges. Its climate and fruits are excellent. At Makhanpur‡, a dependency of Kanauj, is the place of sleep of Shaikh Badiu-d-din,§ better known as Shah Madar and Shah-baz, who was one of the eminent saints of India. Many people, both high and low, believe in His Holiness, and once a year groups of men from distances assemble with golden banners and discharge their vows ; and for some days there is a vast crowd of people and a wonderful spectacle. [He Kanauj

* The temple of Keshava Deva was demolished and a mosque erected on its site in 1669 (I. G x. 54.) Elliot calls it the *Dehra Kesu Rai* and its builder Nar Singh Deo Bundela (vii. 184.)

† The Jama Masjid, built in 1662. (*I. G.* x. 84.)

‡ Now in Cawnpur District. (*I. G.* ix. 215).

§ His life is given in *Ain.* (iii. 370.)

flourished] in the reign of Sultan Ibrahim Sharqi (1401-1440 A. D.)*

The Chambal

In this province are two rivers: one, the Jumna, a detailed account of which has been already given; the other, the Chambal, which issuing from Hasilpur (a dependency of Malwa) passes within eight *kos* of Agra, and through the territory of Bhadaur† and the *mahals* of the *Sarkar* of Irij,‡ and falls into the Jumna near Akbarpur, a dependency of Kalpi.

Extent

In short, east of this province lies Ghatampur; north the river Ganges; south Chanderi; west Palwal. Its length from Ghatampur in Allahabad to Palwal (a dependency of the province of Shah-Jahanabad) is 170 *kos*. Its breadth from Kanauj to Chanderi (appertaining to the province of Malwa) is 100 *kos*. Its *Sarkars* are Akbarabad, Bari, Alwar, Tijarah, Irij, Kalpi, Satuan, Kanauj, Kol, [**26.** *a*.] Narwar, Mandlapur (Mandlaer), Gualior, and [two] others, §—14 *Sarkars* comprising

Revenue

268 *mahals*. Its revenue is 98 *kror* and 18 *lac dam* (Rs. 24, 545, 000) and 65 thousand and 8 hundred *abnah*.

* The A-text is corrupt here.

† Not indentified.

‡ Spelt Irich in *Imperial Gazetteer* (vii, 23), now in Jhansi District. It is close to the Betwah and not the Chambal.

§ Under Akbar, this province had 13 *Sarkars*, 262 *mahals*, and a revenue of Rs. 13, 656, 257-9-6. (excluding *Narnol* which our author assigns to the province of Delhi and not to the province of Agra, as the *Ain* does.) Of the remaining twelve *Sarkars* of the *Ain*, *Bayanwan* may be identified with the *Satuan* of our text, and *Sahar* may be one of the two *Sarkars* left unnamed by our author, while the other ten agree with the list given above. (*Ain*. ii. 311.)

III. ALLAHABAD.

The Broad and Spacious Province of Allahabad.

In Hindu books it is named Prayag and also Tribeni. The Emperor Akbar, having built between the rivers Ganges and Jumna a strong stone fort and excellent mansions, founded a city and named it Illahabas. But the Emperor Shah Jahan, in his own reign, gave it the name of Allahabad.* The rivers Ganges and Jumna mingle together at the foot of the fort. Moreover, a stream issuing from the fort falls into the above mentioned river; it is called Sarsati. For this reason, the place is called *Tribeni* (three braids of hair), that is, "the union of three rivers." But the Hindu books do not speak of the Sarsati issuing from this place. Within the fort there is a very old tree, called the *Akhay Bar*, † that is, the imperishable [Banian tree.] It is narrated in Hindu books that this tree has been always there and will remain undestroyed till the end of the world. By command of the Emperor Jahangir, it was cut down and a cauldron of iron firmly placed over [the stump.] But by the will of God, the tree again raised its head from under this iron and grew high.

Allahabad

Union of three rivers

Sacred Banian tree

In short, the Hindus regard this place as a very ancient and most holy place of worship, indeed, as the king of holy places. In winter, when the Sun enters the Sign of Capricorn (which they call *Makar*), crowds of people assemble together from all sides of the world and, staying here for one month, daily engage in ceremonial ablutions; and every one gives alms to the poor and indigent, as far as he can. They also pay a

Bathing in the month of *Magh*

* *Ain.* ii. 161. *note.*

† Described in the *Imperial Gazetteer*, i. 196.

Pilgrim tax

certain sum per head to the Imperial government. As they consider it meritorious to dissolve the combination of elements (the human body) here, many men in former times used to place themselves in the road* in the hope of final redemption and the obtaining of their desires in the next world. This practice was forbidden in the time of Shah Jahan.

Benares

Thirty *kos* from it is BENARES, which is written as Banarasi (Baranasi) in Hindu books. As it is situated between the rivers Barna and Asi, it is celebrated under that name. It is also written as Kashi. It is an old town, with the habitations forming a bow, while the river Ganges flows by it like the bow-string. On account of its association with Mahadeo,† [26. *b.*] it has been regarded as a place of worship from ancient times. It is a treasury of learning, an assembly-hall of learned men, and the school of those that desire the lore of the Hindus. Brahmans who have acquired learning and perfection and readers of the Vedas who are masters of their condition and speech, have their residence here. And Brahmans and sons of Brahmans, from countries far and near, assemble in this city, live here for acquiring and perfecting knowledge, and derive benefit and grace. Many ascetics and pious men, having by God's grace renounced worldly ties, take up their abode here and remain engaged in praising the Lord of Slaves (God), with a view to making the body free [from passion], which is described in ancient books as the means of salvation in the next world. Aged men and disappointed devotees come here with the desire of dying and surrendering their lives to the Creator of life.

a seat of Hindu earning

* A-text reads "*Khwesh tan ra dar rah miawardand*, 'put themselves in the way,' but the meaning is not clear.

† Worshipped under the name of *Vishweshwar*, Lord of the Universe.

There is a place near it on the bank of the Ganges. Every time that Jupiter enters the Sign of Leo, a hillock becomes visible in the middle of the river and remains so far a month; and many people worship God. This spectacle is one of the miracles manifested by the power of God. A miracle

CHUNARAH is a stone fort situated on a hill,* which is unparalleled in height and strength. The river Ganges flows at its feet. In its neighbourhood, a tribe,† naked from head to foot, lives in the forest by archery and hunting. Chunar

KALINJAR is a stone fort on a sky-reaching hill. Nobody can tell its origin. In this fort there are full-flowing streams, many tanks, and the temple of *Kal Bhairon*‡, about which last marvellous legends are current. Near it is a forest with ebony trees and wild fruit plants. Many wild elephants are trapped in this forest. Near it is a mine of iron; and in many places bits of diamond are found, and the people of the place get a share. Kalinjar Temple Mines

JAUNPUR is a large town. Sultan Firuz Shah founded it in his own reign and named it after Sultan Muhammad Fakhru-d-din Jauna,§ the son of his pater- Jaunpur

* "On a sand-stone rock jutting into the Ganges . . . . . and 80 to 175 feet above the level of the surrounding country. (*I. G.* ii. 346.)

† Probably the Gonds; but the I. G. mentions the Kols and not the Gonds as living in Mirzapur District, in which Chunar is situated.

‡ *Kal Bhairav*, meaning Shiva the Destroyer. "Above the temple is a tank cut out of the solid rock . . . Beyond this is a rock-cut figure of gigantic proportions, representing *Kal Bhairan*, with snakes for a head-dress, in which is set the moon . . . . The figure must be 30 feet high" (*I. G.* iii. 336) See also *Ain*. ii. 159.

§ Jauna and Firuz were the sons of two brothers, Ghiasu-d-din Tughlaq and Malik Rajab, respectively. (Al Badaoni, i. 302.) For the foundation of the city, see Elliot, iii. 307.

nal uncle. As it was situated in the midst of a rebellious district, he ordered the commandant of the fort to keep himself always ready for fighting the rebels and to practise bloodshed and cruelty.

Crops

In short, the whole of this province has an agreeable climate and produces many kinds of flowers and fruits, [27. *a.*] especially melons and grapes, in plenty. Agriculture is excellent. *Moth* (vetch) is scarce, *Jawari* (millet) and *Bajra* (spiked millet) are not met with.

Industries

Jhonah and *mihrkul** and other kinds of cloth are well woven here. The chief rivers are the Ganges and the Jumna. The Gumti, Sarju, Barna, and other rivers are [the smaller ones.]

Extent

Its length from Sinjhauli in Jaunpur to the southern mountain† is 160 *kos*; its breadth from the ferry of Chausa on the Ganges to Ghatampur is 120 *kos.* East of it lies the province of Bihar; west, the province of Akbarabad; north the province of Oudh; south, Bandhugarh (Banda.) Its *Sarkars* are Allahabad, Benares, Jaunpur, Chunarah,

Revenue

Kalinjar, Khura,‡ Manikpur, and [nine] others,—16 *Sarkars*,§ comprising 247 *mahals*. The revenue of this province is 37 *kror*, 60 *lac*, and 61 thousand *dam* (Rs. 9,401,525.)

* Two kinds of cotton cloth mentioned in *Ain* i. 95.

† The Kaimur range (*Ain.* ii. 157 *n.*)

‡ *Korarah* (*Corah*) in Fatehpur District. (*Ain.* ii. 167.)

§ The *Ain* mentions ten *Sarkars*, viz., the above seven and three others—Ghazipur, Bhath-khora, and Karra, (for the last see *Imp. Gaz.* viii. 48.) Under Akbar the province had 10 *Sarkars*, 177 *mahals*, and a revenue of Rs. 5,310,695—7—9. (*Ain.* ii. 160).

IV. OUDH

The Choice Province of Oudh.

OUDH is a large and ancient town. In Hindu books it is called Ajodhya, the birth-place of king Ramchand. His building a bridge over the ocean, his going to Lanka (Ceylon) with a countless host of monkeys and bears, his slaying Ravan (the king of that country), and his recovery of his wife (who was preserved chaste and pure during her captivity under Ravan,) are well-known. The history, *Ramayan*, is an account of his strange and wonderful deeds. As this city was the birth-place of king Ramchand, it is held to be one of the holiest places. One *kos* from it, the river Ghaghar (Gogra) having united with the river Saraju,* passes by the foot of the fort [of Ajodhya.] In the outskirts of the city, they sift dust and get gold. In the town are the tombs of Shish (Seth), the son of Lord Adam (the peace of God be on him!) and Ayub (Job), the prophet,—both places of pilgrimage to Muhammadans. Oudh Muhammadan shrines

At *Ratanpur* is extant the tomb of KABIR,† who at Benares in the time of Sultan Sikandar Lodi, carvad out a path from the material city to the spiritual capital through excess of devotion to the Lord of Slaves, (*i. e.*, died.) Many mysteries of spiritual knowledge and subtle secrets of theological truth, expressed in Hindi verses, remain as his memorial among many people, high and low alike. Kabir's tomb

---

* The *Ain* has by mistake given "*the Sai.*" (ii. 171)

† Kabir lived between 1380 and 1420 A. D. Hunter says that his tomb is situated at *Maghar*, a village in Gorakhpur District, 26.42 N. 83.11 E. (*I. G.* ix. 139.)

Bahraich

Tombs

BAHRAICH is a large [27. *b.*] and old town on the bank of the river Saraju. Its suburbs are charming. Here are the tombs of Salar Masaud *, a relative of Sultan Mahmud of Ghazni) and Rajab Salar,† (the brother of Sultan Ghiasu-d-din Tughlaq Shah and the father of Sultan Firuz Shah—both rulers of Hindustan). Groups of men from distant places come on pilgrimage with golden banners, hold assemblages here, and make many presents.

Mint

Near the city is the village of *Dokon*,‡ which has for a long time been a mint for copper-coinage.

Merchandise

From the northern mountains are brought many articles loaded on the backs of men, goats, and hill-ponies. Gold, copper, lead, musk, *qutas*, honey, the acid *chuk* (which is prepared by boiling together orange-juice and lemon), zedoary (which is called *Kachur* in Hindi), pomegranate, dry ginger, long pepper, amber,§ salt, asafœtida, glass ornaments, utensils, wax, woollens, hawk, tercel, the royal white falcon, the sparrow-hawk, and other articles of the mountains come to this place to be sold ; || and at times there is a great and ceaseless crowd ; merchants from all sides come here, make purchases, and gain profit.

* *Salar* used for *Sipah-salar* or General. Masaud was the son of Mahmud's sister ; he fell in a battle with the Hindus at Bahraich in 1033 A. D. and thus received the rank of a holy warrior. (*Ghazi*) *Ain.* ii. 172 *n.* For his life, see Elliot ii. 515 *et seq.*

† He died in 1316 A. D. (Elliot, iii. 273.)

‡ Not found in Atlas.

§ A-text reads *o audik-i-Hindi*, evidently a corruption.

|| The *Ain*, (ii. 172) speaks of "White and coloured cloths, amber, salt, asafœtida, ornaments, glass and earthen ware" having been carried back by the hillmen in exchange.

Nimkhar sacred tank

NIMKHAR* is a large and famous fort. The river Gumti flows by its feet. Near it is a tank sacred to Brahma.† Within it the water boils and there is such an eddy that one cannot sink in it. Whatever is thrown into it, is cast out. It is regarded as a great shrine. [There were many sacred] books of the Hindus, which, owing to the changes of the revolving heavens, the vicissitudes of time, and revolutions, turned their faces towards non-existence. Learned devotees, by reason of their illumination of mind and excess of spiritual information, bring these books into manifestation anew on the bank of this tank and thus confer favour on the men of the world.

Sacred tank

In the neighbourhood there is a tank, the source of a good stream, one yard broad and four fingers deep, that mixes with the river Godi (Gumti). Brahmans versed in the Vedas read charms and perform worship here. By the power of the All-Powerful, [**28.** *a.*] the figure of Mahadeva suddenly becomes manifest on the sand, and men wonder at it; it quickly disappears. If anybody throws rice and other things into it, no trace of them remains.

Near it is a place named *Charmati*;‡ at the *Holi* festival, torches of fire blaze of themselves and increase the wonder [of spectators].

Luc now

LUCKNOW is a large town on the bank of the river Gumti. Shaikh Mina,§ whom people regard as a

* A town in Sitapur District, 20 miles from Sitapur, and 'a place of great sanctity, with numerous tanks and temples' (*I. G.* x. 336).

† Named *Brahmáwart-kund* in the *Ain.*

‡ Spelt *Charámiti* in the *Ain* (ii. 173). I could not find any such place near Nimkhar in Atlas, sheet 68.

§ The *Imperial Gazetteer* (viii. 505) quotes the *Ain.*

saint, reposes here. *Surajkund* is a holy place ; people resort to it from distances.

Bilgram

The town of BILGRAM has a pleasant climate. Many people of this place are intelligent and skilled in music. There is a well here, the water of which, when drunk for 40 days running, increases knowledge and beauty of appearance.

Rice

In short, all over this province, the climate is pleasant, flowers and fruits are plentiful, and cultivation is excellent ; especially the varieties of rice named *Sukhdas*, *Badrahkir*, and *Jhanuah* * are unparalleled in whiteness, freshness, fragrance, and deliciousness. The *Shali* rice is here sown three months earlier than in other parts of Hindustan. At the commencement of the dry season, the rivers are in flood, and the water covers the land. As the water rises, the stem of the *Shali* also grows longer. If the flood takes place before the grain has been formed, the *Shali* yields no harvest. Wild buffaloes are plentiful. When the plains and deserts become covered with water, the wild beasts come to the human habitations and men have the pleasure of hunting many kinds [of game].

Rivers

The principal rivers are the Saraju, the Ghaghar, the Sai, the Gumti, and the Rudi (Rapti ?).

Extent

The length of the province from the *Sarkar* of Gorakhpur to Kanauj is 130 *kos*,† and its breadth from the northern mountains to Sadhur ‡ (a dependency of Allahabad) is 115 *kos*. East of it lies the province of

* The *Ain* (ii. 171) gives 'Sukhdas, Madkhar, Jhanwah.' But in 'the statistics of the prices of certain articles' (i. 62), the Sukhdas and Jinjiu only are mentioned.

† 135 *kos*, according to *Ain*.

‡ The *Ain* (ii. 170) names it *Sidhpur*. Jarrett has failed to trace it. But Elliot (ii. 534) mentions a *Saddahur*, the same as *Siddhaur*, a town in Bara Banki District in Oudh. (*I. G.* xii. 473.)

Bihar ; west, Kanauj ; north, the mountains [of Hima laya] ; south, Manikpur. The *Sarkars* are Oudh, Gorakhpur, Bahraich, Khairabad, Lakhnau,—five *Sarkars*, comprising 197 *mahals*. The revenue of the province is 26 *kror*, 45 *lac*, and 40 thousand *dam** (Rs. 6,613,500). Revenue

V. BIHAR.

The Province of Eternal Spring,† Bihar or Patna.

PATNA, the capital of this province, is a large town on the bank of the river Ganges. Most of the houses are covered with tiles, which are called *Khaprael* in the language of this country. Patna.

Thirty *kos* south of this city stands the shrine of GAYA, on the skirt of the hills. Hindus, [28. *b*.] having come from distances, make offerings to the souls of departed ancestors. Especially during the 40 days when the Sun remains in the Sign of Sagittarius, many men resort to this place and please the souls of their ancestors by reading spells an making offerings of grains and water (*pinda*). And they regard this as a deed of piety and merit on their own part and the cause of the redemption of the dead. Near it is the quarry‡ of a stone resembling marble. Ornaments are made of it. Good paper is also manufactured here. Gaya.

* In Akbar's time it had the same five *Sarkars*, but 133 *mahals*, and a revenue of Rs. 5,043,954-4 as. (*Ain*. ii. 173).

† This epithet is used for the sake of a pun, the Persian word for Spring being *bahar*.

‡ The *Ain*, (ii. 152) says, 'In the Sarkar of Behar, near the village of Rajgar.'

Monghyr.

In the district of MONGHYR a stone-wall has been built from the river Ganges to the hill. This is regarded as the boundary of Bengal. In this district, on the skirt of the hill, there is a place named the *Jharkhand** of *Baijnath* (Baidyanath), sacred to Mahadeva. Here a miraculous manifestation puzzles those who behold only the outside of things. That is to say, in this temple there is a *peepul* tree, of which nobody knows the origin. If any one of the attendants of the temple is in need of the money necessary for his expenses, he abstains from food and drink,† sits under the tree, and offers prayers to Mahadeva for the fulfilment of his desire. After two or three days, the tree puts forth a leaf, covered with lines in the Hindi character, written by an invisible pen, and containing an order on a certain inhabitant of any of the parts of the world for the payment of a certain sum to the person who had prayed for it. Although his residence may be 500 leagues [from Baidyanath], the names of that man and of his children, wife, father, and grandfather, his quarter, country, home, and other correct details about him are known from the writing on the leaf. The high-priest, writing agreeably to it on a separate piece of paper, gives [it to that attendant of the temple]. This is called the *hundi* (cheque) *of Baijnath*. The suppliant, having taken this cheque, goes to the place named on it, according to the directions contained in it. The man upon whom the cheque has been drawn, pays the money without attempting evasion or guile. A Brahman once brought a *hundi* of Baijnath to the very writer of this book, and he, knowing it to be a bringer of good fortune, paid the money and satisfied the Brahman.

Baidyanath. miracle.

---

* The *Ain*, (i. 340) identifies *Jharkhand* with Chota Nagpur. There is a class of Brahmans named Jharkhandi.

† That is, he sits *dharma*,—a practice of extortionate Brahmans, which has been made an offence by the Indian Penal Code.

More wonderful than this is a cave at this holy place. [29. *a.*] The high-priest enters into the cave once a year, on the day of the *Shiva-brata*,* and, having brought some earth out of it, gives a little to each of the ministers of the temple. Through the power of the Truly Powerful, this earth becomes turned into gold, in proportion to the degree of merit of each man.. *Another miracle*

TIRHUT has long been a seat of learning and a centre of Hindu culture. Its climate is excellent. The curd of this place remains unchanged and pleasant to the taste for one month. If any milkman adulterates his milk with water, some calamity from the invisible world visits him. Its buffaloes are so strong that the tiger cannot hunt them. In the rainy reason, owing to the excess of water, the deer, the elk, and the tiger come down together to inhabited places, and men have the pleasure of hunting. *Tirhut*

In the district of CHAMPARAN, they sow the seed of the vetch *mâsh* without ploughing the soil, and it grows without the labour of cultivation. The long pepper grows abundantly in its jungles. *Champaran*

ROHTAS is a fort on the summit of a lofty hill difficult of access. Its circumference is 14 *kos*. Cultivation takes place here; and there are many gushing fountains. Water is everywhere obtained on digging 4 yards. In the rainy season, more than 200 lakes of water are formed and the water-falls delight the eye and the ear. *Rohtas*

In short, in this province the summer is very hot. The winter is very temperate ; in less than two months [warm quilted] cotton tunics cease to be necessary. The rainy season lasts for six months. The land continues green and moist all the year round, owing to *Climate*

* *Shiva-ratri*, the Night of Shiva, a Hindu holy day.

Agriculture

the abundance of rivers. The wind does not blow violently; dust-storms do not rise. Agriculture is excellent; especially the *Shali* rice is unparalleled for goodness and excellence. Poor men consume a grain named *Khesari*, which resembles *matar* (peas) and causes sickness. Sugar-cane grows plentifully and well. Betel-leaf, especially the *maghi* variety, is very delicate, beautiful in colour, flawless,* fragrant, and sweet to the

Fruits

taste. Fruits are plentiful; the jack-fruit in particular grows so large that a man can carry one with difficulty. The *muchkand*† is a flower like the *dhatura* flower and very fragrant; it is not found elsewhere. Milk is very good and cheap. Horses and camels are less procur-

Cattle

able. Elephants are good and numerous. The castrated Barbary goats [of this province] are good and so fat that they can hardly walk [29. *b.*]; people carry them on *charpoys* (litters). Its parrots and game-cocks are famous. Many kinds of game enhance pleasure.

Manufacture

Various kinds of cloth are woven and articles of gilt glass manufactured here.

Rivers : Sone

There are many rivers here, but the largest of them is the Ganges. The *Son* comes from the south. Its source and those of the *Johila*‡ and the Narbada bubble

* The *Ain*, (ii. 151) reads 'thin in texture.' But A-text reads *be-parm*, 'without cracks,' which has been adopted above.

† Sanskrit *muchakunda*. I have, however, seen this flower blooming in North Bengal. Its petals are thicker and more widely separated at the fringe than those of the *dhatura*; but in other respects the resemblance is striking.

‡ The *Ain*, (ii. 150) has, "The head-springs of these rivers, the *Son*, the *Narbada*, and the *Johila* bubble up from a single reed-bed in the neighbourhood of Garha." In the A-text *Johila* is spelt as *Chala*. The *Johila* is a tributary on the left bank of the *Son* in the upper portion of its course (*I. G.*, xiii. 52.) Garha is a town in Jubbalpur Dist., and the ancient capital of the Gond dynasty of Garha Mandla. (*I. G.* v. 12.)

up from one bush of reeds (bamboos) near Garha. The Narbada flows towards the Deccan. The Son and the Johila, having come in this direction, unite with the Ganges. The *Saraju*, having come from the mountains of the north, falls into the Ganges near Maner.* The *Gandak*, too, comes from the northern mountains and mingles with the Ganges at Hajipur; whosoever drinks its water gets the goitre, which gradually becomes as big as the cocoanut, and is called *joghod*†—especially in the case of children. For forty *kos* [along the course] of this river‡ the *salgram* is found. It is a black stone, considered to be one of the manifestations of the Deity. It is of many kinds, each of which goes by a different name and is worshipped. Saraju Gandak

The *Karamnasa*, having come from the southern mountains, falls into the Ganges at the ford of Chausa. Its water is considered bad; at the time of crossing this river, people take care that no drop of its water may touch their body. The *Punpun*, coming from the southern hills, joins the Ganges near Patna. It is said that up to the city of Patna 72 navigable rivers, flowing from the north and the south, fall into the Ganges. The smaller streams are countless. Karamnasa Punpun

The length of this province from Garhi§ to Rohtas is 120 *kos*; its breadth from Tirhut to the northern mountains is 110 *kos*. Eastwards lies Bengal, westwards Allahabad and Oudh, in the north and south Extent

* The *Ain* has "The *Son*...joins the Ganges near Maner." Our text is wrong, because the Sarju (Gogra) falls into the Ganges near Chapra and not 'near Maner.' (*I. G.* v. 139.)

† In Bihar it is called *ghogha*.

‡ The *Ain* says this of the *Son*, but Jarrett's note mentions the Gandak.

§ *Teliagarhi*, a pass in the Sonthal Parganahs, between the Rajmahal hills and the Ganges. (*I. G.* xiii. 236.)

lofty hills. Its *Sarkars* are Hajipur, Mungir, Champaran, Saran, Tirhut, Rohtas, and others,—eight divisions comprising 240 *mahals*. The revenue of the province is 38 *kror*, 7 *lac*, and 30 thousand *dam** (Rs. 9,518,250.) Revenue

VI. BENGAL.

The excellent Province of Bengal.

The seat of government of this province is *Dhaka* (Dacca) or Jahangir-nagar, which is very spacious. It is beautifully and elegantly inhabited for some *kos*. The commodities and products of the seven climes [30. *a*.] are found here. Men of every race and country live in it. The original name of this country was *Bang*. As the kings of former days constructed embankments 20 yards broad and 10 yards high throughout the province in order to keep out the excessive [flood of] water, and named them *al*†, by the combination [of these two terms] it came to be called *Bangala* in the current speech of the world. The summer here is almost temperate and the winter mild, short, and moderate. It begins to rain at the commencement of the Sun's journey through the Taurus, and the rainy season lasts 6 months; the water covers the land, but the embankments stand above it. Dacca; Derivation of *Bengal*; Climate

The principal cultivation is rice; and there are so many varieties of it that if one grain of each were Agriculture

* The *Ain*. (ii. 153) gives seven *Sarkars* (viz., Behar in addition to the above-mentioned six), 200 *mahals*, and a revenue of Rs. 5, 547,985·1-3. The eighth *Sarkar* was *Patna*.

† From Sanskrit *ali*, a ridge of earth. (*Ain*. ii. 120 *n*.) The word is now applied in Bengal to the low ridges, (about a cubit in breadth and a foot in height,) which divide fields.

taken they would fill a big pitcher. In the same plot of land they sow and reap rice thrice [in the year] and very little is lost. As the water rises, [the stalk] grows taller and the ears of corn do not get under the water; so much so that men who know have seen ears of corn with [stems] 60 cubits in length. The customs of *zabti** and *ghalla-bakhshi* do not prevail here. The rent due is collected in this way: the cultivator for eight months in the year pays rent pie by pie (by instalments), and he is habitually submissive [to the landlord.] The staple food is rice and fish; wheat, barley, and other grains are not to the taste of the people. Nay more, they have not even the custom of eating bread. Having cooked brinjals, herbs, and lemon together, they keep it in cold water and eat it the next day. It is very delicious when mixed with salt. They carry it to distant places and sell it at a high price.

Rent system

Staple food

Flowers and fruits are numerous. The betel-nut† grown here is so good that the mouth is dyed red on chewing it. Diamonds, emeralds, jaspers, and rubies come in plenty from the ports.

Houses are built of reeds (bamboos); and some are so well made that a single one costs five thousand Rupees; and they last a long time. Some mattresses are so finely woven that they look nicer than silk. They also make mattresses which are called *sital-pati*.‡ In this country they travel in boats, especially in the

Bamboo houses

mattresses

* *Zabti* has been interpreted by Jarrett as (1) the subjection of rent-free lands to assessment, (in Bengal) and (2) charging crops at special rates of revenue, (in Bihar) *Ain.* (ii. 153 *n.*) *Ghalla-bakhshi* means the division of grain between the government and the husbandman. *Ain.* (ii. 122, and 338 *n.*)

† Noakhali is famous for it.

‡ Lit. 'the cold mattress.'

conveyances rainy season. In summer people travel in the *sukasan*,* which is such that one can comfortably sit, stretch himself at full length, or sleep within it while travelling. Over it they spread a covering for keeping out heat or rain.† Riding on elephants is pleasant. The people seldom ride horses. In this country the direction of affairs is entrusted to women.‡ Men and women go

Eunuchs naked. Eunuchs come largely from this country and they are of three kinds: the first is called *Sandali* and also *Atlasi*,§ * * the second is called *Badami*, * * and the third is named *Kafuri*, * * In every animal except man haughtiness abates when it is castrated; but in man it increases, so much so that the ill-temper and harshness of speech of eunuchs have become proverbial.

Gaur LAKHNAUTI (Gaur) is an old town, which was the first capital of this province. When the Emperor Humayun graciously came here he renamed it *Jinnatabad*, as its air was pleasant; It has a strong fort. East of it lies a large lake;|| if its embankment were to break, the city would be covered with water.

Sylhet The province of SYLHET is situated within the mountains. Its shields are famous. The fruit called *sang-tarah*,¶ resembling the orange in colour but

* The *Ain*, (ii. 122) names it *Sukhasan*, 'comfortable seat.' In A-text, the word may also be read as *Singasan*, 'throne.' It is a palanquin with a crescent-shaped roof.

† The two texts are corrupt. The A-text reads, *Bar faraz an jehat tabish o barish guzin sair tanahi bar sar bad*. The last five words may also be translated as 'travelling on camels alone is unsuitable.' The B-text reads after *guzin*, '*bazibai bar sazand*,' that is, 'they make [sukhasans] beautifully.' In the translation adopted here I have partly followed the *Ain* (ii. 122).

‡ The B-text has 'business is chiefly transacted by speech.'

§ A few words have been omitted here in the translation.

|| Named in *Ain*, (ii. 123,) *Chhatiapatia*.

¶ Jarrett identifies it with the *citrus decumana*, which is called *Batavi lebu* in Bengal. (*Ain* ii. 124 *n*).

larger and very sweet, the China root,* and aloes wood grow in plenty. At the end of the rains they cut this tree and fell it to the ground. After some time, having guessed its greenness or maturity, they convey it † [to the market.] In this province they make many eunuchs.

In the *Sarkar* of *Ghoraghat* ‡ silk and jute cloth, the *kunt* horse (hill ponies), and geldings are plentiful, and Indian fruits abundant. The *Sarkar of Bagla* § on the sea-coast is well known. There is a forest in the environs of its fort. From the first of every lunar month to the 14th day, the river is filled with waves and they swell like mountains and present a wonderful spectacle. From the 15th day to the end of the month, the waves decrease little [by little.] Ghoraghat Hughli

Near it|| is KAMRUP, also called *Kaonru*. The beauty of the women of this place is very great ; their magic, enchantment, and use of spells and jugglery are greater than one can imagine. Strange stories are told about them, such as the following. By the force of magic they build houses, of which the pillars and ceiling are made of men. These men remain alive, but have not the power of breathing and moving. By the power of magic they also turn men into quadrupeds and birds, so that these men get tails and ears like those Kamrup Female sorcery

* The *Smilax glabra* (*Ibid.*)

† The *Ain* has, 'They give them [the trees] various names according to their greenness or maturity' (ii. 125.)

‡ In Rennell's *Bengal Atlas*, Sheet 6, Ghoraghat is placed 27 m. N. N. W. of Bogra. This *Sarkar* included the Rungpur, Dinajpur, and (part of) Bogra Districts.

§ Hughli, including the Sundarbans.

|| In the *Ain*, which our author copies closely in this part, Kamrup comes just after Kuch Bihar. The phrase 'near it' must not, therefore, be taken literally here.

of beasts. They conquer the heart of whomsoever they like and bring him under their command. They can foretell the movement or repose [of the planets] of heavens, the dearth or cheapness of grains, the length or shortness of the life of any one. [31. *a*] Cutting open the womb of a woman of full pregnancy, they take out the child and read its future.* In this territory there is a wonderful tree; whenever it is pierced a sweet liquid drops from it, and makes the thirsty satiated with water. There is another tree which yields as fruit both the mango and the grape.† In this province there is a flowering plant‡ which will not wither for more than two months after being uprooted, nor lose its colour and smell. They make necklaces of it.

Wonderful trees.

Near this province lies ASSAM, which is very spacious. When any of its rulers dies, his favourites, both male and female, bury themselves alive with him. If any one dies leaving no heir behind him, they bury all his property with him.

Assam

The country of MAHACHIN § is situated near it. From the city of *Khan Baligh*, its capital, to the ocean, for the distance of 40 stages, a canal has been cut, the two sides of which have been embanked with stone

China

* The *Ain* has "They......divine somewhat as to the future" (ii. 127.)

† This sentence is based on our author's misconception of the *Ain*, which says, 'They have also a mango tree that has no trunk; it trails like a climbing vine over a tree, and produces fruit.' (ii. 117).

‡ Probably the *Tulsi*, the trunk of which is cut into beads, which are strung together and worn by the Vaishnavs.

§ Lit., the Greater China. *Khan Baligh* was corrupted into *Cambalo*, which Chaucer mistook for the name of a person: "The other was yclept Camballo" (*Squieres Tale.*)

and lime. King Alexander of Roum * advanced from this country to that. Having traversed the whole of that country, he came [back] by way of the river. By order of King Alexander, eminently wise philosophers have placed on the sea-shore a talismanic human hand, which, whenever a ship comes in that direction, forbids it by a gesture, [as if to say] ' Don't come this way!' †

In the south-east there is a large country named Arracan; the port of Chatgaon lies within it. Elephants abound; white elephants are also found. Horses, camels, and donkeys ‡ are high-priced. Cows and buffaloes are not found at all. There is an animal, piebald and parti-coloured which shares the characteristics of both buffalo and cow. Its milk is drunk. The religion of its inhabitants is different from Hinduism and Islam alike. They marry their own sisters, even twin-born sisters, and abstain only from marrying their own mothers. They call their men of religion and piety *Wali* § and never act contrary to their good counsels. [31 *b*.] It is their custom to station the females of warriors at the court, the men themselves not having to make their obeisance.|| Most of the people are black-complexioned and beardless.

Arracan

Cattle

Strange religion

Near it is a country named *Chin*.¶ One side of this

Pegu

* Alexander of Macedon advanced *from* Tartary *to* India, and not as stated above.

† This traveller's tale finds no mention in the sober pages of Abul Fazl.

‡ The A-text reads *asp o shutar o khar giran*. This goes against the reading proposed by Jarrett (*Ain* ii. 119), 'horses are scarce and of small size.'

§ The A-text reads *Ra-wali*, by wrongly repeating a previous suffix *ra*.

|| I have followed the *Ain* here. In the A-text, the passage may also be translated as 'It is their custom to have female warriors present at the Court, and the men have to bow [to them.]'

¶ The *Ain* gives its alternative name *Pegu* (*i.e.*, Lower Burma.)

country is dry* and contains mines of ruby, diamond, gold, silver, naptha, and sulphur. The inhabitants of this land fight with the tribe of *Magh* (Burmese) for the sake of the mines.

Rivers

In short, this country (Bengal) is extremely spacious. The largest of its rivers is the Ganges in praise of which volumes have been written. The second river is the Brahmaputra ; it issues from the mountains of Kuch [Bihar], then waters the *Sarkar* of Bazuha,† and afterwards enters into the ocean. The length of this province from the port of Chatgaon to Garhi is 400 *kos* ; its breadth from the north to the limits of the *Sarkar* of Madaran is 200 *kos*. East of it lies the ocean, west the province of Bihar, north and south high hills. Its *Sarkars* are Tandah, Fathabad, Jinnatabad, Bagla, Tajpur, Pinjarah, Barbakabad, Bazuha, Sonargaon, Sylhet, Chatgaon, Sharifabad, Sulaimanabad, Ghoraghat, Madaran, and others,—27 *Sarkars*, comprising 1109 *mahals*. Its revenue is 46 *kror* and 29 *lac* dams‡ (Rs. 11,572,500,) with 4,200 guns and 4,400 boats.

Extent

Revenue

* Jarrett reads *Arakan* in the place of *dry*.

† Mymensing-Bogra, (*Ain* i. 520 *n.*)

‡ The *Ain* (ii. 129) gives 24 *sarkars*, 787 *mahals*, and a revenue of Rs. 14,961, 482-15-7, with 4260 guns and 4400 boats, for Bengal and Orissa taken together. The *Sarkars*, in addition to the 15 named above, are Mahmudabad, Khalifatabad, Purniyah, Satgaon, Jalesar, Bhadrak, Katak, Kalang Dandpat, and Raj Mahandrah,—of which the last five belong to Orissa. In the A-text *Pinjarah* may also be read as *Hijrah*.

VII. ORISSA.

The Happy Province of Orissa.

It has 29* *pucca* forts. Its climate is good. The rainy season lasts eight months, winter three months, and summer one month. Fruits and flowers are plentiful, especially the *Nastrin*† (which is very delicate and fragrant) and the *Keorah*. Betel-leaves of many varieties are grown. Paddy is the grain chiefly cultivated. The people eat rice, fish, brinjals, and herbs. They cook in the night, lay the food aside, and eat it the next day. They write books on palm-leaves with an iron pen, which is held in the clenched fist; paper and ink are rarely used. [32. *a.*] Eunuchs are also made in this country, and good cloth is manufactured. Bargaining takes place through the medium of the *kauri*, which is a small white shell of the ocean. Four of these make one *ganda*.‡

Manners of the people

In the southern direction, on the shore of the ocean, within the city of Purushottampur (Puri), stands the temple of *Jagannath*, which was built by King Indradyumna. Its foundation is dated more than four thousand years ago. Near it is a temple § dedicated to the Sun. The revenue of this kingdom for 12 years was spent in constructing it. Its walls are 150 cubits high and 19 cubits thick. It has three doors. Intelligent and fastidious connoisseurs are filled with wonder on seeing it.

Temples at Jagannath and Kanarak

* The *Ain* gives 129 forts. (ii. 126)

† Hindi name, *seoti*.

‡ A *ganda* is one-twentieth of an anna.

§ At Kanarak.

Tehngana

Near it is a country—Taria Raj*—in which the men encrust their bodies with sandal [rubbings] and wear ornaments like women, while the women do not cover their body excepting the private parts. Their coverings are mostly made of the leaves of trees. A woman keeps a husband for a week only. * * [Two lines of the text omitted in the translation.]

Extent

The length of this province is 120 *kos*, and its breadth 100 *kos*. Its *Sarkars* are Jalesar, Bhadrak, Katak, Kalinga, Rajmahendri, and others,—in all

Revenue

15 *Sarkars* comprising 233 mahals; and its revenue is 40 *kror*, 41 *lac*, and 5 thousand *dam*† (Rs. 10,102,625.)

VIII. AURANGABAD.

The Province of Aurangabad,‡ of Auspicious Foundation.

It is stated in some histories that in former times

Deogiri

this town was celebrated under the name of Dharanagari.§ Then it became famous as Deogir. When Sultan Muhammad Fakhru-d-din Jauna, king of Delhi, brought the whole kingdom of Deccan under his rule, he gave

Daulatabad

the name of *Daulatabad* || to the fort of Deogir, and

* This may be a mistake for *Raj-mandria* (Raj Mahendri.)

† The *Ain* assigns to Orissa five Sarkars (the same as here), 99 Mahals, and a revenue of Rs. 3,143,315-15-2, which are included in the area and revenue of Bengal.

‡ It was surnamed *Khujista-baniad.* (Elliot, vii. 256.)

§ The A-text reads *Dharanagari.* Elliot (vii. 41) calls it *Deogir* or *Dharagar.* It must not be confounded with *Dhar*, the capital of Raja Bhoj, which is situated in Malwa. (*Ain.* ii. 197.)

|| Daulatabad is 10 miles north-west of Aurangabad. It was made a capital by Muhammad Tughlaq in 1338 A.D. Aurangabad was the capital of a Mughal province comprising much of the territory of the old kingdom of Ahmadnagar.

made it his capital. After Sultan Muhammad, the whole of this country passed out of the possession of the kings of Delhi. Three hundred years afterwards, in the reign of the Emperor Shah Jahan, the fort of Daulatabad was re-captured (1632 A. D.) The Emperor Aurangzib Alamgir, [32. *b*] when a prince, on being appointed Governor of the Deccan, founded the city of AURANGABAD near the above-mentioned fort at a place which was called the village of KHIRKI* It is undoubtedly a city of great extent and a town of great spaciousness. Its air is always mild like the air of Paradise and delights the spirit and the heart like the spring of April. Its wind, like the wind of spring, is pleasant and cheering. Its air, like intoxicating wine, is stimulating and comforting. Every crop of this place, refreshes the world like the rose. Every morning of it is a means of embellishment to spring. Its winter has the breeze of New Year's Day. Its summer puts forth the splendour of spring. For four months, from the commencement of [the Sun's journey in] the Gemini to [his course in] the Virgo, the clouds shower down rain. Every kind of fruit grows in perfect sweetness. But some fruits are of such species as do not grow in other countries. Various kinds of fresh flowers grow in gardens and woods, too many to be counted. The grains are so good and so plentiful that they always maintain a low price. Many kinds of precious stuffs, and lustrous jewels of high price, can be procured in this city. Its inhabitants, who live happily and well, as lords of fortune and riches and masters of wealth and pomp, its beautiful women, versed in the

Aurangabad

Climate

* The *Imperial Gazetteer* (i. 387) says that the town was founded by Malik Ambar in 1610, and first named *Kirki*. Aurangzib built a palace and the mausoleum of his wife, and made it the capital of a *subah*.

arts of blandishment, and ravishing the heart with their moon-like foreheads, - all these cannot be adequately described in writing.

Extent

Revenue

The length of the province is 150 *kos*, and its breadth 100 *kos*. It has eight *sarkars*, comprising 80 *mahals*. Its revenue is 51 *kror*, 62 *lac*, and 80 thousand *dam** (Rs, 12, 907,000.)

IX. BERAR.

The Province of Berar.

Village officers

This country lies between two mountains in the south. Its climate and agriculture are good. In this country the *Chaudhuri* is called *Deshmukh*, the *Qanongo* is called *Deshpande*, the *Mukaddam* is called *Patel*, and the *Patwari* is called *Kalkarni*.† Wild elephants abound.

owns

Ramgarh‡ is a stone fort on a hillock. Its three sides are enclosed by two streams.§ *Kerla*‖ is a stone-fort on a plain. In the middle of [33. *a.*] it is a hillock, which they worship. Four *kos* from it is a well, which turns into stone the bone of any animal that falls into

---

* The *Ain* does not describe this province as it became included in the Mughal Empire after Akbar's time.

† *Mukaddam*, chief village revenue officer ; *Patwari*, land steward ; *Chaudhuri*, headman of a caste or village ; *Qanongo*, that officer in each district who is acquainted with its customs and land-tenure. (*Ain*, ii. 45-47.) The A-text reads *Kar-karni*.

‡ The A-text reads *Margarh*. *Ramgarh* is a town in Mandla Dist., C. P., situated on a hillock above the Burhner river. (*I. G.* xi. 447.)

§ The A-text has *do rud* ; but the *Ain* (ii. 230) gives *forests*.

‖ The Gond kingdom of Kherla had its centre at Betul, C. P. (*I. G.* ii. 329.)

it. Near *Melgarh* * there is a spring of water which petrifies wood and other things that are thrown into it. [Petrifying well and spring ;] At *Biragarh* † there is a diamond mine ; figured cloths are well woven here. At *Indore* and *Narnal* ‡ there are mines of steel and other metals. [mines.] Charming utensils of stone are carved here. A wonderful cock is found here, with bone and blood of a black colour. Lonar is a very holy place which is (also) called *Vishnu Gaya*. [another Gaya.] It has a very deep tank, one *kos* square and fed by a spring ; a high mountain surrounds it. It contains brackish water ; and the materials for making glass, soap, and saltpetre come out of it and yield a large revenue. Monkeys are numerous in this country.

There are many rivers in this province, the greatest being *Gang Gautami*, also called GODAVARI. [Godavari] The Ganges of Hindustan is sacred to Mahadeva, but this river is sacred to Gautam, who was a famous saint (*Rishi.*) They relate wonderful legends about [it] and do it great worship. It flows from the mountain of *Sahiya* near Trimbak,§ and passing through the country of Ahmadnagar reaches Berar, [then] flows into Telingana, and falls into the sea on that side. When the planet Jupiter enters the sing of Leo, people come here from distances and form a large gathering, which is famous in all parts of the kingdom. Among the other rivers are the *Tali*‖ and the *Tapti*, both of which are [Other rivers.]

---

* *Imp. Gaz.* mentions *Melghat*, a *taluk* in Ellichpur Dist. (ix. 403.)

† This is *Wairagarh*, a village in Chanda Dist., 20.25 N. 80.7 E. "Diamond and ruby mines were formerly worked" (*I. G.* xiii. 513.)

‡ *Narnala*, a hill-fort in Akola Dist., Berar. (*I. G.* x. 213.)

§ In Nasik Dist. (*Ain*, ii. 228 *n.*)

‖ Can it be the *Bel*, which rises, like the Tapti and the Wardha, in the plateau of Multai? The *Imp. Gaz* (ii. 329) mentions another river, the *Tawa*, with a somewhat similar name.

worshipped. Another river, the *Purna*, issues near Dewalgaon,* and one source of it issues 12 *kos* higher up than the source of the Tali.† Another river is the *Munia*,‡ which rises near Deogaon (Dewalgaon.)

Extent

In short, the length of this province from Batiala§ to Biragarh is 200 *kos*; its breadth from Bidar to Hindia is 180 *kos*. Eastwards lies Biragarh, westwards Mahkarabad,|| northwards Hindia, southwards Telingana. Ten *sarkars* comprising 200 *mahals* [belong to it.] Its revenue is 60 *kror*, 72 *lac*, and 70 thousand *dam* ¶ (Rs. 15, 181, 750.)

Revenue.

* The A-text reads *Nulgaon*. *Dewalgaon* is the name of two villages in Buldana, one being 22 m. E. of Ajunta, the other 76. 20 E. 20.5 N. (Letts' Atlas, sheet 3.) The Dewalgaon mentioned in *I. G.* (iv. 235) cannot be the place intended here.

† The A-text reads, *o ek sar-i-an do az dah karoh balatar az chashma-i-Tali bar aid.* But the *Ain* has, "and again the Warda issues forth ten *kos* higher up than the source of the Tali" (ii. 228.)

‡ Evidently the *Murna*, a tributary of the *Purna*. (*I. G.* xi. 320.) The *Ain* reads 'Napta ?'

§ Batiala or Pitalwari was a *Sarkar* which included Chandor (*Ain.*) The *I. G.* (iii. 365) gives *Chandur*, a town in Amaraoti Dist.

|| There is a *Mokheir*, 20.1 N. 74.24 E. in Letts' Atlas, sheet 3. The Mokher of *I. G.* ix. 477 could not have been meant here.

¶ Under Akbar, it had 16 *Sarkars*, 142 *parganahs*, and a revenue of Rs. 14,000,000. (*Ain*, ii. 231.)

X. KHANDESH.

The Province of Khandesh.

BURHANPUR, the capital of this province, is a large city, situated on the bank * of the river Tapti. Many skilful men live in it. In its outskirts are several charming gardens; many sandal trees and aloes and many kinds of fruits and flowers grow here. But in summer dust-storms rise. In the rainy season roses and tulips grow in plenty. The chief cultivation [**33.** *b.*] is *jawari.* In a few places rice and paddy grow excellently, and also abundance of betel-leaf. The cloths *sirisaf, alfia,* and *bhiraun*† are well woven here. *Changdeo*‡ is a village near which the rivers Tapti and Purna unite; it is regarded as a very sacred place and called *chakra-tirtha.*§ Burhanpur. Crops. Cloth manufacture.

In short, there are many streams in this province. The greatest is the *Tali,* which rises between Berar and Gondwana. The *Purna* also rises in the same place. The rivers *Girni* and *Tapti* unite together near *Choprah* || This place being regarded as great in sanctity, people from distant places come to worship here. Rivers.

---

* The *Ain* incorrectly says 'three *kos* distant from the Tapti.' (ii. 223.)

† *Sirisaf* and *bhiraun* are named in the *Ain* (i. 94.) The *alfia* of the text may be a mistake for the *alchah* of the *Ain.*

‡ 21. 2 N. 76 E. (Letts' Atlas, Sheet 6).

§ Curious derivations have been proposed for this word by Gladwin and Jarrett (*Ain*, ii. 224 *n.*) I suggest the following as a more probable one: The word is Sanskrit and means a place hallowed by the descent upon it of any portion of the body of Sati cut off by Vishnu with his *chakra* or discus.

|| The A-text wrongly reads *Junirah.*

Origin of its name

This country acquired its name of *Khan*-desh* from Gharib *Khan*, its king. During the Khalifate of the Emperor Akbar, when the fort of Asir was won by the valiant sword of Shaikh Abu-l-Fazl and this province was presented to Prince Danial, the second son of His Majesty, it was named *Dan*-desh by royal command. The land-owners of this province are all Kolis,† Bhils, and Gonds.

Extent

Its length from Borgaon‡ near Hindia to Laling near the province of Ahmadabad is 75 *kos*; its breadth from Jamod near Berar to Pal (adjoining Malwa) 50 *kos*, East of it lies Berar, west and north Malwa, south Jalna. It has five *sarkars*, comprising 112 *mahals*. Its

Revenue.

revenue is 44 *kror*, 36 *lac* and 19 thousand *dam*§ (Rs. 11,090,475.)

* *Khan-desh*, a hybrid word meaning 'the country of the *Khan* or lord.' Gharib Khan's name is given as Ghizni Khan, with the title of Nasir Shah in *Ain*, ii. 226. Ferishta calls him Nusseer Khan (iv. 286,) and says that he received the title of *Khan* from the King of Gujrat and was the first of his line to assume the ensigns of royalty. (d. 1437 A.D.) There was a Ghizni Khan of Malwa, a contemporary of Nasir. (Ferishta, iv. 194.) The *Ain* has evidently confounded the two names together.

† For the Kolis, see *Ain* (ii. 245 *n*) and Elliot (v. 439.)

‡ *Boregaom*, 12 m. N. of Asirgarh and 65 m. S. W. S. of Hindia. (Letts', Sheet 6.) *Laling*, an ancient fort and the "frontier fortress of the Furrukhi kings," 6 m. from Dhulia, in Khandesh Dist. (*I. G.* iv. 281.) *Jamod* is in Akola Dist. (vii. 132.) There is a *Pali*, 28 m. S. E. E. of Hoshangabad. (Letts, Sheet 6.)

§ Under Akbar it had 32 *mahals* and a revenue of Rs. 11, 382, 355-12-9 (*Ain.* ii. 224.)

XI. MALWA.

Malwa, the Province of Pleasant Climate.

UJJAIN is a large and old town. It was the capital of Rajah Vikramajit, whose era is current even now in Hindustan. It is said to have been very large in that age. The river *Shuparma* (Sipra) flows by its feet. It is regarded as a very sacred place. What a miracle that at times waves of milk flow here and men, filling pots with it, take it away and use it! By the power of God, this miracle has been often manifested. Ujjain.

CHANDERI is one of the large and ancient towns, and has a stone fort, 384 bazars, 360 spacious *serais* and 12,000 mosques. Various classes of men live in it. *Numan* * is a village on the bank of the river Tawa. A perennial spring of water is found here. There is also a large temple in which, if a kettle-drum is beaten, no sound comes out and nobody [outside] can hear it. Chanderi.

MANDU is a large city, 12 *kos* [in circumference.] In the centre of its fort there is an octagonal tower. Formerly [**34**. *a.*] for some period (1387—1526 A. D.) it was the capital. It contains lofty buildings, monuments of the dead, and the tombs of the Khilji kings. It is a miracle that in summer water trickles down from the cupola of the tomb of Sultan Mahmud,† son of Sultan Hushang, and people lay bets on it.‡ It is said Mandu tomb of Sultan Hushang.

* Not identified. The *Ain* has "*Tumun* is a village on the river *Betba*, in which mermen are seen" (ii. 196.) The A-text reads *bar sahal-i-daria-i-Tawa zindah chashma abedar o namodar gardad.*

† A double mistake for 'Sultan Hushang, the father of Sultan Muhammad.' For his tomb, see Ferishta, iv. 190.

‡ The A-text reads *o mardum bad o kardand*; the last word may be a mistake for *garo kunand* (lay bets.) Can it mean rain-gambling?

that in this province there is a stone which turns into gold whatever metal touches it. In the Hindi language it is called *paras.** DHAR is a town which was formerly the capital of King Bhoj and other kings of great state.

Dhar

Climate

In short, in this province the climate is temperate. It is seldom found necessary to wear [padded] cotton tunics in winter, or to cool water with saltpetre in summer. The rains last four months. It inclines a little to cold and at night counterpanes have to be used. The soil of this province is a little high-lying in comparison with other lands, and the whole of it is arable.

Crops.

Both crops [of the year] grow excellently, wheat poppy, sugar-cane, mango, melon, and grape grow well. In some places, especially in Hasilpur, the vine bears fruit twice in the year. Betel-leaf grows wonderfully well. In many forests elephants are numerous. High and low alike give their children opium to eat up to the age of three years. No person, whether a peasant, *bunnia*, artisan, skilled mechanic, or any other, is without a weapon of war.

armed population.

Rivers.

The chief rivers of this province are the *Narbada*, the *Sarakani*, the *Sind*, the *Betam*, the *Godi*, and the *Shuparma.*† At every two *kos* there is a very clear and light stream, on the banks of which the willow grows wild as well as many-coloured and sweet-scented flowers, [esp.] the hyacinth. In the forests, trees and greenswards are numerous.

* Sanskrit *sparsha*, touch.

† The *Ain* (ii. 195) has "the *Narbadah*, the *Sipra*, the *Kali Sind* the *Betwa*, and the *Kodi*." Jarrett identifies the *Kodi* with the *Loni*. *Betam*, is Betwa ; *Shuparma* is Sipra (?) *Godi* is a tributary of the Narbadah. There are three Sind rivers in Malwa, viz., the Sind, the Kali Sind, and the Chota Sind. In the A-text *sarakani o sind* may be a mistake for *Sipra o Kali Sind*, which is the reading of the *Ain*.

The length of this province from the extreme limit of Garha * to Banswara is 240 *kos*; its breadth from Chanderi to Nandurbar is 230 *kos*. In the east lies Bandhu (Banda), in the west Gujrat and Ajmir, in the north Narwar,† in the south Baglana. The *Sarkars* are Ujjain, Raisin, Chanderi, Sarangpur, Bijagarh, Mandhu, Gagron, Kobhri,‡ Hindia, and others,—12 *Sarkars* comprising 309 *mahals*. Its revenue is 36 *kror*, 90 *lac*, and 70 thousand *dam*§ (Rs. 9,225,425.) Extent

XII. AJMIR.

The Province of Ajmir, the abode of goodness.

AJMIR is an ancient town. Near it is the fort of *Bitli*,|| the memorial of Raja Bithal, on [34. *b*] a hillock which is difficult of access. Near the city is a lake, named *Anasagar*,¶ three *kos* in circumference and very deep. Many aquatic animals, crocodiles, &c., live in it. There are royal mansions on its banks. Ajmir Lake

The tomb of the Illuminated Khawajah Muainu-d-din Chishti is situated within the city, on the skirt of the hills, and by the side of the lake *Jhalra*.** This Khawajah, the son of Ghiasu-d-din Chishti, one of the Chishti Sayyids, was born in 537 A. H. (1142 A. D.), at the village of Sijz, in the district of Sijistan. In his 15th year, his eminent father passed on to the other world. Ibrahim Qahandazi, (who was one of the Muainu-d-din Chishti : his life.

* Garha Mandla. † *Narwar*, a town in Gwalior State.

‡ A mistake for Kotri Parayah (*Ain*. ii. 197.)

§ The other three *Sarkars* are Kanauj, Mandesar and Nadarbar. In Akbar's time it had 12 *Sarkars*, subdivided into 301 *parganas* with a revenue of Rs. 6, 017, 376. (*Ain*, ii. 197)

|| *Imp Gaz.*, i. 119. ¶ *Rajasthan*, i. 802.

** A natural spring at Ajmir. (*I. G.* i. 133.)

attendants of the Court of God), cast his eyes upon him. He felt attracted to God, and began to look out for a spiritual guide. At Harun, a dependency of Naishapur, he joined the company of Khawajah Usman Chishti, and practised austerities. In his 20th year, he gathered blessings from Shaikh Abdu-l-Kadir Gilani, *i. e.*, His Holiness Miran Mahiu-d-din. In 588 A. H. (1192 A. D.), when Sultan Shahabu-d-din Ghori conquered Hindustan, he came to Delhi and afterwards went to Ajmir for the purpose of retirement. His precious breath benefited crowds of people. He journeyed to the land of bliss on Saturday, the 6th Rajab, 630 A. H. (1233 A. D.)* His holy tomb is an object of pilgrimage to men.

Pushkar lake

Three *kos* from Ajmir is a very large lake named PUSHKAR.† Nobody can form a guess as to its depth. It is an old place of worship. In the books of the Hindus it is regarded as the guide [chief] of holy places; it is held that if a man bathes in and walks round all other holy places on the face of the earth, but does not come to bathe in this lake, he gains no merit.

Chitor

CHITOR is a famous fort and [the name of] one of the *Sarkars* of this province. There is an iron-mine at *Gangarh*,‡ a dependency of it. Mines of copper exist at *Chinpur*, a place in Mandal. This fort was formerly in the possession of [35. *a.*] the Rana. The Emperor Akbar personally attended to its conquest, and after great fighting and struggle triumphed,—the story of which is famous. In former times, the chiefs of this place were called *Rawals*; but now for a long time

* The *Ain*, (iii. 362) gives 633 A. H. (1236 A. D.)

† *Rajasthan*, i. 792.

‡ Atlas (Sheet 35 N. E.) gives a *Gangrar*, a few miles N. of Chitor, 25. 3N. 74. 40E. *Chenpuria*, 25. 12 N. 74. 29E. (Atlas, Sheet 34 S. W.) The Atlas gives "copper and lead mines," 6 m. south of it. *Mandal*, a town 70 m. N. E. of Udaipur. (*I. G.* ix. 287.)

they have been called *Ranas*. They speak of themselves as belonging to the clan of Gehlote, one of the descendants of Naushirwan the Just. As their ancestor dwelt in the village of *Sisoda*, they have become famous as *Sisodia*. As a Brahman* treated them [kindly in their misfortune,] they are also called *Brahman*. It is customary for the Rana to be marked [on the forehead] with a *tilak* of human blood at the time of his accession to the seat of royalty.† The Ranas.

In SAMBHAR, excellent salt is manufactured. Near the city there is a large lake four *kos* in length and one *kos* in breadth. Its water is extremely briny. Within the lake there are many tracts of land like paddy-fields. After loosening the soil with the spade, they fill it to the brim with the water of this lake. In 15 or 16 days, during which the land absorbs the water, all these tracts of land become full of salt. Having dug it with the spade and thrown it up on the banks, they sprinkle water; the earth becomes separated from it, and pure salt comes out. It becomes blue, red, or white; ‡ several *lacs* of Rupees' worth are annually sold. The Imperial Government levies a tax on it. Sambhar salt lake.

In this province are many deserts; and water comes from a distance [below the surface.] Agriculture depends upon rain. *Jawari*, *bajrah*, and *mot'h* are abundant. One-seventh or one-eighth of the crop is paid to the Treasury. The custom of payment [of rent] in money is rare. The spring harvest is scanty. Winter is almost temperate and summer very hot in many places. The southern mountains and [some other] Crops.

* The Rishi *Harila*, according to Tod, (i. 235.) The *Ain* (ii. 269) reads *Haranj*, with a variant *Marij* (Maricha.)

† For the origin of this custom see *Rajasthan*, i. 233.

‡ "Nearly the whole of the salt extracted is white or slightly discoloured. Some portions are blue and red." (*I. G.* xii. 188.)

places are inaccessible. The inhabitants are Kachwaha,* Rahtor, and other Rajputs. The great haughtiness of this people is due to the desert, which has no water for leagues and leagues. This want of water prevents the Imperial forces from at all reaching the habitations of these people.

Deserts.

The length of this province [35. b.] from Amber† to Bikanir and Jesalmir is 168 *kos*; its breadth from the limits of the district of Ajmir to Banswara is 150 *kos*. In the east lies the metropolitan province of Akbarabad ; in the west Dipalpur in Multan ; in the north the villages belonging to Shah-Jahanabad ; in the south Gujrat Ahmadabad. The *Sarkars* are Ajmir, Chitor, Rantambhar, Jodhpur, Nagor, Sirohi, and Bikanir,—seven *Sarkars*, comprising 123 *mahals*. The revenue of the province is 55 *kror*, 53 *lac*, and 60 thousand *dam* ‡ (Rs. 13, 884, 000.)

Extent

Revenue.

XIII. GUJRAT.

The Pleasant Province of Gujrat Ahmadabad.

Former capitals.

From the histories of the country of Gujrat, esp., the *History of Bahadur Shah* § (a ruler of this country), we learn that in former times its capital was *Pattan* ||, and for some time *Champanir*. When Sultan Akmad, the son of Sultan Muhmmad, the son of Sultan Muzaffar Shah, adorned the throne as king, he in the year 812 A. H. ¶ (1409 A. D.) built on the bank of the river Sabarmatti a strong fort, new houses,

---

* *Rajasthan*, i. 93. † 5 m. N. E. of Jaipur.

‡ Under Akbar it had 7 *Sarkars*, 197 *mahals*, and a revenue of Rs. 7, 210, 038-14-9. (*Ain*, ii. 271.)

§ *Tarikh-i-Bahadur Shahi*, by Sam Sultan Bahadur Gujarati.

|| Pattan, the Hindu capital, 746-1194 A. D. (*I. G.* xi. 82.) Champanir, the Muhammadan capital, 1494-1560 A. D. (ii. 333.)

¶ A mistake for 815 A. H. (Ferishta, iv. 14.)

and a spacious town, which he named *Ahmadabad* and made his capital. It grew up into a large town, as he reigned for 32 years and 6 months, and in the period of his kingship caused it to be well peopled. Outside it 360 places of a special kind (each of which is called a *Porah*)* became inhabited and the essentials of towns are found in every one of them. It contains a thousand mosques, monasteries, and *minars* with wonderful inscriptions. In the *Porah* of *Rasulabad* is the tomb of Shah Alam Bokhari, † who enjoyed the dignity of saintship. Many men were the disciples and believers of His Holiness. Ahmadabad, 1409. Porah

In short, in this town the roofs of houses are mostly tiled, and the walls are of brick and lime; and some have been built prudently on broad stone foundations. [In them] the walls are hollow and there are secret paths for going in, so that in time of need men can seek their safety by escaping by means of these paths. Some wealthy men having built vaults, [36.*a*.] cover the buildings with lime and mortar in such a way that the pure and clear rain-water enters into the cave, which has been made like a tank ‡. It is called tankah (?) in the language of this country. They drink this water all the year round. Painters, inlayers, and other skilful workmen arrange oyster shells in such a way as to form beautiful lines. § Pen-holders, small boxes, and other things are made [in this way]. Cloth of gold tissue, *chirah* (coloured turban), *fotah* (loin-band), *jamahwar* (flowered woollen stuff), velvet, brocade, silk-cloth, and *khara* (undulated silk-cloth), Houses hollow walls Reservoirs of rain-water. Manufactures: Cloth

* A quarter of a town, having its own gateway. (*Ain*, ii. 240 and *I. G.* i. 95.)

† Born 1415 died 1475 A. D., (*Ain*, ii. 372.)

‡ *I. G.* i. 97.

§ The *Ain* (ii. 240) has, "Painters, seal-engravers, and other handicraftsmen are countless. They inlay mother-o'-pearl with great skill and make beautiful boxes and inkstands."

are well-woven here. They imitate various fabrics of Turkey, Europe, and Persia; the *dothi* * especially, is excellently woven, and it is carried to distant lands by way of present. Swords, *jamdhars*, *khapwah*,† and bows are well-made. Lustrous jewels are bought and sold. The silver and gold of Turkey and Iraq are imported. In pleasantness of climate and availableness of good articles, it is unparalleled.

Weapons

Three *kos* from Ahmadabad is the pleasant village of *Batwa*,‡ the place of sleep of many saints, particularly of Qutb-i-Alam, the father of Shah Alam Bokhari. A covering, about one cubit [square] is spread over it. Some people imagine it to be wood, some stone, § some iron; and they relate wonderful stories [about it.]

Batwa

Pattan is an old town; in former times it was the capital of the kings of this country. It has two strong forts, one of stone and the other of brick. In this country excellent cows are found. *Champanir*, a good fort on a rock half a *kos* high, has several gates. At one place they have dug about 60 yards and covered the top with planks, which are removed in time of danger. *Surat*, the famous port, was the capital for some time. There are some other ports ‖ in this [district.] The river Tapti flows by it, and after 7 *kos* falls into the sea. Various fruits, esp., pineapples, are abundant; many kinds of flowers are plentiful, and sweet scents of every kind are found in excellence.

Pattan

Champanir

Surat

* In the A-text this word may be read as *watani*, "belonging to the country." Can it mean the country-made paper for the manufacture of which Ahmadabad has long been famous? (*I. G.* i. 95.)

† Two kinds of dagger. (*Ain.* i. 110.) *Jamdhar* is Sanskrit *Yamadhara*, death-edge.

‡ Hunter's spelling (*I. G* i. 98.) Bayley has '*Batoh*, a suburb of Ahmadabad' (*Gujarat*, 237.)

§ The stone is described by Jarrett. (*Ain*, ii. 240 *n.*)

‖ The *Ain* (ii. 243) mentions *Rander*, *Khandewi*, and *Balsar*.

The sect of Zoroastrians (*Parsis*), having come from Fars and taken up their abode here,keep up among themselves the practice of fire-worship. The Parsis

Between Surat and Nandurbar is an inhabited hilly region called *Baglana*. The country is cultivated and has a good climate. Many kinds of fruit, esp. peach, apple, grape, pineapple, [36.*b*.] pomegranate, lemon, and mango, grow well. It has seven famous forts, of which *Saler* and *Mulher** are [the most] celebrated. The chiefs are of the clan of Rathor. Baglana

Bharonch (Broach) has an excellent fort, and the river Narbada, after washing its feet, falls into the sea. It is a famous port. Some other ports† belong to this district. Many kinds of cloth are woven here ; the *alchah*‡ of this place is especially famous, and merchants carry it to all sides of the world. Broach Cloth manufacture.

The *Sarkar* of *Sorath* (Kathiawar) was formerly a separate State The kings of this land had 50,000 cavalry and one *lac* of infantry, and they did not live on friendly terms with the kings of Ahmadabad. The Khan-khanan of Akbar brought this country under real subjugation. It has a length of 125 *kos* from the port of Ghogha to the port of Aramra,§ and a breadth of 72 *kos* from Sardhar to the port of Diu. Its climate is agreeable, and its fruits and flowers excessive. Grapes and melons also grow here. The country is in scattered tracts, and every tract has an independent ruler. Owing to the abundance of forests and the puzzling intricacy of the hills, they are of a rebellious Kathiawar Its extent

* In the *Nosari* district of the Gaekwar's dominions.

† The *Ain* (ii. 243) names Kawi, Ghandhar, Bhabhut, and Bhankora.

‡ Mentioned in *Ain*, i. 94.

§ *Aramraw* (Letts' Atlas, Sheet 5) is 19 m. N. of Dwarka, with the Beyt Island lying east of it. Sardhar is given as *Surdhaur*, in the very centre of the peninsula, 13 m. S. S. E. of Rajkote. Jarrett has failed to identify it, though it is given both in Bayley's map and in Letts' Atlas.

Junagarh

disposition. *Junagarh* is a stone fort, very strong and firm. Sultan Mahmud, * King of Gujrat, took it by force after a long struggle and built another fortress near it. *Girnal* (Girnar), a fort on the summit of a hill, has many springs of water, and is a very holy place. Near it the stream *Bhadar* falls into the ocean.† Its fish are so delicate that they melt if kept in the sun for a while. Excellent camels and horses are found in its neighbourhood.

Girnar

Somnath

SOMNATH is an old place of worship and is famous in all directions. It lies three *kos* from the sea, and there are five ports ‡ in its territory. The stream *Sarsati* discharges [itself into the sea] near it ; and it is regarded as the greatest of holy places. It is well known that about five thousand years ago, fifty-six *kror* of men of the tribe of *Jadu* sportively took to fighting with one another, between the rivers Sarsati and *Haran*,§ and went down ‖ [to Hell.] Two and a half *kos*¶ from Somnath is a very sacred place, *Bhal ka*,** where an arrow from the hand of a hunter pierced the foot of Sri Krishna, and he passed away to the next world under a *peepul* tree on the bank of the river Sarsati. It is called *Belnir*, †† and is regarded as a very sacred spot. [37. *a.*]

Destruction of the Yadu tribe.

Death of Krishna.

* Mahmud I., Bigarah, 1459-1505 A. D. (Bayley's *Gujarat*, ch. viii.)

† The A-text reads *dar nazdiki-e-an rud-i-Bhadar ta daria-e-shur piwandad mahi chunan* &c. The *Ain* (ii. 245), however, gives, "Near the village of Tunkaghosha, the river Bhadar falls &c."

‡ Named in *Ain*, ii. 246.

§ Letts' Atlas, sheet 5, has *Sursooty* and *Heerny*. They fall into the sea together near Somnath.

‖ Our author, though a Hindu, uses the conventional phrase of Moslem historians in describing the death of infidels.

¶ The A-text reads *O dar nim karohe.* I have followed the *Ain* here.

** The *Ain* reads *Bhalka Tirath* (the shrine of the Arrow), The *Imp. Gaz* (xiii 50) names it *Bhat kund.*

†† The *Ain* reads *Pipal-sir.*

In the town of *Mul** there is a temple of Mahadeo. Every year on a certain day before the rainy season, an animal, (which is called *Sakh*† in the Hindi language) becomes visible here. A little smaller than the pigeon, offensive in odour, and white and black in colour, it alights on the top of the temple, groans, wallows on the ground, and gives up the treasure of life. That day the people of the city having assembled together burn various kinds of incense ; and from the proportion of black and white colour in it [*i.e*, the plumage of the bird] they form their guess as to the rainfall : from blackness they infer rain and from whiteness drought.

Shiva temple :

Miracle.

Near it is DWARKA, also called Jagat. It has a famous shrine. As Sri Krishna, coming from Mathura to this place, chose it as his abode, it is held to be a place of great sanctity. Near it is the village of *Kasi*‡, of which the inhabitants are of the Ahir race and outside the pale of the Hindu religion. They eat food cooked by anybody and marry many wives. When a new governor arrives at this place, they exact a promise from him that no notice would be taken of the unchastity of their women, and then only do they consent to live [under him], otherwise, they emigrate and abandon their homes.

Dwarka

Aboriginal tribe.

Adjoining it, is a land (the *Rann*), 90 *kos* in length. Before the rainy season, the ocean overflows and floods this country. When the rains subside, it decreases, and the land dries up and yields abundance of salt.

The Rann.

* The *Ain* names it *Mul Mahadeo*, Bayley has '*Madhopur* in the perganah of Manglor.' (*Gujarat*, 197). Letts, Sheet 5, has *Madhupoor*, 10 m. N. W. of Maungrote.

† *Sakh* may a corruption of *Suk*, a well-known bird. The *Ain* has *Mukh*.

‡ The *Ain* has, "The *Kathis* are numerous in this tract ; they are of the Ahir caste." For *Kathis* see *I. G.* viii. 89.

Cutch.

KACH is a separate country. Its breadth [is 100 *kos*,]* and length 250 *kos*. West of it lie Sind and many a desert. Camels and goats are plentiful ; the Arab horses of this country are famous. It is said that once upon a time a merchant was conveying Arab horses by way of the river, when the ship was suddenly wrecked and a few of the horses reached the bank on planks and thus arrived in this country. The breed of those horses is still here.

Horses of Arab breed

In short, in this province the climate is temperate. Much of it is desert. The chief crops are *jawari* and *bajrah*, which are the principal articles of food. The spring harvest is scanty. Wheat and other grains come from Malwa and Ajmir, and rice from the Deccan. Around crops and gardens are set thorny plants which form strong hedges. For this reason, the country is hard to travel in. On account of the abundance of trees it does not yield the pleasures of hunting. Mango and other fruit trees are so numerous that the country may well be called an orchard. From Pattan (Anhilwara) to Baroda, a 100 *kos*, is full of mango trees, which yield the finest fruits, some of which taste sweet even when unripe. [**37** *b*]. The fig grows excellently, and the melon can be had in winter and summer alike. Grapes and roses are plentiful. The *cheeta* (leopard) abounds in the desert ; it is trapped every year and trained to hunt. The oxen of this country are famous for their weight, bulk, graceful motion, and swift pace. A pair sells for more than 500 rupees. In half a day they travel 50 *kos*.† The chief rivers of this province are the *Sabarmatti*,

Crops

Thorny hedges.

Fruits.

Hunting leopards

good oxen.

* The A-text is wrong. The correction has been made from the *Ain*.

† The *Ain* (ii. 242) ascribes this feat to the oxen of Pattan.

the *Vatrak*, the *Mahendri*,* the *Narbada*, the *Tapti*, the *Sarsati*, and the *Haran*. There are two fountains, called Jamuna-Ganga. **Rivers.**

The length of this province from Burhanpur to Dwarka is 302 *kos* ; its breadth from Jalor to the port of Daman is 260 *kos*. Eastwards lies Khandesh, westwards Dwarka (situated on the coast), southwards the mountains border it everywhere, nothwards lie Jalor and Idar. In the south are the ports of Daman and Kambhayat. The *Sarkars* are Ahmadabad, Pattan, Nadot, Bahronch, Baroda, Champanir, Godhra, Surath, and Sirohi,—9 *Sarkars* comprising 188 *mahals*, 13 ports, and [a revenue of] 58 *kror*, 37 *lac*, and 90 thousand *dam*† (Rs. 14,594,750). **Extent.** **Revenue.**

XIV. THATHA.

The Pleasure-increasing Province of Thatha.

In ancient times, the capital of this country was a large town named *Brahmanabad*. Its citadel had 1400 bastions, each at the distance of a *tanab* ‡ [from the next one.] Then *Alor*§ became the capital ; many of its bastions and battlements are still to be seen. After that *Diwal*, now [called] THATHA and [also] *Debal*,|| became the seat of government. It is a large town and the emporium of all things, esp., pearls and other **Old capitals** **Thatha**

* The *Vatrak* falls into the *Sabarmatti*, 6 m. N. of Khaira. The *Mahendri* (Mahinadi ?) may be the *Mahi* river.

† Under Akbar it had 9 *Sarkars*, 138 *mahals*, and a revenue of Rs. 10,920,557-8-0. (*Ain*, ii. 252.)

‡ Lit., a chain (60 yds.) ; a measure of length. (*Ain*, ii. 62.)

§ The A-text has the corrupt reading *Adpuri*.

|| The A-text is wrong. I have corrected it with the help of the *Ain*, (ii. 337.)

articles from harbours in plenty. They take a third part of the crop from the peasants [as rent] in this country. The mines of salt and iron yield a large revenue. Six *kos* [from this town] is a quarry of yellow stone; having hewn the stone into the required length or shortness, they use it in buildings. In many places, the people depend upon boats [for conveyance], and they are of many kinds. Taking the big and small ones, the boats will number four thousand. Game, wild asses, hares, the *kotah pachah* (hog-deer), hogs, and fish are plentiful. The staple food is rice, curd, and fish. Having dried the fish and filled boats with them, the people export them to ports and other places. They extract oil from fish [38. *a.*] and use it in boat-[building.] There is a species of fish named *Palwah*,* which is unparalleled in sweetness of taste and flavour. It enters into the river Sind from the ocean and is caught with nets. Nowhere else can it be found. Curd is very well made. Its taste does not change in four months. Flowers are plentiful, and fruits of many kinds, esp. the mango, grow well. Small melons are found in the desert.

Mines

Fish :

the *pala*

The SORCERERS† of this country are notorious in all directions. By glances and spells they take away the livers of men, especially those of children. The glance of the magician has the greatest influence upon all men at the time of eating meals. It is said that in the course of time the sorcerer acquires such power that every one at whom he looks grows insensible. [When the victim is] in that condition, he robs the liver and eats it, sharing it with his brother magicians; and the

Sorcerers

Eating the liver,

* "The chief of the fresh-water varieties [of fish] is the *pala*, nearly allied to the *hilsa* of the Ganges. The local consumption and also the export of dried *pala* are very large." (*I. G.* vii. 14.)

† Lit., liver-eaters.

cup of the life of that unconscious man is filled to the brim, (he dies) When the magician wishes to make anybody like himself, he gives him a bit of the liver to eat and teaches him spells. He rides on the hyena, a carnivorous animal of the woods, tames it by the might of spells, and gets news from a distance [by its help.] When he is caught, expert [witch-doctors] cut open the calf of his leg and extract a grain resembling the seed of the pomegranate. It is given as food to any one who is under the malign influence of sorcerers, and he is cured by the grace of God. These magicians know such magic and incantation that if you throw them into a river after tying a mill-stone round their neck, they do not sink ;* nor do they burn in fire. But when those who are experts in such matters wish to bring back one of them from the path of sorcery, they brand both of his temples, sprinkle his eyes with salt, and keep him suspended in a room for 40 days ; he is given food without any salt, and counter-spells are recited to him. By this process the sorcerer is made to forget his own spells, and he turns back from his wicked ways. The practitioners of witchcraft are mostly women ; only a few are men. I have seen with my own eyes the harm done by these godless persons, who have taken away the livers of children—those tender plants of the garden of life. These godless people live in every town ; but the city of Thatha abounds in them.

and riding the hyena

How to cure of sorcery

Seventy *kos* from Thatha is *Niklaj*,† a place sacred to Durga, and situated between the north and the west, near the ocean. Owing to the difficult character of the

Durga Temple.

*Compare with this the old mode of trying witches in England: "The victim being stripped naked and cross-bound......was cast into a pond or river, in which it was held that it was impossible for her, if guilty, to sink." (Brand's *Popular Antiquities*, 598.)

† Not identified.

path through the desert, the absence of water and the plundering habits of the Bhil tribe, it is hard for any one to reach this place. But some [38. *b.*] *Fakirs*, esp. *Sanyasis* naked from head to foot, having chosen a life of hunger and thirst, reach this place and perform worship. The journey, in going and coming back, occupies more than 15 days and involves many hardships.

Sehwan

The *Sarkar* of SEWISTAN (Sehwan), a dependency of this province, is on the bank of the river Sind. In this tract there is a large lake, two days' journey in length. It is called *Manchur*.* Having constructed platforms on the surface of the water, some fishermen live there and earn a livelihood by the profession of catching fish. Similarly, in the province of Kashmir also, the people construct platforms covered with earth on the surface of water.

Lake *Manchur*

Floating houses

In this province from the limits of Multan and Uch to Thatha and Kiraj-Mekran†, there are high northern mountains of hard stone, where the tribe of *Baluch* and a few Afghans live. Southwards from Uch to Gujrat, are sandhills and the abodes of the *Bhatti* (to which the chief of Jesalmir belongs by birth) and other Rajput clans. From Bhakkar to Nasirpur and Amarkot live the *Soda*‡ and *Jareja* tribes, and others also.

Tribes

* A large lake near the town of Sehwan.

† The A-text may also be read as *Ganj-Mekran*. The *Ain* (ii. 336) has *Kach and Mekran*. Jarrett takes the word *Kiraj* as an Arab corruption of *Kachh* (334 *n*.) Elliot holds that Kiraj was situated in Kachh (i. 391.) In Walker's map, the capital of Mekran is given as *Kedje*, 26° 28′N 62° 28′E.

‡ The Sodah have been identified by Tod with the *Sogdoi* of the Greek historians. Hunter speaks of the Jareja Rajputs as the ruling race in Cutch (*I. G.* iv. 61) and of the Sodah tribe as "formerly the dominant race in Thar and Parkar." (xiii. 266.)

River Sind, the chief highway

The greatest river of this province is the *Sind.* Merchants bring goods and stuffs from Multan and Bhakkar to Thatha in boats over this river. Nay, even travellers in this country and large armies do not travel to Thatha except by way of the river. It would take less time for armies to travel by dry land in this direction ; but in that case they would have to suffer hardships from the intricate woods and scarcity of water.

Extent

The length of this province from Bhakkar to Kiraj-Mekran is 250 *kos* ; its breadth from the village of Badin* to the port of Lahari† is 100 *kos.* Eastwards lies Gujrat Ahmadabad, westwards Kiraj-Mekran, northwards Bhakkar,‡ southwards the ocean. The *Sarkars* are Thatha, Sewistan, Nasirpur, and Amarkot,—four *Sarkars,* comprising 58 *mahals* and 5 ports.

Revenue

The revenue of the province is 9 *kror.* 49 *lac.* and 70 thousand *dam*§ (Rs. 2, 374, 250)

* On the Falaili river, 24·42 N. 68·53 E.

† The *Lahori Bandar* of the *Imp. Gaz.*

‡ The *Ain* has "To the north Bhakkar and Sewi ; to the south, the ocean."

§ According to the *Ain,* it had five *Sarkars* (Hajkan in addition to the above four), 53 *mahals,* and a revenue of Rs. 1,655,284-1-2. Jarrett gives the amount as Rs. 165,383-13-2 ; but here is a double mistake in this ; (1) the rupee equivalent of the *dam* as given should be 165,384, (2) the total amount in *dam* is incorrectly given, as the revenues of the five *Sarkars* when added together amount to 66,251,393 *dam* (Rs. 1,656,284-13-2).

XV. MULTAN.

The Province of Multan, the Abode of Safety.

Multan

The capital, MULTAN, is an ancient town. It has a brick fort. All sorts of people live in it. Various articles of all countries are bought and sold here. Merchants bring horses of Arab breed from Iraq by way of Qandahar, [**39**. *a*] and sell them in this town. The climate is almost temperate in winter; in summer the heat is excessive. The rainy season is short. The people use a dialect * which is a mixture of the tongues of Lahor and Sind. They manufacture excellent flowered carpets and *satranjis* and *chhint*† with figures.

Shaikh Bahau-d-din Zakaria: his life

Within the fort is situated the place of sleep of Shaikh *Bahau-d-din Zakaria*, surnamed Makhdumu l-Alam. A lofty cupola of brick and lime has been raised over the tomb of this Manifestation of Light. This Shaikh was the son of Shaikh Wajihu-d-din Muhammad bin Shaikh Kamalu-d-din Ali Shah Qorishi. He was born at Kot Koror‡ in 565 A. H. (1169 A. D.) His illustrious father died in his infancy. The Shaikh, after busying himself in the acquisition of knowledge and the customary learning, set out on his travels. After travelling in Iran and Turan, he reached Baghdad became the disciple of Shahabu d-din Suhrawardi, and attained the dignity of becoming his successor. Shaikh [Fakhru-d-din] Iraqi and Mir Husaini received their training from him. He came from Baghdad to Multan and resided there. Many believers became his disciples and thus secured grace. He was a great friend

* The *Jatki* or *Multani*, a dialect occupyiug an intermediate position between Sindhi and Panjabi (*I. G.* x. 7).

† A kind of cotton cloth.

‡ 31'12 N. 70 58 E.

of Shaikh Faridu-d-din Ganj-i-Shakkar. They lived together for some time On the 7th of Safar, 665 A. H. (1266 A. D.), a pupil, bringing a sealed letter, sent it within by the hand of Shaikh Sadru d-din, the son of this [Bahau-d-din.] The Shaikh on reading it, surrendered his soul to God ; and from the four corners of the house came a loud voice saying "Friend is united to friend." Many very wonderful stories about his Holiness are told by the people, high and low, of this country. Shaikh *Sadru-d din Arif,* the son of Shaikh Bahau d-din Zakaria, passed away in the year 709 A. H. (1309 A. D.) Shaikh *Ruknu-d-din* (the son of Sadru-d-din), Shaikh Yusuf Kurdezi, Shaikh Musi Gilani, Shamsu-d-din Tabrizi, and many other saints repose in this fortunate city. The tomb of each of these manifestations of light is a place of pilgrimage to multitudes.

Tombs of other saints

Four *kos* south of Multan is the tomb of Sayid *Zainu l-Abidin,* the father of Sultan Sarwar. In summer, men from all sides come on pilgrimage and form a great gathering here Forty *kos* west of Multan, on the skirt of the hills of Baluchistan, on the further side of the river Sind, is the place of sleep of [39. *b.*] SULTAN SARWAR.* This scion of the Sayid family, in early youth conquered the strong evil propensities by hard austerities and very rigorous devotion. Through His blessing the mirror of his heart became polished, and the night of

Sakhi Sarwar

* "*Sakhi-Sarwar,* a famous Muhammadan shrine in Dera Ghazi Khan *tahsil,* founded in honour of Saidi Ahmad, afterwards known as Sakhi Sarwar, the son of an immigrant from Baghdad, who settled at, Sialkot, 12 miles east of Multan, in 1220. The buildings include—the mausoleum of Sakhi Sarwar himself, a monument of Baba Nanak; the tomb of Massamat Bibi Bhai, wife of Sakhi Sarwar. The guardians of the shrine are the descendants of Sakhi Sarwar's three disciples." (*I. G.* xii. 145.)

his soul was illuminated by the light of the candle of spiritual knowledge. By chance a war broke out with the tribe of *Jat Kunwar*. Sultan Sarwar and Mian *Dhudka* (his brother) gained the honour of martyrdom [by falling in this war with infidels.] *Bibi Bhai*, the wife of his Holiness, unable to bear the pang of separation, packed up the baggage of life (*i. e*, died.) Mian *Rana*, his son, who was a little orphan, also went to the other world. They were buried at the foot of the hills, and became famous through [their tombs working miracles like] the tombs of martyrs. Through good luck, a merchant was coming from Qandahar to Multan. When he stopped near the aforesaid tomb, the leg of his camel suddenly got broken. Being too weak to carry himself the load of the camel, he made a vow to the tomb of the martyr. By the will of God, the leg of the camel was instantly set right, and the merchant, thus confirmed in his faith, carried out his vow, and fastening the load on the camel, pursued his journey. This miraculous event became well-known on all sides. Thenceforth that honoured tomb became an object of pilgrimage. Besides that [miracle, there was another:] three persons,—one blind, the second leprous, and the third impotent.—having resolved to devote themselves to the tomb, prayed for the removal of their infirmities. By the grace of God, the impotent man gained virility, the leper health, and the blind man eye-sight. This became the cause of faith to numbers of men, and this wonderful manifestation [of the miracle working property of the tomb] was noised abroad. As the first glance of the aforesaid blind man fell upon a cow and a heron, all of these three men became famous under that name ; and their descendants who devoutly attend at the tomb are still called *Gow-o-gulang*, *i. e.*, cow and heron. In short, vast numbers of different classes of

Holy tombs, working miracles.

Hereditary attendents of the tombs

men from all sides of the country and all places of the world, walk to the tomb of this Illuminated Man, discharge their vows, and pray [40. *a*] for the realisation of their desires. By command of God the Giver of Life, their desires are fulfilled. At the beginning of winter, in particular, large numbers of people come from every side From the city of Multan to the tomb,—a distance of more than four *kos*, the whole road is filled with people, and the assemblage of men in this street is too great to be adequately described

Uch

In the city of *Uch* is the place of sleep of Shaikh *Jalal*, son of Sayid Mahmud, son of Sayid Jalal Bokhari, who was celebrated under the title of *Makhdum-i-Jahanian*. On the *Shab-i-barat* of 707 A. H. (1307 A. D.), he came into the arena of existence. He was the pupil and successor of his illustrious father. He also received a viceregency from Shaikh Ruknu-d-din Abul Fath Suhrawardi. At Delhi, having gone to Shaikh Nasiru-d din *Chiragh-i-Dihli*, he acquired great learning. On Wednesday,* the Id-i-Qurban, 785 A. H. (1383 A. D.) he cast off the material form (died) *Malang* and *Daudai*† dervishes, naked from head to foot, are his disciples in every direction. and they recite his glorious name.

Pattan : tomb of Faridu-d-din, his life

In the city of *Pattan* or Ajodhan, in the *Sarkar* of Dipalpur, west of Multan, is the place of sleep of Shaikh *Faridu-d din* Ganj-i-Shakkar. This Shaikh was the son of Jalalu-d-din‡ Sulaiman, a descendant of Farrukh Shah Kabuli His birthplace was the hamlet of *Knot*

* Thursday, according to the *Ain*. (iii. 369.)

† Jarrett's note has "He is the founder of the descendant *Jalaliya* Fakirs." I have not been able to trace Suhrawardi *dervishes* of the A-text.

‡ The *Ain* gives *Jamalu-d-din*.

*wal** near Multan. In early youth he turned his attention to the acquisition of the usual learning. At Multan, having met with Khawajah Qutbu-d din Bakhtiar Kaki, he gained much grace Having gone to Delhi at his request, he had his desire gratified to the full. Some say that with the permission of the Khawajah, he went from Multan to Qandahar and Sistan, and employed himself in gaining learning, and after that he went to Delhi for the purpose of waiting upon the Khawajah. Having practised austerities and waged war against the evil passions, he gained the victory. With the permission of the Khawajah, he came to the city of Hansi and lived there. Khawajah Qutbu-d-din, at the time of his passing away, ordered that his patched gown, staff, and other things that had come down from the Saint, should be entrusted to Shaikh Faridu-d din That Shaikh, on hearing of the matter, came from Hansi† to Delhi, [40 *b*.] received the trust, returned and fixed his abode at Pattan. Many people gained their desires from the favours which he bestowed, Inasmuch as heaps of earth were turned into sugar at his blessed glance—which had the effect of alchemy,—he became surnamed *Ganj i-shakkar* (the storehouse of sugar). On Thursday, in the month of Muharram, 667 A.H (1268 A.D.),‡ he bade adieu to this transitory world, in the city of Pattan.

Dipalpur, In short, the *Sarkar* of *Dipalpur*§ is a dependency

* The *Ain* has *Khotwal*. There is a *Kaneewala*, 15m. N. E of Multan (Letts' sheet 12.)

† The *Ain* (iii. 364) gives *Jhansi*.

‡ The *Ain* (iii. 364) gives "the 5th of Muharram, A. H. 668," (Monday, 5th Sep. 1269.) Jarrett adds "According to Ferishta, Thursday the 5th Muharram."

§ Identical with the modern Montgomery District of the Panjab.

of this province. The Wattu, Dogar, Gujar,* and other tribes live here, and are notorious for their refractory and rebellious character. In the rainy season, the rivers Biah and Sutlej reach the *mahals* of this *Sarkar* and extend broad and deep for leagues together over the surface of the land, and all the parts of this territory are submerged ; the deluge of Noah seems to be acted again here every year When the water subsidems so many jungles spring up all over this land, owinseems the great moisture and dampness, that a pedestristur all great difficulty in travelling. How then can a every is For this reason, this country is called the *Lakhi* become The wicked men of this plain, owing to the travelling of the river (which flows in many streams by the spring lings of the inhabitants of these tracts) and the shecom afforded by the impassable jungle (which is leagues in length and breadth), become ambuscaders, highwaymen, and thieves The hand of the Imperial commanders cannot reach the chastisement and destruction of these people. In this country winter is temperate and summer heat excessive In the autumn cultivation *jawari* is grown and in the spring wheat.

wild tribes, robbers

Westwards of Multan, five *kos* on the further side of the river Chenab, is the land of the *Baluchis*. In that country are two chieftains : one is *Dudai*, and has 50 thousand horse and 50 thousand foot soldiers of his own ; the other is *Hut*, and commands 20 thousand

Baluchis, two chiefs

* For *Wattu* see *I. G*, ix. 497, and Cunningham's *Sikhs*, 7 *Dogar* is a Muhammadan tribe mentioned in *I. G.* xi. 273 and Cunningham, 8. *Gujar* is a Hindu tribe.

† Lit., 'a hundred thousand forests.' Hunter writes, coarse whole interior upland......consists of a desert plateau, hundred overgrown with brushwood and coarse grass, which are interior ed at places by an impenetrable jungle, impassable alike for with and horse." (*I. G.* ix. 492.)

cavalry and 30 thousand infantry. The two are always quarrelling and fighting about boundaries. By swearing allegiance to the Emperor and paying a fixed tribute, they hold themselves and their principalities in safety. The envoys [41 *a*.] of both of them are present at the seat of government, Multan, and stay there in order to carry out the commands of the Emperor and to perform the mandates of the provincial governor. The kingdom of Baluch is famous for its large population, rich crops of both harvests, abundant wealth, and security from thieves and robbers. It is said that in the reign of Sultan Alau-d-din the Second (1443-1451 A.D.), king of Delhi, the province of Multan passed out of his possession into that of the *Langah* family. Sultan Husain Langah, ruler of Multan, in his own reign settled the territory from Koror Kot to Dhan Kot as *jagir* on Malik Sohrab* and other Baluchis who had come to him from Kiraj-Mekran.

Buffer State But in the reign of the Emperor Akbar, the great Diwan Rajah Todar Mal made over this country absolutely to the Baluchis, fixed them as a strong barrier† between Hindustan and Khorasan, and thus set up a firm rampart on the confines of the two countries.

Bhakkar, a strong fort South of Multan is *Bhakkar*,‡ a strong fort. In old books [it] is named *Mansurah*.§ The river Sind, having

* "One Mullik Sohrab Duvally arrived from Mekran, engaged in the service of Hoosein Lunga, who gave over to them the country lying between Kotgirvur and Dhunkote. Many other Bulochies flocked in great numbers to Mooltan,...till at length all the country lying between Setpoor and Dhunkote was occupied by Bulochies." (Ferishta, iv. 388).

† *Buffer States*, as they are now called.

‡ An island fortress midway between the modern Sukkur and Rohri.

§ The exact locality of Mansurah is doubtful. The province of which it was the capital extended from Alor to the sea. Cunningham locates Mansurah close to Brahmanábád.

become one with the five rivers of the Punjab, reaches the outskirts of this fort, and separating into two streams, two-thirds of it pass by the south and one-third by the north side of the fort It is everywhere famous for its strength of fortification. It is extremely difficult for an army to lay hold of it.

In this province, summer is excessive and the rains scanty. Fruits grow excellently well Between Siwi (Sibi) and Bhakkar is a large desert. In the hot season the Simoom blows for three months. As the river Sind inclines every few years from the south to the north [bank alternately] and destroys the houses of the villages* [by erosion], the people build their houses of wood and grass. The practice of building *pucca* and lasting houses is rare. Climate

The length of this province from Firuzpur to Sewistan is 400 *kos* ; its breadth from Khatpur† to Jesalmir is 125 *kos*, and from ‡ Chandko to Kiraj-Mekran 660 *kos*. Eastwards it adjoins the *Sarkar* of Sirhind, westwards Kiraj-Mekran, northwards Shor Kot, southwards the province of Ajmir. The *Sarkars* are Multan, Dipalpur, and Bhakkar,—three *Sarkars* comprising 96 *mahals*. The revenue of the province is 24 *kror*, 46 *lac*, and 15 thousand *dam*§ (Rs. 6,115,375.) [41. *b*.]. Extent Revenue

* The *Ain* (ii. 328) has "The village cultivation follows its course."

† There is a Khootpur on the Ravi, 25 m. S. W. of Lahore (Letts' sheet 11.)

‡ Here the *Ain* (ii. 326) reads "But since its inclusion, it measures to *Khach* (Gandava) and Mekran, 660 *kos*." *Chandko* is a tract of alluvial land in Sind, on the right bank of the Indus ; chief town, *Ghaibi Dero*. (*I. G.* iii. 359).

§ Under Akbar it had 3 *Sarkars*, 88 *mahals*, and a revenue of Rs. 3,785,090 –8. (*Ain*. ii. 328). Jarrett has by mistake dropped the first zero.

XVI. PANJAB.

The Metropolitan Province of Lahore.

Lahore: founded by Lava.

LAHOR is an old town on the bank of the river Ravi. Its foundation is ascribed to *Lav*, the son of king Ram Chandra In some histories they write [the names] also as Lahu and Laháur. When in the course of the revolution of the revolving heavens long ages passed away and its buildings fell into ruin and few signs of habitation were left, Sialkot became the seat of government of this kingdom. After Sultan Mahmud of Ghaznin had conquered Hindustan, Malik Ayáz, who was acceptable in the eyes of the Sultan and a man of unparalleled keenness of sagacity, decided to restore this town and built a *pucca* fort and newly populated the town. Khusrau Shah and Sultan Khusrau Malik, his son, both descendants of Sultan Mahmud, having reconquered this kingdom, made Lahor capital; and for 38 years* it remained the capital of the dynasty of Sultan Mahmud. After that, none of the kings of Hindustan chose to reside in this city and its population declined from grandeur Afterwards, in the time of Tartar Khan, one of the nobles of Sultan Bahlol Lodi, it again became a seat of government. Thereafter, Kamran Mirza, the son of the Emperor Babar, resided in this city, and its population increased. Then, the Emperor Akbar, in his own reign, turned his attention to the work of peopling it; and having built a strong fort, walls, and a palace, he gave it new splendour. Next the Emperor Jahangir built lofty mansions which are still extant; and his good fortune

Capital of the Ghaznivides.

Buildings of Akbar and Jahangir.

---

* From 1153 to 1184 A. D. (Elphinstone, 391) The two kings mentioned here reigned for 34 lunar years. The text is therefore wrong.

became for a time the means of its increase of splendour. Its habitations were increased by the abodes of the princes and high grandees, esp. the house of Asaf Khan *alias* Abul Hasan, the son of Itimadu d-daulah, which is very large and spacious. In the time of the Emperor Shah Jahan, the population increased daily. In the reign of the Emperor Aurangzib, when the river Ravi encroached upon the town and by its violence destroyed many houses and gardens, in the fourth year from the Emperor's accession, [42. *a*] the Imperial order was issued for building a strong embankment that would prevent the destruction of buildings. The officers constructed a strong embankment, two *kos* in length, and the rampart of Alamgir protects the town like the rampart of Alexander. In many places, by building flights of steps they have made the lip (bank) of the river attractive like the lips of the fair. The high grandees have added to the beauty of the town by building charming houses and pleasant mansions overlooking the river. From the commencement [of the work] to the present time, when more than 40 years have elapsed, repair and construction of buildings on behalf of the Imperial government have gone on, and much money has been spent on it.

Aurangzib's embankment

It is undoubtedly a large city and a big town. Few towns can be pointed out that resemble it in extent of habitation and largeness of population. Various skilled artisans of every country and every class of the handicraftsmen of the age live here. The commodities of the seven climates and the things of sea and land are bought and sold here. Though there are many mosques in every lane and bazar, yet the Emperor Alamgir has built on the bank of the river opposite the lofty palace, a high stone mosque, on which more than five *lac* of rupees have been spent. In the centre of the town is

Mosques of Aurangzib

and Wazir Khan

another mosque, the cathedral of *Wazir Khan alias* Hakim Alimu-d-din of the time of Shah Jahan, which looks like a beautiful mole* on the cheek of the town.

Tombs of Pir Ali Hajuri,

In this town is the tomb of the greatest of great saints, Pir *Ali Hajuri*, who had both learning and piety. Having come from Ghaznin in the company of Sultan Mahmud, he tied up the baggage of life (died) at Lahor. The Sultan ascribed his conquest of Lahor to the auspiciousness of his coming. Many other favourites of the Divine Majesty repose in this town. The august tomb of the Emperor Jahangir is situated on the other side of the river Ravi, near *Shahdra*. Close to it is the tomb of Asaf Khan† (Abul Hasan) of the time of Jahangir.

Jahangir, and Asaf Khan

Garden of Shalimar

Although there are many charming gardens and a thousand pleasant rose bowers in the outskirts of the city, yet the garden of SHALIMAR, which the Emperor Shah Jahan [42, *b*.] laid out in imitation of the garden of Kashmir, ravishes the heart of the beholder. As some parts of the capital have been described, I shall, for the satisfaction of people, write about a few of the other towns of this province.

DOABS :— i. JALANDHAR Doab

In the *doáb* of *Bait Jalandhar* (between the Bias and the Sutlej) is JALANDHAR, an old town. Near it is the tomb of Nasiru-d-din, who enjoyed the reputation of saintship in his life time. In summer people assemble at his tomb on pilgrimage. In the suburbs of this town is also situated the tomb of Shaikh Abdullah of Sultanpur,‡ who was famous for his learning and

Tomb of Mukhdumu-l-mulk

* A mole on the cheek was considered a sign of beauty. The Persian poet Hafiz, in a well-known couplet wishes to give away the kingdoms of Samarkand and Bukhara in return for the black mole on the cheek of his mistress.

† The brother of Nur Jahan.

‡ For his life, see *Ain*. i. 544.

accomplishments, became celebrated under the title of *Shaikhu-l-Islami* in the reign of Salim Shah, and enjoyed the surname of *Makhdumu-l-mulk* in the reigns of Humayun and Akbar. In this *doab* is also the old town of *Bajwara*,* where *sirisaf*, *adhars*, *doriah*, *panch-toliah*, *jhonah*, white *chirah*, *fotah* of gold embroidery and other kinds of cloth are manufactured well. At *Sultanpur*, *chhint*, *dolai*,† and embroidery are finely made. Bajwara : cloth weaving

In the *Bari doab* (between the Bias and the Ravi) is the *parganah* of Ast-purmati.‡ Horses like those of Arabia are bred here ; the price of some of them comes up to ten thousand or fifteen thousand rupees. In the *Chak* of Guru Hargovind, a dependency of Patti Haibatpur,§ there are a large garden and a tank ; on a certain day in *Baisakh* many men assemble here Two or three *kos* from it is *Ramtirth*,‖ an ancient holy place. ii. BARI Doab; Ram-tirth

A few *kos* from it is BATALA,¶ a charming town, with a pleasant climate. The founder of this town was Rai Ramdeo Bhatti, zemindar of Kapurthal and chieftain of his own clan. The legend runs that once on a time, as God willed it, a sort of flood raged in the Panjab, so that all the land from the river Sutlej to the river Chenab, was covered with water, and the houses of the towns and villages were destroyed and many living creatures perished. For some time after the BATALA; Story of its foundation

* Bajwara, a village in Hoshiarpur district, 1½ m. E of Hoshiarpur town. (*I. G.* i 439).

† All the above, except *adhars* and *dolai* are mentioned in *Ain* i. 93—95. *Dolai* is a garment well-known in India even now.

‡ Or, *Purmati.* No such *parganah* is mentioned in *Ain.* Not inentified.

§ *Patti* in the Kasur *tahsil* of Laho.e district, 20 m. N. of Sobraon, 31°17 N. 74°54 E.

‖ *Ramtirath* is 8 m. N. W. of Amritsar.

¶ *Batala* (*I. G.* ii. 215), in Gurdaspur district, 24 m. from Amritsar. Elliot mistook if for *Patiala.*

flood had subsided, this land remained desolate. Afterwards habitations appeared in some places. As the Mughals of Balkh and Kabul [43. *a.*] used to make plundering incursions into the Panjab every year, this country remained desolate on every side, and many tracts of land lay waste; little produce or crop was raised. In the reign of Sultan Bahlol Lodi, Tartar Khan took a lease of it, and by chance became honoured with the honour of [conversion to] Islam, and this became the cause of his advancement. In the year 877 A. H. (1465 A. D.),—1522 of the era of Vikramajit,—during the lease of Tartar Khan, the town of Batala was founded on a site occupied by a lonely forest. The reason of its being so named was that at the time of the foundation of the town there was no good omen; and so, having stopped building at that place, they laid the foundation of the city elsewhere, on a hillock near it. As 'exchange' is called *Batá* in the Panjabi language, the town came to be named *Batála* on account of its change of site The jungle being cut, many hamlets were founded and cultivation took place, and it became recognised as a *parganah*. It has gradually reached such a condition that at present its income comes up to Qarun's* forty treasuries and breathes equality with the treasury of Purviz. At first the population of the town was not so large The eunuch Shamsher Khan, who was the *krori* (revenue-collector) of this *parganah* under Akbar, † increased the splendour of the city

Why so named

Improved by Akbar's governor

* *Korah*, the cousin of Moses, believed by the Muhammadans to have been very rich and avaricious. *Purviz* or *Khusrau Purvis*, grandson of Naushirvan, reigned in Persia 591—628 A. D. (Malcolm's *History of Persia*, i. 125.)

† "Akbar gave it in *jagir* to Shamsher Khan, his foster-brother who greatly improved and beautified the town, and built without it a magnificent tank." (*I. G.* ii. 215).

by building houses worthy of governors, many tanks, and pleasant gardens; and the population of the town increased daily, and it became a heart-ravishing place. Afterwards Shaikh-i-masha-ikh, the *krori*, became the cause of its increase of population, by building numerous edifices and charming gardens. Now in the reign of the Emperor Alamgir, Mirza Muhammad Khan (who bears the title of Wazir Khan) made the shops of the bazar *pucca*, in the 12th year of Alamgir's reign (1669 A. D.), when he was employed as overseer of this *parganah*. Banki Rai, Sujan Singh the Qanongo, and their children have built charming rest-houses, caravan-serais, and *porah*. * Qazi Abdul Hai has established lodging-houses, bazars, caravan-serais, a cathedral mosque, and a garden. These men have been the cause of the splendour and enlargement of the town. Gangádhar, the son of Hiranand-dhar, has sunk a *pucca* well in the bazar, beautiful like a mole on the face; and he has also established a garden and a well with steps in the environs of the city, on the Lahor road. [43. *b*] As the water of both wells rivals the water of the Ganges, their founder is rightly called *Gangádhar*.† Though there are many fresh gardens and pleasant bowers in the suburbs of the city, yet Amar Singh the Qanongo has laid out a garden in imitation of the garden of Shalimar on different planes, with three terraces, and extremely pleasant. The highest terrace overlooks the tank of Shamsher Khan, attracts the gaze of beholders by its freshness and beauty, and gladdens the sightseers of the town.

Buildings of Wazir Khan, Sujan Singh, Abdul Hai, and Gangádhar

Garden of Amar Singh

The outskirts of this town contain many tombs of

Holy tombs

* *Porah*, a set of houses, often enclosed by a wall and forming one ward of a town. (*I. G.* i. 95.)

† "He who holds the stream of the Ganges on his head," *i. e.*, Shiva.

saints such as the Essence of those who have joined the court of the Lord, viz., Shah Shahabu d-din Bokhari, Shah Kharab, Shah Ismail, Shah Niamatullah, and Shaikh Al-Haddad, each of whom was greatly revered in his life-time. Two *kos* off, in the village of ***Miani*** is the tomb of Shah Badru-d-din, who was connected with that saint of saints Miran Mahiu-d-din. Four *kos* from Batala, in the village of *Danal-ti wal*,* a dependency of Kalanor, is the tomb of that Manifestation of Light, Shah Shams, who was one of those that had been admitted to the court of God and of whose miraculous deeds, wonderful legends increase our wonder. One of them is that, in his life-time, a Hindu named Dipali was his favourite servant. Once upon a time the day for bathing in the Ganges came round and groups of Hindus set out [for the river,] Dipali asked of His Holiness permission to journey to the Ganges. His Holiness refused to grant it, and ordered him to remind him of it on the day appointed for the assemblage on the Ganges. When the day arrived, Dipali made his petition and was commanded to close his eyes. As soon as he did so, he found himself on the bank of the Ganges, talking with his brothers and relatives who had set out before him, and bathing in the company of this multitude of people, all of whom saw him there. But as soon as he opened his eyes he found himself in the presence of His Holiness and became puzzled by his own achievement. Afterwards when his brothers came back from the journey to the Ganges and found him already at home, they all cried out, "Dipali was not with us in the [outward] journey; but all of us bathed in the Ganges with him ; and also at the time of our

Shah Shams : his miracle ;

* Not found in Atlas.

return he did not accompany us, and yet he reached home before us " At length, having learnt the truth of the affair [44 a], they were amazed at this manifestation of supernatural power by that Asylum of Saintship. And there was a more wonderful miracle: a few years after the passing away of this member of the Court of Great God, some carpenters at the command of the Governor of Kalanor felled a gum tree which grew close to the tomb and were sawing it into pieces for use in a building, when suddenly by the power of God a terrible sound came out, the earth shook, the trunk of the tree erected itself, and the carpenters grew afraid at this occurrence. The tree again became green and put forth leaves and branches. The legend of this wonder became famous in all corners of the world and served to increase the faith of crowds of men in His Holiness, the Essence of eminent Saints. The tomb of this Manifestation of [spiritual] Light is now a place of pilgrimage to high and low. Every Friday night, especially on the Friday night of the new moon, many people, both male and female, gather together from far and near and make offerings of money and things and also rice, *malida*, and butter and sugar mixed together. Every one makes vows in the hope of gaining his desire, and by the grace of God the wishes are fulfilled. Unlike the tombs of other [Muhammadan] saints, this tomb has for its servants and attendants a family of Hindus, the descendants of the said Dipali. Although the Islamites tried and are still trying to oust these Hindus, they have not succeeded, because the special favour of His Holiness was bestowed upon Dipali. Up to the present time the same family has remained confirmed in the service [of the tomb.]

another miracle

Hindu guardians of a Moslem Saint's tomb,

Near it is a place named *Dhianpur*, in which lived

Baba Lal, a Hindu saint,

BABALAL,* the chief of the lords of condition and speech, and the place of descent (*i. e*, manifestation) of the triumphs of God (who is the Lord of Dignity.) In his own times he was a master of knowledge and a knower of God, eloquent in expressing spiritual truth and wisdom, and the ocean of the waves of various words. Many men, high and low, were believers in him. It is their constant practice and religious duty to repeat his Hindi verses about the truth and knowledge of God. Prince Dara Shekoh, in his life time often interviewed this wise man and conversed with him on the knowledge of God. Munsi Chandrabhán of the time of Shah Jahan [44. *b.*] has penned in a pleasant style in Persian the dialogue between them.

admired by Dara Shekoh.

Sikh Gurus i. NANAK,

Twelve *kos* from Batalah, on the bank of the river Ravi, is the birth-place of BABA NANAK, whose descendants are still living there. In his own days he was the leader of the caravan in the path of truth (*i. e.*, the spiritual guide of a sect,) the torch-bearer in the road of religion, the Manifestation of the splendour of the light of God, and the beholder of the rays of the secrets of the Infinite. He composed Hindi verses on the real character of the True One—the Universal Soul—and thereby proved the unity of the Godhead in an impressive style and clear metaphors. It is said that this Elect One of the world was born at *Talwandi Rai Bhuna*†, in the year 1526 of Vikramajit, corresponding to 880 A. H. (1469 A.D.), in the reign of Bahlol Lodi, and lived at

born at Talwandi 1469,

* The A-text omits his name ; it has been supplied from the B-text.

† "Tulwundee, a village on the Ravee, which was held by one Raee Bhooa, of the Bhuttee tribe." (Cunningham's *Sikhs*, 37*n*).

the same place in his maternal grandfather's house*. As he was predestined to be a receptacle of the victories of God, he exhibited in his 10th year signs of the knowledge of the invisible world, and performed super-human acts and miracles; and many men became believers in him. After having gratified them [with spiritual teaching,] he came to the town of Batala, became a householder (i e., married), and fixed his residence in one of the villages dependent on Batala on the bank of the river Ravi. The fame of his knowledge of God and wise sayings was noised abroad; large numbers of men from all sides of the country came to him and became his disciples. One of his favourites was a musician named Mardána†, who lured men into the snare of faith by singing in a charming manner songs about the Favourites of the Court of the Creator. [Nanak], the chief among the knowers of God, renounced this transitory world‡, between his 70th and 80th years, in the reign of Salim Shah Afghan. Though he had an obedient son named Lakhmidas, § yet, as spiritual wealth was not his share, Nanak, at the time of his death appointed as his successor a Khattri named Lehna‖ (*alias* Teehun), under the title of Guru Angad. He was one of Nanak's dear associates and intimate attendants. After occupying the seat [of Guru] for a

his boyish miracles;

founds the Sikh sect,

dies 1539.

2. ANGAD, d. 1552.

* "Some say that though the father of Nanak was of Tulwandee, Nanak himself was born in Kanakach, 15 miles south of Lahore, in the house of his mother's parents." (*Ibid*).

† "The sweet singer" of the movement, like Charles Wesley among the Methodists.

‡ In 1539, at Kartarpur on the Ravi, 40 miles above Lahor.

§ His second son, the eldest Sree Chund having become an ascetic and the founder of the Oodassee sect. (*Ibid*, 39 *n*.)

‖ Lehna belonged to the *Teehun*, Amardas to the *Bhulleh*, and Ramdas to the *Sodhi* subdivisions of the Kshatriya race. (*Ibid*, 47.)

period of 13 years, he departed (1552 A.D.). As h
3. AMARDAS, had no son, his son-in-law Amardas (*alias* Bhola) wa seated in his chair. He, after acting as the spiritua
d. 1574. guide of men for 22 years, vacated his body. (1574 A.D Though he had descendants [of his own body], yet a the time of his passing away, he seated in his plac
4. RAMDAS, d. 1581. his son-in-law Ramdas (*alias* Sodhi), who lived as th object of adoration of his disciples for 7 years (d. 158:
5. ARJUN, d. 1606. A.D.). After him Guru Arjun*, his son, [.45 *a*] sa in the chair and after 25 years tied up the baggag of life (d, 1606 A.D.).
6. HARGOVIND, d. 1645. Then Guru Hargovind†, his faith ful son, adorned the chair for 38 years. When he diec (1645 A.D.),
7. HAR-RAI, d. 1661. Guru Har Rai, whose father Guru Dutt ‡ had died in the life-time of Guru Hargovind, sat in th place of his illustrious grandfather, and for 17 year acted as the guide of the believers (d. 1661).
8. HAR-KISHEN, d. 1664. After him his young son, Guru Har Kishen, sat in the chair fo 3 years (d. 1664).
9. TEGH BAHADUR, d. 1675. Then Tegh Bahadur, the younge son of Guru Hargovind, occupied the chair for 15 years, but at last he was captured by the Imperial officers and, in 1081 A.H. (1675 A.D.) corresponding to the 17th year of the reign of Alamgir, executed at Shah-Jahanabad by command of the Emperor. At the time
10. GOVIND RAI. of writing this book, Guru GOVIND Rai, § the son of Guru Tegh Bahadur, has been seated in the chair for 22 years.

The Sikh religion : In short, among the followers of Baba Nanak there

* He made Amritsar the seat of the religion, compiled the *Adi Granth*, and organised the Sikh community. (*Ibid*, 49).

† He first formed the Sikhs into a military body. (*Ibid*, 53). Died at Kiritpur, on the Sutlej.

‡ Eldest son of Har Govind.

§ He made the Sikhs an aggressive power in order to combat the Muhammadan faith and power, and established the theocracy of the *Khálsa*. He died in 1708 A.D.. (*Ibid*, 65 and 71.)

are many ascetics, men agreeable in speech, austere devotees, and persons whose prayers have been heard [by God]. The essence of the worship of this sect is the recital of the verses of their Guide, which they sing with instrumental and vocal music and with a heart-ravishing chant. They have removed the effects of foul [worldly] attachments from their minds and cast away from their hearts the obscuring veil of impediments [to spiritual progress.] In their eyes, kinsmen and strangers are alike, friends and enemies are the same. They live with devotion to their friends, and without quarrel with their enemies. The reliance which this sect has on its leader is seldom seen in other sects. In the name of their Guide (which they continually repeat on the tongue), they consider it an act of great piety to attend on travellers. If a wayfarer arrives at midnight and takes the name of Baba Nanak, every such stranger and unknown man,—unless he happens to be a thief, highwayman, or person of evil notoriety,—is treated as a brother and friend and served in a worthy manner.

chanting holy verses, universal brotherhood, devotion to the Guru, hospitality.

Two *kos* from Batala [45. *b*.] is *Achal*,* a place sacred to Syam Kartik, the son of Mahadev ; it is an old shrine. Here is a large lake the water of which rivals that of Kausar in pleasantness and good taste. At the commencement or middle of [the Sun's journey in] the Libra, which is the time of the equinox and the merry season among the men of the world,—thousands of mendicants of austere devotion and many anchorites bent upon benefiting others, come to this place. And all classes of people, fashionable, respectable, great and small, male and female, having come from all parts of the country, assemble together for six days. This vast crowd of men and assemblage of private and public personages covers leagues [of ground]. Many get their

Achal

Mela

vast gathering:

* Not found in Atlas.

ascetics — temporal and spiritual desires gratified by interviewing and frequenting the company of the religious medicants who know God. Others make merry by meeting and sitting with their shines. Some, by watching the throng of all species of men, understand the rare power of the Creator (who shines in dignity.) Multitudes by beholding the beauty of the moon-faced fairy-like [fair ones], gratify their wishes. Groups of pleasure-seekers and lovers of good cheer fill the stomach of their desire with every sort of eatables. Numbers of the sick, by the holy prayers of the benevolent, get curative medicines. And in this merry gathering, in one part of the bazar, on the two sides of the road, are arranged on trays and dishes many kinds of eatables, confects, fruits of spring and autumn, perfectly sweet and fresh. In another quarter of the assembly, music, song, dance, and pantomime delight the sightseers and the audience. At another place, clever buffoons and eloquent story-tellers, by their rare speeches, excite the laughter of the spectators. Elsewhere strong-armed athletes and strong men of iron-like grasp perform the feats of Rustam* and Isfandiar in wrestling. [**46.** *a.*] At another place jugglers of extraordinary capacity perform strange and clever tricks in sleights of skill and rope-dancing. Elsewhere many matchless pictures of heroes, of banquet and war, of mountain-like elephants and strong-limbed horses, and of other objects, create a second picture-gallery of Manes† upon the walls, and make the beholders stand absorbed in the sight like figures on a wall. In another quarter the bazar grows

Margin notes: beautiful women; food stuffs; confects; singing; gymnastics; jugglery; pictures

* Rustam, the celebrated Persian hero, and son of Zal. (Malcolm's *History of Persia*, I. 19 *et seq*) Isfandiar, a son of Gushtasp, King of Persia. (*Ibid*, I. 46 *et seq*.)

† The founder of the sect of Manichæans, and a celebrated painter, according to Muhammadan myth.

warm with the buying and selling of many kinds of arms, accoutrements, and the various implements used by men and women, and children's toys. The ears of the heavens are deafened by the shouts of men, the din and bustle of the crowd, and the sounds of the large brass drum, the tabor, the tambourine, the cymbal, the lute, &c. The great dust chokes up the eyes of the sky. Undoubtedly this is a sight to behold which the sky opens its thousand eyes ; and the stars grow in wonder as they gaze at it. The Sun, which does not stop for a moment in its swift revolution, stands in the sky to behold this assembly. The Moon, which illuminates the gathering of night, every day puts forth its face out of the window of the East in order to see it. Travellers of the habitable world and tourists of hill and forest have never seen such a gathering or spectacle in any other place. The people of Batala, even when they happen to be a hundred leagues away from their home and in the enjoyment of power, pleasure, comfort, and wealth, invariably wish to come to this place at the time of the gathering. As the birth-place of the author of this book is the pleasant land of Batala, he has thought it fit to record a few of the things of that happy town and this delightful fair. | weapons | din and bustle.

In this *doab,* 50 *kos* from Batala in the northern direction in the hilly region is the fort of *Kangra,* famous for its strength. At the foot of that fort is a place named NAGARKOT,* sacred to Bhawani, and an old place of pilgrimage. [46. *b.*] Twice a year, in September and February, people come here on pilgrimage from distant places,—sometimes after a year's journey,—and get their hearts' desire. What is more | Kangra | Nagarkot

* Situated on the northern slope of a hill which is surmounted by the fort of Kangra. "The temple of Devi ranks among the oldest and most wealthy shrines in India." (*I. G.* vii. 430.)

devotee cut out their tongues

wonderful is that some, in order to realise their wishes, cut out their tongues ; these tongues are restored in a few hours in the case of some, in two or three days in the case of others. Another miracle is that in this place some men sever their heads from their trunks ; their friends place the heads on the bodies and they again get life by the grace of God.

and heads

Jawalamukhi.

Ten *kos* from Nagarkot is *Jawálámukhi,** in many spots of which tongues of fire shoot up like torches. Men make pilgrimages to this place also, and throw into the fire all sorts of things, which are reduced to ashes. This is regarded as auspicious.

iii. RECHNA Doab.

SIALKOT its founder Shalya

or Salivahan.

an old capital,

In the *doab* of Rechnau [between the Ravi and the Chenab] there is an old town, SIALKOT, also called Salkot. Its foundation is ascribed to Raja *Sál* (Shalya) the general of the Pandus.† In the book *Mahabharat*, since the composition of which about 5,000 years have passed away, mention is made of the aforesaid town and Raja. It is called Sialkot in connection with Raja Salivahan,‡ whose memory is preserved by a *pucca* fort. Formerly it was the seat of government of the Panjab, and the habitations covered 2 or 3 *kos*. It was famous and had a larger population than any other town in this province. In 580 A. H. (1184 A. D.), when

* It has "a very holy shrine, surpassing even that of Kangra. The temple stands above certain jets of combustible gas, issuing from the ground, and kept constantly burning, as a manifestation of the goddess Devi." (*I. G.* vii. 162.)

† He was really a general on the side of the Kurus.

‡ "Sialkot, founded by Raja Sál or Shál, an uncle of the Pandava princes. Restored about 65 or 70 A. D. by Salwán or Salivahana, otherwise called Vikramaditya, father of the great Punjab hero, Rasálu......In the centre of the town stands the remains of an ancient fort, popularly believed to have been the original stronghold of Raja Salwán" (*I. G.* xii. 451.)

Sultan Shahabu-d-din Ghori came for the fifth time with the purpose of conquering Lahor and besieged it without success, he turned to Sialkot, and, after repairing and renovating its old fort, left his army in it.* After a long time, Raja Man Singh of Akbar's court, when he was Commandant of Jummun and fief-holder of Sialkot, turned his attention to the repair of the fort and the improvement of the town. After that, Masdar Khan of Jahangir's time, who also was Commandant of Jummun [47. *a.*] and had this *pargana* as his fief, rebuilt the fort and battlements. Since then many governors have repaired it. In short, this delightful town is adorned with all sorts of beauty; the buildings of the *Qanongoes* of the [Jain] tribe of *Bhabra* and of some other persons are extremely delightful and heart-attractive. Good paper† is manufactured in this town, especially the *Mansinghi* paper and silken paper of very good texture, white, clean and durable. These are exported in all directions. Embroidery with silk and gold threads and many kinds of *bafta*, *chira* (scarf). *fotah* (sheet), *sozani*, *adsaka*‡ table-cloth, tray covers, and small tents with figures in gold thread, are well manufactured here. Every year about a *lac* of rupees' worth of embroidered fabrics are bought and sold and sent to all parts of the world. The *jamdhar*, *katari*,§ and lance are well made.

fort repaired by Shahabud-din,

Man Singh,

and Masdar Khan.

Manufactures: paper,

embroidery

arms

In the environs of the city are pleasant and charm-

* Elliot, ii. 294.

† "The distinctive industry of the place is the manufacture of paper, carried on in 3 hamlets forming suburbs of the city...... Under the Mughal Emperors, Sialkot paper was noted for its excellence, being largely used at the Delhi court." (*I. G.* xii. 452)

‡ All these are mentioned in *Ain.* i. 93-95, except *adsaka.*

§ *Ain.* i. 110.

ing gardens, esp., the garden of Nazar Muhammad, where plants and fruits of every kind are grown.

River Aik

Near it flows the stream of *Aik*, which issues from the mountain of Jummun. This stream after leaving that town, for ten *kos* extends over the ground and gets the name of *Khelri**, and, branching off on all sides, disappears.

water sports at Sialkot

In the rainy season when this canal becomes flooded, many people of Sialkot, both high and low, strip themselves naked from head to foot and with only a waist-band on, get upon [inflated] skins and perform water-sports in this canal with happiness and joy. If any inhabitant of this town happens to be at a distance at that time, the memory of the water-sports of the town makes him cheerful. In this charming place is the tomb of Imam Ali-al-Haq, the son of Imam Zainu-l-Abidin.†

Tomb of a holy warrior

It is said that he came to Hindustan from the west in the company of many Muhammadans with the intention of waging a holy war. By chance he reached Sialkot, and having fought with the Hindus [47. *b*.] received the honour of martyrdom. The tomb of this Manifestation of Light is a place of pilgrimage to high and low.

Scholars of Sialkot :

This happy town is a seat of learning and the resort of learned men, a mine of scholarship and the abode of scholars.

Kamal

In the reign of the Emperor Akbar, Maulana *Kamal*, that essence of the masters of condition and speech, getting angry with Husain Khan the governor of Kashmir, came to Sialkot in 971 A. H. (1564 A. D.) engaged himself in teaching pupils, and thus gave currency to learning in this town.

Hakim

In the reign of Shah Jahan, Maulvi *Abdu-l-Hakim*—the most accomplished of the accomplished, the most perfect of

* *Khilree*, a river directly south of Wazirabad is also called *Aik*, though it is distinct from the *Aik* which flows by Sialkot.

† Zain was a nephew of Hasan, the son of Ali.

scholars, the manifestation of the upright nature, the ocean of the waves of learning and perfection, the man of unrivalled accomplishments and beneficence,—spread learning still further. By writing marginal commentaries on some books, he interpreted the meaning of difficult passages; the pupils who joined his blessed school from far and near, attained to many accomplishments. When he passed away, that leader of the men of God and guide of the creatures of the Deity, Maulvi *Abdulla*, the second son of the saved soul [Abdul Hakim], engaged himself in increasing the glory of the school and in guiding the pupils. He made his internal virtues match his external learning and his religious poverty the close associate of his scholarship. As he promoted sweeter manners and acted as the guide of all classes of men, this great man was surnamed "the Imam of the Age." He passed on to the Eternal world in the 26th year of Alamgir's reign (1682 A. D.)

Abdulla

Twelve *kos* from Sialkot is *Dhonkal*,* a place associated with Sultan Sarwar. It is a place of pilgrimage at all times; but in summer crowds of people come from all sides of the country and offer presents, and for two months there is a great gathering here.

Places of Pilgrimage: Dhonkal

Fifteen *kos* from Sialkot is *Purmandal*,† in the midst of the hills of Jummun. It is sacred to Mahadev. When the Sun enters the Sign of Virgo, which [**48.** *a.*] is called *Baisakhi*, large numbers of people, coming from all sides of the world, form a great gathering. And the kings of the hilly region, coming with pomp and grandeur, construct high platforms and practise archery. A rare spectacle is seen.

Purmandal

The river DEGH issues from this place. After leaving it and passing by the limits of villages of the

River Degh.

* 4 miles south of Wazirabad.

† 14 miles S. E. E. of Jummoo city.

*parganas** of Zafarwal, Haminagar, Pasrur, and Aminabad, it reaches the foot of the bridge of Shah Daula,† which is on the high way. Flowing by the *parganas* of Daulatabad, Mihrabad, Manish, Faridabad, and others, it unites with the Ravi. This *pargana* is called Degh-Ravi.

Bismuth

In *Jummun* there is a mine of bismuth. Taking gravel from the river Tavi (which flows at the foot of Jummun city) and setting it on fire, they make bismuth. No other place produces bismuth of such whiteness, hardness, and durability.

SODHRA

SODHRA‡ is an old fort on the bank of the river Chenab. In the reign of the Emperor Shah Jahan, *Ali Mardan Khan,* the premier noble, founded a city near the aforesaid village and named it Ibrahimabad after his own son. He laid out a pleasant garden, which rivals the garden of Shalimar, and built lofty houses, spending six *lac* of rupees on these buildings, garden, and a canal§ which brings the river Tavi to the garden-house. The Imperial government has assigned to the premier noble 2,000 villages of Sodhra rent-free for the repair of the aforesaid garden and city.

Ali Mardan's garden, city, and canal.

iv. CHINHUT Doab.

Gujrat,

In the *doab* of *Chinhut,*‖ [between the Chenab and the Bihat] is the town of Gujrat which was populated in the reign of the Emperor Akbar ; and villages having

* Of these 8 *parganas*, Zafarwal, Pasrur, and Aminabad are given in Atlas ; Haminagar and Daulatabad are mentioned in *Ain.* ii. 319 ; the remaining three have not been identified.

† Given in Atlas, Sheet 30, as *Pool Shah Dowla*, 31.54 N. 74.25 E.

‡ Four miles N. E. of Wazirabad.

§ Ali Mardan's canal "brought the waters of the Tavi to supply the Imperial gardens at Shahdara," on the Ravi, opposite Lahor city. (*I. G.* xii. 441.)

‖ Also spelt *Jenhat* or *Jechna.*

been detached from the *pargana* of Sialkot, a separate *pargana* was formed. At first the town was not so splendid as now. But SHAH DAULA, the Essence of saints, fixed* his habitation here, and constructed a tank, wells and mosques. [48. *b.*] He also built a bridge over the river, which, flowing from the hills of Bhimber †, had been doing injury to the above town. He thus became the cause of its growth in population and splendour. It is said that Shah Daula in early life was the slave of Khema Bhadra,‡ an inhabitant of Sialkot, and loved Faqirs excessively. He particularly served his Holiness Mian Midna. When the time of departure of Mian Midna arrived, his gracious look fell on Shah Daula, and by the influence exerted at that time he was turned to another way of life, and his interior was illuminated with the light of spiritual knowledge. Leaving Sialkot for Gujrat, he resided there. As he was illuminated at heart, many treasure-troves became revealed to him, and he built houses and bridges in many places; in particular he built a strong bridge—such a substantial structure as no rich man even has constructed—over the river Degh on the highway, 5 *kos* from Aminabad in the direction of Lahor. While this Asylum of Saintship lived, many people used to make pilgrimages to him from all parts of the world, and present him with cash and kind. This knower of the secrets of the unseen [world] used to bestow cheerfully on other pilgrims more than what had been presented to him [by his devotees.] Every day he used to keep open the hand of gift and charity to such an extent that the liberality of the whole life-time of Hatam was

the abode of Shah Daula

his life

charity and public works;

* In the reign of Shah Jahan. (*I. G.* v. 196.)

† West of Jhilum city.

‡ Kshema-bhadra, or probably Kshema of the Jain tribe of *Bhabra*, mentioned by Hunter as living in Sialkot.

not a tenth part of a tenth part of his [daily alms.] At last in the 17th year of Alamgir's reign (1674 A. D.) he departed to the Eternal World. Near the city stands the tomb of this great man, an object of pilgrimage to many. This town is the abode of all classes of men and a store-house of the articles of all countries and the rare things of the age. Swords and *jamdhars* are well made, and more embroidery is done than at Sialkot. Here are bred horses resembling the Arab, some of which fetch prices up to one thousand rupees.

his tomb.

Manufac. tures

v. SIND SAGAR Doab : Rock salt

In the *doab* of *Sindh Sagar* (between the Jhilum and the Indus), rock salt is obtained near Shamsabad* [49. *a*.] at the foot of the mountain. The salineness and delicate taste of this salt are renowned as surpassing those of the salts of [other places on] the surface of the earth. It is called the *Sindh* salt, † *i. e.*, the salt produced in the *doab* of the Sindh river. By the power of God, the Creator of rare things, the whole mountain has been formed of salt, though its length exceeds a hundred *kos*. In the *Zafarnama* and the *Akbarnama* it is called "the mountain of Judha." Judha was the chief of the tribe of Janjuah,‡ under whose name the hill is famous and whose descendants still hold sway over the *parganas* of Kirjhak, Pandna, Makhiala,§ and others, which are situated at the skirts of the hills. In short, men called *Aldsha-kash* are engaged in extracting the salt. Digging a mine of more than 200 or 300

vast deposits

how salt is extracted

* It seems to have been situated near Pind Dadan Khan. There is a *Shamsabad* 10 m. S. E. E. of Atak, but it could not have been meant by our author.

† Sanskrit *saindhava lavana*, 'salt of the sea,' the meaning of *Sindhu* being 'sea.'

‡ A pure Rajput tribe, mentioned by Hunter (vii. 168.)

§ *Kirjhak* (or Girjak) and *Makhialah* are mentioned in *Ain.* (ii. 324) *Pandna* cannot be traced.

yards deep in the hill side, each man, naked from head to foot, with torch in hand and pick-axe on shoulder, goes into the dark mine, digs out lumps of salt three *maunds* in weight, and comes out carrying them on the back. They get wages from the superintendents of this work. As they are well accustomed to this work, they do not feel any fear or bewilderment in going into the darkness, digging salt, and bringing it out of the mine. By the grace of God, inside the mines it is not hot in summer nor cold in winter, but temperate like spring in all seasons. Although rock salt is got from many places, yet *Khuhra* and *Keohra** are two large mines near Shamsabad, from which several *lacs* of *maunds* of salt come out every year. The Imperial government gets from them a royalty amounting to the [total] revenue of other places. Many skilled artisans make trays, dishes, dish-covers, and lamps of salt.

the best mines

art ware of salt.

Near it is situated a quarry of sweet lime which is used in whitewashing the inside of the houses of wealthy men. Of this stone also they make dishes, cups, and other things.

Sweet lime

Near it, within the territory of Makhialah is *Kota Chhina*,† a lake, the depth of which no man knows. [49. *b*.] It is regarded as an ancient place of worship. On holy days, such as the time of the entrance of the Sun into the Sign of Aries, and such others, groups of Hindus assemble here for bathing. It is their belief that the Earth has two eyes,—the right eye is the lake of Pushkar near Ajmir and the left eye is this lake.

Sacred lake

* Given in Atlas (Sheet 15.) *Keora*, 32°39 N. 73°4 E., *Khoora* 4 m. N. E. of Keora. "The Mayo mines in the neighbourhood of the village of Kheura, a few miles N. E. of Pind Dadan Khan, in Jhelam Dist." (*I. G.* xii. 171.)

† Not identified. The only lakes here are the *Kallar Kahar* and the *Sun*|*Sukesur Kahar*.

Balnath Tilla

On the summit of this mountain, *7 kos* from the fort of Rohtas is a cave of austerities, *Balnath Jogi.* It is [also] called *Tilla,** and is situated four *kos* high (?) On appointed days, especially on the *Shiva-ratri* (which is a day sacred to Mahadev), at the end of winter, many men and crowds of *Yogis* assemble here and perform worship.

resort of ascetics.

Rivers of Panjab :

A few of the famous places of the five *doabs* have been here set down. It is now necessary to write a true account of the six rivers of this province which enclose the five *doabs.* The first river, the SUTLEJ, issues from the mountain of Bhu Tibbat and passes by the territories of Kullu and Bashahr.† Then it travels among the mountains, and reaching the limits of Kahlur encloses that country on three sides. The King of Kahlur by reason of the strength afforded by this river, the inaccessibility of the hills, and the security of his residence,—the city of Bilaspur is his seat of government,—swerves from [obedience to] the Imperial officers. This river, after issuing from the hills, parts into two branches, passes by the fort of Mako-wal‡

1. SUTLEJ :

its course in the hills

and plain

* Tilla, the sanitarium of the Jhelam Dist., 3242 ft. high, according to Hunter, (but 3215 ft. acc. to Atlas, sheet 29, where it is spelt *Jogi-tila,*) 32·51 N. 73·30 E.

† *Kullu,* the territory round Sultanpur, 32·5 N. 77·2 E. (Letts' Sheet 11.) *Bashahr,* a hill State, lying N. E. E. of Simla (*I. G.* ii. 182) *Kahlur,* a hill State N. W. of Simla. (vii. 293.)

‡ *Makowal,* 20 m. W. of Bilaspur city. *Kiratpur,* 'a place bestowed upon Hurgovind by the hill chief of Kuhloor.' (Cunningham's *Sikhs,* 56.) *Rupar* is in Umbala District ; *Machhiwara* is midway between Rupar and Ludhiana ; *Talwun* (Atlas, Sheet 30), 23 m. S. of Jullundur city ; *Tulwarrah* is 4 m. W. of Aliwal, on the south bank of the Sutlej. *Bauh* is not found in Atlas, though Jarrett speaks of a *Baupur. Mandi* and *Suket* are given in Letts' Sheet 11. *Hindun* is probably a mistake for *Nandaon,* 16 m. S. of Kangra fort.

(which was the abode of Guru Govind Rai) and Kiratpur (in which lived Gurus Har Govind and Har Rai), and then forms one stream again on arriving near the village of Rupar. Thence passing by the village of Machhiwara, it reaches the neighbourhood of Ludhiana. In this *mahal* is a royal road. From this place it passes by the villages of Talun and Tharah, and unites with the river Biah near the *mauza* of Bauh, a dependency of the *pargana* of Haibatpur Patti. The tract between these two rivers is called the *doab* of *Beth Jalandar* and [also] *Siharwal.* unites with the Bias.

2. BIAS : its course in the hills

The second river, BIAH (Bias), also rises in the hilly country of Bhu Tibbat, from a lake. Passing by the town of Kullu, it arrives at the city af Mandi. [50. *a*.] Then, flowing through the territories of Suket, Sachchan, and Machalmuri, it reaches the foot of the town of Hindun,—the residence of the Commandant of the hill country. Thence it passes by the limits of Dhual, Sabnah, and Gualiar. Though Gualiar is a small country, yet its Raja has often defied the Imperial officers by reason of the strength of the river and the inaccessibility of the hill. Then this river passes by the villages of Purnur * and descends from the hills. After reaching the plains and passing by the fort of Kanuahan, (which is one of the Emperor's appointed places of hunting), and the village of Rahila, it reaches the foot of the city of Govind-wal. Here is a royal road. After leaving this place, it unites with the river Sutlej near the *mauza* of Bauh. The tract between these two rivers is called the *Beth* of Jalandhar. [The united stream of] both these rivers passes by the towns of Firuzpur and Mamdot. Thence reaching the territory

and plain

junction with the Sutlej

* A mistake for *Nurpur*, which is midway between Chamba and Batala *Kanhwan*, 10 m. S. of Gurdaspur town. (Atlas. Sheet 30) *Govindwal*, 14 m. S. W. W. of Kapurthala.]

of the *mahals* of the *Sarkar* of Dipalpur,* it widens in the rainy season. Leaving Dipalpur it bifurcates: one branch flowing southwards gets the name of Sutlej, the other flowing northwards by way of Qabwal and Kata-i-Baldi gets the name of Biah. Both these streams, after a few leagues, unite again. Passing by the limits of Fatehpur, Khiror,† and other places, the river reaches the territory of Khalu Ketarah and gets the merges in the Indus. name of *Kanarah*,‡ [but] in the territory of the Baluchis it gets the name of Sindh river.

3. RAVI: The third is the river RAVI. Between the Biah and this river lies the famous *doab* of Bari and Manjhah. The Ravi issues from the mountain of Man Mahes, a its upper course dependency of the country of Chamba, which is a place sacred to Mahadev and has the snow and climate of Kashmir and Kabul, and produces many sweet and delicious fruits. The kings of this place breathe the spirit of independence on account of the extent of their country, its large population, the inaccessibility of the hills, and the strength of their fastnesses, as this river forms a barrier to the Imperial army. After coming out of [50. *b*.] Chamba and flowing to the boundaries of the land of Besuhli, § it reaches the foot of the town of four canals issuing from it. Shahpur, a dependency of Nurpur. Near Shahpur‖ have been taken out of this river a royal canal which goes to the garden of Shalamar in Lahor, a second canal which

* 30°40 N. 73°43 E. (*I. G.* iv. 303).

† Both given in Letts' Sheet 12, N. E. of Bahawalpur.

‡ Atlas (Sheet 30) gives 2 canals as branching off from the Sutlej and named Kutora and Kanwah. Our text seems to be wrong here.

§ 20 m. W. of Chamba (Letts' Sheet 11).

‖ 32°23 N. 75°44 E. (Atlas, Sheet 29), north of Pathankot. The main Bari Doab canal issues from *Madhupur*, 7 m. N. W. of Pathankot. Ali Mardan Khan's canal commenced a little below this point (*I. G.* ii. 153).

goes to the *pargana* of Pathan [-Kot], a third [canal which goes] to the *pargana* of Batala, and a fourth [canal which goes] to the *pargana* of Biar (?) Patti Haibatpur.* These canals do good to the crops of the *mahals*. After leaving this place and flowing by the limits of the *parganas* of Pathan [-Kot], Katuhah, Kalanor, Batala, Pursarwar, Eminabad, and other *mahals*, this river increases the splendour of the capital Lahor. [It acts as] a highway at the feet of the Imperial buildings. After this place, passing by the limits of Sindhuan, Faridabad, Degh-Ravi, and Multha, it unites with the rivers Chenab and Bihat (Jhilum), which flow together, near Sarai Sindhu, † 20 *kos* from Multan, and gets the name of Chenab.

its lower course

unites with the Chenab.

4. CHENAB

The fourth river is the CHENAB. The region between the Ravi and this river is famous under the name of *Rechnau doab*. In Hindu books the Chenab is written as the Chandrabhaga. It is believed to have come out of the country of Chin. When [the Chenab ?] after passing by the limits of the land of Chamba reaches Kishtwar‡, (the saffron of which place is famous), the river Chandrabhaga, having come from the direction of Thibet, joins [it] and gets the name of Chandrabhaga§. From this place, travelling by way of Hasial and Bahwal, at the feet of the towns of Ambara and Aknoor‖, it descends

its upper course

* The Sobraon branch of the Bari Doab canal goes to Patti. *Biar* is inexplicable to me.

† *Sindhuan*, probably Syadwala, 4 m. S. W. of Faridabad. *Faridabad*, 31·8 N. 73·37 E. *Deg-Ravi*, in Montgomery District. Letts' Sheet 12 has *Sarai Sidhu*, 42 m. N.N.E. of Multan.

‡. 33·14 N. 75·45 E. (Letts' Sheet 11).

§ The *Ain* (ii. 310) has "From the summit of Kishtwarah issue two sweet water streams, the one called *Chandar* and the other *Bhaga*, which unite near Kishtwar."

‖. *Aknoor*, 32·42 N. 74·48 E. *Ambarah* is 2 m. N. of it. *Tarakota*, given as *Trekotta Temple*, 3·3 N. 75 E. (Atlas, Sheet 29).

14

from the hills with a hundred lustres. Passing near the hill of Tarakota, (a dependency of Jummun,) which is a famous place sacred to Bhawani, at the feet of Ambara and Aknoor [it] emerges from the hills with a hundred lustres * In this place is [seen] a wonderful spectacle and [it is] a theatre of strange things. Its water in perfect deliciousness equals the *elixir vitæ*, and this is due to the reason that there is a similarity of spelling between *Ab-i-Chenab* (the water of the Chenab) and *Ab-i-haiat* (the water of life). After leaving this place it flows

and lower course

in 18 streams [**51**. *a*.] On reaching the foot of the city of Bahlulpur, at a distance of 12 *kos*, it again becomes one stream. Passing by the villages of the *pargana* of Sialkot and the foot of the town of Sodhra,† it arrives at Wazirabad. Merchants bring *sal* and the famous teak wood by the river highway from the hilly country of Chamba and elsewhere to Wazirabad, and make profit. Having built rafts with the wood, they carry them for sale along this river to Bhakkar and Thatha. At Wazirabad there is a highway. Then it flows by the feet of the towns of Jakubar [Chuk Bhuttee ?], Diudhath, Bhuna, Mizl, and Hazara.‡ Four *kos* from Hazara, on the bank of the river, is situated the tomb of Dhundu *Ranjha*, who was famous for his love of the lady *Hir* ; the people of the Panjab have made rare pictures and wonderful verses about the love-madness of this pair, and sing heart-ravishing ditties and songs. After leaving this place, it passes between two hillocks, near the old town of Jind-niwat (?), and forms a

* The text is evidently corrupt here.

† *Behlolpoor*, 32°41 N. 71°30 E. *Sodhra*. 4 m. N.E. of Wazirabad.

‡ *Bhowana*, 25 m. N N.E. of Jhang. *Huzara*, 32°8 N. 73°18 E. in Shahpur District (Atlas, Sheet 30). The others cannot be identified.

wonderful spectacle. In this town is the tomb of Shah Burhan, who was famed as a saint, and in whom many people [still] believe. After passing by this place and uniting with the river Bihat [at Timmu] near the town of Jhang-sialan,* (the residence of Hir, who became famous for the love of Ranjha), it proceeds onwards. junction with the Jhilum.

The fifth river is the BIHAT (*Jhilum*). The *doab* between the Chenab and this river is known as the *Chunhat*. The Bihat issues from a lake [*Ver*] in the hills and having reached the city of Kashmir (*i.e.*, Srinagar) passes through the bazar and streets. Bridges have been built at various places in the town. Many heart-attractive gardens, delightful buildings, charming promenades, and unparalleled houses are situated on its banks. After leaving Kashmir, it is joined by the river *Kishengang*† within the limits of Pakli. Thence it reaches the foot of the town of Dangali, the seat of government of the chief of the Ghakkars. Afterwards, passing by Mirpur and other places in the Ghakkar territory, it comes below the city of Jhilum,—in which *mahal* there is a highway,—and gets the name of Jhilum river. Thence, flowing by‡ Girjhak, Zhandna, Shamsabad, Bhera, Khushab, and Khurd-khana, it unites with the waters of the Chenab [at Timmu] near the town of Jhang-sialan, and gets the name of Chenab.

5. JHILUM

its source

junction with the Kishan Ganga

and with the Chenab

* *Jhang* was founded by Mal Khan, a *Sial* chieftain, in 1642, and its principal inhabitants are Sials (hence the name), and Khatris. (*I. G.* vii. 213).

† "At Muzaffarabad, just before entering British territory, the Jhilum receives the Kishan Ganga, which rises in Baltistan or Little Tibet." (*I. G.* vii. 165). *Dangali*, a Ghakkar stronghold, near Hilan or Hil, a ferry on the Jhilum. (*Ain.* i. 457 *n.*)

‡ *Mirpur*, 33·10 N. 73·55E. *Girjhak*, the Hindu name for Jalalpur (acc. to Cunningham.) *Bhera*, on the left bank of the Jhilum, 10 m. S. W. of Pind Dadan Khan. *Khushab*, 32·16 N. 72·14 E. The others cannot be traced.

6. INDUS: The sixth river is the SIND. [51. *b*.] Between the Bihat and this river lie the land of *Ponhuhar** and the *Sind Sagar doab*. This stream intervenes between Hindustan, Kabulistan, and Zabulistan (Ghaznin).

its course in the hills Its source is not known, but according to travellers it issues from the country of the Qalmuqs. After passing by the limits of Kashghar, Tibbat, and Kafiristan, and the countries of Kashmir, Pakli, and Dantur,† it reaches the land of the Yusufzais.

at Attock At the foot of Atak Banaras fort, the river *Nilab* (the Kabul) having come from the direction of Kabul, mixes with some other streams.

violent current As the river has little breadth here, it flows narrow and swift with great violence, so that the eyes of beholders cannot rest firmly on it and the sight of onlookers grows dim. Its dashing waves turn the bile of fish into water, and break into fragments the rocks and black boulders upon which they beat In this *mahal* is a highway. The rapidity of the current makes boats travel quickly and arrive at the opposite bank in the twinkling of an eye.

a black rock fatal to boats On the western bank of this river is a black rock which is called *Jalali*.‡ Boats have often sunk by striking upon this fatal rock and the passengers have been drowned in the river of non-existence. Hence it is always dreaded by boats. The common people say that on the top of this rock is a great tomb which bears the the name of Jalali; but the [true] reason of its being so

* According to Blochmann (*Ain*. i. 487 n) this is a mistake for *Pothwar*, the country between the Jhilum and the Sohan, from Margalah to Hatia.

† Dhantawar, a district near the Kashmir frontier, close to Naushahrah. (Cunningham's *Anc. Geo.* 131.)

‡ "Below their junction, a dangerous whirlpool eddies between two jutting precipices of black slate, known as *Kamalia* and *Jalalia*, from the names of two famous Roshnai heretics, who were flung from their summits during the reign of Akbar." (*I. G.* i. 381.)

named is reported to be the following:—In the reign of the Emperor Akbar, an Afghan named Jalali* became notorious for wrong-doing, rebellion, and highway robbery. The Emperor once wished to cross this river for the purpose of travelling to and hunting in Kabul. All of a sudden his treasure-boat struck against the rock and went down, and the Emperor remarked, "This rock has proved a Jalali." As a king's word becomes the king of words, thenceforth the rock got the name of *Jalali*. Near it is a stone house of the Raja of Hudi,† who held sway over this country in former times.

named Jalali by Akbar

On the east bank of the river is situated the fort of Atak. [52. *a.*] There is no other road for the coming and going of travellers than [that through] the fort. There are pleasant houses overlooking the river; especially, the houses of the governors on the river-side wall of the fort are extremely delightful. It is a city of temperate climate, midway between Hindustan and Kabulistan, so that on this bank the manners, customs and language are Indian, while on the other bank are the houses of the Afghans and Afghan customs and speech.

Attock fort,

the ethnic frontier of India.

In short, this river, after leaving this place and passing by the hills of Afghanistan, Khatak (Kohat?), &c., reaches the plains at Sanail‡ within the limits of

* "A Hindustani soldier had come among the Afghans, and set up an heretical sect. He gave himself the title of *Pir Roshanai.* His son *Jalala*...raised disturbances, shut up the roads between Hindustan and Kabul." (Elliot, v. 450.)

† "Babar attacked the Ghakkar capital, Pharwala. It was defended with great bravery by its chief *Hati* Khan" (*I. G.* xii. 24.) "*Hatia*, which was built by a Gakkhar of the name of Hathi" (*Ain.* i. 486 *n.*)

‡ Can it be *Sanawan*, the northern *tahsil* of Muzaffargarh District? (*I. G.* xii. 193)

The Indus is joined by the other 5 rivers.

Afghanistan. Thence it passes on to the territories of Baluchistan and Multan. The five rivers of the Panjab, which have been described above, all come out of the northern mountains, and on the other side of Multan within the limits of Baluchistan, they unite with this river one after another. All of them then get the name of Sindh and proceed to the swelling ocean.

Bhakkar

Thatha.

Port of Lahori.

Then, at the foot of the fort of Bhakkar, it branches off into two and surrounds the fort. This cause has led to the fort being famous for strength and difficulty of conquest. Thence it goes to the *mahal* of Thatha by way of the land of Sewistan Thirty *kos* from the city of Thatha it ends in the ocean near the famous port of Lahori.

Climate of Panjab

crops

Irrigation by water-wheels.

Washing gold.

In short, the province of Lahor has a pleasant climate and matchless beauty. Summer is very hot and winter colder in comparison with Hindustan. Its melon and vine are like those of Persia and Turkestan; its mango resembles that of Hindustan; its rice is better than that of Bengal, and its sugar-cane sweeter than that of the Deccan. Cultivation depends upon irrigation from wells; old mechanics make water-wheels which require 360 large and small pieces of wood and more than 100 small pots. So skilful is their mechanism that a pair of oxen can turn such a wheel, at every revolution of which many hundred (?) maunds of water come out of the well in the pots and benefit cultivation. The autumn crops and cheapness of grains depend upon rain. In some places, especially in the rivers Biah and Bihat, they obtain gold by sand-washing. In some places in the northern mountains there are mines of gold, copper, brass, and iron, [52. *b*] which yield profit to the finders and revenue to the Imperial government.

Extent

The length of this province from the Sutlej to the

river Sindh is 180 *kos*, its breadth from Bhatar to Chaua Kandi 87 *kos*.* Eastwards lies Sirhind, westwards Multan, northwards Kashmir, southwards Dipalpur. It has five *Sarkars* or *doabs* comprising 316 mahals, and a revenue of 89 *kror*, 33 *lac*, and 80 thousand *dam*† (Rs. 22,334,500.) Revenue.

XVII. KASHMIR.

The Paradise-resembling Province of Kashmir.

SRINAGAR

The capital of this country is SRINAGAR; it has been inhabited for a long time, and its habitations extend over four leagues. The rivers *Bihat* (Jhilum), *Mar*, and *Lachmah*‡ pass through it. All classes of artisans, skilled mechanics, experts of every trade and profession and learned and accomplished men live in it. Woollen stuffs, especially *shals* are well made and sent to the seven climes [of the world] by way of present. Soft and beautiful broad-cloths of wool are manufactured. *Pattu* (woollen) sheets in two pieces are also well woven. It is not their custom to hold bazars; they transact buying and selling in their own houses. Woollen manufactures

---

* The *Ain* (ii. 310) has 'from *Bhimbar* to Chaukhandi, one of the dependencies of Satgarah.' Satgarah is 13 m E. of Gugaira on the Ravi.

† Under Akbar the province had 232 *mahals*, and a revenue of Rs. 13,986,460-9-2. (Jarrett has dropped the zero.) *Ain*. ii. 315.

‡ The *Mar* is the *Nalli Mar* which flows into the Sind near Shadipur, connecting the *Auchar* with the *Dal*. (*Ain*. ii. 355*n*.) "The canal now known as *Lacham Kul* brings the waters of the Sind River *via* Amburher to the northern suburbs of Srinagar, and empties itself into the *Mar* canal near the bridge called Kadi Kadal." (Stein, p. 150.)

wooden houses

All the houses are built of wood, with four storeys or more. On the ground floor are kept the animals and furniture; the second storey is the residence; the third and fourth are for keeping articles. On account of the abundance of wood and the frequency of earthquakes, they do not make the roof with stone or brick. It is not their custom to build walls [of brick or stone] The whole house is built with wood. On the roof tulips are planted and form a nice spectacle in spring. There are no snakes, scorpions, and other oppressors of life in this town. Bugs, lice, gnats, and flies abound. Near the city is a very big lake, some leagues in length, called the *Dal*. It remains full of delicious and tasteful water all the year round. The water does not get a bad smell even after many days. One side of it adjoins the *pargana* of *Phak*.* In travelling in the hilly part, men carry big loads on their backs, but boats are mainly used in transporting heavy articles. Hence, boatmen and carpenters drive a roaring trade.

earthquakes

Fauna

Lake *Dal*.

Many Brahmans live here. Though the country has a language of its own [53. *a*], yet learned works are written in the Sanskrit language and Hindi characters. They generally write on the bark or leaf of a tree† that is peculiar to this country; all old books are written on it. The ink made is so excellent that it cannot be washed away.

Writing on barks

Though the Hindus regard the whole of this country as sacred and narrate wonderful legends [about its sanctity], yet some certain places are described as more

Holy places :

* It comprises the tract lying between the east shore of the Anchiar, the range towards the Sind Valley and the hills which enclose the Dal on the east and south." (Stein, p. 157.)

† The *Ain* names it *Tuz*, which Dr. King identifies with the birch *Betula Bhojpattra*. (*Ain*. ii. 351 *n*.)

sacred [than the rest.] Near *Sendha Brari** is a spring which remains dry for 6 months. On a fixed day, peasants come to the place for worshipping and slaughter sheep and goats as sacrifices. Through the power of God, water gushes out and irrigates the crops of all the villages. When [the water] inclines to excess, they perform worship in the aforesaid manner and the water decreases. Near it is a fountain named *Kukar Nag*, the water of which is very light, cool, and tasteful. If a hungry man drinks it he is satiated, while in the case of a satiated man it increases the appetite. *Samdhya* spring *Kukar Nag*

In the village of *Pampur*,† there are 12,000 *bighas* of SAFFRON-land, which ravish the sight even of fastidious observers. The time for its cultivation is the end of March and the whole of April. The soil is ploughed and softened ; and then with shovels they make small perterres fit for cultivation. The bulbs of saffron are next placed in the soil. In one month they turn green (*i.e.*, send forth sprouts) and at the end of the *Ilahi* month of September, are fully grown. They do Saffron cultivation : its process

* The *Ain* (ii. 3,6) has "First in one corner of it is a cavity like a mortar called *Sendh brari* : when this becomes full, &c." "*Bring* (pargana) contains one of the holiest of Kasmir Tirthas in the sacred spring of the goddess SAMDHYA, the modern *Sundabrar*. It is situated south of the village of Devalgom, circ. 75.22 long. 33.32 lat. During uncertain periods in the early summer it flows intermittently, three times in the day and three times in the night. Owing to the analogy thus presented to the three-fold recitation of the Gayatri (*Samdhya*), it is held sacred to the goddess Samdhya...... The *Kukar Nag* lies about a mile above Bidar. It is a spring of very great volume, referred to as Kukkutesvara" (Stein, p. 181.). It is 5 m. N.E.E., and *Sundabrar*, 4 m. E. of Vernag (Shahabad) in Stein's *Map*.

† 74.59 E. 34.1 N. Described in Vigne's *Kashmir*, ii 31. Stein (p. 122) has "Its cultivation has apparently from an early time specially flourished about Padmapura, the present Pampar, where the Udar lands are still chiefly utilized for it."

not grow taller than a span. The stalk is of a white colour. When it grows equal to a finger*, it begins to flower ; the flowers cluster one to another up to 8 flowers. And [it puts forth] six lily-like petals. In most of them six filaments,—three yellow and three red,—are found. The term saffron denotes the three latter. When the flowering is over, the stem turns green. One planting yields flowers for six years. In the first year they are few ; in the second ten to thirty [times the first year's crop] is produced ; in the third year the crop reaches its maximum ; and so on for six years. [Then] the bulbs are dug out. If, however, they are kept in the same place, they deteriorate. Hence† they are taken out and planted elsewhere.

Sacred spring

In the village of *Zewan*‡ are a spring and a reservoir, considered sacred [53 *b*.] It is believed that the seeds of saffron originate in this spring. At the time when cultivation is begun they perform worship at this spring and make offerings of cow and goat milk. If the offering sinks into the water, it is held to be a good omen and the saffron grows to their heart's desire. But if it floats on the water, it is a bad omen.

In the midst of Tibbat§ is a big cave and within it

* A-text has dropped the word 'finger.' (*Ain.* ii. 357.)

† A-text reads *lekan.* The *Ain* (ii. 358) has 'but if taken up, they may be profitably transplanted.'

‡ *Ibid.* There is a *Zebanwan* peak, 8813 ft. high, 4 m. S. E. Srinagar in Stein's *Map.*

§ The *Ain* has 'Between Great Tibet and the above-mentioned *parganah* is a cave.' Amarnath is situated 75'33 E. 34'13 N. (Stein's *Map.*) See Vigne, ii. 8. Stein (p. 94) writes "It is now the most popular of Kashmirian pilgrimage-places ; ...... in the month of Sravana attracts many thousands of pilgrims from all parts of India. Their goal is a cave formed by a huge fissure on the south side of a snowy peak, 17300 ft. high. In this cave there is a large block of transparent ice formed by the freezing of the water which

Amarnath cave and idol.

is an idol of ice named AMARNATH. It is a very great shrine. When the Moon comes out of [her] throne of rays, there is manifested in the cave a bubble of ice ; and it increases daily up to the 15th day, when it measures ten* Imperial yards. When the Moon begins to wane, this figure also decreases, and at the end of the [lunar] month, no trace of it remains. This is known to be the figure of Mahadeva, and is considered as an instrument of the success of undertakings.

Shakar Nag spring

Shakar Nag† is a fountain which remains dry all the year. In the month of which the 9th day falls on Friday, water wells up and flows from morn to eve. Many people assemble [here on pilgrimage.]

Banahal temple : miracle

Banihal‡ has a temple sacred to Durga. Whosoever wishes to learn the future of himself or of his enemy, fills two pots of rice,—one in his own name and the other in that of his enemy—and the two are left in the temple and its doors are closed. On another day, after performing worship he inquires about the future. Of the two persons, his undertakings are sure to succeed whose pot is found to be filled with roses and saffron ; but that person's affairs are ruined whose pot is found to be full of ashes and rubbish. A greater wonder is that in the case of a quarrel in which the right is hard to ascertain, the two disputants are sent to this temple

another miracle

oozes from the rock. It is worshipped as a self-created (*svayambhu*) Linga, and is considered the embodiment of Siva."

* The *Ain* (ii. 360) has 'two yards of the measure of the right determined by His Majesty.'

† *Ibid*, 361. Not found in Stein's *Map*, which, are ruined whose the *Shesha Nag Peaks*, 75·35 E. 34·3 N. (Stein, p. 71).

‡ The Banahal Pass is situated 75·19 E. 33·31 ashes and rubbish "The Banahal Pass, 9200 feet above the sea, is worshipped as oozes from the Pir Pantsal Range on which communication inquires about stopped by snowfall." (Stein, p. 71).

with two fowls or two goats ; the two animals are administered poison, and the men rub their hands on them. He who has justice on his side sees his poisoned animal reviving, while the other dies.

Deosar tank

miracle

Deosar * is a tank twenty yards square, from the interior of which water gushes out. Whosoever seeks information about the prosperity of the year and his good or bad prospects, fills an earthen pot with rice, writes his name on its side and having closed its mouth throws it into the water. After a time the pot comes up to the surface of the water. It is then opened ; if the rice is found hot and fragrant [**54**. *a*], the year becomes prosperous or his condition happy ; but if mud earth and rubbish cover it, then his condition becomes adverse.

Kothar fountain

At *Kothar* † is a fountain which remains dry for 11 years ; when Jupiter enters Leo, it flows on Thursday. In the course of the week it becomes dry ; but the next Thursday it is filled [with water.] And this continues for a year.

Heronry

At the village of *Matalhana*‡ is a forest in which herons perch, and pen-quills are collected. The food of these birds is assigned [by the State.]

---

*. "In *Devsar* in the village of Balau is a pool called Balau Nag." (*Ain.* ii. 362.) "The Pargana of *Divasar* adjoins Shahabad-Ver on the west." (Stein, p. 183.)

† *Ain.* ii. 362. *Kothair*, 7 m. S. E. of Islamabad. (Stein's *Map.*) "The Tirtha of KAPATESVARA, close to the village of *Kother.* The name of the latter is undoubtedly a derivative of *Kapatesvara.* The place of pilgrimage is the sacred spring of *Papasudana* ('sin-removing'). In it Siva is believed to have shown himself in the disguise (*kapata*) of pieces of wood floating on the water......The sacred spring rises in a large circular tank, enclosed by an ancient stone-wall with steps leading into the water." (Stein, p 179).

‡ Not given in Map. See *Ain.* ii. 362 *n.*

At *Nagam* * is spring named NILA NAG ; its basin is 40 bighas and the water is of the purest blue colour, It is regarded as a place of worship ; and many people throw away the baggage of their lives into fire (*ie*, burn themselves alive) around it. It is marvellous how they take omens from it : they quarter a walnut and throw it into the water ; if an odd [number of quarters] floats they consider it as an augury of good ; if not, it is considered an evil omen. In ancient times a book † named the *Nilmata* [*Purana*] came out of the spring. The distinctive features of Kashmir and the descriptions of its temples are written in detail in it. The story goes that there is a populous town with lofty buildings under the water.‡ In the reign of Badu

***Nila Nag* spring**

its *Purana*

submerged city

* "About 5 miles south of Arigom we find a small lake known as Nilanag. Abul Fazl, by some curious misapprehension transfers to it the legends of the famous Nilanaga (at Vernag) He adds to them what appears like a garbled version of the story of the city submerged in the Volur lake." (Stein, p. 190). There are two *Nagams* ; one, 75'18 E. 33'32 N., in Shahabad District, only 5 miles N. N. E. of the greater *Nilanag* ; the other 74'45 E. 33 56 N., a village in Nagam District, near the lesser *Nilanag*. If we take the former, Abul Fazl is quite correct, and one of Dr. Stein's two strictures is misapplied.

† "The oldest extant text which deals in detail with Kasmirian Tirthas is the *Nilamata-purana*. This work claims to give the sacred legends regarding the origin of the country and the special ordinances which Nila, the lord of Kasmir Nagas, had revealed for the worship and rites to be observed in it. To use Prof. Buhler's words—"a real mine of information, regarding the sacred places of Kasmir and their legends." The *Nilmata* in its present form could not be older than the 6th or 7th century of our era." (Stein, pp. 46,47.)

‡ This legend is related about the Volur lake (Sanskrit, *Maha-padma*.) "The Muni Durvasas, not receiving hospitable reception in this town [Chandrapur], cursed it and foretold its destruction by water...The Mahapadma Naga...converted the city into a lake, hence-forth his and his family's dwelling place." (Stein, p. 115).

Shah, * a Brahman [used to go] under the ground and come out after two or three days, bringing rare presents and giving information [about what he had seen below.]

Holy waters

In this neighbourhood, two streams flow apart side by side; one of them is very cold, and the other very hot. It is considered a sacred place The bones of the tenement of flesh are here reduced to ashes. In the midst of the hills is a large tank, into which the bones and ashes of the dead are thrown,—this being considered a means of their translation to the neighbourhood of God. If the meat of any animal is thrown into the water, then it rains and snows heavily.

Spring curing leprosy.

Bhutiser temple

In the village of *Birua* † is a fountain in which white lepers bathe on Sunday morning and regain their health. *Bhutiser* ‡ is a place secred to Mahadeva. If any body goes to it on pilgrimage the sound of [musical] instruments of worship reaches his ears, but nobody knows whence it comes.

Wular lake

Near it and adjoining Lesser Thibet is a big lake named *Wular*, 28 *kos* in circumference. The river [**54**. *b*.] Bihat falls into it and disappears [in it for] a part [of its course.] Near *Kargaon* § is a pass named *Soyam*. Here for one month, while Jupiter is in Leo,

Soyam volcanic phenomenon

Kashmir from 1422 to 1472 A. D.

† Modern *Biru* (=Bahu-rupa), 74°39 E. 34°1 N. (Stein, p. 192.)

‡ *Buthiser*, 75°1 E. 34°20 N. "A series of interesting temple ruins marks the importance of this Tirtha." (Stein, p. 92)

§ Not found in Map. *Soyam* is misspelt *Evatam* in A-text. It is situated 74°10 E. 34°24 N. Stein, (p. 204) writes, "The sacred site of SVAYAMBHU (the 'Self-created Fire'), known to the villagers as *Suyam*. ...In certain years steam has been known to issue from the fissures. The ground then becomes sufficiently hot to boil the Sraddha offerings of the pilgrims who at such times flock to the site in great numbers. The phenomenon...was last observed in 1876."

a tract of land, ten chains in area, becomes so hot that the trees burn Kettles filled [with raw articles of food] are placed on the ground and they are cooked [by the heat.] Near it is a populous village.

Gold dust from rivers

[From] *Kamraj** is a defile ; on one side it adjoins Kashghar ; on the west lies Pakli. In the fords of the river the people spread the bark of the *Bar* tree †, around which they place stones, so that the current may not sweep it away, After two or three days it is taken out, left in the Sun, and when dry shaken, yielding gold up to three *tolas*. It is met by a second pass, named *Gilgit* ‡, which also adjoins Kashghar. Here gold is got by dust-washing

Two days' journey from *Hayahom* § is a river [the

* "A part of the plains of Kashmir, which lies...to the north of...the Wulur lake and the Jylum in its course thence to Baramula,...is known by the name of *Kamraj*" (Vigne, ii. 157.) "The Valley of Kasmir has from early times been divided into two great parts, known by their modern names as *Kamraz* (Sanskrit, *Kramarajya*) and *Maraz* (Sanskrit *Madavarajya*.) The boundary was indicated by a line drawn through the capital. The term Kamraz has occasionally been used also in a more restricted sense for the designation of the [the several small] Parganas to the west and north-west of the Volur lake, grouped together in one Pargana for administrative purposes." (Stein, p. 133.)

† "The skins of long-haired *goats* are spread" (*Ain*. ii. 365) But the A-text has *post-i-darakht-i-bar*.

‡ Mis-spelt *Galgasht* in A-text.

§ The *Ain* (ii. 365) wrongly names it *Haehamun* and the river *Padmati*. Stein writes, "*Hayahom* (ancient designation *Hayasrama*)...There is a route leading past it to Sardi. ...The temple of the goddess Sarada, among the foremost Tirthas of Kasmir,...was well known even far beyond the frontiers of Kasmir. Situated circ. 74 15 E. 34'43 N. on the right bank of the Kisanganga. An ancient temple is still extant at the site. Immediately in front of it the sacred stream of the Madhumati falls into the Kisanganga." (p. 206, 207.) Hayahom is given in Stein's Map, 74'18 E. 34'34 N.

Madhumati], which comes out of the Dardu country. Gold is found here. On its bank is a stone temple named *Sarada*, sacred to Durga and held in great reverence. On every eighth night of the waxing moon,* [a shaking takes place here]

Sarada temple

PAKLI

The *Sarkar* of *Pakli*† is included in this province. It is 35 *kos* long and 25 *kos* broad. The snow falls here as in Turan, and the winter is very rigorous, the rainy season is like that of Hindustan. Three rivers confer plenty on it : the *Kishan-Gang*, the *Bihat* Jhilum), and the *Sind*. The dialect of this country resembles that of Kashmir and not of Hindustan or Zabulistan. Gram and barley grow very well Apricot, peach, and walnut here grow wild, as also the fruits of Kashmir. Game, horses, mules, cows, buffaloes of medium size, goats, and fowl are plentiful.

language

crops

Praise of Kashmir

In short,‡ Kashmir is a heart-attractive kingdom. If we call it a garden of eternal spring or a heaven-founded fortress, it would be only appropriate. If it be called the bower of bliss of jolly spirits or the place of retirement of recluses, it would be quite true. Its water delights the taste; its waterfalls charm the ear; its meadows exhilarate the spirit; its flowers everywhere are fresh and innumerable [55. *a.*] The rose, the tulip, and especially the narcissus, grow wild in abundance. Its Spring and Winter are very wonderful. All fruits, except the *shah-alu* (plum) and the *shah-tut* (mulberry), are abundant. Melons, apples, peaches, apricots, and water-melons are excellent. Grapes are plentiful, but seldom good; they are mostly trained on

flowers

fruits

* The A-text is here defective. The sentence has been completed from the *Ain*.

† West of Muzuffarabad. 73 E. 34·10 N.

‡ Nearly the whole of this florid description is borrowed from the *Ain*. (ii. 348).

mulberry trees. Mulberry is little eaten by men, as its leaves are used in feeding silk-worms. Its seeds are brought chiefly from Gilgit and Lesser Tibbat. The *shali* rice is not of fine quality. Wheat is small in grain, black, and scanty. *Mung** is rarely eaten ; pulse and barley are very scarce.

silk worms

grain

The soil is of two kinds : (1) soft and moist, and (2) hard and black. In all parts the division of crops [between landlord and tenant] is at the ratio of 3 to 9. Assessment of crops at special rates and transaction in gold and silver are not customary. A portion of the *sair jihat* [cess is paid in cash.] Payments in cash and kind are calculated in *Kharwars*.† There is a species of sheep resembling the *Kuhcha* goat ; it is called *Hundu*‡ Its meat is delicious, sweet in taste, and well-flavoured. Strong horses, capable of travelling over hilly ground, are plentiful. Elephants and camels are not found. The cows are black and ugly, but their milk and butter are excellent The staple food is rice, fish, many kinds of liquor, and vegetables. These [last] are dried and preserved. After cooking rice they keep it for the night and eat it the next day. Notwithstanding the large population and the scanty means of subsistence, there are few thieves ; but the beggary and meanness of the inhabitants of this country are proverbial. As for their dress, one coat of leather serves for a year.

Land-tenure :

division of crops

payment in kind.

sheep

horses

cows

Food of the people.

No thieves.

Twenty-six roads lead into this country from Hindustan ; the Bhimbhar § and Pakli roads are the best.

Routes

* A kind of pulse.

† A *kharwar* of grain is 3 maunds and 8 seers of Akbar's standard. (*Ain.* ii. 366)

‡ The *'Ain* has *Handu*, and Jarrett mentions the rejected reading 'like the *Kadi*.'

§ *Bhimber* is a town, 74·5 E. 33. N. "The pass known as *Pir Pantsal*, 11400 feet high. The route which crosses it has

The first is nearest and has many branches. Troops
miracle mostly enter by the Pir Panjal road. If a cow or horse is slaughtered in these mountains, instantly clouds and wind rise, and it snows and rains.

Extent. The length of this country from Qambar* to the river Kishan-Ganga is 120 *kos*; its breadth is 80 *kos*. In the east lie Peristan and the river Chenab; east and south lie Banihal and [the Jummu] mountains; east and north, Greater Tibbat; westwards Pakli and the river Kishan-Ganga; west and south are the Ghakkars; west and north Lesser Tibbat; on all [55. *b.*] the four sides are sky-reaching mountains. It has 46 *mahals*,

Revenue. with a revenue of 12 *kror*, 62 *lac*, and 85 thousand *dam*,† (Rs. 3, 157, 125) and 2, 400 pen-quills.

from early days to the present time been the most frequented line of communication from Kasmir to the central part of the Panjab." (Stein, p. 72.)

* The *Ain* has *Kambar Ver*. Neither name is found in Map. There is, however, a *Phamber*, 75°34—75°46 E. 33°30—33°40 N. *Peristan*, 75°5 E. 33 N. (Vigne's Map).

† Under Akbar the province had 38 *mahals* with a revenue of Rs. 15,52,826. (*Ain*. ii. 368).

CHAHAR GULSHAN.

[The numbers in **antique type** enclosed within square brackets represent the leaves of the manuscript in Khan Bahadur Khuda Bukhsh Khan's Bankipur Oriental Library, while *a* or *b* stands for the front or back page of each leaf. The words enclosed in square brackets are the translator's.]

BOOK FIRST.

NORTHERN INDIA OR HINDUSTAN.

(Abridged Translation.)

I. DELHI.

[**36.** *b.*] **Holy Places** of the Hindus :—KURUKHET, at Thanesar, 60 *kos*. from Delhi, vast gathering of pilgrims at the solar eclipse. HAR MANDIL, in Sambhal, where the last incarnation *Kalki* will be manifested in the house of a Brahman. NANAK MATA, near Sambhal. NAGAMBUDH, where the Fish incarnation appeared. [**37.** *a.*] Badrinath, Badri Kedarnath, Rikhikesh (Hrishikesh), and Bhupa, which is a village on the bank of the Sarsati, 10 *kos* from Thanesar, and contains an ancient shrine. [**37.** *b.*] NARNOL has a deep and sacred well, the water of which flows of itself whenever the *amawav* (conjunction of the moon) happens to be a Friday. PRAVASKUND [a spring] in Islamabad ; on the summit of a hill, adjoining the *pargana* of Sahna, 14 *kos* from Delhi, is a spring from which hot water issues.

Mela : The *mela of the Ganges*. Between Barapula and Tughlaqabad, for a space of 5 or 6 *kos*, a vast gathering of the people of the city takes place, esp. on the 9th day of the waxing moon of the month of Kumar (Aswin). The *pheri* of Mahadeo, on the 14th of Chait. JOGMAYA, an old place of worship, near the *dargah* of Khawajah Qutbu-d-din and the garden of Mihr-parwar Begum ; men make a pilgrimage to it on the 14th day of the moon in the month of Falgun. *Chhri Debi*, where pilgrims assemble in the months of Kumar and Chait. *Mela of the Ganges at Garh Mukhteswar* [**38.** *a.*] which is 40 *kos* from Delhi ; lacs of pilgrims assemble here in the month of Kartik after the Dewali festival, and the *mela* lasts 15 days, during which a space of 10 or 12 *kos* on the bank of the Ganges becomes peopled with men. [Description of the bazar and the merrymaking on land and on rafts floating on the Ganges.] [**38.** *b*] *Mela at Hardwar* in Baisakh : the largest gathering takes place in the year in which Jupiter enters the Sign of Aquarius, and is called the *Kumbh mela.* Lacs of laymen, Faqirs, and Sanyasis assemble here. If any Faqirs of Prag [or Bairagi ?] come here, they are attacked by the Sanyasis. *Parsun*, the abode of the ascetic Parashar, the chief of hermits (*Rishiswar*), 2 *kos* west of Faridabad, near the hill. *Surajkund*, a reservoir of water, near the *serai* of Khawajah Bakhtawar Khan ; pilgrims bathe here on the way to Parsun.

The procession of Ramchandra on the *Dashahara* [**39.** *a.*] *Tej Sanwan* (?) **Chhri** : The *Chhri of Khawajah Muainu-d-din* Chishti, on the 7th Jamadu-s-sani, at the *dargah* of Khawajah Qutbu-d-din. The *Chhri of Zahir Pir*, goes towards Mewat. The *Chhri of Ghazi Mian*. Opposite the ghat of Khizrabad, a pilgrim gathering takes place in the month of Bhadon, in honour of the saint Khizr. In the village of *Bhath*, on the 10th Rabiu-s-sani, on the further side of the Jumna, illumination takes place in honour of Rashid Abdulla.

[**39.** *b.*] The *Chhri of Sarwar Sultan*, starts on Monday in the Hindu month of Magh and goes to the Lakhi-jungle. The *Chhri of Shah Madar* starts from Barapula in the month of Jamadu-l-awal, and reaches Makanpur on the 17th of that month.

Rivers : Ganges, [**40.** *a.*] Jumna, Sarsati, Hindun, Khagar, and Dhangar. The canal of Ali Mardan Khan.

[**41.** *a.*] **Statistics** of the province : This province has 12 *Sarkars*, with 248 *mahals*, 45,088 *mauzas* (villages), 6,93,56,572$\frac{18}{20}$ *bigha* of measured land (excluding the *Sarkar* of Srinagar on the skirt of the hills, the records of which have not been obtained) ;

a revenue in *dam* of 1,05,86,35,698 (=Rs. 2,64,65,892-7-2) excluding the *mahals* on the skirt of the hills ; and a revenue in cash of Rs. 1,31,33,115-6 as. for six months. [This would yield Rs. 2,62,66,230 12 as. for the entire year, an amount less than the Rupee equivalent of the *dam* given above.]

[41. *b*.] DETAILS OF SARKARS.

1. Shah-Jahanabad......51 *mahlas*, of which 4 are *manduyat* (granary ?), and of one more the area is unknown. Remaining 46 mahals ; area 1,21,456 *bighas* ; 5,499 *mauzas* ; revenue, 24,65,21.713 *dam* (Rs. 61,63,042-13-2).
2. Badaon...20 *mahals* ; area 1,65,928 *bighas* ; 12,177 *mauzas* ; revenue 11,68.89,788 *dam* (Rs. 29,22,244-11-2).
3. Tijara...18 *mahals* ; area 2,00,376$\frac{13}{20}$ *bighas* ; 253 *mauzas* ; revenue 3,22,92,880 *dam* (Rs. 8,07,322).
4. Hissar...28 *mahals*, of 7 of which area unknown. Remaining 21 *mahals* ; area 71,48,184 *bighas* ; 2,373 *mauzas* ; revenue 8,83,79,328 *dam* (Rs 22,09,483-3-2).
5. Rewari...11 *mahals* ; area 13,95,535$\frac{6}{20}$ *bighas* ; 1,207 *mauzas* ; revenue 4,10,79,328 *dam* (Rs. 10,26,983-3-2)
6. Srinagar...7 *mahals* ; revenue Srinagar *pargana* 4 *lac*, Kohil *pargana* 31 *lac*, Chandi *pargana* 10 *lac*, detached *parganas* 19 *lac*, total revenue 64 *lac dam* (Rs. 1,60,000).
7. Sambhal...49 *mahals*, of one the statistics are unobtainable. Remaining 48 *mahals* ; area 47,53,321 *bighas* ; 7,392 *mauzas* ; revenue 14,16,73.745 *dam* (Rs. 35,41,843-10).
8. Shahranpur...28 *mahals*, of 2 of which area unknown. Remaining 26 *m* ; area 36,29,315 *bighas* ; 2,197 *mauzas* ; revenue 10.91,07,306 *dam* (Rs. 27,27,682-10-5).
9. Sirhind...38 *mahals*, of 3 of which area unknown. Remaining 35 *m*. ; area 1,57,86,388 *bighas* ; revenue 24,32,49,082 *dam* (Rs. 60,81,227-0-10).
10. Faizabad...12 *mahals*, 2 of which unsettled, Remaining 10 *m*. ; area 14,51,707 *bighas* ; 1,380 *mauzas* ; revenue 3,72,95,612 *dam* (Rs. 9,32,390-4-10).

11. Kumaon...7 *mahals*, of 6 of which the statistics are unobtainable. Remaining 1 *m.*; 88 *mauzas*; revenue 1,68,00,000 *dam* (Rs. 4,20,000).

12 Narnol...15 *mahals*; area 68,04,356 *bighas*; 1,655 *mauzas*; revenue 7,68,32.754 *dam* (Rs, 19,20,818-13-7).

[Some of the above figures must be incorrect, because by adding together the figures for the different *Sarkars* we get a total (named 'S') which differs from the provincial total (named 'P') written fully *in words* in the text just above these "Details". The total for Akbar's time is given as 'A' :—

Total.	*Sarkars.*	*Mahals.*	Area in *bigha.*	*Mauzas.*	Revenue in *dam.*
S.	12	284	4,14,56,566$\frac{18}{20}$	34,221	1,15,65,21,536
P.	12	248	6,93,56,570$\frac{18}{20}$	45,088	1,05,86,35,698
A.	8	237	71,26,107$\frac{17}{20}$	...	12,30,12,590]

II. AGRA.

[45. *a.*] **Statistics** of the Province :

This Province has 12 *Sarkars*, comprising 254 *mahals*, 28,350 *mauzas*, 5,58,79,207$\frac{2}{10}$ *bighas* of measured land, [45. *b.*] a revenue in *dam* of 89,66,44,429 (=Rs. 2,24,16,110-11-7), and a revenue in cash of Rs. 1,16,83,129-12 as. [If the last amount be for six months only, then the annual cash revenue would be Rs. 2,33,66,259-8as.]

Details of Sarkars.

1. Agra......48 *mahals*, of three of which statistics unobtainable and of two more area unknown. Remaining 43 *mahals*; area 2,00,97,473 *bighas*; 6,737 *mauzas*; revenue 60,24,045 *dam* (Rs, 1,50,601-2-0.) [In the text the line for *kror* in the revenue portion of the column has been worm-eaten. The revenue in *dam* for this *Sarkar* must have been several *kror*, judging from the provincial total. The area is also wrongly given as 30 *kror*, which I have emended into 2 *kror*.]

2. Irij......20 *mahals*, of 1 of which area unknown, and of 3 statistics unobtainable. Remaining 16 *mahals* ; area 33,43,777$\frac{18}{20}$ *bighas* ; 4,259 *mauzas*, revenue 8,89,61,866 *dam* (Rs. 22, 24,046-10-5.)

3. Alwar......43 *mahals*, of one of which statistics unobtainable. Remaining 42 *mahals* ; area 24,57,410 *bighas* ; 1,412 *mauzas*; revenue 9,59,34,232 *dam* (Rs. 23,98,355-12-10).

4 Bayanwan......30 *mahals*, of 7 of which area unknown. Remaining 23 *mahals* ; area 12,49,197 *bighas* ; 1,520 *mauzas* ; revenue 3,53,67,346 *dam* (Rs. 8,84,183-10-5).

5. Sanor (?)......6 *mahals* ; area 13,94,335 *bighas* ; 1,297 *mauzas* ; revenue 2,00,00,000 *dam* (Rs. 5,00,000.)

6. Sahar..... 7 *mahals* ; area 14,27,148 *bighas* ; 826 *mauzas* ; revenue 2,45,47,552 *dam* (Rs. 6,13,688-12-10).

7. Kanauj......30 *mahals* ; area 54,62,569 *bighas* ; 2,115 *mauzas* ; revenue 10,00,55,467 *dam* (Rs 25,01,386-10-10).

8. Kol......13 *mahals* ; area 26,69,310 *bighas* ; 1,443 *mauzas* ; revenue 4,45,69,557 *dam* (Rs. 11,14,238-14-10)

9. Gualiar....23 *mahals* ; area 41,46,148$\frac{12}{20}$ *bighas* ; 3,292 *mauzas* ; revenue 9,96,18,141 *dam* (Rs. 24,90,453-8 5).

10. Mandlaer......15 *mahals*, of 5 of which statistics not received. Remaining 10 *mahals* ; area 47,92,462$\frac{11}{20}$ *bighas* ; 2,155 *mauzas* ; revenue 2,00,21,350 *dam* (Rs. 5,00,533-12).

11. Narwar......23 *mahals* ; area 41,46,147$\frac{2}{20}$ *bighas* ; 3,292 *mauzas* ; revenue 1,63,60,100 *dam* (Rs. 4,09,002-8).

12. Kalpi......14 *mahals* ; area 47,92,565$\frac{11}{20}$ *bighas* ; 2,269 *mauzas* ; revenue 4,00,01,132 *dam* (Rs 10,00,028-4-10).

[The total for all the *Sarkars*, the Provincial total, and Akbar's total are given below :

Total	*Sarkars.*	*Mahals.*	Area in *bighas.*	*Mauzas.*	Revenue in *dam.*
S.	12	272	5,59,78,523$\frac{8}{20}$	30,617	59,13,60,788
P.	12	254	5,58,79,207$\frac{8}{20}$	28,350	89,66,44,429
A.	13	262	2,78,62,189$\frac{18}{20}$	......	54,62,50,304]

III. PANJAB.

[47. *a.*] **Hindu Shrines**—JAWALAMUKHI......SUKANT MANDAVI is a place where there is a very [large] tank named Ravansar; a hill [47. *b.*] appears on the surface of the water. When suppliants pray. "We have come from distant places for the purpose of worshipping [thee ;] honour us by showing thyself," this hill moves and comes close to them and they worship it. If they wish they even step upon it; when it is over, the hill goes back to its place. If it came by the right side it returns by the left, and if by the left it goes back by the right. ACHAL-TIRTH, 2 *kos* from the hills, sacred to Syam Kartik the son of Mahadeo. The CHAK-i Guru Nanak, near Hastpurmati (Haibatpur Patti ?), where Govind, the 5th Guru, built a beautiful garden and tank. RAM-TIRTH. BALNATH JOGI, also known as the *Tilah of Balnath*. There is a lake named...[left blank in the text], near Gujrat, in which crowds of pilgrims bathe on the *Mesh-sankranti*, *i.e.*, the turning of the Moon into the Aries. It is said that the earth has two eyes, one being [the lake of Pushkar near Ajmir] and the other this.

Forts.—Lahor, [48. *a.*] Sialkot, Atak, Rohtas.

[48. *b.*] *Dasanpur*, the abode of Babalal, the chief of those who know God. The Garden of Ibrahim Khan, in the village of Sodhra which is famous as Ibrahimabad, was laid out by Ali Mardan Khan, in the name of his son Ibrahim Khan; and a canal was brought from river Tuhi to this garden at a cost of 6 *lac* of Rupees.

[49. *a.*] **Statistics** of the Province –There are 5 *doabs* (instead of *Sarkars*), comprising 329 *mahals*, 30,256 *mauzas*, 2,43,19,960 *bighas* of measured land (excluding the *mahals* whose areas are not known and the *mahals* outside these 5 *doabs*,) [49. *b.*] and a revenue in *dam* of 58,11,90,59) *dam* (Rs. 1,45,29,764-15-17.) [In the number of *mauzas* the text reads 3 thousand, evidently a mistake for 30 thousand.]

DETAILS OF DOABS.

1. Bait Jalandhar......69 *mahals*, of 15 of which records not received, of 7 more area unknown. Remaining 47 *mahals*; area 39,39,518$\frac{4}{20}$ *bighas*; 5,784 *mauzas*; revenue 14,37,50,069 *dam* (Rs. 35,93,751-11-7.)

Hilly......	28 *mahals*......	2,71,00,070 *dam*
Plain......	19 „	......11,65,80,069 „
	47 „	......14,36,80,139 „

2. Bari *doab*......57 *mahals*, of 21 of which records not obtained. Remaining 36 *mahals*; area 52,39,857 *bighas*; 4,678 *mauzas*; revenue 19,73,50,057 *dam* (Rs. 49,33,751-6-10.)

3. Rechna *doab*......49 *mahals*, of 6 of which area unknown. Remaining 43 *mahals*; area 98,52,01c *bighas*; 4,693 *mauzas*; revenue 4,26,43,515 *dam* (Rs. 10,66,087-14-0.)

Mandyat (?)	12 *mahals*	34,13,340 *dam*
Baharjat (?)	26 „	4,20,30,440 „
	38 „	4,54,43,780 „
Parganahs	30 „	20,12,94,241 „

4 Chunhat *doab*......22 *mahals*, of 3 of which records not received; of 5 more area unknown. Remaining 14 *mahals* area 40,41,809 *bighas*; 7,583 *mauzas*; revenue 9,26,88,735 *dam* (Rs. 23,17,218-6.)

Hilly	11 *mahals*	1,75,55,699 *dam*
Plain	11 „	7,51,33,241 „
	22 „	9,26,88,940 „

5. Sindh Sagar *doab*......48 *mahals*, of 17 of which records not received, of 19 more area unknown. Remaining 12 *mahals*; area 12,56,771$\frac{11}{20}$ *bighas*; 2,177 *mauzas*; revenue 14,05,99,371 *dam* (Rs. 35,14,984-4-5)

Hilly	36 *mahals*	11,10,83,571 *dam*
Plain	12 „	2,95,15,500 „
	48 „	14,05,99,071 „

[The text has dropped by mistake 2 *kror* in the *dam* for "Plain."]

6. Kangra (outside the *doab* region), 63 *mahals*, of 32 of which records not received, of 25 others area unknown. Remaining 6 *mahals* ; 311 *mauzas* ; revenue 5,80,53,832 *dam* (Rs. 14,51,345-12-10.)

[The different totals (inclusive of Kangra) are given below :—

Total	*Sarkars*	*Mahals*	Area in *bigha*	*Mauzas*	Revenue in *dam*
S.	5	308	2,43,29,965$\frac{18}{20}$	25,226	67,50,85,579
P.	5	329	2,43,19,960	30,256	58,11,90,599
A.	5	232	1,61,55,643$\frac{3}{20}$	......	55,94,58,423.]

IV. MULTAN.

[51. *b*.] **Statistics :** 4 *Sarkars*, comprising 113 *mahals*, 9,257 *mauzas*, 44,54,206$\frac{15}{20}$ *bighas* of measured land (excluding one *Sarkar* the area of which is not obtainable), a revenue in *dam* of 18,36,31,458 *dam* (Rs. 45,90,786-7-2), and a revenue in money of Rs. 22,86,431—4 as. for six months. [The annual total would be Rs. 45,72,862-8as.]

DETAILS OF SARKARS.

1. Multan......53 *mahals*, of which 17 unsettled. Remaining 36 *mahals* ; 3,532 *mauzas*, revenue 12,72,27,352 *dam* (Rs. 31, 80,683-12-10.)
2. Bhakkar......15 *mahals* ; of which 2 are *sair*. Remaining 13 *mahals* ; 680 *mauzas*, revenue 2,43,87,248 *dam* (Rs. 6,09, 681-3-2.)
3. Dipalpur...24 *mahals*, of one of which statistics not obtained. Remaining 23 *mahals* ; area 44,54,206$\frac{15}{20}$ *bighas* ; 4,643 *mauzas* ; revenue 2,63,97,258 *dam* (Rs. 6,59,931-3-2.)
4. Sewistan......21 *mahals*, of one of which records not received. Remaining 20 *mahals* ; 347 *mauzas*, revenue 1,26,29,600 *dam* (Rs. 3,15,740.)

[The three kinds of total are given below :

Total	*Sarkars*	*Mahals*	Area in *bigha*	*Mauzas*	Revenue in *dam*
S.	4	113	44,54,206$\frac{15}{20}$	12,202	19,06,41,458
P.	4	113	44,54,206$\frac{15}{20}$	9,257	18,36,31,458
A.	3	88	32,73,932$\frac{4}{20}$	......	15,14,03,619.]

V. THATHA.

[53. *a.*] **Statistics.**—In this Province are 4 *Sarkars*, comprising 60 *mahals*, 1,325 *mauzas*, a revenue in *dam* of 6.93,17,526 (Rs. 17,32,938-2-5), and a cash revenue of Rs. 66,530-10 as. [The annual total would be Rs. 1,33,061-4 as. Evidently the last number has been incorrectly transcribed]

DETAILS OF SARKARS.

1. Thatha...24 *mahals*, of which 3 are *mir-bahari* (admiral's ?). Remaining 21 *mahals*; 755 *mauzas*, revenue 3,19,75,648 *dam* (Rs 7,99,391-3-2).
2. Chakarhalah [spelt in the text *Chakhala*]...10 *mahals*, 116 *mauzas*, revenue 1,72,15,519 *dam* (Rs 4,30,387-15-7).
3. Hajkan [spelt in the text *Khwaj-kan*]...14 *mahals*, 248 *mauzas*, revenue 81,69,500 *dam* (Rs 2,04,237-8.)
4. Nasirpur [spelt in the text *Nasirabad*]...10 *mahals*, 176 *mauzas*, revenue 1,20,56,858 *dam* (Rs 3,01,421-7-2).

[The three kinds of total are given below :

Total.	*Sar.*	*Mah.*	Area in *bigha.*	*Mauz*	Rev. in *dam.*
S.	4	58	......	1,295	6,94,17.525.
P.	4	60	......	1,325	6,93,17,526.
A.	5	53	......	...	6,62,51,393.]

VI. KASHMIR.

[58. *a.*] **Statistics.**—Qazi Ali fixed the revenue at 30,63,050 *kharwar* and 11 *tarak*; each *kharwar* is 3 *maunds* 8* *seers* of Akbar's measure [and 16 *taraks* make one *kharwar*; the revenue paid in money being] 1,20,22,183 *dam* (Rs 3,00,554-9-2). The revenue settled by Asaf Khan† was 30,79,443, *kharwar*, of which 10,11,

* The text wrongly reads *bist* (twenty) for *hasht* (eight.) The correction is from *Ain*. ii. 366.

† "The country having been recently annexed, was assessed very lightly at 22 lacs of *kharwars*, which was 2 lacs more than before, the *kharwars* being reckoned at 16 *dam*. For this sum, Akbar handed over Kashmir to Mirza Yusuf Khan." (*Ain*. i. 346).

330½ *kharwar* was paid in money. [The average price of each *kharwar* in kind was 29 *dam*, and of each *kharwar* in money 13$\frac{8}{25}$ *dam*. (*Ain* ii. 367). At the latter rate Asaf Khan's cash revenue would be 1,34,70,922 *dam* (Rs. 3,36,773-0 10.)] The cesses *baj* and *tamgha** were remitted by the Imperial command. The Province [now] has 7 *Sarkars*, 75 *mahals*, of 10 of which the details are not known, 5,352 *mauzas*, and a revenue of 21,28,20,099 *dam* (Rs 53,20,502-7-7.)

DETAILS OF SARKARS.

1. Environs of the capital (Srinagar)...36 *mahals*. [Text reads *haweli-e-Kashmir*].
2. Srinagar...3 *mahals*.
3. Kamraj...22 "
4. Northern region...7.
5. East and South of Kamraj ..11.
6. North and West...some certain *mahals*.

[The three kinds of total are given below:

Total	*Sarkars*	*Mahals*	Area	*Mauzas*	Revenue in *dam*.
S.	6	79+?	...	...	...
P.	7	75	...	5,352	21,28,20,099.
A.	1	38	...	...	6,21,13,040.]

VII. ORISSA.

[60. *a.*] **Statistics.**—This Province has 12 *Sarkars*; 258 *mahals*, of which 29 are unsettled; measured land 5,95,079$\frac{1}{2}\frac{7}{0}$ *bighas* of the measure of Bir Singh which, at the rate of 55 yards of Sikandar's measure, would be 1,19,17,590 *bighas*, but according to the *tanab* of 60 *yards* would be 9,01 26,259 *bighas*; 26,000 *mauzas*; revenue in *dam* not known

---

"In the 39th year [of Akbar's reign], Acaf was sent to Kashmir, Mirza Yusuf Khan having been recalled...The revenue was fixed according to the assessment of Qazi Ali, *i e.*, at one lac of *kharwars* at 24 *dams* each." (411.)

* *Baj* was used loosely for any toll or tax. *Tamgha* meant (1) a demand in excess of the land revenue, or (2) inland tolls. (*Ain.* ii. 367. *n.*)

DETAILS OF SARKARS.

1. Jalesar, 28 *mahals*. 2. Bhadrak, 7 *m* 3. Katak, 21 *m*. 4. Kalang Dandpat, 27 *m*. 5 Raj Mahendri, 16 *m*. The statistics of the other *Sarkars* are not obtainable. ["Sultan Sikandar Lodi introduced another *gaz* (yard) of the breadth of 41½ *Iskandaris*. This was a copper coin mixed with silver. Humayun added a half and it was thus completed to 42. Its length was 32 digits. Till the 31st year of the Divine Era (*i.e.*, of Akbar's reign), although the *Akbar Shahi gaz* of 46 fingers was used as a cloth measure, the *Iskandari gaz* was used for lands. Akbar abolished the variety of measures and brought a medium *gaz* of 41 digits into general use. He named it the *Ilahi gaz*." (*Ain*. ii. 61.)

	Sarkars	*Mahals*	Measured land in *bigha*	*Mauzas*	Rev. in *d*.
Provincial Total	12	258	9,01,26,259	26,000	......
Akbar's Total	5	99	......	...	12,57,32,638]

VIII. BENGAL.

[63. *a*.] **Statistics.**—This Province has 28 *Sarkars*, 1,243 *mahals* (the records of 156 of which have not been received, leaving a remainder of 1,187 *mahals*) ; measured land 3,34,775 *bighas*, 1,12.788 *mauzas*, and a revenue in *dam* of 56,29,09,019 *dam* (Rs. 1,40.72,722 15-7), all [paid] in money, so that the collection is some *kror* of Rupees,

DETAILS OF SARKARS.

Sarkars	*Mahals*	*Mauzas*.	*Sarkars*	*Mahals*	*Mauzas*.
1. Udner	...	376	9. Jinnatabad in Bengal	73	1,030
2. Udaipur	...	103	10 Jinnatabad in Kamrup	55	4,469
3. Purnia	11	1,353	11. Mahkar in Kamrup	15	1,865
4. Marauhar (?)	2	51	12 Khalifatabad and Bankar	24	681
5 Bazoha—Barbakabad	5	1,879	13. Sharifabad—Khalifatabad	15	2,899
6. Pinjara—Barbakabad	47	9,327	14. Dakhan kol Sharifabad	29	6,359
7. Tajpur—Sakhra (or Pinjara ?)	26	3,389			
8. Bengal Tajpur	30	1,546			

	Sarkars	*Mahals*	*Mauzas*
15.	Bihar-i-Dakhan Sikol	...	1,030
16.	Salimabad near Bihar	2	291
17.	Balgaon—Salimabad	37	6,618
18.	Sonargaon—Balgaon	72	1,897
19.	Madaran—Sonargaon	52	2,899
20.	Fatihabad—Madaran	14	3,548
21.	Mahmudabad and Fatihabad	38	2,506
22.	Ghoraghat—Mahmudabad	98	7,155
23.	Sylhet—Ghoraghat	16	3,885
24.	Jinnat (?)—Sylhet	124	2,891
25.	Maljih—Jalih (?)	1(98 *mali*)	19
26.	Tappa Kori Maljih	25 (of 10 of which area unknown)	13,354
27.	Farmandihi Tappa Kori	4 (6,600 *mali*)	136
28.	Satgaon—Farmandihi	7	
29.	Khuldabad—Satgaon	53	
30.	Sulaimanabad—Khuldabad	53	
31.	Sulaimanabad	31	

[The three kinds of total are given below :

Total	*Sarkars*	*Mahals*	Area	*Mauzas*	Rev. in. *d.*
S.	31	959	...	81,558	...
P.	28	1,243	3,34,775	1,12,788	16,29,09,019
A.	19	688	...	...	47,27,26,681]

IX. BIHAR.

[64. *b.*] **Statistics.**—This Province has 8 *Sarkars*, 252 *mahals*, [65. *a.*] 55,476 *mauzas*, a revenue in *dam* of 37,84,17,380 *dam* (Rs. 94,60,434-8 as.) and a revenue in money of Rs. 94,65,432-8 as. [The text here incorrectly adds "for six months."]

DETAILS OF SARKARS.

1. Bihar (Patna)...58 *mahals*, of 7 of which details not known and of 11 others area unknown. Remaining 40 *mahals* ; area 67,09,647 $\frac{11}{20}$ *bighas* ; 17,036 *mauzas* ; revenue 17,41,391 *dam* (Rs. 43,534-12-5).
2. Tirhut...102 *mahals*, of 19 of which area unknown. Remaining 83 *mahals* ; 8,246 *mauzas* ; revenue 2,94,83,210 *dam* (Rs. 7,37,080-4 as.).
3. Champaran...3 *mahals* ; 1,264 *mauzas* ; revenue 96,24,121 *dam* (Rs. 2,40,603-0-5).

4. Hajipur...11 *mahals* ; 5,676 *mauzas* ; revenue 4,53,27,400 *dam* (Rs. 11,33,185).
5. Rohtas...7 *mahals*, of 3 of which area unknown. Remaining 4 *mahals* ; area 10,45,275 *bighas* ; 7,220 *mauzas* ; revenue 2,82,82,017 *dam* (Rs. 7,07,050-6-10).
6. Saran...27 *mahals*, of 5 of which area unknown. Remaining 22 *mahals* ; area 22,37,856 *bighas* ; 5,772 *mauzas* ; revenue 3,53,28,800 *dam* (Rs. 8,83,220)
7. Shahabad...12 *mahals*, of 3 of which records not obtained. Remaining 9 *mahals* ; area 18,81,368 *bighas* ; 4,545 *mauzas* ; revenue 2,84,12,018 *dam* (Rs 7,10,300-7-2 .
8. Monghyr...40 *mahals*, of 6 of which records not received. Remaining 34 *mahals* ; area 12,78,698 $\frac{5}{20}$ *bighas* ; 5,516 *mauzas* ; revenue 4,02,23,024 *dam* (Rs 10,05,575-9-7).

[Some of the above figures must be inaccurate, especially the revenue of the *Sarkar* of Bihar, which was 8,01,96,390 *dam* under Akbar. The three kinds of total are given below :

Total	*Sarkars*	*Mahals.*	Area in *bigha*	*Mauzas*	Rev. in *dam.*
S.	8	260	1,31,52,844 $\frac{18}{20}$	55,275	21,84,21,981
P.	8	252	....	55,476	37,84,17,380
A.	7	200	24,44,120	...	22,19,19,404.]

X. ALLAHABAD.

[65. *b.*] **Saint.**—Shaikh MINA, a saint of Lucknow, was in his childhood brought up in the service of Shaikh Qawamu-d-din Abrakhi. Then he became a disciple of Shaikh Sarang. It is said that Shaikh Qawamu-d-din had a son named Mina, who owing to his [thoughtless] youth went to one of the kings for service. As the kings of this country were often the disciples of this family, the father was displeased. Although [the son] was in service, the father was not at all pleased with him. He adopted a *dervish* named Shaikh Alam as his son, and gave him the name of Mina. He found favour in the eyes of the Shaikh (Qawam) and reached the perfection of holiness. He (Qawam) cursed his son, [66. *a.*] and on that very day the son died. His (Mina's) tomb is at Lucknow.

[**67.** *a*] **Hindu Shrine.**—Prayag (Allahabad.) In former times there was a saw here ; if a man cut off his head with it, every desire that he had was fulfilled. In the reign of Shah Jahan this practice was forbidden.

[**67.** *b.*] **Statistics**—This province has 17 *Sarkars*, 269 *mahals*, [or, excluding the *Sarkars* whose records are not to hand] 156 *mahals* ; 47,328 *mauzas* ; measured land [**68.** *a.*] 1,97,03,983$\frac{16}{20}$ *bighas*, excluding the unsettled *mahals*, the area and number of *mauzas* of which are not known ; revenue in *dam* 29,02.32,270 *dam* (Rs. 72,55,806·12 as.), revenue in money Rs. 63,00,925 for 12 months.

Details of Sarkars.

1. Allahabad·· ··11 *mahals* ; area 15,53,607$\frac{10}{20}$ *bighas* ; 5,512 *mauzas* ; reveuue 3,87,65,894 *dam* (Rs. 9,69,147-5-7).
2. Muhammadabad Benares ·····9 *mahals*, of one of which area unknown. Remaining 8 *mahals* ; area 4,53,354$\frac{11}{20}$ *bighas* ; 1,420 *mauzas* ; revenue 54,30,000 *dam.* (Rs. 1,35,750).
3. Ghazipur ·····17 *mahals* ; area 17,33,349$\frac{14}{20}$ *bighas* ; 5,464 *mauzas* ; revenue 1,45,53,445 *dam* (Rs. 3,63,836-1).
4. Kora ·····8 *mahals* ; area 13,57,817$\frac{8}{20}$ *bighas* ; 1,181 *mauzas* ; revenue 5,75,67,342 *dam* (Rs. 14,39,183-8-10.)
5. Barhar* ·····18 *mahals*, of 3 of which details not received and of 2 more area unknown. Remaining 13 *mahals* ; area 3,29,368 *bighas* ; 1,218 *mauzas* ; revenue 1,73,78,800 *dam* (Rs. 4,34,470.)
6. Karrah ·· ··12 *mahals*, of 2 of which area not known. Remaining 10 *mahals* ; area 14,17,127 *bighas* ; 2,346 *mauzas* ; revenue 3,71,65,617 *dam* (Rs. 9,29,140-6-5) [**68.** *b.*].
7. Jaunpur ·· ··42 *mahals* ; of 2 of which area unknown. Remaining 40 *mahals* ; area 54,51,118$\frac{16}{20}$ *bighas* ; 19,361 *mauzas* ; revenue 10,38,83.516 *dam* (Rs. 25,97,087-14-5)

* Not identified, as the word seems to have been incorrectly transcribed in the text. There is no name in the *Ain* at all approaching it in form.

8. Kalinjar......10 *mahals*, of 3 of which area not obtained, Remaining 7 *mahals*; area 43,38,324 *bighas* ; 1,375 *mauzas* ; revenue 4,70,00,030 *dam* (Rs. 11,75,000-12.)

9. Manikpur .....14 *mahals* ; area 21,01,324$\frac{5}{20}$ *bighas* ; 3,575 *mauzas* ; revenue 6,02,50,818 *dam* (Rs 15,06,270-7-2.)

10. Chunarah .....15 *mahals* ; area 7,40,686$1\frac{8}{20}$ *bighas* ; 1,345 *mauzas* , revenue 35,00,000 *dam* (Rs. 87,500)

11-17. Bitha* and other *Sarkars*, which are unregulated and whose areas have not reached the Court.

[The three kinds of total are given below :—

Total	*Sarkars*	*Mahals*	Area in *bigha*	*Mauzas*	Rev. in *dam*.
S.	11+?	156	1,93,76,077$\frac{18}{20}$	42,797	37,54,95,432.
P.	17	156	1,97,03,983$\frac{15}{20}$	47,328	29,02,32,270.
A.	10	177	39,68,018$\frac{8}{20}$	......	21,24,27,819]

XI. OUDH.

[69. *b*.] **Statistics**—This province has 5 *Sarkars*, with 149 *mahals*, 52,691 *mauzas*, measured land 1,90,22,908 *bighas*, a revenue in *dam* of 33,24,00,617 *dam* (Rs. 83,10,015-6-10), and a revenue in money of Rs. 41,55,420-12 as. for six months. [This gives an annual revenue of Rs 83,10,841-8 as.]

Details of Sarkars. [70 *a*.]

1. Suburban area of Oudh......22 *mahals* ; area 43,83,869 *bighas* ; 7,846 *mauzas* ; revenue 5,72,93,615 *dam* (Rs. 14,32,340-6.)

2. Bahraich......12 *mahals*, of 4 of which area not known, Remaining 8*m* ; area 27,52,378 *bighas* ; 6,838 *mauzas* ; revenue 2,51,97,173 *dam* (Rs. 6,29,929-5-2.)

3. Gorakhpur......57 *mahals*, of 1 of which statistics unobtainable, and of 2 more area not known. Remaining 54 *m*. ; area 53,04,601 *bighas* ; 9,641 *mauzas* ; revenue 11,19,13,684 *dam* (Rs. 27,97,842-1-7.)

4. Lucknow......34 *mahals* ; 17,076 *mauzas* ; revenue 5,52,00,005 *dam* (Rs. 13,80,000-1.)

* Evidently the *Bathhhora* of *Ain*. ii. 166.

18

5. Khairabad......24 *mahals*, of one of which area unknown. Remaining 23 *m.*; area 65,46,458 *bighas*; 11,460 *mauzas*; revenue 8,17,95,850 *dam* (Rs. 20,44,896-4.)

[The three kinds of total are given below :—

Total	*Sarkars*	*Mahals*	Area in *bigha*	*Mauzas*	Rev. in *dam.*
S.	5	149	1,89,87,306	52,861	33,14,00,327
P.	5	149	1,90,22,908	52,691	33,24,00,617
A.	5	133	1,01,71,180	...	20,17,58,172]

XII. AJMIR.

[71. *a.*] **Towns.**—Chitor. [71. *b.*] Fort of Bitli (Ajmir), Sambhar, and Jaipur.

[72. *a.*] **Statistics**—This province has 8 *Sarkars*, with 238 *mahals*, 7,905 *mauzas*, measured land 1,74,09,684 *bighas*, excluding the *mahals* whose area and statistics are not known, a revenue in *dam* of 70,11,93,170 *dam* (Rs. 1,75,29,829-4) and a revenue in money of Rs. 88,28,232-12 as. [Evidently the last figure is for 6 months; the total annual revenue then would be Rs. 1,76,56, 465-8.]

Details of Sarkars.

1. Ajmir......30 *mahals*, of 2 of which statistics not received, and of 3 more area unknown. Remaining 25*m.*; area 64,25,670 *bighas*; 1,176 *mauzas*; revenue 1,06,47,773 *dam* (Rs. 2,66, 194-5-2.)
2. Chitor......35 *mahals*, of which 28 are in *jagir*. Remaining 7*m*; area 9,35,507$\frac{18}{20}$ *bighas*; 250 *mauzas*; revenue 9,85,21,787 *dam* (Rs. 24,63,044-10-10.)
3. Jodhpur......27 *mahals*, of 21 of which statistics not received, and of 6 others area unknown. 1,000 *mauzas*; revenue 26,52,00,000 *dam* (Rs. 66,30,000.)
4. Ranthambhor......83 *mahals*, of 2 of which statistics not to hand, and of 3 more area unknown. Remaining 78*m.*; area 82,64,551$\frac{18}{20}$ *bighas*; 830 *mauzas*; revenue 12,34,14,375 *dam* (Rs. 30,85,359-6.)

5. Nagor......31 *mahals*, of one of which statistics not obtainable, and of 28 more area unknown. Rem. *2m.* ; area 17,83,354 *bighas* ; 1,664 *mauzas* ; revenue 7,95,60,686 *dam* (Rs. 19, 89,017-2-5.)
6. Jesalmir......8 *mahals* ; statistics wanting ; revenue 87,30,000 *dam* (Rs. 2,18,250.)
7. Bikanir (the abode of Raja Karan*)......area and details not known ; revenue 1,00,00,000 *dam* (Rs. 2,50,000.)
8. Kumbhalmir †......revenue 50,80,000 *dam* (Rs. 1,27,000.)

[The three kinds of total are given below :—

Total	*Sar.*	*Mah.*	Area in *bigha*	*Mauzas*	Rev. in *dam.*
S.	8	214	1,74,09,083$\frac{5}{20}$	4,920	60,11,54,621
P.	8	238	1,74,09,684	7,905	70,11,93,170
A.	7	197	2,14,35,941$\frac{7}{20}$		28,84,01,557.]

XIII. GUJRAT.

[74. *b.*] **Holy places** of the Hindus.—Somnath, Bhal-katirth, Mul, [75. *a.*] Uana—where there are 2 reservoirs, the Jumna and the Ganges, the fish of both of which have 3 eyes,‡—Manglor, Satrunjaya §—a fort on a hill, not much inhabited, but considered very sacred by the Jains,—and Dwarka.

[75. *b*] **Towns.**—Ahmadabad, Mahmudabad,‖ Jhalwar, Champanir, Surat, Rander, Broach, Sorath (Kathiawar). [76. *a.*] Pattan—on the sea-coast and having a stone fort,—New Surat,¶ Salher and Mulher, and Kathi**—a village.

Statistics.—The province has 10 *Sarkars*, with 256 *mahals*, of 39 of which records not received ; 10,370 *mauzas* ; measured land

---

* Kurrun succeeded his father Rae Sing in 1632 A. D. and died about 1660 A.D. (Tod, ii. 1018.)

† It may be a mistake for *Sirohi.*

‡ *Ain.* ii. 247.

§ Palitana.

‖ 12 *kos* from Ahmadabad. (*Ain.* ii. 241.) Jhalwar (*Ibid*, 242.)

¶ *Ibid*, 245.

** The *Ain.* (ii. 248) speaks of the Kathis as a tribe living in Baghelkhand ; our text wrongly calls them a *village.*

(excluding 170 *mahals* the record of whose area is unobtainable) 1,27,49,374$\frac{8}{20}$ *bighas* ; revenue in *dam* 53,02,89,319 *dam* (Rs. 1,32, 57,232-15-7) and revenue in money (excluding those *mahals* whose area and statistics are not to hand) Rs. 70,28,326-[76. *b.*] 9 as. for six months.* [This would yield an annual revenue of Rs. 1,40,56,653-2 as.]

DETAILS OF SARKARS.

1. Gujrat (Ahmadabad)......34 *mahals* of 6 of which records not received and of 8 others area not known. Remaining 20*m.* ; area 63,76,319$\frac{4}{20}$ *bighas* ; 1,880 *mauzas* ; revenue 27,11,27, 162 *dam* (Rs. 67,78,179-0-10)
2. Baroda......4 *mahals*, of 2 of which area unknown. Remaining 2*m.* ; area 9,85,415$\frac{12}{20}$ *bighas* ; 335 *mauzas* ; revenue 2,92,11, 846 *dam* (Rs. 7,30,296-2-5)
3. Champanir......10 *mahals*, of 4 of which area not known. Remaining 6*m.* ; area 3,72,184$\frac{12}{20}$ *bighas* ; 492 *mauzas* ; revenue 3,27,42,695 *dam* (Rs. 8,18,567-6)
4. Pattan......16 *mahals*, of 5 of which records not received and of 7 more area not known Remaining 4*m* ; area 24,23,308 *bighas* ; 1,284 *mauzas* ; revenue 4,06,47,362 *dam* (Rs. 10,16, 184-0-10)
5. Surat ......37 *mahals*, of which 6 are *jharat* (jungles ?) and of 15 more area not known. Rem. 16 *m* ; area 7,23,000 *bighas* ; 330 *mauzas* ; revenue 7,86,22,832 *dam* (Rs. 19,65,570-12-10).
6. Islamnagar......15 *mahals*, of which 5 are mints, and of 10 others area not received ; 730 *mauzas*.
7. Broach......14 *mahals*, of 4 of which statistics not to hand. Remaining 10*m.* ; area 28,69,141$\frac{10}{20}$ *bighas* ; 584 *mauzas* ; revenue 5,65,01,619 *dam* (Rs. 14,12,540-7-7)
8. Sorath (Kathiawar)......63 *mahals*, of 7 of which statistics not to hand. Remaining 56*m.* ; 1,754 *mauzas* ; revenue 4,68,50, 388 *dam* (Rs. 11,71,259-11-2.)

---

* After this the text has *lekan mulk besiar hasil ast.* If we suppose *sair* to be understood after *besiar* (from the example of p. 80. *b.*) then it may mean 'much *sair* (cess) is realised [in this] country.'

9. Godhra......11 *mahals* ; area not known ; 209 *mausas* ; revenue 16,20,100 *dam* (Rs. 40,502-8)

10. Nandot......12 *mahals*, of which 4 are unsettled. Remaining 8 *m.* ; 119 *mausas*.

[The three kinds of total are given below :—

Total	*Sarkars*	*Mahals*	Area in *bigha*	*Mausas*	Rev in *dam*.
S.	10	216	1,37,49,368$\frac{18}{20}$	7,717	55,73,24,004
P.	10	256	1,27,49,374$\frac{6}{20}$	10,370	53,02,89,319
A.	9	138	1,69,36,377$\frac{8}{20}$	...	43,68,22,301]

XIV. MALWA.

[79. *b*.] **Towns**.—Ujjain, Chanderi, Tumun—where mermen are found on the bank of the Betwa,—Mandu, Dhar, and Hindia. [80. *a*.]

Statistics—The Province has 11 *Sarkars*, with 259 *mahals* ; 18,678 *mauzas*, measured land (excluding the 119 *mahals* whose area has not been received) 1,29,64,538 *bighas*, revenue in *dam* 36,01,83,719 *dam* (Rs. 90,04,592-15-7), and [80. *b*] revenue in money Rs 45,02,874 for six months ;* [this would yield an annual revenue of Rs. 90,05.748.]

DETALS OF SARKARS.

1. Ujjain...13 *mahals*, of 2 of which records not received. Remaining 11 *m.* ; area 42,02,057 *bighas* ; 1,561 *mauzas* ; revenue 5,24,72,658 *dam* (Rs. 13,11,816-7-2).

2. Chanderi...49 *mahals*, of which one *mahal* is *amran* (?) Remaining 48 *m* ; 3,353 *mauzas* ; revenue 9,24,83,592 *dam* (Rs. 23,12,089-12-10).

3. Raisin†...38 *mahals*, of 11 of which details not to hand, of one other area not known, and of 26 more records of

---

* After this the text reads *lekan een mulk besiar ser hasil ast aksar az shashmah do chand pidast o seh chand.*

† Our text names it *Phil* or *Bhil*. This may be (1) a mistake for *Raisin* which has 35 *mahals* or (2) a corruption of *Bhilsa*, which is one of the *mahals* of Raisin (*Ain*. ii. 199).

statistics not received. Area 89,850 *bighas* ; 8,774 *mauzas* ; revenue 8,14,16,346 *dam* (Rs. 20,35,408-10-5)

4. Shahabad...7 *mahals*, area 10,49,586 *bighas* ; 366 *mauzas* ; revenue 90 *lac dam* (Rs. 2,25,000).

5. Sarangpur...24 *mahals*, of one of which details unobtainable and of 7 others area not known. Remaining 16 *mahals* ; area 39,93,213 *bighas* ; 2,323 *mauzas* ; revenue 1,02,71,663 *dam* (Rs. 2,56,791-9-2).

6. Garh*...55 *mahals*, of 49 of which statistics not received. Remaining 6 *mahals* ; 759 *mauzas* ; revenue 2,21,30,000 *dam* (Rs. 5,53,250).

7. Gagron...12 *mahals*, of 5 of which details not obtained. Remaining 7 *mahals* ; area 6,63,374 *bighas* ; 300 *mauzas* ; revenue 1,74,42,700 *dam* (Rs 4,36,067-8).

8. Kotri Parayah...9 *mahals*, of 5 of which area not known. Remaining 4 *mahals* ; area 6,12,508$\frac{14}{20}$ *bighas* ; 702 *mauzas* ; revenue 1,82,33,683 *dam* (Rs. 4,55,592-1-2).

9. Mandsor...16 *mahals*, of 4 of which details not to hand and of 11 others area not obtained Remaining 1 *mahal* ; area 43,400 *bighas* ; 1,061 *mauzas* ; revenue [blank]

10. Mandu...23 *mahals*, of 4 of which details not to hand and of 4 others area not known. Remaining 15 *mahals* ; area 17,05,818$\frac{6}{20}$ *bighas* ; 1,553 *mauzas* ; revenue 2,94,47,452 *dam* (Rs 7,36,188-12-10).

11. Hindia†...13 *mahals*, of 8 of which details not obtained and of 4 others area not known. Remaining 1 *mahal* ; area 4,91,627 *bighas* ; 833 *mauzas* ; revenue 11,45,000 *dam* (Rs. 28,625)

[The three kinds of total are given below :—

Tot.	*Sarkars*	*Mahals*	Area in *bigha*	*Mauzas*	Rev. in *dam*.
S.	11	258	1,28,51,434	21,585	33,40,43,094
P.	11	259	1,29,64,538	18,678	36,01,83,719
A.	12	301	42,66,221$\frac{8}{20}$	...	24,06,95,052]

* This is identical with the *Sarkar* of Kanauj of *Ain* ii. 192, which contains 57 *mahals*, one of them being named *Garha*.

† Our text incorrectly reads *Handia*.

BOOK SECOND.

SOUTHERN INDIA OR DECCAN.

(Full Translation).

[**84**. *a*] That portion of the kingdom of the Deccan which came into the possession of the Chaghtai [Mughal] Emperors, was marked out into six *Subahs* (provinces), each with a certain number of *Sarkars* (districts). The Deccan is a very spacious country, on three sides [**84** *b*.] bordering on the ocean. Many *Paligars* live here. In the Deccani language, *Paligar* is the name for Rajas and chiefs. When these provinces were included in the protected Empire [of Delhi], they were divided thus: (1) the province of *Berar*, (2) the province of *Khandesh*, (3) the province of *Aurangabad* Khujista-buniad ("of auspicious foundation"), (4) the province of *Haidarabad* Farkhanda-buniad ("of fortunate foundation") also called Daru-l-jihad ("the seat of holy war"), (5) the province of Muhammadabad *Bidar*, also called Zafarabad ("the abode of victory"), and (6) the province of *Bijapur* Daru-l-zafar ("the seat of victory").

Revenue.—At the end of the reign of his Majesty now in heaven (Aurangzib), these six provinces paid to the Treasury, at the six-monthly rate, Rs. 17,92,50,735-12¾ as, and for the entire year Rs. 35,85,01,470 in money. The revenue in *dam* of these provinces was formerly 6,20,02,22,140 *dam* (Rs. 15,50,05,553-8). As some other kingdoms of the Deccan have been added to the protected Empire, the revenue in *dam* now paid is 14,35,87,40,135 *dam* (Rs. 35,89,68,503-6).

XV. BERAR.

Its original name was *Warda-tat*,—revenue in *dam* of these a river and *tat* meaning 'bank'. It province of *Bijapur* Daru

---

* The *Wardha* rises in the hills of were divided on the ocean. (*I. G.* v. 242.)

climate. Length from Batiala to Biragarh 200 *kos* and breadth from Bidar to Hindia 180 *kos.* Eastwards lies Biragarh, north Hindia, south Telingana, west [**85.** *a.*] Mahkar. *Mahkar** has much inhabited territory. [This province is situated] between two hills; the one in the south is called BANDAH† and on it are *Gawil* (21·22 N. 77·18 E.), *Narnala* (21. 18 N. 77 E.), and *Melgarh*; and that which is in the north is named SAHYA and on it are *Mahor* and *Ramgarh.* Its climate is excellent. The Gang Gotami, which is also called Ganga *Godavari,*—its name Gotami being due to its connection with the sage Gotam,—issues from the Sahya hill near Nassik, and comes from Ahmadnagar to Berar. When Jupiter enters Leo, men having come from distant places worship it. The other rivers are the *Napi* (?), the *Tapti*, and the Purna; this [last] issues from Dewalgaon Another stream comes out of the spring of the *Napi*, and [yet] another, the *Lunia*,‡ flows near Deogaon. In this country, the Chaudhuri is called *Deshmukh*, the Qanongo *Deshpande*, the Muqaddam *Patel*, and the Patwari *Kulkarni*

Elichpur is a large town; it was the capital of the kings of this country. Here a flower is found, violet-coloured and very sweet-scented; it is called *bhun champa.*§ *Gawil* is a large fort without an equal. It contains a spring with [the water of] which they give lustre to weapons. *Punar*‖ has a stone fort on a hillock; two streams enclose it on three sides *Kherla* is a stone fort on the plain. Inside it is a small circular hillock which is worshipped. Four *kos* from it is a well which turns into stone the bone of any

* Evidently the modern Buldana district of Berar. It contains the town of *Maikur*, 20. 9 N. 76. 22 E. (Letts, Sheet 3.)

† *Banda*, a branch of the Satpura range. *Melghat*, 21.42N. 77.3E. *Mahur*, 19.51N. 77.58 E., but not "on a hill." *Ramgarh* cannot be the town of the same name situated 22·47N. 81 E. (*I. G.* xi. 447.)

‡ Evidently a mistake for *Murna*, which rises near Dongaom. (Letts, Sheet 3)

§ *Ain.* ii. 229 *n.*

‖ *Pannera*, on the bend of a river, 20·40N. 76.7E. (Letts, Sheet 6) and not Pownaur, 20 45N. 78.38E.

animal that falls into it. *Biragarh* has a diamond mine; cloth is well [woven] here. Besides this, [it has a spring; whatever] falls into it, is turned into stone. *Mahur* is an excellent fort [85. *b*] on a hill; there is a temple here, sacred to Durga and known in this country as *Jagdatiá* (Jagaddhatri.) *Manik doorg* (19·46 N. 79·9E) is a fort on a hill, surrounded by many deserts; near it is Chandá. *Telangána*, which is also called Telangia, has a mine of steel. Heart-ravishing stone-pestles are made [here.] In this country a cock is found, the blood and bone of which are black. *Lunar** is the name of a *tuppa* (division) of Mokheir; on it is a great place of worship. VISHNU GAYA: Three places bear the marks of Gaya; one is in the province of Bihar and is called *Brahma Gaya*, the second is *Shiva Gaya* in Bijapur, and this [third one is a reservoir, very deep, one *kos* in length and breadth, and situated on a hillock. The water is saline, but on digging from the middle to the border, sweet water issues † The materials of soap and glass are found in it There is another spring on the summit of a hill; its mouth, [that is] the place whence the water pours forth, has been made like a cow's mouth (*go-mukh*) in figure The water never flows from it to the reservoir, except when the *amáwas* [conjunction of the moon] falls on a Monday. Monkeys abound here. Within its limits are four temples hewen out of the rock in the middle parts of the hills ‡

This province has 10 *Sarkars* and 200 *parganas*; the total number of its *mauzas* (villages) is 10,008; its measured land is

---

* "Lunar is a place of great sanctity...The Brahmans call it Bishan Gaya" (*Ain.* ii. 230.) "The Province has but one natural lake, the salt lake of LONAR, in Buldana District. It is shut in by a ridge of well-wooded hills, and is perfectly circular. The circumference is 5½ miles" (*I. G.* v. 259.) "The salt lake of Lonar (19.58.50 N. 76. 33 E.), the fabled den of the demon-giant Lonasur, who was overcome by an incarnation of Vishnu...The salt is chiefly used for the manufacture of country soap." (*I. G.* viii. 489.)

† The *Ain* has, "The water is brackish, but when taken from the centre or at the sides, it is sweet"

‡ "In the sides of the hill 24 temples have been cut each containing remarkable idols." (*Ain.* ii. 231.)

2,00,28, 100 *bighas* and 13 *bisua*, excluding the *mahals* whose area has not reached the Court. [86. *a*] Revenue in *dam*, 90,24,00,000 *dam* (Rs 2,25,60,000); revenue in money Rs. 1,14,90,043—12 as. [If the last amount be for six months, then the annual revenue in money would be Rs 2,29,80,087—8 as]

DETAILS OF SARKARS.*

1. Pathri......11 *mahals*, 546 *mauzas*, area 6,443 $\frac{8}{20}$ *bighas*. [The figure for *lac* in the column of *bighas* has been evidently dropped.]
2. Basim......8 *mahals*, 307 *mauzas*, area 19,24,181 *bighas*.
3. Pitalwari......9 *mahals*, 109 *mauzas*, area 49,012 $\frac{17}{20}$ *bighas*.
4. Panár......4 *mahals*, 734 *mauzas*, area 7,93,023 $\frac{13}{20}$ *bighas*.
5. Kallam......28 *mahals*, of 3 of which area unobtainable. Remaining 25 *mahals*, 1880 *mauzas*, area 19,89,880 *bighas*.
6. Mahur......21 *mahals*, of one of which area unobtainable. Rem. 20 *m*; 1188 *mauzas*, area 21,57,999 *bighas*.
7. Mohkar......22 *mahals*, 827 *mauzas*, area 23,18,830 *bighas*.
8. Narnala......37 *mahals*, of 3 of which area unknown. Rem. 34 *m*; 1589 *mauzas*, area 48,18,541 *bighas*.
9. Gawil......46 *mahals*, of 5 of which area unobtainable. Rem. 41 *m*; 2.335 *mauzas*, area 43,85,326 *bighas*.
10. Kherla......24 *mahals*, of 12 of which statistics not received. Rem. 12 *m*; 3,711 *mauzas*. area 7,30,779 $\frac{12}{20}$ *bighas*.

[The three kinds of total are given below:

	Sarkars	*Mahals*	*Mauzas*	Area in *bigha*	Revenue in *dam*
S.	10	210	12,307	1,91,74,016 $\frac{11}{20}$	....
P.	10	200	10,008	2,00,28,100 $\frac{13}{20}$	90,24,00,000.
A.	16	242	......	......	64,26,03,272]

* "Berar has now six Districts, Akola, Buldana, Basim, Amraoti, Ellichpur, and Wun." (*I. G.* v. 258.) The *Ain.* (ii. 231) gives to the Province 16 *Sarkars*, of which 14 only are named in detail, viz., the above ten and *Manik drug*, *Telinganah*, *Ramgarh*, and *Chanda*. The 14 have a total of 242 *parganas* (incorrectly given by Jarrett as 142), and a revenue of 64,60,07,246 *dam*, (though the provincial total of the revenue is given by Abul Fazl as 64,26,03,272.)

XVI. KHANDESH.

In the reign of the Emperor Akbar, when this province was presented to Prince Danial [as his viceroyalty], it got the name of *Dandesh*. This province is in the second climate. Length from Borgaon adjoining Hindia [86. *b*.] to Laling adjoining Ahmadnagar, 75 *kos*. Eastwards lies Berar, north Malwa, south Galna (Jalna),* west Mandhu in Gujrat. Two streams rise between Gondwana and Berar. The *Tapti* rises in the same direction, and the *Purna* [unites with it at Changdevi.] And the *Girni* flows [into it] near Choprah. Its air increases cheerfulness; winter is temperate here. The chief cultivation is *jawari*, which,† in some places, bears three crops in the year. Its stalk is so delicate and pleasant in flavour that it is considered as a sort of fruit. Rice grows well; betel leaf is abundant and good. *Siri-saf* and *bhirun*, two kinds of cloth, are manufactured at Dharangaon. [20·57 N. 75·16 E. in Letts, Sheet 6.]

Asir is a lofty fort and the residence of the governor; it has three other forts [as its dependencies.] It is itself unrivalled in strength and height. At its foot is a large and populous town.

Burhanpur is a large town on the bank of the Tapti. Its situation is 118°20′ long. and 29°40′ lat.‡ It has many gardens. Sandal grows here.

AHMADNAGAR§ has a strong fort and many gardens, of which

---

* Jalna 19·53 N. 76 E.

† Text reads *barkhe ja shali ham se bar barad, tar-i-an chunan* &c. In the translation I have followed the *Ain*.

‡ Or, calculating from Greenwich, 21.18.′33″ N. 76.16.′26″ E.

§ "Half a mile to the east of the city stands the fort, built of stone, circular in shape, about 1½ miles in circumference, and surrounded by a wide and deep moat." (*I. G.* i. 109.) The garden of *Husht Behist* (8 heavens), enclosing a palace, was formed north of the fort by Boorhan Nizam Shah I. (Ferishta, iii. 298) Mrs. C. Mackenzie wrote on 21 April, 1850, "Colonel and Mrs. Parr took us to see a fine villa of the kings of [Ahmad-] Nagar, called the *Ferrier Bagh*. It is rare that one finds any remains of the dwellings of the Mussalman conquerors: durability seems to belong only to their tombs.

Fara-bagh is unparalleled in the power of increasing cheerfulness, and *Behisht-bagh* is exactly a sample of the heaven above and heart-attractive. After Shaikh Abul Fazl had accomplished the conquest of Asir, he was ordered to conquer Ahmadnagar and also to suppress the rebellion of Rajwari (?) and other wicked men of this zilla (1597 A. D.) At that time CHAND BIBI, the sister of Ibrahim Nizam, giving him the title of Nizamu-l-mulk, placed him on the throne, and herself discharged the work of the *durbar* (Court.) Shaikh Abul Fazl, besieging the fort [**87.** *a*], made the condition of the [men of the] fort so hard that at last Chand Bibi, finding that she had no power of resistance and disdaining to be made captive, drowned herself* in the ocean of non-existence in a well (*báwli*) within the male apartments (*mardana*) of the fort. (1599 A. D.) From 935† to 1008 A. H. (1529-1599 A D.) this country was in the possession of the Nizamu-l-mulk dynasty. Then it came into the possession of the Emperor Akbar. May God keep it for ever in the Chaghtai line! The writer of these pages once went to visit it, at the end of the time of the Emperor Alamgir. The men of the place said that Chand Bibi at first loaded her cannon with balls of gold and silver;‡ and when the turn came to the iron balls, [or, they were exhausted?] she drowned herself. But I have not seen this incident recorded in any history; probably, it is a pure myth

This is a two-storied building of octagonal shape. We ascended the ruinous stair......and from the top of the domed roof enjoyed a beautiful view of the hills, the wood, and the sunset." (*Life in the Mission &c.*, 2nd edition, ii. 244.)

* According to Ferishta (iii. 312), Chand Bibi was slain by her mutinous soldiery under Humeed Khan, in her *private* apartments, in 1008 A. H.

† Really from 895 A. H. (1490 A. D.)

‡ Elphinstone mentions the legend (*History*, p.524 footnote). An American traveller wrote in 1856, "The common tradition among the natives is, that during the siege, after the supply of cannon balls was exhausted, she loaded her guns successively with copper, with silver, and gold coins, and did not consent to make terms until the only missiles remaining were her jewels." (R. B. Minturn's *From New York to Delhi*, 367.)

*Adilabad** is an excellent town; near it is a tank, which is regarded as a place of worship. Raja Jasrath (Dasharatha), the father of Ram Chandra, having inadvertently committed a 'slip of the foot' [*i e*, unintentional sin], sought atonement in this holy place. It is full to the brim all the year round. *Changdevi* (21.2 N. 76. E. Letts, Sh. 6.) is a village near which the Purna and the Tapti unite. *Chakar-tirth* is considered a place sacred to Mahadeo. There was a blind man who always carried about him and worshipped the idol of Mahadeo † One day it fell down from his hand and he lost it. He made a similar image with sand and performed his worship. By the miracle of Destiny it was turned into stone, and is still extant. Near it is a fountain, which is regarded as the Ganges. An ascetic used daily to go to the Ganges and come back [after his bath.] [87. *b*.] One night the river told him in sleep, "Bear needless hardship no longer. I will flow in thy corner."‡ In the morning a trickling appeared, which has flowed up to this day.

Amarni § is a populous village; near it is a reservoir from which hot water constantly bubbles up. *Chopra* (21·19 N. 75·14 E.) is a large town Near it is a temple [named] *Ramisar*. The Girni and the Purna|| unite together here and men from distant places come here to worship. The native Kolis and Bhils tame tigers so well that they obey their orders and do violence to none.

Revenue : 46,00,30,000 *dam* (Rs. 1,15,00,750) It has not been divided into *Sarkars*, but comprises 133 *mahals* and 6,339 *mauzas*. Revenue in money Rs. 57,49,972-14¼ as. [The last figure, if it stands for the six-monthly collection, represents an annual revenue of Rs. 1,14,99,945-12½ as.]

---

* Probably *Idulabad*, 21.1 N. 76 3 E. (Letts, Sh. 6.)

† *Ain*. ii. 224.

‡ *Ain*. ii. 224.

§ The *Ain* reads *Damarni*, but mentions *Damri* in the list of *mahals* (ii. 225) None of these names is found in Letts's Atlas.

|| This should be *Tapti*.

Details of Sarkars.

The whole province forms one *Sarkar*, with 133 *mahals*, of 25 of which the records of division and area are not obtainable. Remaining 108 *mahals* ; 6,339 *mauzas*. (i) The *mahals* whose area has reached the court : 33 (? 108) *mahals* ; area 88 *lac bigha* 16 *bisua* ; 2,832 *mauzas*. (ii) The *mahals* whose area is not obtainable : 85 (? 25) *mahals* ; 3,507 *mauzas*.

[The two kinds of total are given below :

	Sarkars	*Mahals*	Area in *bigha*	*Mauzas*	Rev. in *dam*.
P.	1	133	88,00,000$\frac{16}{20}$	6,339	46,00,30,000
A.	1	32	...	...	45,52,94,232].

XVII. AURANGABAD.

We learn from histories that in former times this town was called *Dharanagari*. After some time it became famous as *Deogir* or Daulatabad. When Sultan Fakhru-d-din Jauna, king of Delhi, brought the whole of the Deccan into his possession, he named the fort of Deogir *Daulatabad*, and [**88**. *a*.] made it his capital. The fort came back to the possession of the Muhammadan Emperors [in 1632 A D], 300 years after the time when the country of Deccan passed out of the hands of the kings of Delhi. When Prince Muhammad Aurangzib Alamgir was appointed Viceroy of the Deccan, he founded a town near it, at the village of *Khirki*, perfectly beautiful and strong, and named it *Aurangabad*. It is in the 2nd climate. Eastwards is the frontier of Muhammadabad Bidar, west Salhir* and Mulhir, south Bijapur, north Burhanpur and the river Pambra (?). The town is situated 111° long. 20°30′ lat.†

Daulatabad is a town, 2 *kos* from Aurangabad. Many precious things of all countries can be had here. In the reign of the Emperor Shah Jahan, this fort, which was among the forts of the Nizamu-l-mulk dynasty, was annexed to the Empire [of

* ***Salhir***, 20°43 N. 73°58 E. ***Mulhir***. 20°46 N. 74°8 E. (Letts' Sheet 6.)

† ***Aurangabad***, 19°54 N. 75°22 E. of Greenwich. (*I. G.* i. 387.)

Delhi]. This province has 145 forts, of which many are on the summits of hills, some in inaccessible forests, and all unrivalled in strength and power.

The revenue in *dam*, in the time of Alamgir (now in heaven), was 1,18,00,00,073 *dam*. (Rs. 2,95,00,001-13-2). The province comprises 11 *Sarkars*, 116 *mahals*, and 5,950 *mauzas*. The measured land is 2,55,70,950$\frac{9}{20}$ *bighas*. [88. *b*.]

DETAILS OF SARKARS.

1. Daulatabad...19 *mahals*, of which one is a mint. Remaining 18 *mahals* ; 1,147 *mauzas* ; area 25,37,388 *bighas*.
2. Ahmadnagar...20 *mahals* ; 112 *mauzas* ; area 37,21,877$\frac{3}{20}$ *bighas*.
3. Jalna...10 *mahals* ; 112 *mauzas* ; area 23,36,113$\frac{13}{20}$ *bighas*.
4. Islamabad Konkan...7 *mahals*, of 5 of which records not obtainable. Rem. 2 *m* ; 1,136 *mauzas* ; area 4,01,456 *bighas*.
5. Sholapur...3 *mahals* ; 112 *mauzas* ; area 4,47,803$\frac{17}{20}$ *bighas*.
6.* Jooner (?)...13 *mahals*, of 5 of which statistics not obtainable. Rem. 8 *m.* ; 1,223 *mauzas* ; area 42,05,394$\frac{12}{20}$ *bighas*.
7. Pattan (?)...3 *mahals* ; 165 *mauzas* ; area 3,74,651$\frac{3}{20}$ *bighas*.
8. Sir (?)......1 *mahal* ; area 28,23,363$\frac{15}{20}$ *bighas*.
9. Purainda (?)......19 *mahals* ; 5,599 *mauzas* ; area 20,05,475 *bighas*.
10. Sakha (?) ......11 *mahals* ; 1,353 *mauzas* ; area 32,57,368$\frac{3}{20}$ *bighas*.
11. Fatihabad......11 *mahals* ; 430 *mauzas* ; area 12,02,132$\frac{18}{20}$ *bighas*.

In this province fruits are plentiful, especially *sugar-cane* and mango are of great excellence. The former is of a black colour and soft ; people even go so far as to say that its juice can be pressed out by the nail [of the finger] ; it grows to such weight

---

* The transliteration of the names which are followed by the note of interrogation is doubtful, as the text is hopelessly illegible. *Jooner*, 19·16 N. 74 E. *Pattan* 19·31 N. 75·26 E. *Purainda*, 18·17 N. 75·30 E.

that more than 5 *seers* of clear juice can be pressed out of one sugar-cane. The latter (*mango*) weighs about $1\frac{1}{2}$ *seers*; and is very sweet, full of juice, soft, having a small stone, and free from fibres. But this [species] is hard to get. Those weighing $\frac{1}{2}$ *seer* are abundant in the bazars, and grow everywhere The flower *Keora* is plentiful. The *cocoa-nut* palm is numerous. In summer and the rainy season, men bring basket-loads of its green fruits and sell them cheap, giving 2 or 3 for one Alamgiri *pice*. When they are cut open, from [89. *a*] the interior a tasteful and sweet milky fluid comes out. The *shali* grows well and is of various kinds. *Betel* leaf is plentiful; one species of it, the *Kankiri* (? *Gangiri*) is very delicious and soft. If a man eats it, his tongue never corrupts.

[The first two kinds of total and that supplied by the *Khulasat* are given below :

Tot.	*Sarkars*	*Mahals*	Area in *bigha*	*Mauzas*	Rev. in *dam.*
S.	11	117	2,33,13,023$\frac{18}{20}$	11,389	......
P.	11	116	2,55,70,950$\frac{8}{20}$	5,950	1,18,00,00,073
K.	8	80	......	...	51,62,80,000.]

XVIII BIJAPUR.

This province is in the 2nd climate. In the east lies Gulburga (17·22 N. 76·54 E.), in the west Til-kokan,* in the south Adoni (15·37 N. 77·21 E.) and the river Kishna, in the north Aurangabad. The situation of the city is 105 long, 16·20 lat. (16.49.15 N. 75. 46·5 E. of Greenwich.) In 1096 A. H. (1686 A.D.), on Monday, the 2nd Jamadu-s-sani of the 28th year from the accession of the Emperor Aurangzib, the siege of the fort of Bijapur began. In 2 months and 28 days it was captured. The following is a detailed account of it :

On the 23rd Rajab of that year, Prince [Muhammad Azam] was appointed to this work. On the 26th of the same month Ghaziu-d-din Khan Firuz-Jang was appointed [to assist him] with

* Not found in Map. There is a *Tull Ghat*, 19·40 N. 73·32 E.

the troops of his command, viz, 16,995 cavalry Khan Jahan Bahadur with 15,000 cavalry, and Ruhulla Khan with 11,000 troopers and 250 [? blank in the text] were ordered to join the Prince in the siege of the fort and manifest energy and effort [in the work.] A total force of 77,105 horse and foot, was appointed to besiege the fort But as the siege was protracted, the Emperor also turned to the work and on the 22nd Shaban of the 29th year [of the reign] [89 *b*] arrived at the foot of the fort of Bijapur. At Rasulpur, within (? outside) the fort, was the entrenchment of the army. On Monday, the 7th of Ramzan, His Majesty himself rode out to inspect the entrenchments and honoured [with his presence] the trenches of Saf Shikan Khan. The men of the garrison then aimed their cannon so that one ball passed by the head of His Majesty and some others fell in front of him. On the 17th the assault (?) was delivered on the outer works (?). The enemy fled into the fort. On the 10th Shawwal of the 30th year, the filling up of the ditch began and it was finished in 2 days. That day [the 12th] His Majesty left his tent for the purpose of making the assault, went to the foot of the rear of the entrenchment, and desired the fort to be taken by assault. When Sikandar Adil Shah, lord of the fort, was convinced that the fort would be conquered in a day or two, he, on Monday the 4th Zi-qada, sent a message to Ghaziu-d-din Khan Bahadur and Saf Shikan Khan, requesting that they would take him to His Majesty after procuring a pardon for his offences. On the very day he was [allowed] to wait upon His Majesty. Ghaziu-d-din Khan advanced to the door to meet him. Adil Shah was at first riding in a palanquin ; but the above-named Khan sent one of his own riding horses and seated him on it ; and the two riders met together and the kissing of hands took place.

It was decided that he should at first live in the house of the Khan and afterwards enter into the white tent, which had been pitched for him. At night he came away from the fort to the Court of the Emperor. On Wednesday he waited upon the Emperor at Rasulpur. His Majesty held audience in the Bath.

Jumlatu-l-mulk Madaru-l-maham (chief minister) Asad Khan, Mahabat Khan and [90. *a*] Ruhulla Khan went out to meet him, [the last two] near the *Nakkdr-khdna* and Jumlatu-l-mulk Asad Khan near the canvas walls of the door of the Bath. When he came to His Majesty, he had the good fortune of kissing the [Emperor's] feet and was informed by the tongue of the most holy [Emperor], "It is for thy good. Have peace of mind." After being thus reassured he was permitted to stand face to face [with the Emperor] on the left hand of the silver railing of the throne. On the 15th Zi-hijja of the 30th year, the Emperor favoured him with perfumery (*attar*) and betel-leaf in the private tent and said, "You should not live at a distance. Remain near me in an adjoining tent." When he came to that place (?) all his furniture was confiscated. Ihtamam Khan and Sardar Khan were appointed to guard his tent ; he was mounted on an elephant and brought with a mounted escort (*sawari.*) One *lac* of Rupees was settled on him as his annual pension, and his name was changed into Sikandar *Khan.**

122 forts, full of war materials, were in this province. All of them came into the possession of the Emperor. Among them, *Turna garh*† in the *Sarkar* of Nurkal is a lofty and strong fort ; it was given back by Sultan Mahmud of Bijapur to Sultan Bahlol [Lodi] king of Delhi, who came from Hindustan. The walls of the fort have been built of stone and clay on the top of a hill, at some places 5 *zira* (=yard or cubit). at other places 4 *zira*, and elsewhere half a *zira* thick. This fort was founded when Ram Raja built the fort of Nagarkot in [the province of] Haidarabad. It has two gates, of which the southern one has been closed and the northern one [90 *b*] is open. The circumference of the fort is 1395 *zira* ; it has 24 towers and 389 parapets. A dry ditch 9 *zira* broad surrounds it ; in the rainy season it is filled with water at some places. The fort has one large well of brackish

* *Khan* or nobleman, as distinguished from his former title, *Shah* or king.

† *Torna*, a hill-fort, 18.14 N. 73'17 E.

water within it, and a tank of sweet water outside. It is [in the road] from Bijapur to the Karnatik which adjoins the ocean.

The fort of *Tel kokan* adjoins the ocean. West [of it] is a mountain between the countries of Salhir and Mulhir, in the northern hills. The rebel *Sambha[-ji]* fixed it as his residence. It appertains to Bijapur. The following is a detailed account of its capture :

On the 5th of the holy month of Ramzan, in the 25th year of the reign, corresponding to 1090 A.H. (1680 A.D.), the Emperor, who had set out for the Deccan, halted at Aurangabad* and deputed Prince Muhammad Muazzam for the chastisement of the malefactors of the Konkan. He himself, on the 2nd Zi-qada of that year, marched towards Ahmadnagar. The Prince entered Konkan from the mountain-pass of *Ram-ghat* ; in a short time all the country fell at the feet of the ever-victorious army, and plunder binding and imprisoning took place. This country has 8 *mahals*, a revenue [in *dam*] of 10,14,90,000 *dam* (Rs. 25,37,250) and a [cash] realisation amounting to Rs. 12,88,320 [for six months.] Eight *parganas* belong to it [**91.** *a*]

DETAILS OF SARKARS.

1. Kubir or Bhagundá (?)†...348 *mauzas* ; revenue 3,93,00,045 *dam* (Rs. 9,82,501-2) and a cash realisation of Rs. 4,91,819 [for six months ?].

* "Aurungzebe remained at Burhanpoor for some months. He first ordered Sultan Mauzum to proceed in advance from Ahmednugur and reduce Sumbhajee's southern territory, whilst Sultan Azim was directed to reduce his northern forts about Candeish, Buglana, and Sungumnere, and to commence by besieging the important fortress of Salheir. Accordingly Sultan Mauzum descended into the Concan by the Ambar-durray Ghaut, near Nassuck, and...advanced to the southward, where he plundered and burnt the country from Raigurh to Vingorla." (Duff's *Mahrattas*, i. 325,) "After Aurangzeb reached Aurangabad, Prince Muhammad Muazzam was sent to take the forts and punish the infidels of Ram-darra in the Kokan...[He] penetrated into the Kokan, and passing through its inmost recesses, passes and thick woods, he laid the country waste in all directions ; and put many infidels to the sword. (Twenty-fifth year of the reign ; 1092 A.H., 1681 A.D.)" Elliot, vii. 311.

† Most of the names of *Sarkars* as given in the text baffle all attempts to decipher them.

2. [Left blank in Text]...92 *mauzas*; revenue 27,00,000 *dam* (Rs. 67,500), cash realisation Rs. 63,763.

3. Muzaffarabad...revenue 1,33,50,000 *dam* (Rs. 3,33,750); cash realisation Rs 1,66,875 [for six months ?].

3. [Left blank in Text]...revenue 36,00,000 *dam* (Rs. 90,000); cash realisation Rs 45,000

5. Kodána (?) ... 56,000 *mauzas*; * revenue 57,05,000 *dam* (Rs. 1,42,625), cash collection Rs. 71,332

6. Sarangah (?) ... revenue 27,00,000 *dam* (Rs. 67,500), cash collection Rs 33,750.

7. Muzaffarabad or Khálo (?), 265 *mauzas*; revenue 1,33,50,000 *dam* (Rs 3,33,750), cash collection Rs 1,66,875. [This is a mere repetition of No. 3, except in the *mauzas*.]

8. Sáhli (?)...52 000 *mauzas*; revenue 36,00 000 *dam* (Rs 90,000); cash collection Rs. 75,000 [This is a mere repetition of No 4; though the cash collection has been incorrectly given as 75,000.]

[The two kinds of total are given below :

	Mahals	*Mauzas*	Rev. in *dam*	Rev. in money
S.	8	813	8,43,05,045	Rs. 11,14,314
P.	8	...	10,14,90,000	Rs. 12,88,320]

The fort of NAGARKOT is concealed in the ground. Ram Raja, the *Zemindar* of the Karnatik, built it on the frontier of his territory. It has 2 gates, one in the S E and the other in the N. The river *Diali* (?) [is] in it. In one (?) the water is abundant, the other is dry. The distance between the rivers Krishna and Bahat by way of Ladarbadri is 4 *kos*. In length... Ladarkola (?) 10 *kos*. There are many other forts in this province, the number of which has been already given. They will be detailed separately, if God wills it.

Collection in cash, Rs. 3,36,84,771. The statistics of the *Sarkars* of this province are not at Court. As is well-known, Nizamu-l-mulk Asaf Jah [91. *b*.] carried away with himself the

* Evidently the numbers of *mauzas* given for *Sarkars* 5 and 8 are wrong. I take them as 56 and 52 respectively in calculating the totals.

papers of every one of the six divisions [Text reads *mahals*] o the *Subah* of Deccan during his own viceroyalty. [He left Delh for the Deccan about 1720 A.D.] Therefore, they have not reached the author of these pages, who writes in his own place

XIX. HAIDARABAD.

[The town] was at first known as *Daru-l-jihad*, [the place of religious war], then it became celebrated as *Farkhanda-buniad* In former times it bore the name of *Bhagnagar* * It is in the first climate. The situation of the city is 102 30 long. and 19'30 lat. (17° 21'45 N. 78° 30'10 E. of Greenwich) The fort is situated on a hillock†, which is enclosed by another mountain. The ocean is near [the province The region commencing] from this place is called the territory of Abul Hasan Qutbu-l-mulk, whom the common people call Tana Shah. He was the unique of his age and the son of a noble of Iran. He came travelling from Hamadan, in the guise of a *Faqir*. The ruler of this place, Qutbu-l-mulk Abdulla (1611—72 A. D.) had no son, and, being pleased with his sagacity and acuteness of genius, accepted him as his son-in-law. When Abdulla bade farewell to the world, the Pillars of the State (chief officers). giving Abul Hasan‡ the title of Qutbu-l-

* "Haidarabad was founded in 1589 by Kutab Shah Muhammad Kuli...... on the banks of the Musi river, 7 miles from Golconda. He called it *Bhagnagar*, 'Fortunate City,' from his favourite mistress Bhagmati ; but after her death he named it Haidarabad." (*I. G.* v. 254 ; also Elliot, vii. 336.)

† "It stands on a height of about 1700 ft. above sea-level. The city is 6 miles in circumference, with a stone-wall, flanked with bastions, encircling it" (*I. G.* v. 254.)

‡ "Abu Husain (*sic*)......notorious for dissipated habits. He fell entirely under the influence of a Maratha Brahman named Madhuna Panth, who became his Prime Minister....In 1687, Aurangzeb formally declared war against Abu Husain. The king bravely defended the fort of Golconda for 7 months, lost it at last by treachery, and was sent a captive to Daulatabad, where he resided until his death. Abu Husain was a very popular monarch, and many anecdotes of his virtues are still current in the Deccan." (*I. G.* v. 256.)

mulk, placed him in authority. He was liberal, charitable, and indifferent to the world and its concerns. His night passed into day and his day wore on into night in attending dances and songs. The Pillars of the State looked after the work of government. Summoning many of the skilled artisans of the country, [he] assigned them quarters in his town. The handicrafts of the place have remained famous in the world up to this day. The Brahman *Madna* became his *Vizier* and the [**92** *a*] knot of his sovereignty. As Abul Hasan by always drinking to excess ruined his earthly realm and mental kingdom, the subjects of the country were oppressed by tyrannical men. Till at length their complaint reached the Emperor Aurangzib. He resolved to free the country from the hands of its oppressors, and for this purpose appointed his son, Prince Muhamad Azam Shah, with a large army and materials of war and siege. An acconnt of it is given below.

In this province there are 53 lofty forts, which rival the hill of *Alwand* [in Hamadan, Persia.] in strength and firmness. One of them is the fort of *Golconda*, of the capture of which the following is an account : [Not translated.]

[**93.** *b.*] Details of the property of Abul Hasan which was confiscated to the Imperial Treasury.—The cash reaching the treasury and spent as *tamghah** amounted to 31,05,000 *hun*, or Rs 93,35,000 ; [**94.** *a.*] and Rupees in cash 6 *lac* ; altogether amounting to Rs 1,04,81,849-12 as The money which was spent as *tamghah*, was an additional Rs 11,46,700. Besides the above, the price of the jewels and gold which Bhamdas (?) brought

---

"The king Abul Hasan, though indolent and voluptuous, was popular ; and his government and finances were ably conducted by Madna Pant, a Bramin. But the exclusive employment of this minister was odious to the Mussulmans." (Elphinstone's *India*, 652).

* "The word also signifies a royal grant under the seal of some of the former native princes and recognised by the British Government as conferring a title to rent-free land in perpetuity." (Wilson's *Glossary*.) But here the word seems to mean prize-money or royal grant.

in amounted to Rs 35,52,441-11as. [and they were kept] in charge of the Imperial officers.

Revenue in *dam*, 1,09,28,35,000 *dam* (Rs 2,73,20,875), collection in cash, Rs. 2,99,00,678, comprising the produce of the cesses which were levied in the time of Abul Hasan, the *dbwáb** being forbidden [The Province has] 12 *Sarkars.* As the records of this Province, like those of Bijapur, are not at Court, I cannot give the statistics of the *parganas* and *mauzas* and its area.

DETAILS OF SARKARS.†

1. Devalkundal‡...18 *mahals* ; revenue 3,44,666 *hun* 9¾ *anna* ; revenue in Rupees, Rs. 13,33,399-10¼ as.
2. Warangal, on the further side of the Krishna,...10 *mahals* ; revenue 1,22,512 *hun* 15¼ as.; revenue in Rs., Rs. 3,67,528 13¾ as.
3. Rajgopal, on the further side of the Krishna,...8 *mahals* ; revenue 3,72,486 *hun* ; revenue in Rs., Rs. 11,11,458-6 as.
4. Kambhim-mandi......5 *mahals* ; revenue 70,512 *hun* ; revenue in Rupees, Rs 2,30,427-13 as.
5. Ibrahim-pattan,§ on the further side of the Krishna,......revenue 2,24,266 *hun* ; revenue in Rupees, 6,72,780 12 as. [94. *b.*]
6. Nizam-pattan,‖ on the further side of the Krishna.........5 *mahals* ; revenue 10,66,214 *hun* ; revenue in Rupees, Rs. 31,00,000
7. Muhammadánagar......5 *mahals* ; revenue 32,92,04,500 *dam* (Rs. 82,30,112-8) ; revenue in Rupees, Rs. 37,71,284-1½ as.

* Cesses in excess of the original assessment (Fallon).

† At present the State of Haidarabad comprises the following 18 Districts, grouped in Divisions : (*a*) In the Eastern Division,—Kamamet, Nalgonda, and Nagar Karnul. (*b*) In the Northern Division,—Mehdak, Indoor, Yelgandal, and Sirpur Tandur. (*c*) In the Western Division,—Bidar, Nander, and Naldrug. (*d*) In the Southern Division,—Raichor, Lingsagar, Shorapur, and Gulburgah. (*e*) In the N. W. Division,—Aurangabad, Bhir, and Parbaini ; while the capital forms the City District. (*I. G.* v. 240.)

‡ *Daver-condah,* 16°42 N. 78°59 E. (Letts.)

§ 17 m. S. E. of Haidarabad City.

‖ 15°55 N. 80°45 E. (Letts.)

8. Kulpur (? or Gilpur) on the further side of the Krishna,...... 8 *mahals* ; revenue 3,68,331 *hun* 4 as. ; revenue in Rupees Rs 11,04,393-12 as.

9. Rajmahendri...12 *mahals* ; revenue 6,27,857 *hun* 11¾ as. ; amount in Rupees, Rs. 18,23,579-2¼ as

10. *Mahals* on the further side of the Krishna,...19 *mahals* ; revenue 11,46,392 *hun* ; amount in Rupees, Rs. 34,18,270-5¼ as.

11. [*Mahals*] on this side of the Krishna,...6 *mahals* ; revenue 32,92,04,510 *dam* (Rs. 82,30,111-12) ; amount in Rupees, Rs. 37,71,294-1½ as

12. *Mahalat i-sáir* : (1) Mint, 52,339 [*hun* ?] Income from *sendhi* (juice of the date palm, toddy,) 19,000 *hun*. *Mandúyát* (marts, emporia ?) 3 houses, 1,000 *hun*.
   (2) Income from reservoirs 1,375 [*hun* ?] Grass, 3,225 *hun*.
   (3) Income from *Bándher* (?) 16,365 *hun*. *Kotwali chabutra* (police-station) 39,300 *hun*.
   (4) Diamond mines 2,00,055 *dam* (Rs. 5,001-6) ; 52,339 *hun*, Rs. 7,57,017 12 as *

XX. BIDAR.

This provinee is in the second climate...Eastwards lies Haidarabad, westwards Aurangabad, south-west Gulburga, north Burhanpur. In the time of the Emperor Alamgir, the fort of Bidar was conquered along with some other forts. Of them five are very strong, viz, Muhammadabad, Raigarh, Firuzgarh or Ibrahimgarh, Kalliangarh,† Muzaffarnagar or Balkhan‡ In this

* The total revenue in Rupees for all the *Sarkars* added together is Rs. 2,13,21,434-8, while the Provincial total is given as Rs. 2,99,00,678.

† *Kullianee*, 17'53 N, 77'1 E (Letts, Sheet 3.)

‡ There is a *Balkhi*, 18'5 N. 77'17 E. (*Ibid.*)

province the excellent and valuable *Bidri* pots are manufactured, [such as] the *pán-dán*, *ab-khora*, [**95.** *a.*] *rekabi*, small and large cups, *hukka*, candle-stick and other things ; different sorts of flowers are inlaid on them with gold and silver by the artisans of this place, so delicately and nicely that even a painter cannot picture them in his imagination. Fruits and flowers abound in all the provinces of the Deccan. The heat [of summer] is not great ; in the rainy season one has to wear the *shal* and *doldi* morning and evening. Winter is temperate This province has 4 *Sarkars*, 54 *mahals*, 3791 *mauzas* ; its measured land is 78,72,194 $\frac{18}{20}$ *bighas* ; revenue in *dam* 62,05,50,000 *dam* (Rs. 1,55,13,750) ; revenue in money Rs. 66,59,801-12$\frac{3}{4}$ as.

DETAILS OF SARKARS.

1. Bidar...8 *mahals*, 549 *mauzas*, area 15,65,198 $\frac{9}{20}$ *bighas*.
2. Kallian...2 *mahals*, 147 *mauzas*, area 2,04,137 $\frac{13}{20}$ *bighas*.
3. Rúmgarh...1 *mahal*, 107 *mauza*, area unknown.
4. Mándir...43 *mahals*, of one of which area unknown. Rem. 42 *mahals*, 2,886 *mauzas*, area 66,02,888 $\frac{8}{20}$ *bighas*.

[Text wrongly gives the number of *mauzas* for No. 4 as 93. The two kinds of total are stated below :

	Sark.	*Mah.*	*Mauzas*	Area in *bigha*	Rev. in *dam*.
S.	4	54	3,689	81,71,624 $\frac{18}{20}$	......
P.	4	54	3,791	78,72,194 $\frac{19}{20}$	62,05,50,000.]

In many places of the Deccan, cloth and other articles are very well manufactured. The gold *bádla*, *do-patta*, [**95.** *b.*] bordered *korta*, *chirah*, and *sarpech* are well woven. *Do-patta*, *kamar-band*, and *sar-pech* of lace are excellently made. In the territory of the Karnatik *chhint* is well manufactured ; and abundance alsc called *chhint*, is woven, of which the warp that even a painter of the hair of the cow. It is very nice, cloth and flowers abound Many men make dresses of it.

In this *Zilla*, *jaifal* (nut-meg) and the warp different sorts of grow in abundance. Of the former they that by the artisans of fruit). The present writer brought one even a painter cannot *murabba*. European *badam* (almond) grows in Haidarabad ; its size is one foot or less than one foot in length, and 12 fingers—more or less—in breadth. Four [kernels are found] in one [fruit.] It matures in 7 months. Its taste is like that of the [Indian] *badam*. (*Terminalia catappa*) *Mauz*, i.e. plantain, is numerous. One variety of it, called the *suhan kela* is smaller ; its pith is so delicate that if you place it on hot rice it melts into water and sinks down. Another variety is called the *gokeli kela* ; its pith is used after being dried. Its flavour resembles that of *khobani* (apricot). *Fofal*, i.e., betel-nut, is plentiful, and its trees are numerous. It has a slender trunk, the fruits and leaves growing in clusters ; among the leaves it has bunches [of fruits] like the date-tree ; its good flavour makes it fetch a high price. one *seer* costing as much as ten rupees. With the wood of the trunk they make very strong spear-shafts. Other precious things are abundant ; I have no space to write of them. The *karaunda* (the corinda, *Carissa carandas*) bears good fruits at certain places ; one of it weighs 2 or 3 copper coins. Its taste is sweet and sour blended together, and it pleased the palate of the Emperor Alamgir. Whoever presented him on the way with one *seer*—more or less—of it, [96. *a*] got one gold coin by way of reward

Account of the **Kings** of the Deccan, [not translated].

[116. *b*.] The **Forts** of each of the six Provinces of the DECCAN given separately :

I. THE FORTS OF THE PROVINCE OF AURANGABAD.

(144 *Forts*.)

1. Kaliáni.	10. Bhamri.	19. Ratangarh.
2. Bakhári.	11. Dhánkhora.	20. Sárdá-durg.
3. Púri.	12. Dargáhikhora.	21. Sakatrá (?).
4. Qila Mánik.	13. Barálaf.	22. Songarh.
5. Qila Masi.	14. Bahrángarh.	23. Surplárak (Surpál durg ?)
6. Qila Balgarh.	15. Barili (?).	
7. Qila Manranjan.	16. Durg-garh	24. Koliána.
8. Mankar-garh.	17. Sardári.	25. Kúrgarh.
9. Sarmar-rái (?)	18. Rámpuri.	26. Kaláná-khurd.

27. Kanak-durg (Gang-durg ?).
28. Ghósála.
29. Mát-garh (?).
30. Mánik-garh.
31. Madh-garh.
32. Balá.
33. Mandal-garh.
34. Mulk-garh
35. Basant-garh.
36. Haidar-garh.
37. Manpálgarh.
38. Mór-garh.
39. Isá-garh.
40. Go-ganj.
41. Bháskar.
42. Deo-dand
43. Uniri (?)
44. Unakdanda (?)
45. Mulk-garhi.
46. Chánd-bari (?).
47. Dhák.
48. Koplás (?)
49. Konkána.
50 Udurg.
51. Bisrám-garh.
52. Bhúri
53. Saudágir.
54. Padam-durg.
55. Partáb-garh.
56. Púrna.
57. Chandan-garh.
58. Ráj-garh.
59. Ráj-durg
60. Karúr.
61. Khánderi.
62. Kotwal-garh.
63. Kalman-garh.
64. Kánu.
65. Bari.
66. Makarand-garh.
67. Dabdal-garh.
68. Wánúba (?).
69. Bansli (?).
70. Sakota (?)
71. Ahangarh.
72. Bandágarh.
73. Kijr-garh (?).
74. Suádas.
75. Harsal.
76. Khujista-buniad (Aurangabad).
77. Begampur.
78. Daulatabad
79. Ajláu.
80. Ahmad-nagar.
81. Islamabad or Júlna.
82. Azim-garh.
83. Buna.
84. Amúr.
85. Aud-gir.
86. Usa (?).
87. Undh (?).
88 Islamabad or Ráiri
89. Anjráni (?).
90. Alang.
91. Anki-banki.
92. Ahuhat.
93. Bahádur-garh or Bikapur.
94. Bula (?).
95. Buhár [117 *a.*]
96. Sardári.
97. Báni-garh (?).
98. Malih (Mulher ?).
99. Sálih (Salher ?).
100. Purainda.
101. Nand-gáon.
102. Bhim-garh.
103. Bamar-bank (?).
104. Warangal-dári.
105. Júdhan.
106. Jaula.
107. Chándpur.
108. Parand.
109. Chanún (Jaiún ?).
110. Dharat.
111. Dabhra.
112. Rájmand.
113. Rájkot.
114 Rásanj.
115. Rúla.
116. Sinkhar.
117. Sadhú-durg.
118. Ságar-garh.
119. Son-garh.
120. Sholápur.
121. Qandhár.
122. Fatihabad or Dhári.
123. Gúlbarga.
124. Khadása.
125. Kahan-garh.
126 Kálubi.
127. Khajar bajar (?).
128. Nakhra.
129. Kurang.
130. Gúldhar.
131. Kánra.
132. Kurang.
133. Kalul-garh.
134. Kar-garh.
135. Lauh-garh
136. Muftáhu-l-fatuh or Kúnila
137. Badh.
138. Márkand.
139. Máhuli.
140. Mánik-ganj.
141. Máhur.
142. Nal-durg.
143. Sar-bas (?)
144. Harchand-garh.

II. The Forts of the Province of Khandesh or Berar (19 *Forts*).

1. Burhánpur.
2. Asirgarh.
3. Rudi.
4. Mánik.
5. Hargarh.
6. Maurágarh.
7. Panála.
8. Fatihábád.
9. Bhátnir Mul.
10. Mujha (?)
11. Sultángarh.
12. Sánula (?).
13. Songarh.
14. Gáwil
15. Kámla.
16. Barnála (? Narnala)
17. Nauágarh.
18. Báila (?)
19. Bábhal-garh (?)

III. The Forts of Bidar. (5 *Forts*).

1. Muhammadábád (Bidar).
2. Rámgir.
3. Firuzgarh [or] Ibrahimgarh.
4. Kalián.
5. Muzaffarnagar or Balkhan (Balkhi ?)

IV. The Forts of the Province of Bijapur. (120 *Forts*).

1. Bijápur.
2. Islámgarh.
3. Alang.
4. Achalpur.
5. Amalánk (?)
6. Rewni.
7. Aniráj-durg.
8. Andarud.
9. Ast-garhi.
10. Rang-durg.
11. Táru.
12. Panch-durg.
13. Him-durg.
14. Mahim-garh.
15. Sudar-garh.
16. Badnur.
17. Sák-durg.
18. Nau-madár-garh.
19. Bái-buzáni (?)
20. Mákhárái.
21. Mákhárali.
22. Banli (?)
23. Sálliki.
24. Sadh-garh [117 *b*.].
25. Nupar-garh (?)
26. Sapandan-durg (?)
27. Susar.
28. Siáh-durg.
29. Kalki.
30. Kisán-garh.
31. Lakhmir.
2. Lúmsi-garh (?)
33. Nádar-garh (Naradgarh ?)
34. Bhál-garh.
35. Mahammat-garh.
36. Mandhi-garh.
37. Nándu-garh (?)
38. Bálápur.
99. Harang.
40. Dang-pur.
41. Bhúkhan-garh.
42. Múdgal (Mu ktul ?)
43. Súsal.
44. Barad.
45. Mandpál.
46. Saubat-durg.
47. Bundi-kotha.
48. Gokal-pur.
49. Chhilam.
50. Luná.
51. Bundi.
52. Kotpur.
53. Khua.
54. Rasúlgarh.
55. Kandal-garh.
56. Kulár-garh.
57. Júb-garh.
58. Bhúm-garh.
59. Rahim-garh
60. Ruin-garh.
61. Sháhmandar.
62. Wazir-garh.

63. Viláit-garh.
64. Humá.
65. Bankábalá.
66. Harbans-garh.
67. Chandan-garh.
68. Mahál-garh (?)
69. Gulaband-garh.
70. Gandharb-garh (?).
71. Mor-garh.
72. Naulpur.
73. Mardán-garh.
74. Súram-sakh.
75. Kumbar-álál.
76. Khadi.
77. Ladhá sadha.
78. Asgharnagar or Aklúj.
79. Azimnagar or Malkápur.
80. Imtiár-garh.
81. Kabúrah.
82. Máráni.
83. Banal-garh.
84. Basuámin.
85. Baldá-garh.
86 Bikánur
87. Bhus-garh.
88. Pádsháh-pur.
89. Bánsi (?).
90. Máthúra.
91. Núrgal.
92 Mangalkot.
93. Khabrá.
94. Dhubri.
95 Rájbans-garh.
96. Athsli-garh.
97. Anmál-garh.
98. Sánkúla.
99. Sadhúr.
100. Sadánand-garh.
101. Sribast-garh.
102. Harkona-garh
103. Kanúl-garh.
104. Martazábád.
105. Mangal-band.
106. Múdgal (16·1N. 76.30E.)
107. Baldatpi.
108. Máham.
109. Haidar-garh (Chandargarh ?)
110. Sabanján-garh (?).
111. Mandalgarh.
112. Mahmán-garh.
113. Nasir-ábád.
114. Nand-pál.
115. Dárá garh.
116. Bijuli (?).
117. Huli-garh.
118. Hali-hál.
119. Huli-honúr.
120. Húnmali.

V THE FORTS OF THE PROVINCE OF HAIDARABAD.

(54 *Forts.*)

1. Bhágnagar or Haidarabad.
2. Danúrgarh.
3. Muhammadabad.
4. Rasápur.
5. Khúlás.
6. Martaza-nagar.
7. Kalúh-bádar (?).
8. Makha [1'8. *a.*]
9. Kúmal-garh.
10. Mustafa-nagar.
11. Haidar-nagar.
12. Basant-nánam (?)
13. Kúbháúli (?)
14. Tubal kandan.
15 Mandakrápur.
16. Hasab-nasab (?)
17. Kanji-kúp.
18. Jangal-pet.
19. Másrúr (?)
20. Naumalgarh.
21. Golkonda.
22. Sadah-danam (?)
23. Habur.
24. Arganúr.
25. Wálmák.
26. Makahkúr.
27. Bhu-garh.
28. Karúdh.
29. Bans-dhar.
30. Har-mali (?)
31. Urksla.
32. Uárun.
33. Mánkal.
34. Khulirah.
35. Karábkali.
36. 'Absi.
37. Kumin.
38. Ubúr.
39. Panchla.
40. Lundhá-e.
41. Korúr.
42. Kalá-pur.
43. Kúli.
44. Bámin.

45. Abdulla-garh.
46. Bidli-garh.
47. Sundam-bár.
48. Manjádurg.
49. Kha-ram-war-dar.
50. Khajla (?)
51. Nimi.
52. Khim.
53. Dharamrám.
54. Kúni (Guti ?)

The **Saints** of the six Provinces of the Deccan [not translated.]

[**119.** *a*] **Hindu Shrines** in the Province of Deccan.—*Shiva-Ganga* [not translated, as it is a repetition of p 85 *b* of the text.] [**119.** *b*.] *Tank near Adilabad* [a repetition of p 87. *a*] *Chakar-tirth Ibid.*] *Reservoir at Amarni* [*Ibid.*] *Ramisar* [*Ibid*] *Lachhman-chati* : He [Lachhman] was the brother of Rám, who was an incarnation [of Vishnu] ; his shrine is on a hill difficult of access, [where] a large temple has been built to him ; every day presents are offered at the place, and they are spent on paupers and *faqirs*.

The **Rivers** of the Provinces of the Deccan.--The *Kishna* coming out of the hill near Balkokan, unites with the ocean near [the province of] Haidarabad [**120** *a*] The *Bhimra* flows from between the territories of Bijápur and Aurangabad The *Bángangá* [first] comes into sight in the territory of Bijapur and [then] flows on to the province of Aurangabad. The *Narbada*, descending from the hill of Mangal which is in Bengal, reaches the Deccan and falls into the ocean The Hindus call it a *nad*, i. e.. a male [river] All rivers are of the feminine gender [*nadi*], except seven, which are called *nád* The *Kahúr* (?) flows out of the Purná near Fardápur. The *Tapti* flows from Deogáon in the province of Berar ; the city of Burhánpur is on its bank ; at the village of Cháng-devi it unites with the Purná. The *Gangá Gotami*, also called *Godávari*, is connected with the *Rishi* Gotam It comes from Ahmadnagar into Berar. Its stream is [first] seen near the hill of Sahyá. When Jupiter enters Leo, men come from distant places to perform worship here. The *Girni* and the *Purná* : the former flows near Chopra, and the latter at Deogáon. They unite with the Tapti at the village of Chang-devi.

BOOK THIRD.

ON THE STAGES AND DISTANCES.

I write of the royal road (*sháh-ráh*) from Bijapur to Shah-Jahanabad and [those] which extend on the four sides of Delhi, east and west, north and south, together with the distances and [halting] places, as far as they are known. From Bijapur to a 100 *kos* [south] is the limit of [the territory of] Adil Shah ; thence to Setu-bandh Rameswar is the dominion of Rám Rája.

[The following tables, each occupying a page of the text, have been here reproduced verbatim, the only change that I have made being the transposition of the columns so that the pages which in the text read from the right to the left are here made to read from the left to the right. The numbers enclosed in brackets have been supplied by me, while those outside brackets are as found in the text A note of interrogation has been placed after doubtful unidentified names. In the footnotes *A* stands for the *Indian Atlas* (1" = 4 miles) issued by the Survey of India Office, *L* for Letts' *Popular Atlas*, and the number immediately following these letters for the number of the sheet in the Atlas.]

[120. *b*.]

			Aurangabad, which was formerly named *Khirki*, and then *Khujista-buniad*.	
Bijápur Fort			35 Poolmurry (8).	
Bijápur [City]	Golkonda			
Kanwalápur			3 Pathri	River of Nagpur
Nandgáon (1)	Bidar		3 Alund (9)	
Chambhar-goonda (2)	Qandhar (7)		Serái-kámán	
Izdábád (3)			Ki Salur (10)	
Ahmad-nagar Fort	Ahmadna-gar city		Gola-gáon Fardápur	
Bihisht-bágh (4)	Ellichpur		Gháti Fardá-pur	River of Nag-pur ?
Ban-ganga [river]	Takht-bahzád ?		Serai-Hátam Beg	The stream Purna comes from Berar.
Durjanpur			Bikhári ?	
			Adilábad (11)	
Village			Antri (12)	
Village	River Tapti		Bahári ?	On this side is Burhanpur.
Village	Asir Fort	Sorath of Gujrát	Ujjain city (13)	Serai-Dádan Gháti-Tubri ?
8 *Cutcha* Serái	River Mándhár?	Burhán-pur	Firozpur vil-lage	Serai-Bádli .
3 Bheekungáon (5)		2 Serái-Jolá	Serai-Sultan Mahmud	Serai-Nukrá-nia ?
Nagpur 6 Ghorágaon (6)		3 Serái nim		Badshahi Serai

(1) There is a *Nimbgaon*, 18·5 N. 74·58·30 E (A 39 S E)
(2) 18·37 N 74·45 E. (L. 3) ; named *Shrigonda* in A 39 N. E.
(3) Probably *Kalarabad* or Mandavgan, 17 m. N. N. E. of Shrigonda (A. 39 N. E.)
(4) A garden north of Ahmadnagar, see p. 148.
(5) 21·49 N. 76·1 E. (L. 6)
(6) Probably *Gogaon*, 6½ m. S. of Multan (A. 37 N. E.).
(7) *Kandahr*, 18·53 N. 77·17 E. (L 3.)
(8) 15 m. N of Aurangabad (L. 3)
(9) 13 m. N. E. of Poolmurry, 20·13 N. 75·39 E. (*Ibid*).
(10) *Sailoor*, 8 m N. E of Alund (*Ibid*).
(11) Probably *Idulabad*, 21·1 N 76·5 E. (L. 6.).
(12) Not t e Antri which is 11 m. S. of Gwalior.
(13) 23·10 N. 75·48 E. (L. 6).

[121. *a.*]

*	†			‡	
6 Multhán (1).	10 Serai-Mandhár.		Serai-Sang-in-Kaman.	Serai-Cha-har-dah (4)	Dargah of Shah Mastan ?
Serai-Mál-chand.	2 Mandu.		Road from the side of Ujjain.	Sihore village	Road.
Akbarpur.	3 Daudnagar.		Shahjahanpur (3)	Serai-Nimak	Daghwara ?
				Duraha	Tomb of Shah Karmun.
Jahangir-nagar.	3 Serai-Bir ?				
Nau-nahra	3 New Serai		Village.	Serai-Bhatkhera	Shrine of Shah Ali.
Dikthan	3 Serai.		Deodha village.		Mewatian-Nakhraj ?
Dipalpur	3 Serai Baharankata ? (2)	Imperial Serai.		*Cutcha* Serai	Abode of Mandiburj
Fatihabad [also] known as Juria.	8 Serai-Chinpur			Nala Bhuanala ?	Imperial nala.
				Serai of Baroda village	Asafabad.
Garden of Aurangzib	Narmada River.			Serai-Basant baria ?	Eastern direction :
	8 Serai-Nim			Serai-Kankar ?	Chanderi (5)
Darband *or* the gate of Ujjain (?) 15 *kos*.	4 Charwah village			Serai-Niuária ?	Sironj city
	Serai-Beli				This river of Sironj
	Serai-Bijhula ?				
	Hindia village				
	Tomb of Mulla Dopiaza.	Serai of Murshid Quli Kotwal			
	Serai-Nurbari ?	Ghati Fardapur ?			

* This column comes immediately after the *Ghoragaon* of the previous page. † This column comes immediately after the *River Mandhar* of the preceding page. ‡ This column comes immediately after the 2nd column of this page, and the fifth column follows it, while the 3rd column of the page follows the 1st.

(1) 22 N. 75'47 E. (L. 6.) There is another *Multhan* (A. 36 N.E.) 23'5 N. 75'16 E. *Akbarpur* 22'9 N. 75'31 E. (A. 37 N.E.) *Dikthan* 22'34 30 N. 75'32 E. (A. 36 S.E.) *Dipalpur* 22'53 N. 75'32 E (L. 6.) *Fatihabad* 23'1 N. 75'44 E. (A. 36 N.E), 12m. S. S. W. of Ujjain. There is a village named *Jharolia*, 1½ m. N.W. of it.

(2) Probably *Bhamghur*, 15 m. S.W of Chainpur (L. 6) *Chainpur* 21'48 N. 76'43 E (L. 6) *Charwah* ?? N. 76.52 E. (L. 6) *Hindia* 22'29 N. 77'3 E. (A. 53 S.E.) The pass of Fardápur, 32 *kos* from Aurangabad. (Elliot vii. 307).

(3) 23'24 N. 76'16 E. (L. 6.), 34 m. N. E. of Ujjain. *Deodha* is probably *Dupara*, 14 m N. of Shah-Jahanpur (A. 53. N. W.)

(4) Probably *Ichhawar*, 23'2 N. 77. 5 E. (A. 53 N.E.) *Sihore*, 23'12 N. 77.7 E. *Duraha* 23.24 N. 77'13'30 E. *Bhatkhera* 23'38 N. 77'38 E (*Ibid.*)

(5) The *Chanderi* meant here seems to be the one at 24'3'30 N. 77'20 E., 26 m. W. of Sironj. (A. 52 S.E.) *Sironj*, 24 7 N. 77'45 E. (*Ibid.*)

[121. *b*.]

Continuation of the royal road of Sironj. This river flows below Sironj, but nobody drinks its water.		Serai Tamawaj (?) built by order of the Emperor Alamgir [but] not used.		Serai Rajhula(?) was renovated in the time of Alamgir, and became a village of the name of Rajhula.
		Serai Maláncha ?		River Chambal
Stone Serai.		River Nun		Dholpur (10)
Serai-Mughal (1).	Ghati.	Village of Nun		Serai Sádiq
Serai-Afghan		Serai-Nun		Fatihabad
Serai Kachner(2).		Serai-Sardar Khan	Built by order of the Emperor; the Prince Akbar sold it.	Serai Begam
Shah-daura (3).	Old serai.			Serai Shaikh
Serai of the village of Madhkati ?		*Cutcha* Serai		Serai Than ? (11).
		Antri was a village named Guna (8)		Serai Abu Said Hassan.
Village of Kalabagh (4).		Serai Sarmast		Jamal-nagar.
		Serai Gajpati in the city ?		
Serai Abul Hassan	Aknapi ?			Serai Sambha ?
Tumadu-nagar ?		Gwalior city		Serai Sikandra (12).
Village of Rajhulá ?		Serai-Jándwarán ?		
		Serai-Ud Singh		Serai Sara.
Serai Sa'id.	A *pucca* serai has been purchased by order of the Emperor from the Prince.			
Serai-Badridas (5).		Serai Mihr Ali	Distance of other cities from Akbarabad†	Village of Kakuba.
Village of Sawari (6).		Serai-Sank ? (9)		
		Garden of Khan-Jahán *	Celebrated as Ambar Khan.	Serai Muluk-chand.
Serai-Dongri (7)	!Ghati			
Narwar city.	Narwar.	The river Sánkh		!Serai Kanwari?

(1) 14 m. N. of Sironj (A. 52 S. E.). (2) 24'26 N. 77'4 E. (A. 52 N. E.).

(3) 24'37 N. 77'39 E. (*Ibid.*) (4) 16 m. N. of Shahdaura; 3½ m. S. of it is *Nai Serai*, but 3½ m S. E. is *Hasanpur*. (*Ibid.*)

(5) There is a *Kailaras*, 15 m. S. of Sipri (A. 51 S. E.)

(6) Should be *Sipri*, 8 m. S. W. of Dongri. (7) 25'30! N. 77'49 E. (*Ibid*) 14 m. N. E. of it is *Nurwur*.

(8) *Antri*, 11 m. S. of *Gwalior*; near it is a village named *Ningona* (A. 51 N. E.) 14 m. S. of it is the river *Noon*.

(9) There is a river named *Sank*, 8 m. W. of Gwalior.

* Here there are two lines in the text which cannot be read correctly. The last column of this page is very puzzling. At first sight *Sadiqpur* (7 m N. N. E. of Dholpur) and *Fatihabad* (17 m S. E. of Agra) seem to indicate that the road proceeds N. E. from Dholpur, avoiding Agra in the west. But from the context it seems to be the last portion of the road from Gwalior, via the Sank river, to Agra. I take it as the latter.

(10) 26'41 N. 77'58 E (A. 50 S. E) (11) May be a mistake for *Thanro*, 10½ m. N. of Dholpur. (12) *Sikandarpur*, 11½ m. S. of Agra, and *Kakuba* 4 m. N. of Sikandarpur. (*Ibid.*)

† After this comes the information at the top of the next page of the text.

[122. *a*.]

[Distance in *kos* from Agra to] Burhanpur 245, Mandhu 202, Azimabad Patna 356, Jaunpur 141, Etawah 4 [should be 40], Allahabad 15 [should be 150] Mathura 18, Delhi 80, Kabul 391 [should be 591], Lahor 282, Kashmir by the road of Dhantaur *via* Pakli, 274 [should be 374] The fort of Akbarabad on the river Jumna was formerly a village named Agra and a dependency of Biana.

From Akbarabad to Shah Jahanabad.		From Banchari to Shah Jahanabad Delhi Khana Kathra (2).		From Shah Jahanabad to the capital Lahor.		Continuation of the road.
Sikandra (1).	The tombs of Akbarabad are here.		4	Badli (5).		Duraha (8).
Serai Farah			6	Narela.		Ludhiana
			8	Sonepat.		River Sutlej.
			6	Ganaur.		Phulour.
Jhandipur from Sikandar ?		Mitrul (3).	6	Samalkha		Nurmahal.
Ganu-ghat ?	*Pucca* Serai commanding the Jumna.	Bahamni Khera (4).	8	Panipat.		Nakodar.
		Serai-Palwal.	7	Gharaunda	Firuz's canal which has been dug from Mukhlispur (from which place Shah Jahanabad is 100 *kos*.)	Dakhni
		Baghaula.				River Biah.
		Pir-thala.				Sultanpur.
		Sikri.	4	Serai-pul (6).		Fatihabad.
		Chahar Sihli ?	4	Karnal (7)		Nauranga-bad.
Serai Koila		Ballabgarh.				Nuru-d-din Hassan.
Naurangabad	Over-looking the Jumna.	Faridabad.				Serai Amanat Khan.
Mathura, birth place of Sri Krishna-ji.						Darkah Pul ? †
Akbarpur.			7	Taraori-Azimabad.	The river *Sarsati* between Thanisar and Shahabad. *Kuru Chhatra*, which is a great holy place of the Hindus, is here.	
Serai Cháta* *pucca.*	was a village named Chata.		9	Shahabad Thanisar.		

* Between the Cháta and Khana Kathra of this page intervenes the 1st column of the next page (Deotana). After Faridabad comes the 2nd column of the next page (Serai-Khawajah Bakhtawar Khan.) Between the Thanisar and Duraha of this page intervenes the 3rd column of the next page (Umbala.)
† After this comes the *Hushiar Khan* of the next page.

(1) *Sikandra*, 5 m. N. W. of Agra. *Farah* 13½m N. W. W. of Sikandra. *Jhandipur* 3 m. N. of Farah, and *Koila* 5 m. N. of Jhandipur. (A. 50 N. E.) *Naurangabad* is given at 9½ m. from Farah (*Agra and Calcutta Gazetteer*, vol II. pt. I. p. 37 *n*.) *Akbarpur*, 12 m. N. W. of Mathra. *Chata*, 27. 44 N. 77. 34 E. (A. 50 N. E.)

(2) *Khataila* 4 m N. of Banchari (A. 49 S. E.); it is named *Kuttehla* in the *A and C Gazetter* p. 132. (3) *Mitnaul* 6½ m. N. of Banchari (A 49 S E.) spelt *Metrolee* in the *A and C Gazetteer*. (4) *Khera Serai*, 2½ m N. of Mitnaul, and 2 m S. of *Tikri Brahman* (A. 49 S. E.); the *A. and C. Gazetteer* calls it *Baminee Khera*. (p 132) *Palwal*. 28. 9 N. 77. 23 E. *Baghaula*, 4 m. N. of Palwal. *Pirthala* 6½ m. N. of Palwal. *Sikri*, 3 m. N. of Pirthala. *Ballabgarh* 28. 21 N. 77. 23 E. There is a *Sihi*, 1½ m. N. E. of it. *Faridabad* 5½ m. N. of Ballabgarh and 16 m S. of Delhi. (A. 49. S.E.)

(5) *Badli*, 8 m. N. W. of Delhi. *Narela*, 7 m. N. N. W. of that. *Sonepat* 29 N. 77. 5 E., 11½ m N. W. of that. *Gunaur* 9 m. N. W. of that. (A. 49. N. E.) *Samalkha* 29. 15 N. 77. 4 E. 10½ m. S. of Panipat. (A. 49 N. W.) *Gharaunda*,

10 m. N. of Panipat (A. 48 S. W.) (6) Probably the *bridge* over the canal, at the 6th mile from Gharaunda, mentioned in the *A. and C. Gaz*, p. 25 *n*. (7) *Karnal*, 10 m. N. of Gharaunda *Taraori*. 9 m. N. W. of Karnal (*Azimabad* is given at the same locality in *L* 9 as Taraori is in *A*.) *Thanesar* 29. 58 N. 76. 54 E. (A. 48 S. W.) *Shahabad* 30. 10 N. 76.55 E., 13 m N. of Thanesar (A. 48 N. W.)

(8) *Douraha ke Serai*, 25 m. from Sirhind (*A and C. Gaz*. p 23.) *Ludhiana* 30. 52. 30 N. 75. 54 E. *Phulour* 10 m N. N. W. of that (L. 11.) *Noor-mahal*, 7 m. E. of Nakodar. *Nakodar* 31.7.30 N. 75. 32 E. *Dukhnee*, 5 m. N. W. of that. *Sultanpur* 13 m. W. of that, here is the ferry over the *Kalna* river. *Futtehabad*, 31. 23 N. 75. 10 E, *Nowrungabad*, $4\frac{1}{2}$ m. S. E. E. of Tarn Taran. (A. 30.) *Nooroddeen Surace*, 6 m. N. W. W. of Tarn Taran (L. 11), given in *A* 30 as *Pindoree Husun*. *Surai-Amanut Khan*, 31. 31 N. 74. 45. 30 E. (A 30.)

[122 *b*.]

Continuation of the road from Akbarabad to Shah-Jahanabad.

Stage	Remarks
Deotána (1)	
Serai-Kosi	A *pucca* serai with red stone gates on two sides.
Hodal	
Banchári	Old town

* Kábul	Multán	Azimabad	Jaunpur
616	447	......	221
Etáwa	Abád	Muthrá	Kashmir
102	195	62	294
Sirhind	Jalal	Peshávar	Lahor
100	556	518	200

The citadel of Láhor was in ancient times named Laháwur ; and some called it Lahápur. It was founded by Lav, the son of Ramchandra, one of the 10 Incarnations. It over-looks the river Ravi. Some ascribe the foundation of the fort to Malik Ayáz, a favourite of Sultan Mahmud. The Emperor Akbar repaired the wall surrounding the town.†

Kábul	Multán	Ravi
305	236	......
Ajmir	Kasur	Delhi
67	2	200

Continuation of the road from Banchari to Shah-Jahanabad Delhi.

Stage	Remarks
Serai-Khawajah Bakhtáwar Khan.	Raushanu-d-daula peopled it
Badarpur (2)	Serai Jalpá-dikan ?
Tank of Raja Kishan Das (3)	Siráj Shaikh Sharf ?
Serai-Mahábat Khan.	
Bárapula (4)	

Serai, in which the stipendiary Arabs live, known as the *Serai-Arab*. Near it Sher Shah built a fort. On [the foundation of] the fort of Shah Jahan in the city [it] became the old fort (?)

Continuation of the road from Shah-Jahanabad to Lahor.

10 Umbala
4 Serai-Nun
2 Serai-Hajjám
3 Todar Mal
7 Aluah (5)
7 Sirhind
7 Khanná
4 Serai-Lashkar Khan

Continuation of the road from Douraha

Hushiar Khán (6)
Shah-ganj

(1) *Dotana*, 3 m. N. W. of Chata. *Kosi*, $3\frac{1}{2}$ m. N. W. of Dotana *Hodul* m N. W. of Kosi (A. 50 N. E.) *Banchari*, 27. 56 N. 77. 25 E. (A.49 S. E.) $3\frac{1}{2}$m I. of Hodul.

* Distances in *kos* from Delhi to other towns. *Abad* is a mistake for *Ilahabad*, † Distances in *kos* from Lahor to other towns.

(2) Probably *Madanpur*, 5 m. N. E. E. of Tughlaqabad (*Ibid.*)

(3) Not given in Atlas. But the *A. and C. Gaz.* (ii. 132) mentions it, as situated at 11 m. from the Turkooman gate of Delhi.

(4) There is a *Barapula bridge* near Delhi.

(5) *Aluwa*, 11 m. S. E. of Sirhind (A 48 N. W.) *Sirhind* 30 37 N. 76. 27 E. *Khanna*, 10½ m N. W. W. of Sirhind. *Serai-Lashkar Khan*, not given in Atlas, but mentioned in the *A. and C. Gazetteer* (ii. 26 *n*) as situated at 20 m. from Sirhind. (6) *Hosheear Nugur*, 5 m N. of Surai Amanut Khan, and only 2¼ m S. of the road from Amritsar to Lahor (A. 30) *Shahganj* was probably the point on this road at which it was joined by the Delhi-Lahor road.

[123 *a*.]

From Láhor to Atak fort	Continuation of the road from Lahor to Atak	The stream Surkhab. From the canal Surkhab to Kabul. Another road from the canal Surkhab to Kabul goes from the hilly village (?)		From Gujrat, which is on the bank of the river Chenab, the road goes towards Kashmir. The same road comes from Shah-Jahanabad and above it, which [portion] has already been described.	
12 Sháhdera (1) 6 Fazılábád 2 Juáhir mal 6 Eminabad 7 Hakimabadpur 6 Cheemah-Ghakkar River of Wazirabad (Chenáb) 2 Gujrát 4 Khwaspur 4 Kinári 8 Khariáli 3 Serai-Alamgir Ferry over the river (Jhilum) 6 Said Khán 3 Nauranga-bad 4 Chokuha 4 Khurda-Jalál 4 Mahsa ? 15 Paka	Rabát (2) Laskari ? Rawalpindi Hazira ? Kálápáni Hassan Abdál Madrota Atak fort overlooks the Atak river. The Atak river. From Atak to Pesháwar : Khairábád Qasári ? Akhora Sindh ? Khánkhánán Pesháwar fort Jamrudh Lundikhána Dah Ghulámán Ali Masjid Dhaka	Jái ? Chárbágh-khurd Chárbágh-kalán Serai-Chilla? Gandamak (3) Malik Ali Jagdalak Barang badehat ? Serdhána Piri ? Qahar Jabbár Kábul khurd Khák Sat ? Bagrami Kábul fort ——— Surkh-diwár ? * Ali-Boghan Jalalabad on the bank of the stream Surkh-ab	Said Asrafnagar † Mir Ali Mansur Hajikhel Kunis ? Kamálpur Hausli ? Kár fort Place of crossing ——— This is a canal which reaches the wall of the fort.	Daulatabád (4) Bhimbar Chauki-hati Naushahra Chekand-hati ? Ináyetpur Rájáur Thana Baramgaon Poshána Serai Ali Mardan Khan Said Hala ? Hirpur Shádimarg Khánpur	From Rajaur the middle road goes towards Kashmir Saifábád Poonch (5) Aliabad Oori Bhaniar ? Bára mula

Lahor ‡	Atak	Jalálábád	Peshâwar
305	142	64	124
Delhi	Akbarabad	Multán	Kashmir fort

The Jhilum flows apart from the Chenab

This small column comes between *Dhaka* and *Jai*.

No name in this column has been traced.

These are distances in *kos* from Kabul.

(1) *Shahdura*, 3 m. N. of Lahor fort. *Fazilabad* is mentioned by Tieff. as 12 m. N. of Lahor. *Eminabad*, 9 m. S. of Gujranwala (A 30) *Ghukur Cheemah* 10 m. S. of Wazirabad. *Wazirabad*, 32. 27 N. 74. 11 E., 9 m. N. of it is *Gujrat*. *Khanwaspoor* 11 m. N. N. W. of Gujrat. *Kinūri* may be *Kharian*, 10 m. N. W. of the last stage, while 5½ m. further N. W. is *Kharyalah*. *Suraee Alumgeer* and *Naurangabad* are both 3 m. S. E. of Jhelum city and 3 m. N.W. of Kharyalah (A. 29) *Chokuha*, 10 m. N. of Rohtas, *Serai-i-Jalal Khan* 10 m. onward, and *Paka* 10 m. further on. (Tieffenthaler, i. 114.)

(2) *Rowat*, 33. 30 N. 73. 16 E. (A. 29) *Kalapani* 5 m. S. of Hassan Abdal (Tieff.),but A 14 gives *Kala ka Serai* 9 m. S. E. of that place, 33. 45 N. 72. 52 E. *Madrota* 7½ m. E. of Atak. *Khairabad*, on the W. bank of the Indus, opposite Atak. *Akora* 34. N. 72.10 E. Can *Sindh* &c. be Serai-i-Khankhanan ? *Jumrood* 11 m. W. of Peshawar, *Ally Musjid* 10 m. on, *Lundee Khana* 12½ m. further on, (34. 6 N. 71. 5 E.)*Dhaka* 34. 12. 30 N. 71. 2 E. *Surkh Dewar* is mentioned in *A. and C. Gaz.* (ii. pt. 1, 57.) *Ally Boghan*, 7½ m. S. E. of Jelalabad, which is at 34. 25 N. 70. 25 E. (A. 29) (3) *Gandamak* 29 m. S. W. of Jelalabad, *Jagdalak* 17 m. N. W. of the former. Tieff. mentions *Sher-Dahan* 5 m. from Jagdali and *Tesi* 8 m. onward. *Kahar Jabar* 18½ m S. E. of Kabul. *Khurd Kabul* is 6 m. W. of K-J.*Bagrami*, 6 m. E. of Kabul and 10 m. N. W. of Khurd Kabul (L. 12.)

(4) *Daulatnagar*, 12 m. N. of Gujrat ; 16 m further north is *Bhimbar*; 16 m. further north is *Nowshera* (A. 29) *Chauki-hati* is mentioned by Tieff. (p. 88) as 4 royal miles N. of Bhimbar and as having a beautiful lake and a cave with two *elephants* carved on the rock. *Chekand-hati* may be *Changis-hati*, 4½ m. N. of Nowshera (Tieff.) *Rajaori*, 33. 23 N. 74. 22 E., 16 m. N. N. E. of Nowshera. *Thana* 4½ m. from Rajaori, *Baramgula* 3½ m. further on, *Poshana* 2 m. on, *Serai-i-Muhammad Kuli* 3½ m. on (Tieff 88 and 89.) Between| Poshana and Hirapur, Tieff. (p. 87) gives *Serai Aliabad* (=Serai Ali Mardan Khan ?) and *Serai Sokhta* (=Said Hala ?) *Hirpur* (10 m. N. of Poshana, acc. to Tieff.) 18 m. S. S. W. of *Khanpur* (which is 11 m S. of Srinagar, in Stein's Map.) For *Shadimarg*, Tieff. (p. 88) gives Shajamarg, 6 m. from Hirapur. (5) *Poonch* 33. 46 N. 74. 9 E. *Oorie* 34. 5 N. 74. 6. 30 E. *Bhaniar* 8½ m. N. E. E. of it. *Baramoola* 10 m. further E. (Stein's Map).

[123. *b*.]

From Kashmir to Atak.	From Lahor to Multan.	From Delhi to Ajmir.	From Ajmir to Gujrat.	From Multan to Bhakkar.	Continuation of the road from Multan.
Bridge on the river Jhilum.	Abul Hasan	Serai of Alawardi (2).	Garh Bithli [*i. e.*, Ajmir].	Rindarpan? Kanpur (4). Akanmasti	Abar-dhan. Oobari (5). Fort Bhakkar.
Manzil Gahi?	Aurangabad	Patudhi.	Jhalor fort (3).	Kháki. Dipalpur vilage.	River Chenab passes on the further side by the city.
Baliás.	Nowshahra (1).	Rewari.	Gujrat 12 *kos*? from Ajmir.	Chauki-bhai?	From Oobari the road goes to Thatha.
Serai Gajpati?	Mophalkama..			Jalalpur.	
Nimdurg?	Satghara.	Kotputli.	Gujrat.	Alipur.	
Sárghar.	Kamal.	Barduráyán?		Sujaatpur.	Bahrnalu?
Serai Saudagar.	Chauki Fatu.	Chuksar?		Jahangirabad.	Kist. Pargana Kanri
ManzilSarhad.	Harapa.	Sambhar village.		Murtaza Khan.	Laliputrá. Pargana Kala.
Sultanpur.		Muranda.		Daran.	Hakandi.
Manzil Sahá.	Chichawatni.	Sarsara?		Uchh-barg. Muhammad Waris.	Pargana Bakas.
Atak Banaras.	Ali Sahwa.	From Ajmir to Thatha, the road is a sandy desert, without any habitation.		Janpuri.	Pargana Nasarpur.
Atak fort already described.	Talumba.			Hamid-be-mahni? Fatihdari.	
From Atak to Rohtasgarh.	Sard.	Fort Bahkran? within the jurisdiction of Jesalmir, Amarkot, Manu? Pargana Bákr? Pargana Jun.		Palthunala? Murakh? Bhawanidas.	
River Jhilum.	Khalid?	Cross [to] Thatha [over] the same Chenab which has been described.		Baqr-pur.	
Ferry over the Kalapani.	Mardánpur.				
Randirasi?					
Bahsand?		Fort Thatha.			
Holi.					
Masnu?					
Mahra.					
Máru.					

Tamarwara.	Dakajir-
Muhammad Dani.	Guzar-Khana
Multan.	River Chenab. (Haiat?) a stream which coming out of the
Banla.	
Sarkar of Bhakkar.	
Adilpur Sultanpur.*	

Chenab unites with the ocean.

* From this place the road from the Chenab to Thatha already described, goes to the aforesaid town.

(1) Surai *Nowshehra*, 31. 11 N. 73. 53 E. *Shutgurrah*, 30. 55 N. 73.34. 30 E. There is a *Mopalkee*, 13 m. S. W. of the former and 13½ m N. of the latter. (A 30) *Hurruppa*, 12 m N. E E. of *Cheechawutnee* (which is 30 34. 30 N. 72. 45 E.) *Sahwa Gureeb*, 6 m. W. of Ch. *Tulumba* 30 31 N. 72. 18 E. (A 17) *Sird* 19 m. W. of Tulumba, *Kulalpoor* 8 m. N. W. of Sird, *Mundalpoor* 36 m. N E. of Multan (Walker, India, xii.)

(2) *Alawirdi* 1 m. N. of Gurgaon Railway Station, 28. 30 N. 77. 5 E. (A 49 S. E.) *Pataudi* 28. 19. 30 N. 76. 50. 30 E, *Rewari* 13 m. S. W. of the last

(A. 49 S. W.) *Kot* 27 . 42 N. 76.16 E. *Putli* is 1 m. S. W. of it. (A 50 N. W. *Sambar* 26. 55 N 75. 15 E. Chuksar may be a mistake for *Jubner* 13½ m N.N.E of Sambar. Muranda may be a mistake for *Momana* 10½ m. S. W. of Sambar (A. 33 S. E.) (3) *Jhalor* 25. 22 N. 72. 37 E.

(4) 29. 59 N. 71. 21 E., 9 m S. E. of Muzuffergarh. *Jalalpur*, 29. 30 N 71. 17 E. (A. 17) Janpuri may be *Khanpur* 28. 40 N. 70. 42 E (L. 12)

(5) *Oobaro*, 37 m N. E. of Bukkur (L. 12.)

[124 *a.*]

Kabul fort. From Kabul to Ghaznin and from Ghaznin to Qandhár. Though all these three places belong to the country of Turan, yet, as they were for some time in the possession of the Emperors of India, I am writing of them.

Sufid-sang (1).
Chár-asia.
Laghmán ?
Deh-nau.
Danbara ?
Bakhsawand ?
Haft-ásia.
Shash-gáon.
Ser-i-dana.
Tomb of Sultan Mahmud. Ghaznin fort.
From Ghaznin.
Dera Náni
Farábágh.
Bárik-diwár.
Boundary of Qandhár
Shastal.
Ab-i-tazi.
Sar-i-asp.
Kalát-i-Ghilzái ?

Road of Multan.
Maruf (2)
Diar-maskir
Ranj-had-ándar.
Kafir-cháh.
Qaba-khel.
Farkhu.
Kulab.
Bakhil-ward.
Aria-quama.
Birah-durg
Lahumu-khel.
Mir Hussain Mulla-khel.
Bandana Mandar khel.
Laut Ali.
Jarkhand.
Ganjur-hadahami.
Kul-had-nau-khan.
Kaski.
Ekalut
Sar Manzil.
Bila ?
Aski ?

Pass of Greater Qandhár
Road of Atak.
Kári.
Biáh-maruf.
Khâma sir.
Dámudar.
Wárun ?
Chalkari.
Dera-Shaikh.
Kul-tur.
Sakam-bara.
Dilir qom-Abdáli.
Ujha ?
Mihr Ali-Ghilzai.
Kishu Ghilzai.
Kalu Ghilzai.
Kaliá-bahudi.
Karkas-dádar.
Kundar-dadar.
Kakluh.
Sarna.
Hukánhák ?
Tuli ?
Kákar-pup.

Another road to Atak between the hills.
Du-kalán.
Laili-Majnun.
Chashma-siáh
Pucca bridge.
Cháh-Alam.
Pura.
Arti.
Kuásir ?
Kub-Mahmud.
Pakuna.
Pari.
Wari fort.
Ma-Makrani ?
Hati fort.
Rud-Balkh.
Sang-bakhsh.
Lashkari.
Dháká.
Hajja-fort.
Dehâia-Hajja (3
Kuchah.
Duráha.

(1) The *A. and C. Gaz.* (II. pt 1. 57) mentions a *Suffaid Sung* "a large white stone the powder of which is said to cure manifold diseases !" But it is situated near Gundamuk. *Char-asia*, 9 m. S. of Kabul, *Shashgao* 14 m. N. of Ghazni, *Sher-i-dana* 3 m. south of Shashgao. (L. 12) *Haftasia* 3 m N. of Shash-gaon. *Nani* 12 m. S. of Ghazni. *Sir-i-asp*, 10 m. N. E of Kalat-i-Ghilzai (L. 12) Another map gives *Ab-i-tazi* 26 m. N. E. of Kalat-i-Ghilzai, which is 75 m. N. E. of Kandahar and *Shaftal* 5 m. further north.

(2) There is a *Maruf* 82 m. E. of Kandahar (L. 12) Another map gives *Kafir Chah* 50 m. E. of Maruf.

(3) Deh-i-Haji, 19 m. S. E. of Kandahar (L. 12).

[124 *b*.]

Continuation of the road of Multan.	Continuation of tho road of Atak.	Continuation of the road of Atak	From Akbarabad to Allahabad and from that place to Patna.	If from the Delhi road one goes to Patna by the road of Barili, the route will be the following :
Khar-Mákran	Jalál-Bábar fort	Bhang-dera	Kabra of Wazir Khán (2)	Shah-Jahanabad
Dera Ismail Khan	Zoráih Sahi	Chandar-wáli	Firuzabad	Cross the river Jumná
Ferry over the river	Aurangabad	Chabutra	Shikoh-abad	Shahdra (3)
River of Atak	Israd-ánkár	Ali-siri	Etáwah	Serai-Basant ?
Continuation of the road of Multan :	Musa-khel	Fort of Ghazi Khan	Jumná	River Hindun
Fort of Dariá Khan (1)	Nabirah-Malik-qom	River Atak	Rajpura	Ghaziu-d-din nagar
Chatah appertaining to Ibrahim	Qabr-i-Hanud?	Continuation of the road of Atak	Kora	Dásna
Kot Korur	Road of Pábar	Ferry of Qareshi (?)	Hatgaon	Kálan-deh-ni
Mankuána	Continuation of the road of Atak	Nurwala	Shahzádpur	Hápur
Kusuála	Ganj fort appertaining to Gházi Khan ?	Máru	Fatihábad	River Kálini
Ráhr	Well of Bhábra	Barkhakar ?	Allahabad, also called Prayag and Tribeni.	Bagsar
Hasli-Chenáb	Well of Kashkuri		Báns Barili	Rath-sahi ?*
	Dardara		Hanuman-nagari	Garh-Mukhtesar
			Malikpur fort	River Ganges
			Shahjahanpur	Bagri village
			Sándha	Amroha
			Mullá Lusad-wáli ?	Moradabad
	Lucknow	City of Lucknow		

Some other roads go from Kabul to Atak, such as the one from the neighbourhood of Surkháb and other places, but [they are] very difficult.

* Bridge of Bábá Dargáhi, a *faqir* following Guru Nának.

(1) *Duria Khan*, 10 m. E of D. Ismail Khan. *Kuror*, 31. 31 N.71 E (L 12)

(2) Probably *Itimadpur*, 14 m E. of Agra. Can the author be referring to the tomb of Itimadu-d-daula (the father of Nur-Jahan) on the left bank of the Jumna, which splendid mausoleum was completed in 1628 A. D.? *Firuzabad*, 27. 9 N. 78. 28. 30 E. *Shikohabad*, 11½ m. S. E E. of it ; *Etawah*, 26. 46 N 79. 5 E. (A. 68) *Rajpoor* 13 m N. N. W. of Kalpi. *Koorarah*, 10 m. W. of Hamirpur, 25. 59 N. 80. 3 E (A. 69 N. E.) *Hutgaon* 17 m W of Manikpur on the south bank of the Ganges ; *Futtypour* 9 m. N. W. of Allahabad (Rennell, xiii) *Shahzadpur* 32 m. N. W. of Allahabad, on the S. bank of the Ganges (L. 10) *Hoonoomangunj* 10 m. E. of Allahabad fort. *Sundha*, 25. 18 N. 82. 38. 30 E. (A. 88).

(3) *Shahdara*, 3 m. E. of Delhi. *Ghaziabad*, 11 m. E. of Delhi (given in L. 9 as *Gazoodeenugur*) *Dasna* 6 m. E. of Ghaziabad ; *Hapur* 16 m. N. E.E. of Dasna. *Bagsar*, 6½ m. W. of *Garh Muktesar*, which is 28. 47 N. 78.19. 30 E. (A. 49 N. E.) *Bagri* 10½ m S. W. W. of Amroha, which is 28. 54 N. 78. 32 E. *Moradabad*, 18½ m E of Amroha (A. 67 N. W.)

[125 *a*.]

Conclusion of the Delhi-Patna Road. Rai Barili (1). Selun Kathra. Dia-Mái ? Banáras, on the Ganges. Serai-Said Raji ? Ghazipur. Buxar. Raniságar. Bisambhar. The River Son—whatever falls into it is turned into stone. The Province of Bihar or Azimabad Patna.	River Hindun. Bridge of Barhána.	Another road goes towards Kol from Shah Jahanabad : At the foot of the city [the river] is crossed. Patparganj (2). Chalera. *Pucca* Serai of Bhakar ? Serai Khási ? Begampur. Sikandra. Khurja. Well of Sitárám. Chandaus. Kol. Harduáganj. At this place Sábit Khan built Sábit-garh now known as Rámgarh.

(1) *Rae Bareli*, 49 m. S. E. E. of Cawnpur. *Selon*, 21 m. S. of R. B. (A 88) *Ghazipur*, 25. 35 N. 83. 39 E. *Buxar*, 25. 34. 30 N. 84.2.30 E. *Raneesagur* 25. 37 N. 84. 24 E. (A. 103) There is a *Bisumhur pur*, 10½ m. N. N. E. of Arrah, and west of the place where the Son falls into the Ganges.

(2) · 3½ m. S. E. of Delhi, on the eastern bank of the Jumna. *Chalera*, 5 m. S. E. E. of P, *Begampur*, 28.29.30 N. 77.31 E. *Sikandarabad*, 28.27 N. 77.45 E., 15 m. S. E.E. of B. *Khurja*, 16 m. S. of Sikandarabad. *Chandaus*, 11½ m. S. of K. (A 49 S. E.) *Koil*, 2 m. S. of Aligarh. (A. 50 N. E.) *Hurdouhgunge*, 6 m. E. of Coel (L. 9.); not given in the *Indian Atlas*.

CORRECTIONS AND ADDITIONS.

Page x, line 3, *for* thougb *read* though.

P. xiii, l. 17, *for* stan *read* tan.

P. xv, l. 13, *insert bracket after* Things.

P. xxi, l. 28, *for* has been *read* was.

P. xxxii, column of 1700, line of Ajmir, *for* 1,50,74,500 *read* 1,50,74,506.

P. xxxv, line of 1700, *for* 3,03,23 753 *read* 3,05,73.753.

P. lxxvii, l. 22, for *cost price of* read *cost price of a maund of.*

P. 1, l. 2, *for* D. 153 *read* D 156.

P. 4, l. 27, *for* aud *read* and.

P. 7, margin, *for* Imperia *read* Imperial.

„ l. 32, *for* coolnes *read* coolness.

P 10, foot note † *for* cclebrated *read* celebrated

P. 12, l. 17, *for* Abdu-l-Kadr *read* Abdu-l-Qadir

„ l. 30, *for* 1165 *read* 1166.

P. 13, margin, *for* Paniapt *read* Panipat.

„ footnote † *add* 30 7 N. 76 12 E

P. 14, l. 24, *for* Bejaur *read* Pinjaur.

„ *omit* foot-note § *and read in its place* Pinjaur, a town in the Patiala State, 30·48 N. 78·59 E., situated at the confluence of two tributaries of the Ghaggar. (*I. G.*, xi. 184) Thornton's *Gazetteer* mentions that it has "a garden which has been laid out on the natural slope of the ground in *six* separate and *successive terraces, one below another.*" Fidai Khan Azim Khan, the *Koka* or foster-brother of Aurangzib, died at Dacca in 1088 A. H. (1678 A. D.) while acting as Governor of Bengal. His life is given in the *Maasiru-l-Umara* i. 247.

P. 21, l. 13, *for* from *read* form.

P. 22, foot note §, *add* Under Akbar this province had 8 *Sarkars* and 237 *mahals.* (*Ain.* ii. 285).

P. 24, foot-note ||, *add* but commonly called *Polo.*

P. 26, l. 20, for *abnah* read mangoes.

„ l. 26, *for* excluding *read* including.

„ l 30, *for* aud *read* and.

„ l. 31, *for* above (Ain. ii. 311) *read* above excluding *Bari* (*Ain.* ii. 182).

Page 28, l. 4, *for* in the road *read* under a saw [i e., severed their heads].

„ margin, *for* earning *read* learning.

„ *omit footnote* *

P. 31, l. 20 *for* carvad *read* carved.

P. 33, margin, *for* Luc now *read* Lucknow.

P. 35, l. 17, *for* an *read* and.

P. 36, l. 27, *for* upon *read* on

P. 42, l. 9, after *Sandali* insert [30. *b.*]

P. 43, l. 8, for *kunt* read *gunt*

P. 50, l. 12, for *Kalkarui* read *Kulkarni.*

„ margin, *for* owns *read* Towns.

P. 51, l. 6, *to* wonderful cock *add note*

Bernier refers to it, saying that the skin alone is black ; Constable (p. 251 footnote) quotes from Linschoten's *Voyage to the East Indies,* "There are [in Mozambique] certain hens that are so black both of feathers, flesh, and bones, that being sodden they seen as black as ink, ... whereof some are likewise found in India."

„ l. 23, *for* sing *read* Sign.

P. 52, foot-note ¶, *for* 142 *parganahs read* 242 *parganahs* (wrongly printed as 142 in Jarrett's translation).

P. 57, l. 8, *insert in margin* Revenue.

P. 62, l. 16, *to* Pattan *add note* Anhilwarra, 23°51'30 N. 72°10'30 E., and not Somnath, though both of them were called Pattan.

P. 67, footnote *, *after* Mahi river *insert* (Elliot, v. 435 *n.*)

P. 71, footnote §, *for* R1,655,284-1-2 *read* R1,656,284-13-2.

P. 75, l. 17, *for* viceregency *read* vicegerency.

P. 80, l. 28, *for* his *read* this.

P. 90, l. 21, *for* 1081 A. H. (1675 A. D.) *read* 1084 A. H. (1674 A. D.)

P. 98, l. 9, *to* bismuth *add note*

The text uses the word *qal'i,* which also means tin. From the description it seems as if the author meant to speak of lime.

P. 103, l. 8, *to* Bauh *add note*

The *Indian Atlas* (Sheet 30) gives *Baoopur,* on the eastern bank of the ferry over the Bias, 31°15'30 N. 75°10'30 E., 5½ m. N. W. of Sultanpur and 15 m. E. of *Puttee.*

Page 106, l. 24, *to* Dhundu Ranjha *add note*

Ranjha and Hir were two Muhammadan lovers. "They are celebrated in the Panjab as the types of constant lovers, much in the same way as Abelard and Heloise in Modern Europe, or as Laili and Majnun in Arabic, and Farhad and Shirin in Persian story. Hir's tomb is about half a mile from the civil station of Jhang, and is marked on the survey map as "Mookurba Heer," which stands for "Maqbara-i-Hir," or Hir's monument. A *mela* is held at the tomb in the month of Magh." "Hir was the daughter of Chuchak, a Syal of Rangpur, in the Muzaffargarh District. Ranjha's true name was Didho ; he was by caste a Ranjha Jatt, and is known almost exclusively by his caste name. His father Manju was a Chaudhri or Revenue Collector, at Takht Hazara in the Gujranwala District." (Captain R. C. Temple's *Legends of the Panjab*, vol. ii, 177) Their love-story is given below : Hir fell in love with Ranjha, a buffalo-herd, but her mother forced her to marry a youth named Shida. She ran away with Ranjha, and the two lived together at Jhang ; but in the end her caste-fellows murdered her, and Ranjha in grief caused himself to be buried alive in her grave. In later legends Ranjha figures as a wonder-working *faqir*.

Poems were composed by the following bards among others in connection with the above story : (1) Namodar Patwari of Jhang, (2) Waris Shah of Takht Hazara, (3) Hafiz Ahmad of Jhang, (5) Makbil, and (5) Roshan Shah.

P. 121 }
P. 122 } heading, *for* PANJAB *read* KASHMIR.

P. 123, l. 10, for *amawav* read Namodar

P. 124, l 1 and elsewhere, *for* Chhri *read* Chhattar

P. 125, l. 8, *for* (granary ?) *read* (emporia)

P. 126, l. 13, *for* 6,93.56,570 *read* 6,93,56,572

P. 128, l. 30, *for*-15-17 *read*-15-7

P. 133, l 20, *for* Rs 1,40,72,722-15-7 *read* Rs 1,40,72,725-7-7

P. 137, l. 13, *for* 156 *read* 269.

P. 142, l. 20, *to* revenue *add note* By deducting the revenues of the other 10 *Sarkars* from the total provincial revenue, we get 2,61,40,625 *dam* (Rs. 6,53,515-10) as the revenue of Mandsor.

P. 155, l. 15, *after* this country *insert* [*i. e.*, Kokan]

„ l. 19, *after* SARKARS *insert* OF KOKAN.

„ l. 20, *for* 348 *read* 748.

Page 156, l. 5, *for* 3 *read* 4.

" l. 11, *for* 265 *read* 235.

" l. 15, *for* 75,000 *read* 45,000.

" l. 27, *to* Ladarbadri *add note* This obscure passage is cleared by a reference to Tieffenthaler (p. 503), where we read that in going from Nagarkot to Bijapur one has to cross the Krishna and the Kahati rivers, and that in going from Bijapur to this fort the road is 30 miles if the Krishna is crossed at the *ferry of Badari*, and 24 miles if the Krishna is crossed at Golar. Therefore, Ladar badri = the ferry (*guzar*) of Badari, Ladar kola = the ferry (*guzar*) of Golar, and Bahat = Kahati.

P. 157, l. 1, *for* Text *read* text.

P. 158, l. 21, *to* property *add note*

Khafi Khan. (Elliot, vii. 335) gives "8,51,000 *huns* and Rs. 2,00,53,000, altogether Rs. 6,80,10,000, besides jewels &c......The total in *dams* was 1,15,16,00,000 *dams*, which was the sum entered on the records."

P. 159, l. 19, *for* 6,72,780 12 as *read* 6,72,780—12 as.

P. 164, column 2, *for* 99 *read* 39.

P. 165, col. 1, *for* Imtiar-garh *read* Imtiaz-garh

P. 168 col. 1, *after* Ban-ganga *insert* (Pain-Ganga)

" footnote (3), *for* N. N. E. *read* N. N. W

" footnote (12), *for* Not t e *read* Not the

P. 170, col. 2, *for* Serai-Jandwaran *read* Serai-i-Khan-dauran.

" col. 3, *for* Ambar *read* Ma'sir ?

P. 171, footnote (5), l. 1, *for* 8 m. *read* 7 m. *and for* 7 m. *read* 8½ m

" " l. 2, *for* 9 m. N. W. *read* 9 m. N.

P. 172, footnete (8), l. 6, for *Suraee*, 6 m. read *Suraee* 3½ m.

" " l. 7, for *Pindoree Husun* read *Nooroodeen.*